BESPOKE HOME

BATES MASI + ARCHITECTS

ORO EDITIONS

INTRODUCTION BY PAUL GOLDBERGER

CONTENTS

INTRODUCTION

BY PAUL GOLDBERGER

I first encountered the work of Bates Masi + Architects a decade or so ago, when I agreed to serve on a jury to select the winners of the annual design awards of the regional chapter of the American Institute of Architects on eastern Long Island. The jury of architectural experts spent a rainy afternoon going through photographs of several dozen new and renovated houses in East Hampton, Southampton, Bridgehampton, Sag Harbor, and the other communities that make up the heart of this unusual and special region, and came up with a first prize winner, a second prize winner, and some honorable mentions.

Almost all of the best houses we reviewed that day—and a disproportionate number of the winners—turned out to be by a local firm called Bates Masi. I had never heard of them. I remembered that there had been an architect named Harry Bates who did some fine modern beach houses back in the 1960's and 1970's, but Bates is a common name and I had no reason to believe that this Bates was that Bates. As for who Masi was, I had no idea whatsoever.

I soon learned that Bates was indeed the same Harry Bates, and that Masi was Paul Masi, a gifted architect younger by a generation—actually more than that, since there is a difference of more than 40 years in their ages—and that they had formed an unlikely and extraordinarily fruitful partnership. Together, Harry Bates and Paul Masi were producing some of the most compelling modernist residential architecture in the Northeast. The designs of theirs that so impressed the jury on that rainy afternoon were widely varied, but they all had an unmistakable degree of self-assurance, and they were marked by a consistent but very subtle kind of elegance. You could say that they had both inventiveness and gravitas, two things that rarely go together, especially in the category of new domestic architecture in the Hamptons.

Those houses from the early years of the Bates Masi partnership marked the beginning of nearly two decades of noteworthy architecture, and by now it is fair to say that the *oeuvre* of Bates Masi takes its place within the important heritage of modernism in the Hamptons. Their architecture is good enough to be taken seriously if it were anywhere, but it is particularly meaningful situated where it is.

It makes sense to digress for a moment and say something about the nature of the place in which the firm does most of its work. The set of communities by the sea at the eastern end of Long Island evolved long ago from farming and fishing villages to resorts, and from casual summer communities whose tone was set by artists and writers to grander places where fortunes made on Wall Street and elsewhere are oft expressed in the building of enormous new houses that now, more often than not, are designed to look like old ones. That kind of house is not, needless to say, what Bates and Masi build. Their work connects to another part of the Hamptons' history, the tradition of modern houses by architects like Richard Meier, Charles Gwathmey, Norman Jaffe, Andrew Geller, Julian and Barbara Neski, Paul Lester Weiner, Pierre Chareau and Robert Rosenberg, not to mention Harry Bates himself.

It is a tradition that fell out of favor when the fashion for making new houses in the manner of the great Shingle Style mansions of the early twentieth century began in the early 1980's. At first, those houses were an intriguing curiosity, and not unwelcome. The motive behind them was understandable: by the 1980's, it was easy to feel that modern domestic architecture in the Hamptons, which in the 1950's and 1960's seemed to hold promise of a bright new world, had lost its groove so to speak, faded along with the innocence that had helped to make much of that work so appealing. By then, even the sharp, lively geometries of Harry Bates' early houses did not seem as fresh as they had in 1966, when a magazine like Better Homes and Gardens could swoon over a modest and simple Bates design, publishing it under the headline "Gift for a Lifetime: A Vacation House." Times had become more jaded. They had also become wealthier, and houses were getting much bigger in the 1980's. Most of the notable modern houses in the Hamptons were small. The best of them were visually exciting and explored interior space with great inventiveness, but no one ever claimed that their appeal came from their grandeur.

Such restraint would not do in the 1980's, when along with new wealth came a desire for a level of opulence that the modernist tradition, at least then, seemed unable or unwilling to provide. Within a few years, the neo-Shingle Style houses that had first seemed an appealing alternative became more and more common, spreading everywhere, each seemingly bigger than the previous one, and each appearing to give birth to two more. I found myself yearning for the directness, clarity, and understatement of the modern houses, particularly since all too many of them were literally disappearing before our eyes, purchased by wealthy Hamptonites only to tear them down and put enormous shingled mansions in their place. The new modernist houses that were built in the 1980's and 1990's were few and far between.

That was the picture in 1996, when Paul Masi, a young architect who had been working for Richard Meier in New York City, first came to work with Harry Bates in his small office on eastern Long Island. Bates was past seventy and had stayed the course of modernism, but he was not entirely sure how bright the future was, and the thought had crossed his mind to consider retiring from architecture altogether. Masi was in his twenties, due shortly to leave for Harvard to get a graduate degree in architecture, and he saw his time with Bates as no more than a summer job. The two got along so well that Bates invited him back the following year, and then, once he finished at Harvard, proposed that he join him permanently. Bates found that the presence of his younger colleague reignited his own creative instincts. If Masi would forego his original intention of joining a large corporate firm and instead become his partner, Bates told him that he, in turn, was prepared to forego any thoughts of retirement. Masi, realizing that with Bates he would have the opportunity to design entire houses rather than toil away on minor details of huge projects, which is what he would have been doing if he joined a large corporate firm, agreed, and Bates Masi Architects was born.

It was a propitious moment, in large part because the architectural culture was beginning to shift again. While there were still plenty of traditional houses being built, by the early 2000's there was an increasing interest in the potential of modern architecture in the Hamptons, as well as a renewed respect for the houses of the first, mid-century modernist generation that remained. And implicit in this rediscovery of modernist architecture was the recognition that the omnipresent Shingle Style did not have sole possession of the region's architectural traditions: modernism, too, was a part of the Hamptons architectural DNA, with an important history that was waiting for a creative architect to mine.

Bates and Masi have succeeded at doing that, but they have also succeeded in another related realm, which is in connecting their work to the important, and all too often ignored, architectural vernacular of eastern Long Island. The first wave of postwar modernist houses made little reference to their context. They were shaped primarily by their architects' imaginations, adjusted, to a greater or lesser degree, to accommodate the programmatic requests of their clients. For the most part they ignored the potato barns, the seventeenth and eighteenth-century houses, the fishing shacks, and the other structures that were in some ways a deeper part of the area's heritage than the great and oft-imitated Shingle Style houses. The simple forms of these vernacular buildings were ripe for reinterpretation by a new generation of modernists, and they have been a consistent and strong influence in Bates Masi's work, especially in projects such as Pierson's Way, Northwest Peach Farm, and Genius Loci. Pierson's Way illustrates with particular eloquence Bates and Masi's ability to abstract vernacular buildings, turning these familiar, everyday forms into clearly articulated, simple, and modern geometric shapes.

Bates and Masi are devoted to materials: to finding new ones, to using old ones inventively, to assuring that every material fulfills its utmost potential. Their houses are built of many kinds of wood, stone, glass, and metal, often combined in unusual ways: elegant mahogany siding may cover the exterior as well as the inside walls and ceiling, as in the house at Sam's Creek; or copper is installed as shingles, as in Northwest Peach Farm; or Corten steel juxtaposed with cedar siding and screens, as at the house in Sagaponack, where the two join to make an exquisite abstract composition. To do this kind of thing well you need to understand materials in the deepest sense, to know what they are capable of, and to know where not to use them, which can often be as important as knowing where they will mean the most. To be able to use industrial materials in a residential design and sacrifice none of its domestic feeling is an accomplishment. Bates and Masi pull it off because of their inherent sense of restraint and appropriateness. They make wood feel like wood, concrete feel like concrete, and metal feel metallic. What enables this—what needs to go hand in hand with this close affinity for materials—is an ability to detail consistently and well. In every Bates Masi house, there is a myriad of tiny, alluring details that invite your eye. They are often among the most inventive elements of the design, and they can shape the experience of being in the house as much as anything bigger.

Every Bates Masi house is different: as the title of this volume reminds us, these are all bespoke houses, designed for the needs and aspirations of different clients and for the demands of different sites. Yet they are also all of a piece. Beyond a rich sense of materials and superbly conceived details, they share a commitment to light, a modesty of scale—at least by comparison to many houses built today, if not to their modernist forebears—and, perhaps most important, and most subtle, a sense of texture. This is not modernism as super-sleek or high-tech, and it is not modernism as a series of spectacular, space-age curves. You wouldn't confuse Bates Masi with Norman Foster on the one hand, or with John Lautner on the other. Harry Bates and Paul Masi are not wedded to any particular shape, but I think it is fair to say that they prefer straight lines to curving ones, and they prefer quiet, understated effects to flamboyant ones. In this sense, their work really does extend themes begun by Harry Bates, whose early work did not so much break out of the box as make boxes into lively, rhythmic compositions. No Bates Masi house is a glittering, perfect sculptural object, the kind of architecture that seems to say "look, but don't touch." These houses have the opposite effect. They make you want to touch them, not to look at them from afar. They are sensuous, and they call for engagement.

Few of these houses are made up of a single, large structure; many are broken down into units that are carefully arranged into a serene composition—at its best a kind of architectural still life. Pierson's Way, with its series of connected, barn-like masses, epitomizes this. Here, Bates and Masi have turned the image of the barn into something truly sumptuous, and made of it the theme of what could almost be called a small village. Mothersill is a different kind of composition altogether. It consists of a long, L-shaped main structure set into a site that slopes down toward the wetlands; the façade is two stories high facing the wetlands, and appears to be a modest single story on the entry side. Even more notable here is the way the long, L-shaped structure plays off against two small outbuildings on the property that were designed more than fifty years ago by Andrew Geller, which Bates Masi restored and integrated into their design, literally demonstrating the bridge between the old modernist

generation and the new that all of the firm's work alludes to symbolically.
It is not only the larger houses that are handsomely composed, however. The smaller buildings, like Paul Masi's own house, Elizabeth II, contain the same appealing balance of elements: solid and void, horizontal and vertical, hard and soft, textured and flat, neatly and tightly bound together into a smaller package. (The details are just as inventive here, too. Rough vertical boards are placed over concrete as exterior siding and also used as cabinet fronts inside. In each case, they are both punctuated and decorated by stainless steel clips that are both fastening clasps and handles. And then they are used again on white interior cabinets, creating a subtle tie between different materials throughout the house.) In another instance, Bates and Masi condensed their ideas and their design skill still further, in a small house recently completed in Beach Hampton in the Amagansett dunes: a tightly composed box of glass, steel, and concrete, it stands as a reminder that the modesty of the houses of the earlier modernist generation has not been entirely lost.

For Bates and Masi modernism is a language, not a doctrine. Neither of them has much interest in approaching architecture from the standpoint of theory. Their shared commitment to modernism carries with it a freedom from dogma and a belief that the modernist vocabulary can be every bit as flexible, as attuned to demands of program and site, and as visually pleasing as any traditional architectural language. And while they take obvious pleasure in connecting their work to the history of modernism in the Hamptons, as well as to Harry Bates' own history, they are emphatically not limited by that history, and they would be no more likely to design a house today that looked like Harry Bates' early work than they would be to design a shingled McMansion.

Harry Bates and Paul Masi are producing houses for the twenty-first century, and they acknowledge, and even celebrate, the differences between their time and that of the mid-century modernists. Their work takes advantage of what is almost invariably a larger budget, a more expansive program, a wider choice of materials, and an altogether different level of technology than that which was available to a previous generation of modernist architects. I think it is fair to say that their deepest commitment is to producing architecture that proves that modernism continues to evolve, that it has ongoing, fresh life within it, and that it can yield as much warmth and serenity as any traditional architecture. Bates and Masi's work aspires to extend the history of modernist architecture in the region, to situate it properly in its time and place—and to prove that as far as the history of modernism in the Hamptons goes, there are meaningful chapters still to be written.

TREE HOUSE
1967

On a National Seashore island with divergent communities, this two-level house, referred to by its Owner as his "tree house", is situated in a dense grove of pines and hollies. Served for the most part by wooden walkways, the island is primarily seasonal with a lively social scene in the warmer months and a more reflective atmosphere in the cooler days and nights.

After briefly considering renovating an old waterfront house, the Owner, an interior designer, bought the heavily wooded lot close to the bay that he wanted to see from the main living level. His aesthetic was simple, opting for the architecture and natural surroundings to be the dominant elements.

The approach to the closely positioned cubes leads to a walled deck and glass entrance. Two guest bedrooms, bath, and guest deck are on the first floor with a steel stair leading to the living, dining, kitchen, master suite, and deck on the second floor with views of the bay and treetops.

All exterior and interior wall surfaces and cabinets are rough-cut cypress; the flooring is bleached oak. The ceilings are exposed fir structural members, and doors and windows are aluminum. The wall-hung fireplace provides heat on cool spring and autumn days and evenings. The 1" X 12" cypress vertical louvers on the high windows reduce the intensity of the southern sun. The east and west walls of the house have selected views but are virtually blank because of the close proximity of the neighbors and a community walkway.

Whether alone or with guests and coupled with the often erratic weather, the serenity of the elevated spaces was a welcome respite for the Owner for many years from a crowded and busy professional life in the city.

Community walkway

Harry Bates, 1967

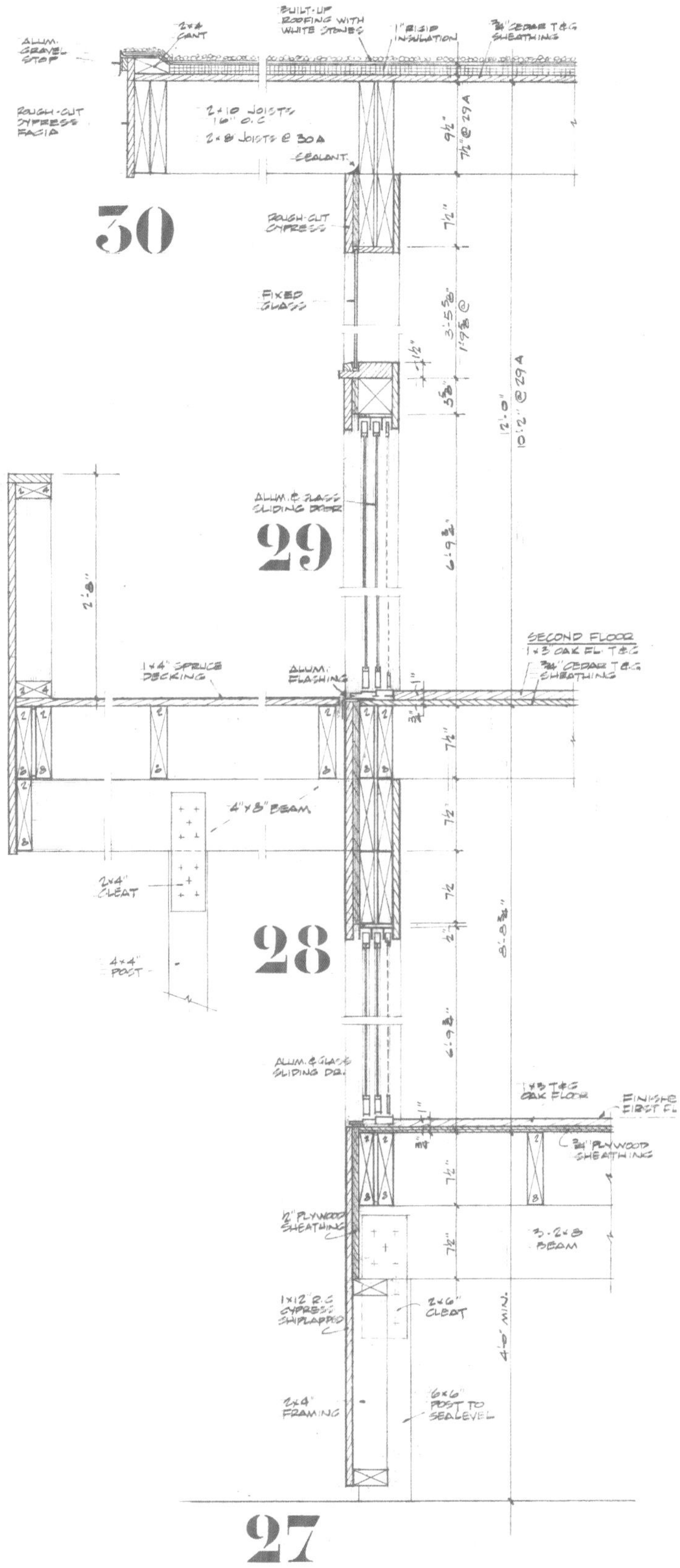

Wall section

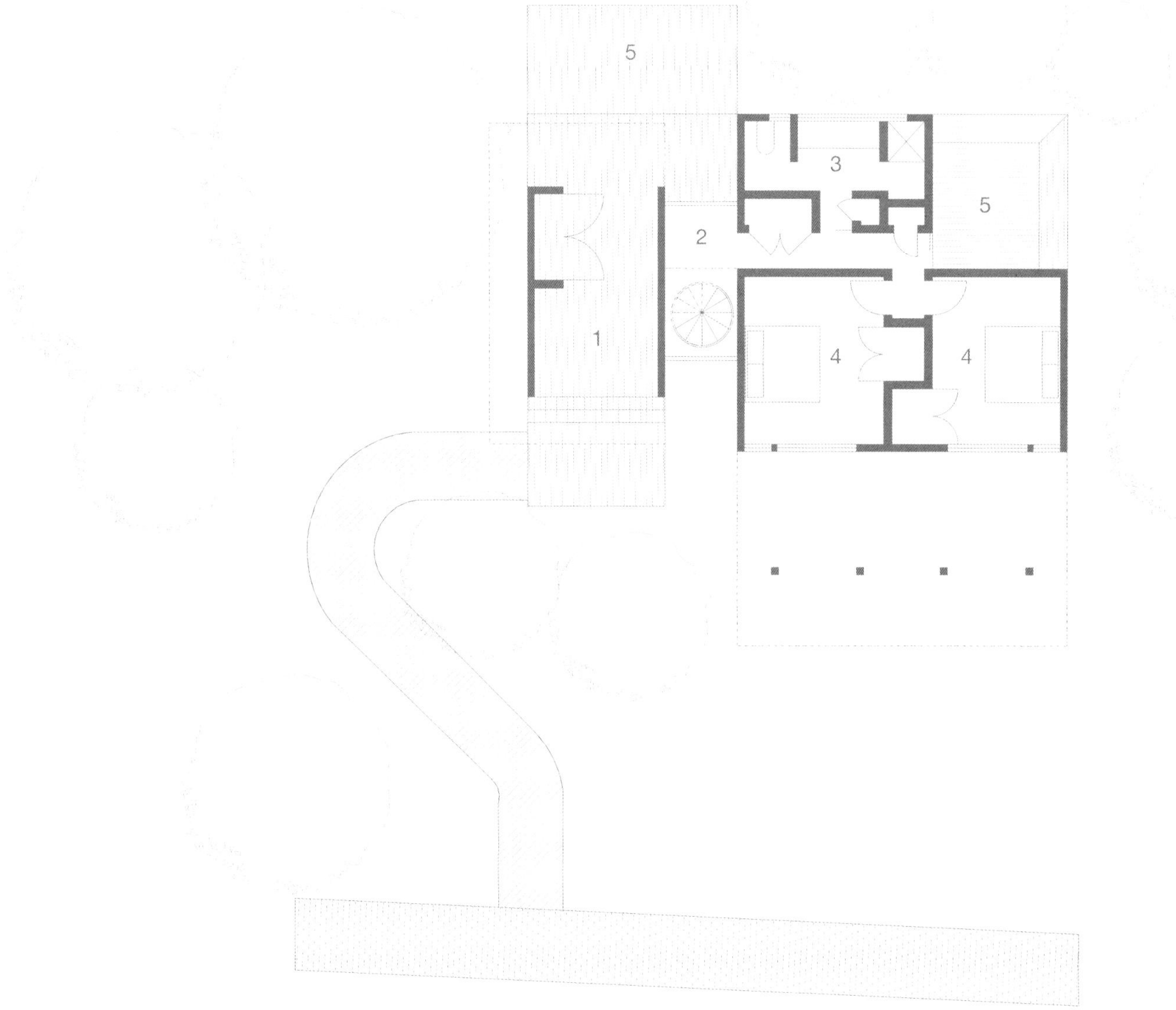

ENTRY LEVEL PLAN

1. Entry Deck
2. Entry
3. Bath
4. Bed
5. Deck

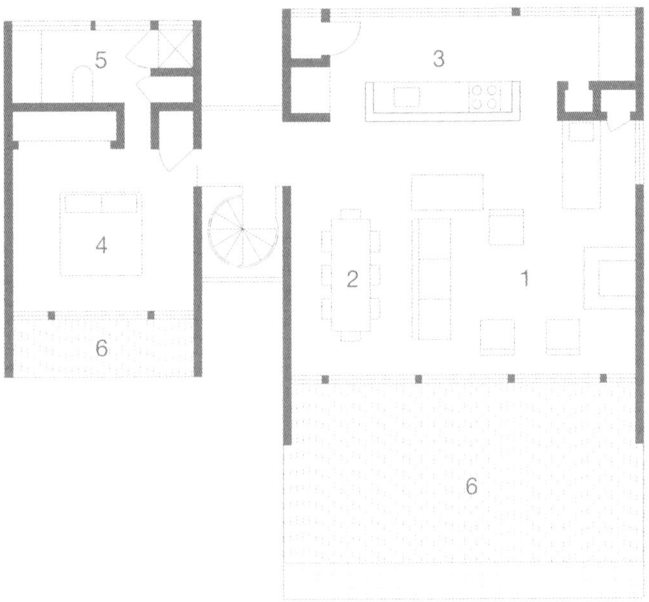

UPPER LEVEL PLAN

1. Living
2. Dining
3. Kitchen
4. Bed
5. Bath
6. Deck

RECOVER
1968 + 2006

Thirty-five years after the firm originally designed this vacation residence, its new owners sought to rejuvenate the house while preserving its spaces, seasoned tones, and texture. Clad inside and out almost entirely in twelve-inch-wide cypress boards, the original house exuded a straightforward simplicity the owners wished to maintain. By constraining the palette of materials and reusing salvaged parts of the existing house, the line between new and old becomes nearly imperceptible, limited only to minimal inflections in finish.

In the enlarged and updated baths, and in the modernized kitchen and dining terrace, dense glacial sedimentary sandstone is used for its fine workability into a variety of finishes. In this way the stone varies subtly – only in texture – as it is reapplied from one surface to another: horizontal walking surfaces are rendered with a smooth honed finish, vertical wall surfaces with a rough flamed finish, and countertops in a glossy polished finish. This tactile language is traced consistently from room to room.

Little of the material seen in the addition is in fact new. As the south wall and deck of the house were dismantled to make room for the new construction, the cypress boards and cedar decking were carefully salvaged and machined into new siding, fine scrim material, stair treads and risers. Reused, this cladding bears precisely the same patina as the other surfaces in the house – an effect impossible to achieve with new construction materials. Only on close inspection is new texture and color revealed at the boards' freshly cut edges.

In enhancing the simplicity of the original design, a subtle complexity has emerged. Splices, cuts, and finishing techniques inflect upon otherwise homogenous materials, recording the methods of craft and workmanship. Over the next thirty-five years, the patina that naturally accrues over time will continue to refine the delicacy of these inflections.

Resawn cypress siding

كراش

Flamed, honed, and polished sandstone

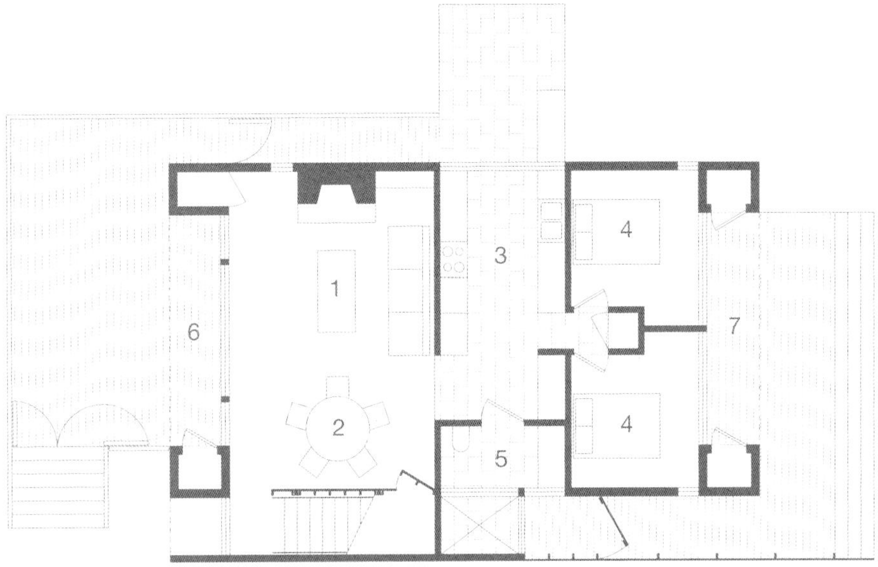

GROUND LEVEL PLAN

1. Living
2. Dining
3. Kitchen
4. Bed
5. Bath
6. Entry Deck
7. Deck

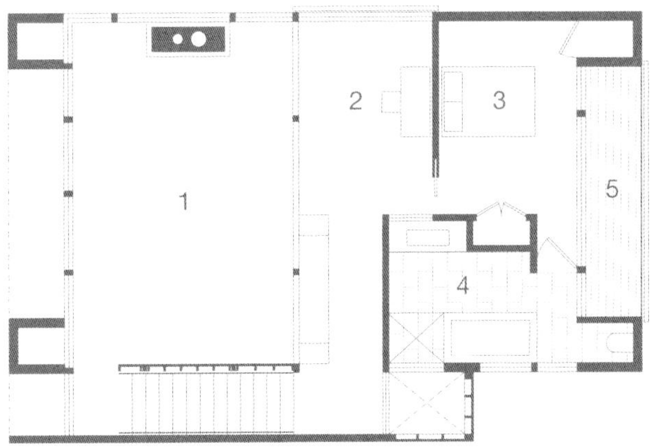

UPPER LEVEL PLAN

1. Open to Below
2. Office
3. Bed
4. Bath
5. Deck

PRYOR
2008

The house occupies a hill in Montauk with a distant view of the ocean. A site that the owners, a couple with two young boys, spent years to find. It is the couple's reprieve from their home in the city, a place to share the outdoor lifestyle with their family and to remember their teenage years together in Montauk. The house design prompts the owners to interact with the surrounding environment, evoking experiences of camping.

A departure from typical residential planning, the house is entered through multiple areas for different guests and occasions. Large glass doors slide open to the living, dining, and kitchen area for a large gathering; a smaller-scaled swing door for an occasional guest opens to the center hall with a view of the ocean; and a sequence of auxiliary spaces – beach equipment area, outdoor shower, sand and mudroom – creates a seamless ritual of the daily activities for the family and their friends. In all living areas and bedrooms, glass doors and insect screens slide in and out from wall pockets, transforming rooms to screened porches or spaces completely open to the landscape.

The double-height kitchen, dining, and living area has thirty-six-foot-wide glass doors that pocket into southern and northern walls. When open, the dining room becomes a picnic area, and the living room fireplace becomes a campfire. Multiple layers of bronzed metal fabric at the clerestory windows in the living area unfold to adjust sunlight for optimal brightness and temperature. These operable architectural elements use the natural environment to create suitable living conditions.

The house is environmentally friendly in its overall construction and planning, with such specifics as geothermal heating and cooling, shading and venting systems, solar panels, and organic finishes and materials. Lending to the structure's sustainability, the house is assembled, rather than built, with a prefabricated foundation, panel siding, and efficient built-ins that minimize construction debris and toxins, such as concrete foundation tar, on the site. With the owner's initial premise of camping, the design and functionality of the house promote a memorable experience for friends and family in the natural environment.

Local beach pavilion

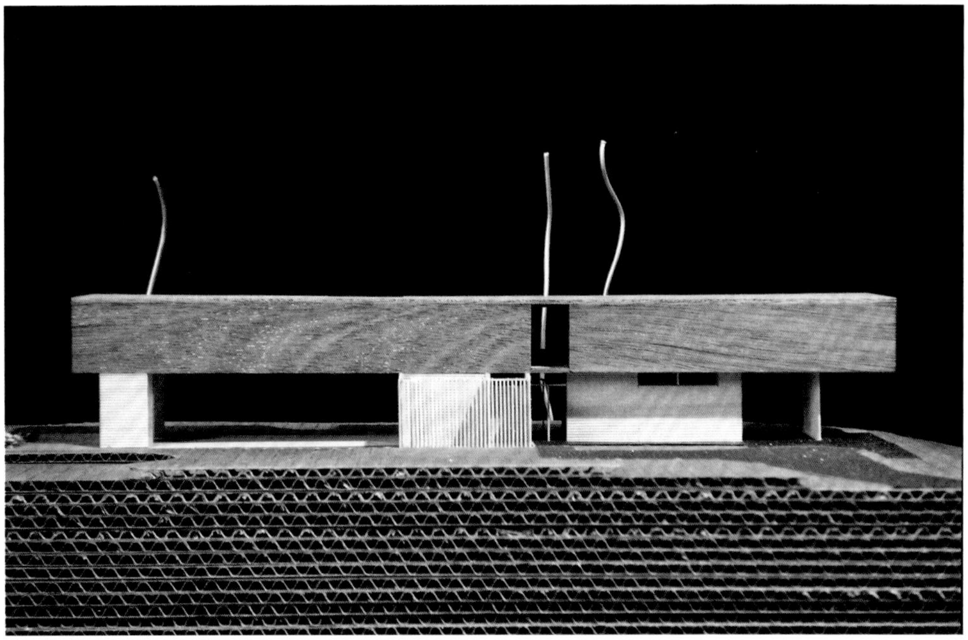

F-4

Installation of panelized construction

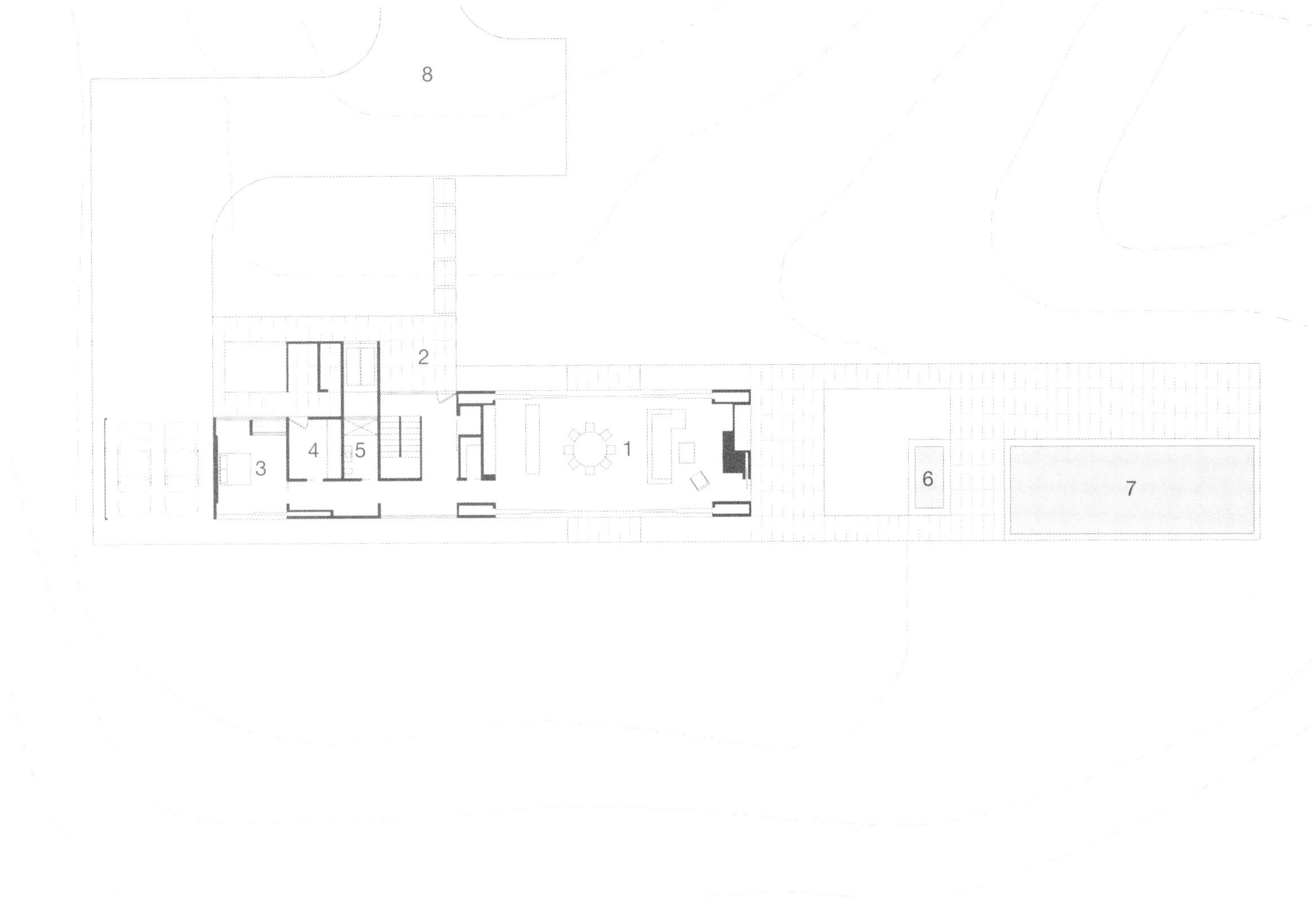

SITE PLAN

1. Living/Dining/Kitchen
2. Entry Patio
3. Guest Bed
4. Mud
5. Guest Bath
6. Spa
7. Pool
8. Driveway

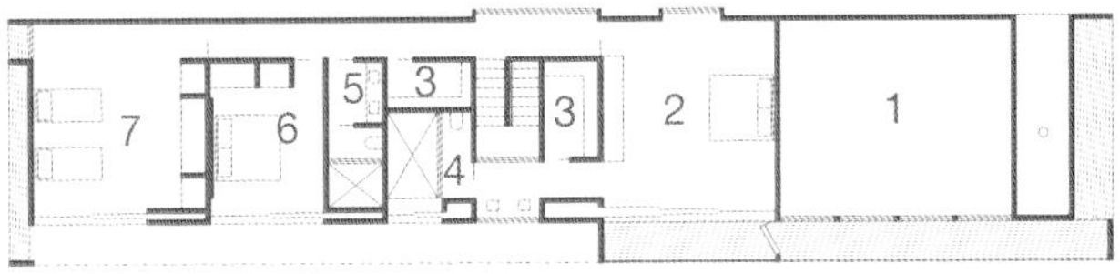

UPPER LEVEL PLAN

1. Open to Below
2. Master Bed
3. Master Closet
4. Master Bath
5. Guest Bath
6. Guest Bed
7. Kids Bed

NORTHWEST PEACH FARM
2008

In a market that treats houses as commodities, designed to maximize resale value after a few summers of enjoyment, the owners of this home have a uniquely long-term vision. Coming from a European perspective, the owners think of a country home in terms of generations, not seasons. They want the house to be a venue for their young childrens' future weddings and a playground for the grandchildren they hope for someday. The home is to be a family heirloom.

To remain a treasured heirloom despite changing fashions and styles, the design of the home must be timeless. On a former peach farm, the house is comprised of a series of gable-roofed pavilions that appear to have accumulated over time. The size and form of each piece are in keeping with more modest vernacular buildings. Similarly, the siding references local building traditions in texture and scale. These traditional forms are subtly adapted in this house to establish its own rare and timeless character.

The materials and systems were chosen to withstand the elements with little or no maintenance. The life span of the copper shingles cladding the roof and walls is over 100 years. The doors and windows were selected with durability in mind as well. A British company has manufactured the same industrial steel windows for over 150 years, with many early examples still in use. Future energy concerns are addressed with a geothermal heating and cooling system, green roofs, and triple-glazed windows.

To further knit the house together with the family, it is designed to slowly change over time with them. As the extended family gathers for their annual visits, they will notice the copper shingles slowly changing from brown to green and the weathering limestone transitioning from cream to brown. And as the family's cherished wine collection grows over time, the pixelated pattern of shadows the bottles cast on a glazed wall of the entry will gradually expand.

The final means of establishing the house as an heirloom is to design it to encourage lasting family memories. Toward that end, unique details transform daily rituals into memorable events. In the kitchen, rolling cutting boards ride in tracks down the long island, turning meal preparation into an assembly line for everyone's participation. The dining table can be reconfigured to make every meal special. Stainless steel tubes running the length of the table can be rotated to reveal candleholders, flower vase holders, or flat surfaces for hot dishes. For parties, the tubes can be removed and the trough filled with ice for chilling drinks. The house surrounds a large lawn, terraced to create large areas for play or for a future wedding.

The clients look forward to many summers together in the house, each one made more memorable by thoughtful design.

Patinaed copper

Weathering of copper over time

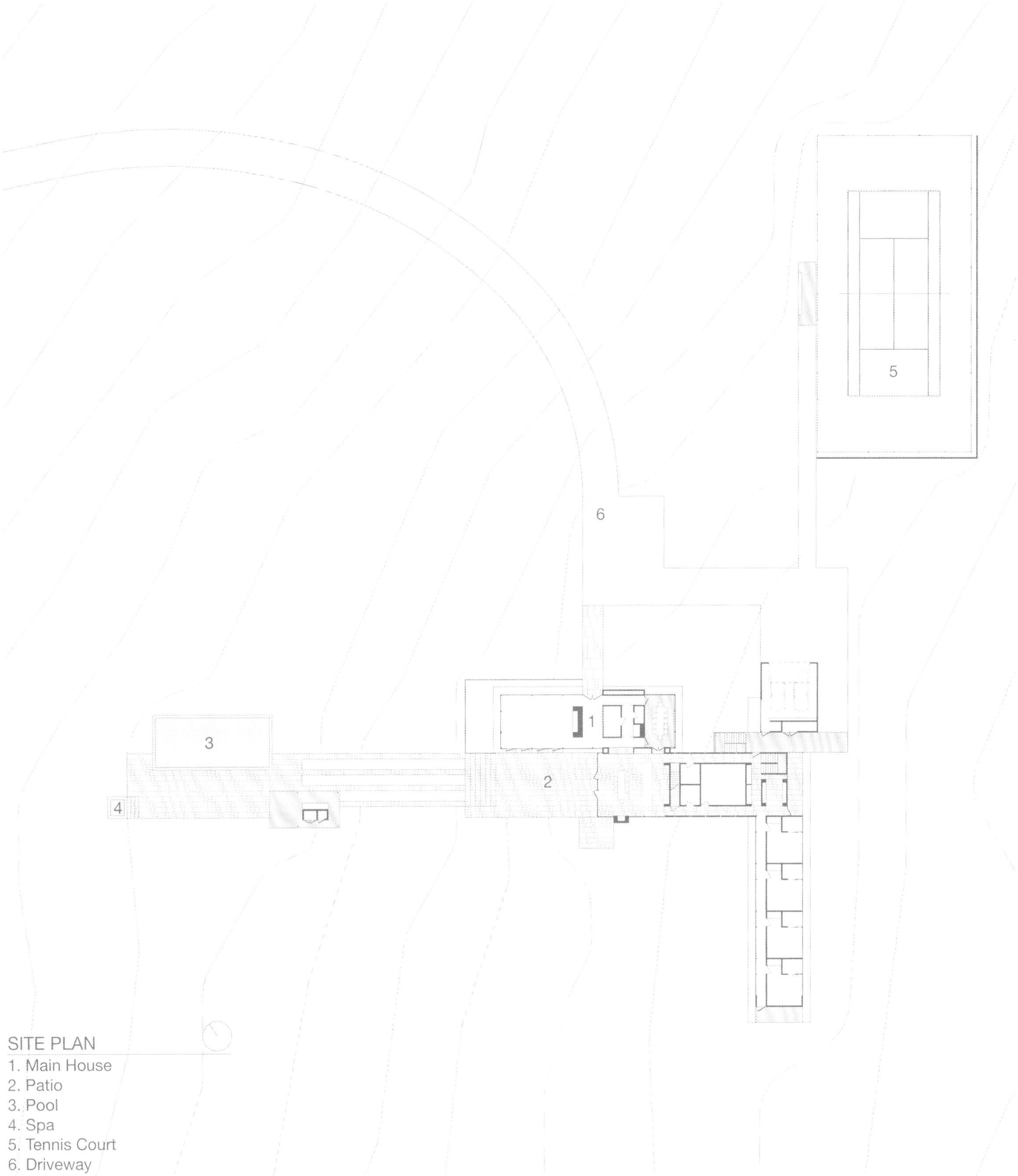

SITE PLAN
1. Main House
2. Patio
3. Pool
4. Spa
5. Tennis Court
6. Driveway

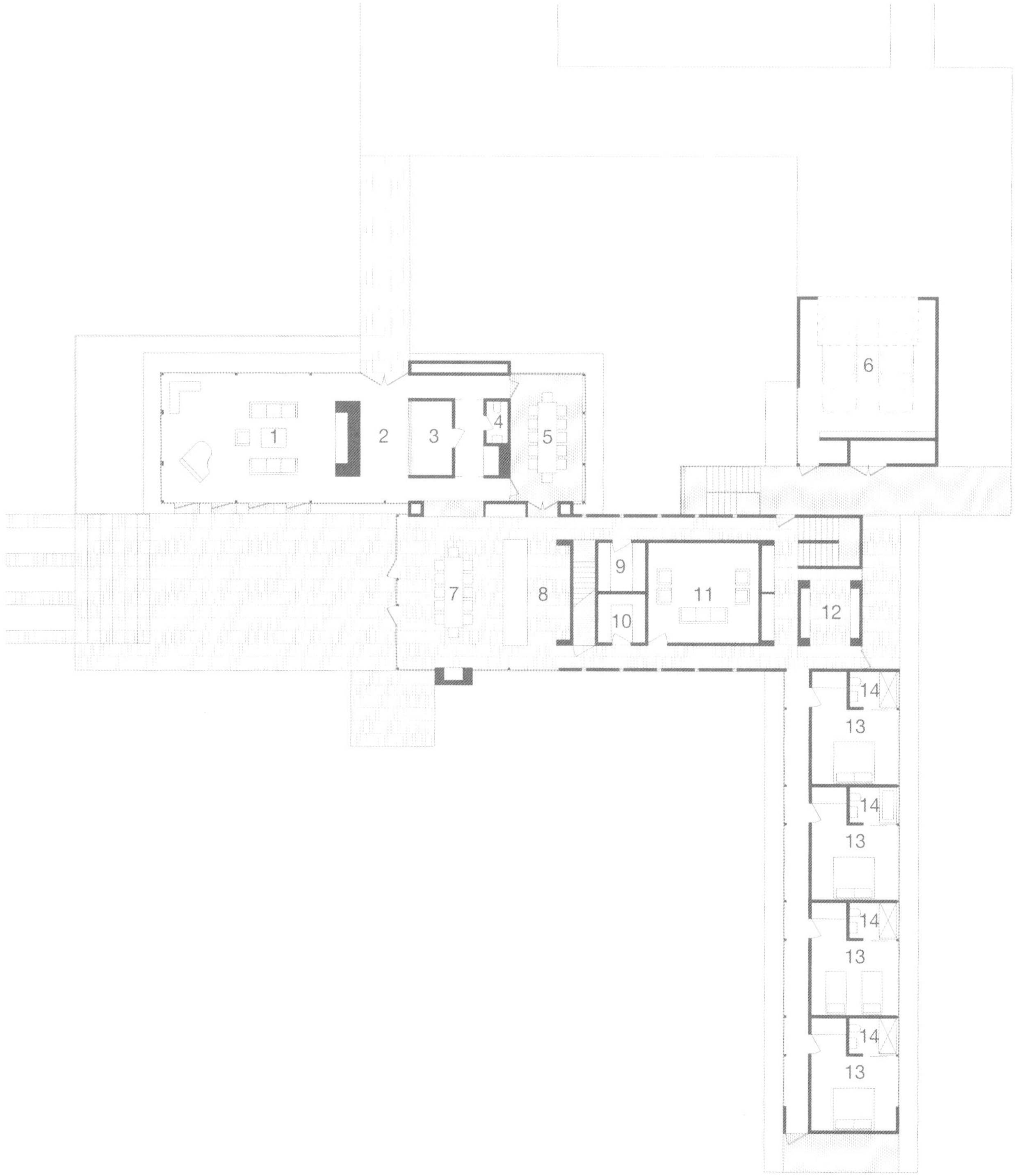

GROUND LEVEL PLAN

1. Living
2. Entry
3. Wine
4. Powder
5. Porch
6. Garage
7. Dining
8. Kitchen
9. Laundry
10. Pantry
11. Den
12. Library
13. Bed
14. Bath

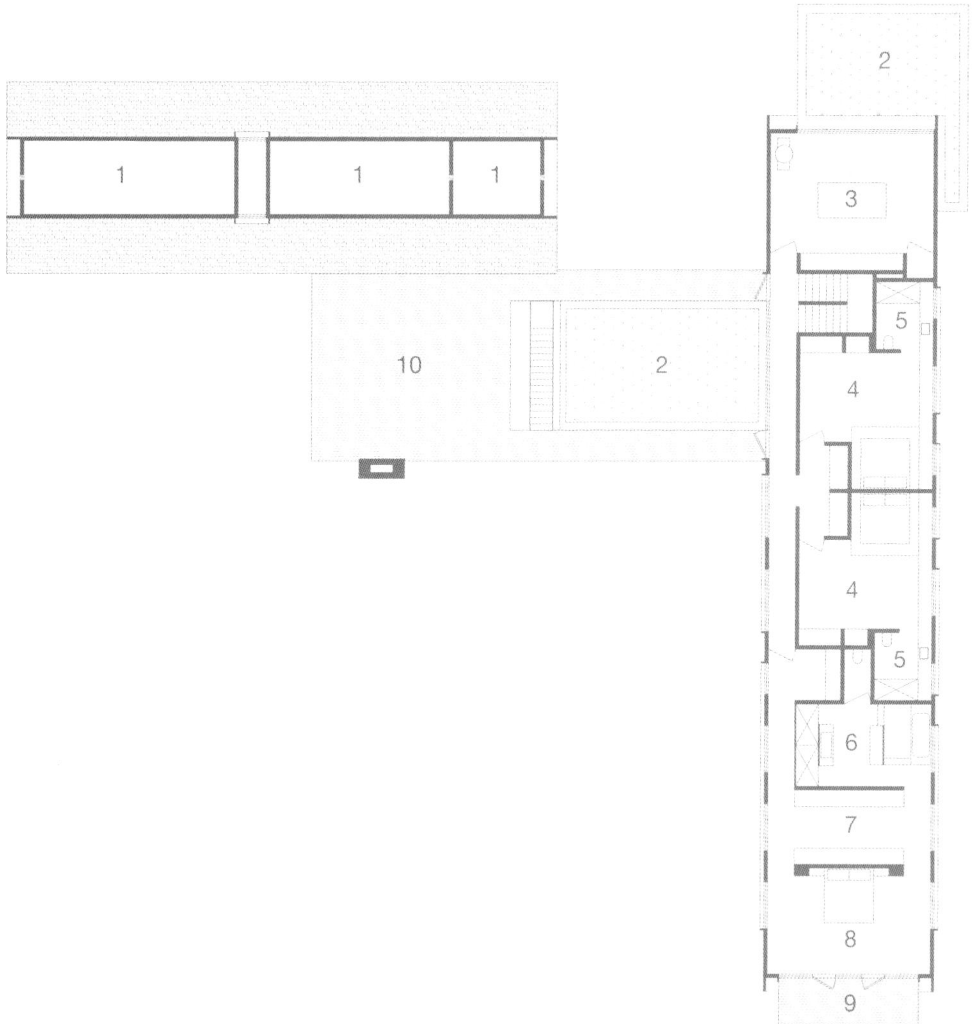

UPPER LEVEL PLAN

1. Open to Below
2. Roof Garden
3. Recreation
4. Bed
5. Bath
6. Master Bath
7. Master Closet
8. Master Bed
9. Master Deck
10. Roof Deck

NOYACK CREEK
2009

The client, a New York actor, sought a retreat for relaxation and casual entertaining on a restrictive narrow lot fronting the tidal estuary of Noyack Creek. The house became a study in architectural theater: a series of spaces in a carefully scripted sequence that subtly reflect his professional life.

The path begins at the front door, where perforated privacy screens slide apart like a curtain, revealing the loft-like living and dining spaces. The direction of the deck boards that make up the flooring is altered to demarcate the path through the space, emerging seamlessly to an exterior waterside deck. A broad stair to the second level, parallel with an interior stair along a glazed wall, acts as tiered seating for entertaining and looking at the water view beyond. Beneath the stair, hidden backstage for maximum privacy, the guest room shares the water view through a nearly hidden sliding door. Guests emerge as if through a trapdoor.

Continuing up the stair to the second floor, the final destination is the master suite and balcony. The master bedroom is connected to the bath by a bridge overlooking the public spaces below, which are lit by the glazed stair wall. Lined with a guardrail of stainless steel cables recalling a fly loft and catwalk, the path culminates in the master bedroom, with its glazed wall overlooking the water.

Windows throughout the house are carefully placed to provide maximum daylight and water views while maintaining privacy from nearby neighbors and street. The siding system is manipulated for varying degrees of privacy as well. Comprised of Skatelite, a natural resin panel typically used in skateboard ramps, the siding is water-jet cut with tight joints in areas demanding privacy and loosely spaced in other areas to admit light and air. The texture and color of the siding, in keeping with the budget of the house, reference a black box theater.

In the end, a house that could have been limited by its small site and budget was elevated by its conception as a stage for lasting experiences.

Local outdoor theater

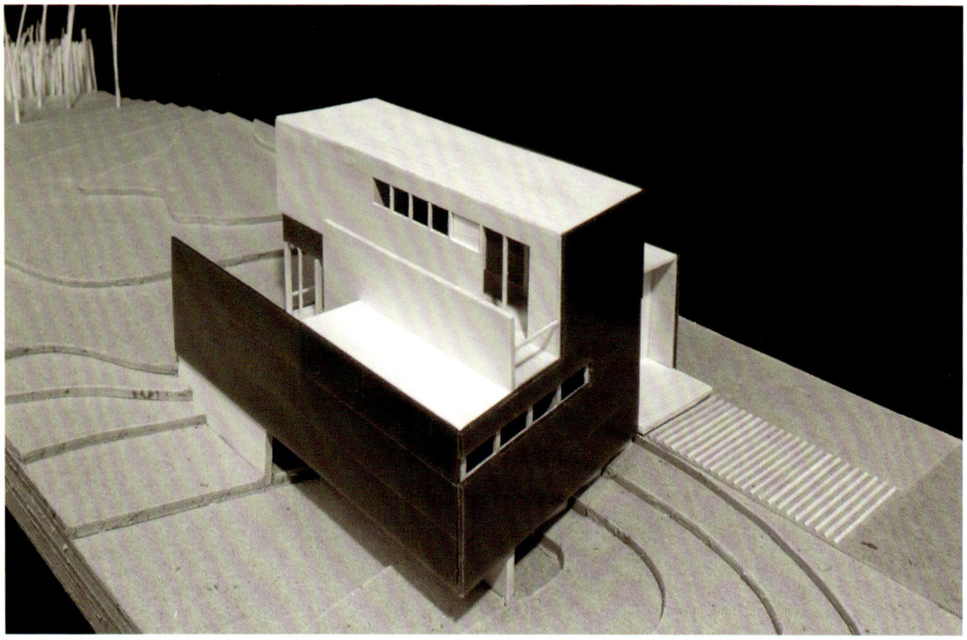

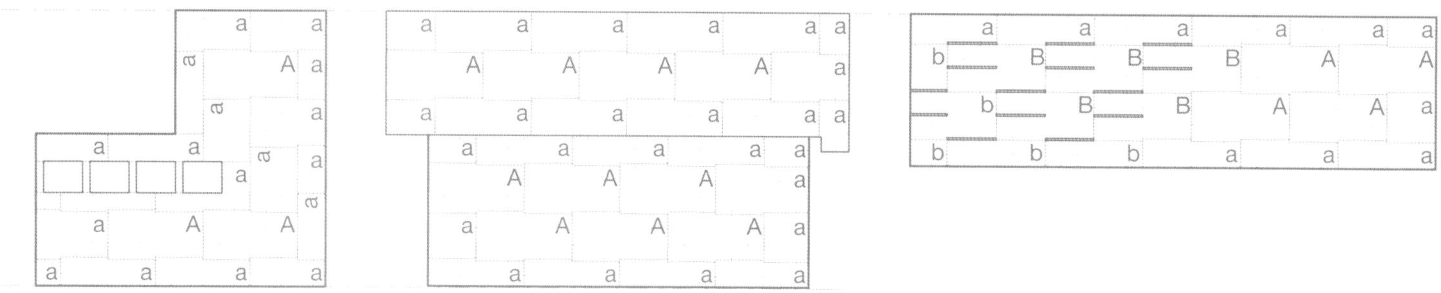

A: Full Type A Panel
a: Cut Type A Panel
B: Full Type B Panel
b: Cut Type B Panel

Water-jet fabricated resin panel installation diagram

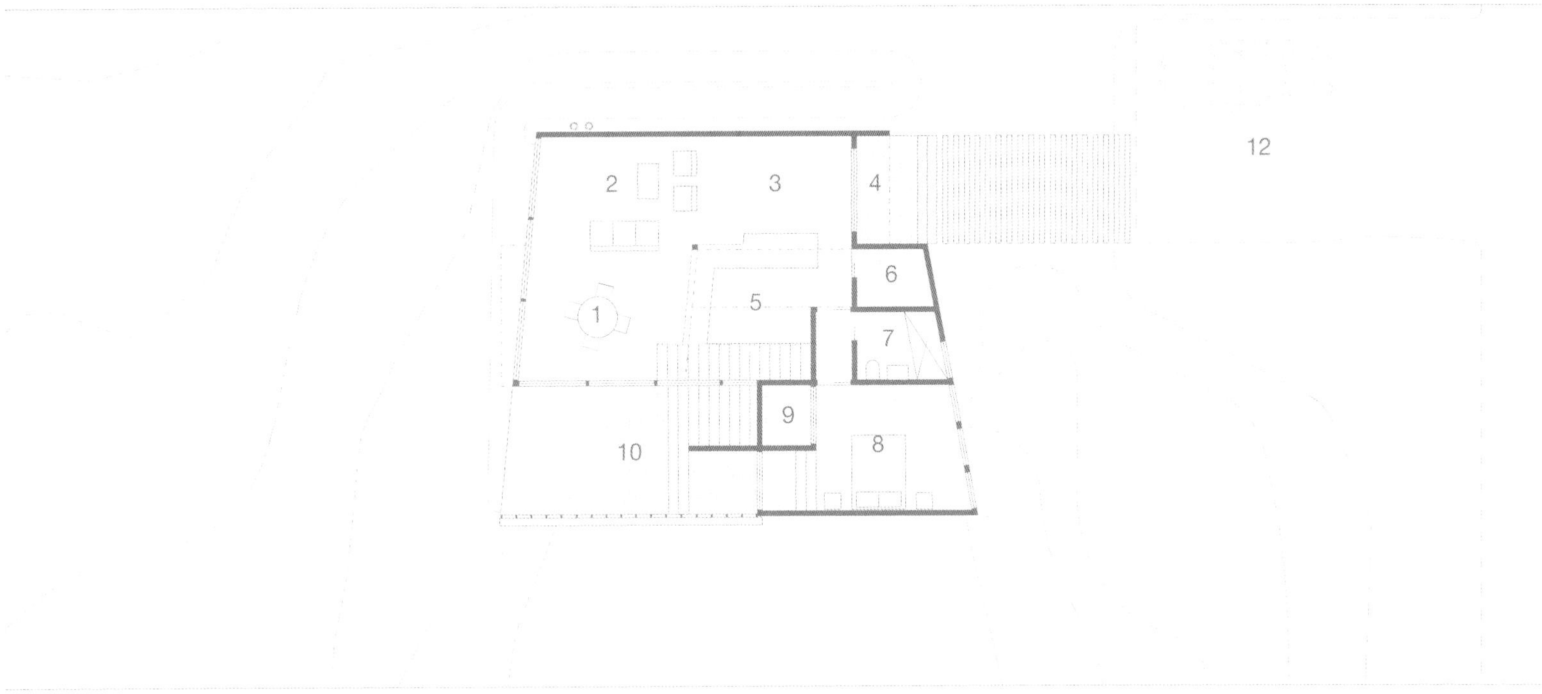

GROUND LEVEL PLAN

1. Dining
2. Living
3. Entry
4. Entry Deck
5. Kitchen
6. Pantry
7. Guest Bath
8. Guest Bed
9. Closet
10. Deck
11. Creek
12. Parking

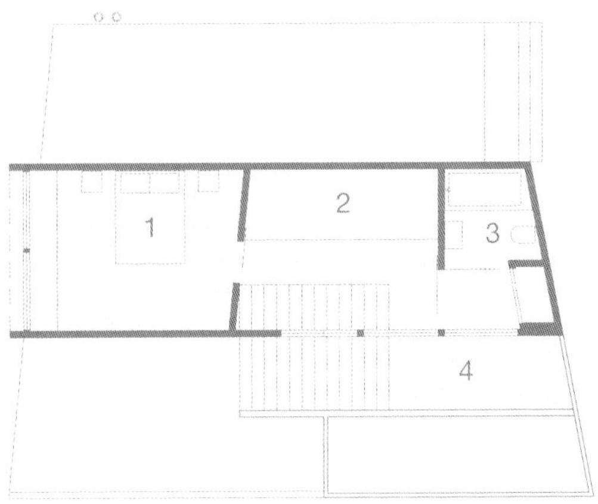

UPPER LEVEL PLAN

1. Master Bed
2. Open to Below
3. Master Bath
4. Roof Deck

GENIUS LOCI

2011

Montauk, NY, at the eastern end of Long Island, may appear to be like any other small seaside community upon first glance; however, it possesses unique characteristics that imprint lasting memories. The weather is unpredictable with banks of heavy fog and gusty winds. History is closer to folklore than truth, with stories of the Montauk Project Conspiracy, German submarines and, most recently, the Montauk Monster blurring the line between fact and fiction. Structural remnants of the past, such as a radar tower and bunkers, are scattered throughout the landscape. Socially, there is a seasonal migration and mix of economic classes. The clients could have chosen to vacation anywhere in the world, but were lured to Montauk by the characteristics that identify it from other areas. These characteristics embody the "Spirit of Montauk", and the clients challenged the architect to design a house that would capture this spirit in the architecture.

The house responds to the site's context and strengthens the "spirit of place". Formerly a horse ranch, the rolling green pasture of the site is located at one of the highest elevations in Montauk. The extensive program is terraced and embedded into the steep slope of the hill without compromising access to the exterior or natural light. Approaching from the south, the house appears to be two modest and separate one-story ranch houses. Circling around to the north, the house unfolds to reveal a more extensive project. In this case, the conventional Montauk building typology of the low-pitched gabled roof is modified by the geometries of the allowable building envelope and height restrictions of the site. The geometric anomaly is apparent upon entry and it is unexpectedly clear that the ridge is offset and the walls converge, directing one's view west to the lake. The optical illusion caused by the parabolic roof is visible on the south side and invites a second look, as do numerous other details. Architectural details throughout the house occur at surprising moments. A wood, screen-covered bridge unifies the two separate, cedar-shingle-clad volumes, allowing light into the grass paver courtyard below. The cedar screen of the bridge reads differently from day to night. It appears flat during the day, but as darkness falls, light seeps out in an undulating pattern, showing the wedge shape cut in the back of the boards. In front of several clerestory windows, a milled bluestone screen is similarly detailed. The stone appears weightless, as alternating stones are removed from the stone wall pattern to let light into the guest area. These unusual details reinforce the larger idea of capturing the unexpected.

For the occupant there is no prescribed path of circulation, encouraging different encounters, much like the social experiences of Montauk. One can enter beneath the bridge that frames the sky beyond and up a series of terraced planter steps, which reveal the pastoral rolling hills and ocean in the distance. This path draws a visitor directly into the landscape, bypassing the house. One can also climb the exterior entry stair that directly connects to the interior stair, separated by a wall of glass, and choose to enter the house or continue the journey to the outdoor fireplace, dining area, and out to the pool. A guest staying at the house can privately come and go by a stone terrace that wraps the exterior of the guest area from the entry courtyard around to the pool with no need to enter the house.

The house celebrates the "spirit of the place" where it is located. With the rise of technology and rapid transmission of information through the internet, the identity of place can be lost. This project explores regionalism and evolves from the community where it is located.

Montauk beach with bunker remnants

Stone screen

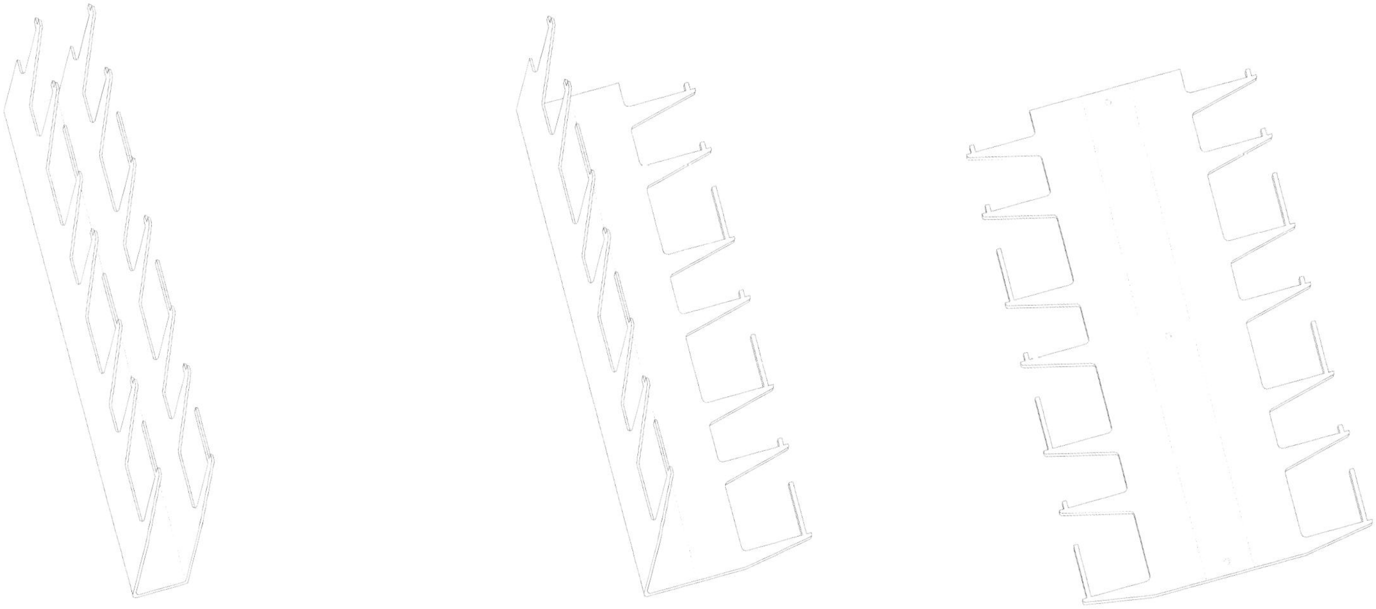

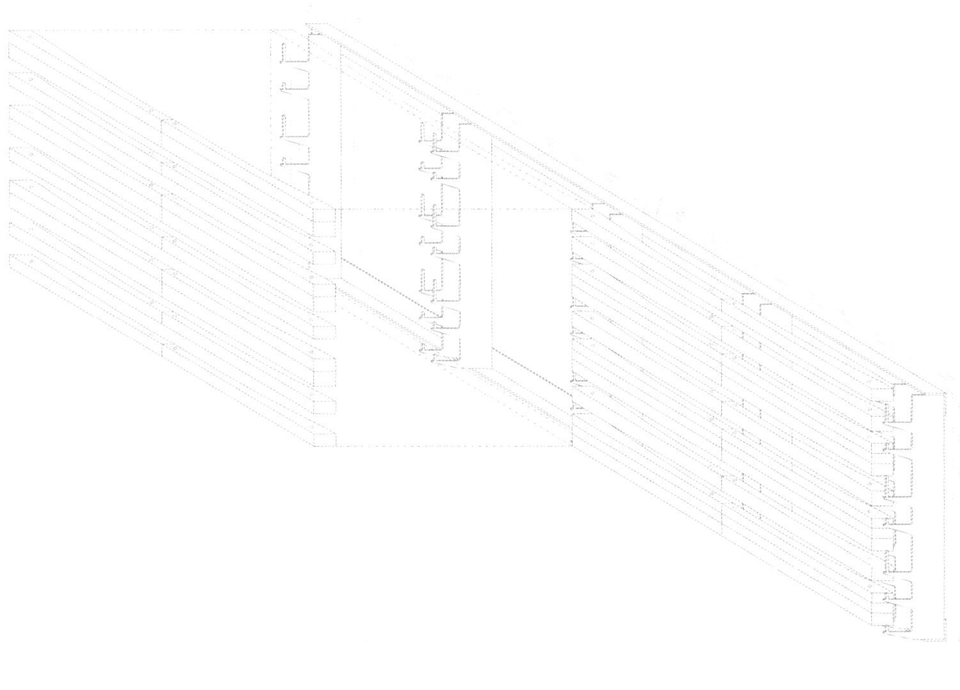

Armature folding diagram and assembly of stone onto armature

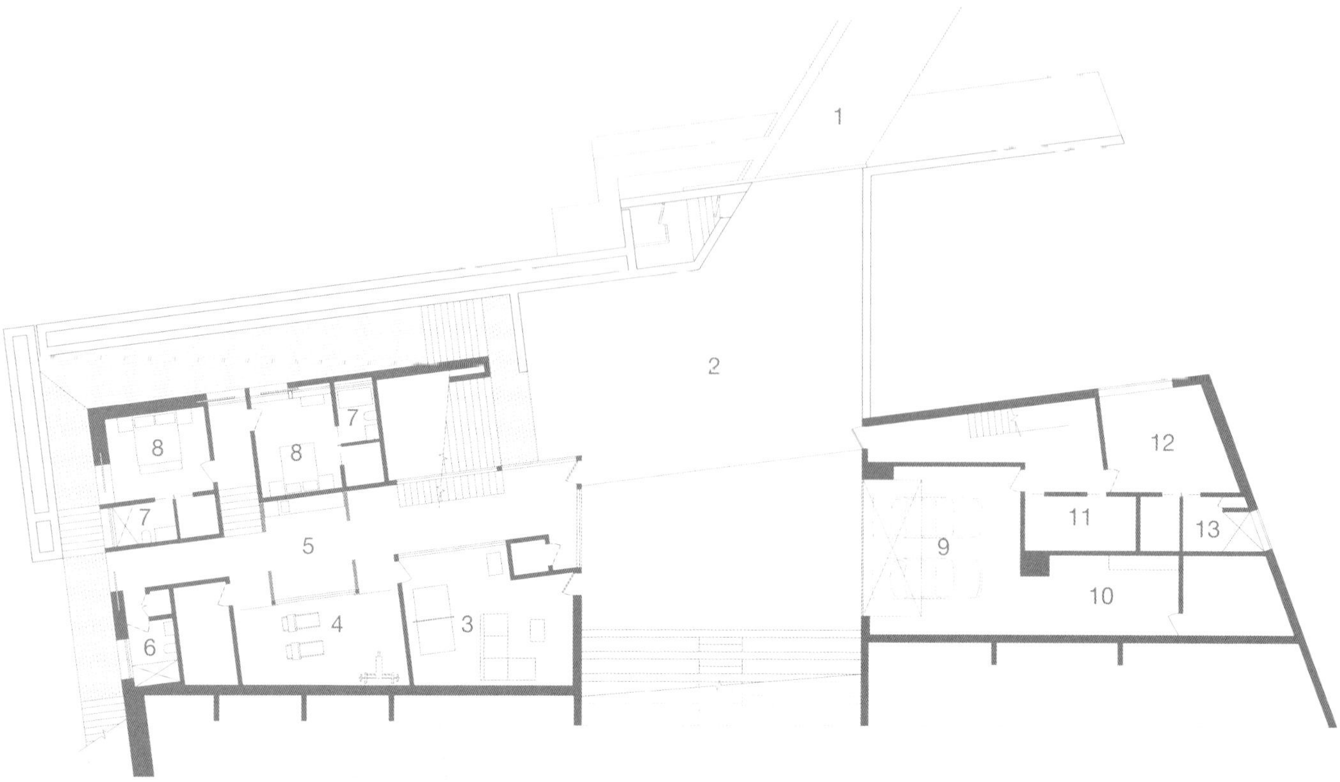

LOWER LEVEL PLAN

1. Driveway
2. Parking
3. Recreation
4. Gym
5. Common
6. Pool Bath
7. Guest Bath
8. Guest Bed
9. Garage
10. Storage
11. Laundry
12. Maid's Bed
13. Maid's Bath

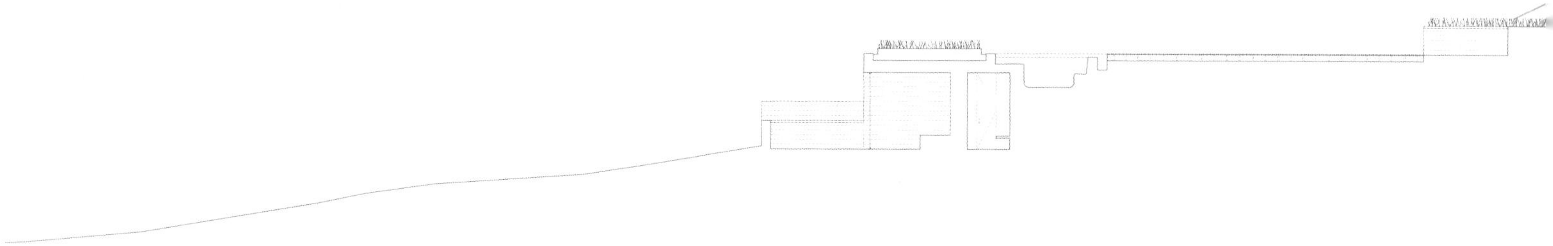

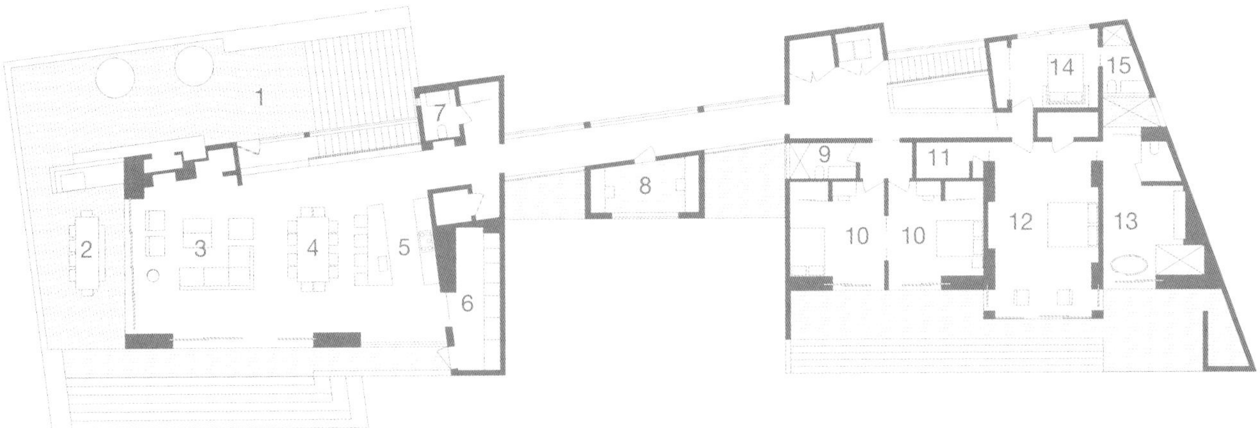

UPPER LEVEL PLAN

1. Entry
2. Deck
3. Living
4. Dining
5. Kitchen
6. Pantry
7. Powder
8. Office
9. Kid's Bath
10. Kid's Bed
11. Closet
12. Master Bed
13. Master Bath
14. Nursery Bed
15. Nursery Bath

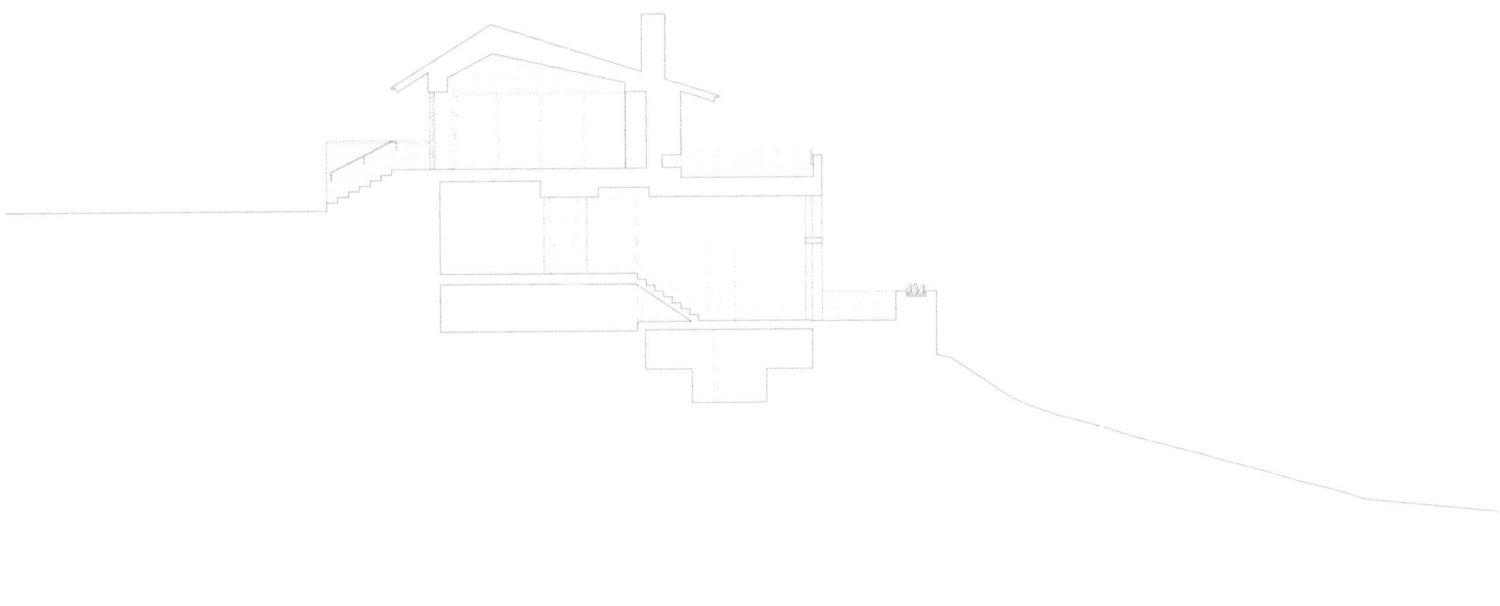

SAM'S CREEK
2011

We live in a time where smartphones and tablets are in everyone's hands and multitasking is the normal way of life. Influenced by the clients' multitasking lifestyle, a diverse set of requirements developed for a new home. The clients, one of whom is the owner of a public relations company, requested that multiple activities could happen throughout the house without interruption; a dinner party could take place while simultaneously entertaining a group of children, or guests could come and go without disturbing the rest of the family. These programmatic requests diagrammatically divide the site, as well as establish view corridors from front to back. Transparency through the house puts concurrent activities on display and provides a setting where guests can see and be seen.

A series of open-ended boxes, each tailored to a portion of the architectural program, focuses the view from the street through the house to the landscape in the rear. Mahogany boards wrap floors, ceilings, and the sides of the boxes to heighten the perspectival view and provide privacy from neighbors. Each box has independent audio, video, and climate control to operate autonomously, and the scale of each box is tailored to its program. On the exterior, interstitial spaces between the arranged boxes form gardens and patios. The overlap of the boxes on the interior creates thresholds with unique spatial relationships. With each box occupying a specific program, the multitasking of different events is accommodated.

A limited material palette provides continuity and serenity amidst the diverse activities. Mahogany is used inside and out for its inherent durability without the need for harsh stains or finishes. Travertine is used as flooring for the terraces and as cladding on portions of the open-ended boxes. To use the stone as an exterior cladding, a custom hanging system was designed. The travertine siding is held at the top and bottom by a CNC-wire-formed frame and overlapped by the following course above. The proportion and repetition of the siding references the wood shingle vernacular ubiquitous in the area.

The gas fireplace, a utilitarian object and a crafted sculptural work of art, is a moment frame which supports lateral loads to allow for the large, open-ended volume of the living and dining room. It also houses a coat closet and HVAC components. The overlapping, repeating bronze components were digitally fabricated and assembled on-site. Different patina processes were studied to achieve the dark bronze facing the room and the polished bronze on the interior of the hood. Sunlight from above is reflected by the polished bronze and filters through the spaces from the overlapped construction. Similar construction methods were utilized for the master bedroom headboard, using repeating strips of belting leather.

The large, flat roofs hide photovoltaic panels, which reduce the energy demands of the house. Geothermal heating and cooling, interior light wells, overhangs, integrated operable awnings, and organic finishes further reduce the home's environmental impact.

The separation of program into individual volumes allows the multitasking lifestyle of the clients to continue into their home. Where multitasking on a daily basis can seem chaotic, a new order is developed by the architecture. The clients' new home allows them to keep up with their busy lifestyle while also providing respite from it.

Grouping of rocks at local beach

Custom stone shingle and clip

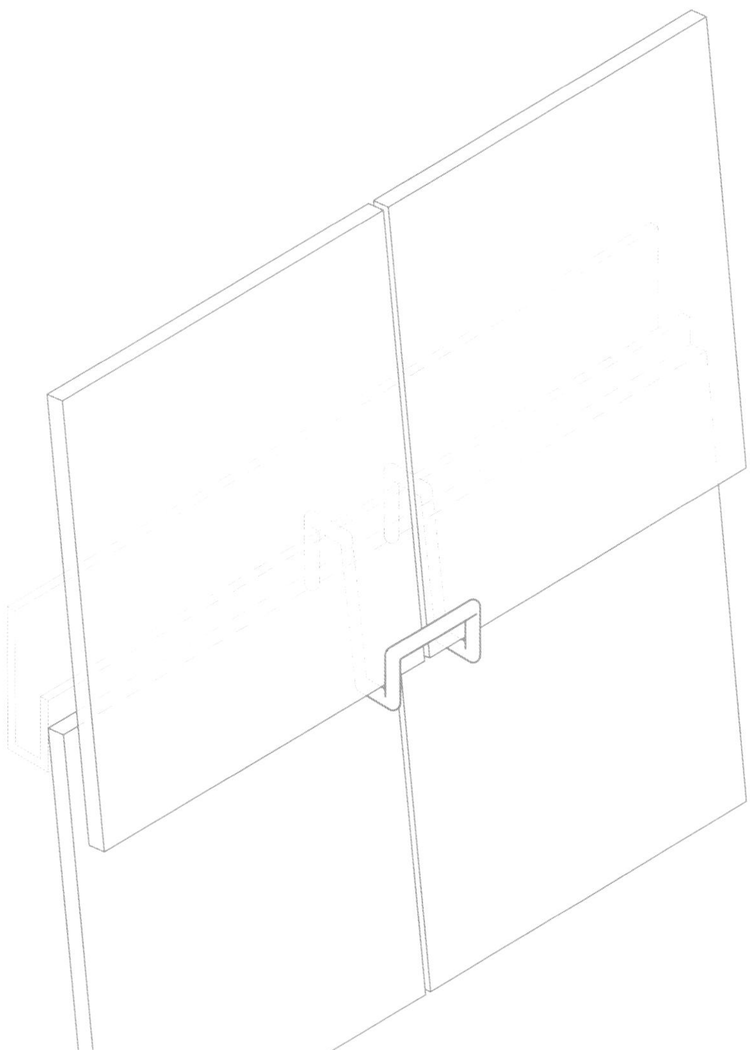

Shingle and clip diagram

GROUND LEVEL PLAN

1. Entry
2. Dining
3. Living
4. Family
5. Kitchen
6. Pantry
7. Powder
8. Laundry
9. Garage
10. Outdoor Shower
11. Patio
12. Guest Bed
13. Guest Bath
14. Master Bath
15. Master Closet
16. Master Bed

UPPER LEVEL PLAN

1. Open to Below
2. Kid's Bed
3. Kid's Bath
4. Guest Bed
5. Guest Bath

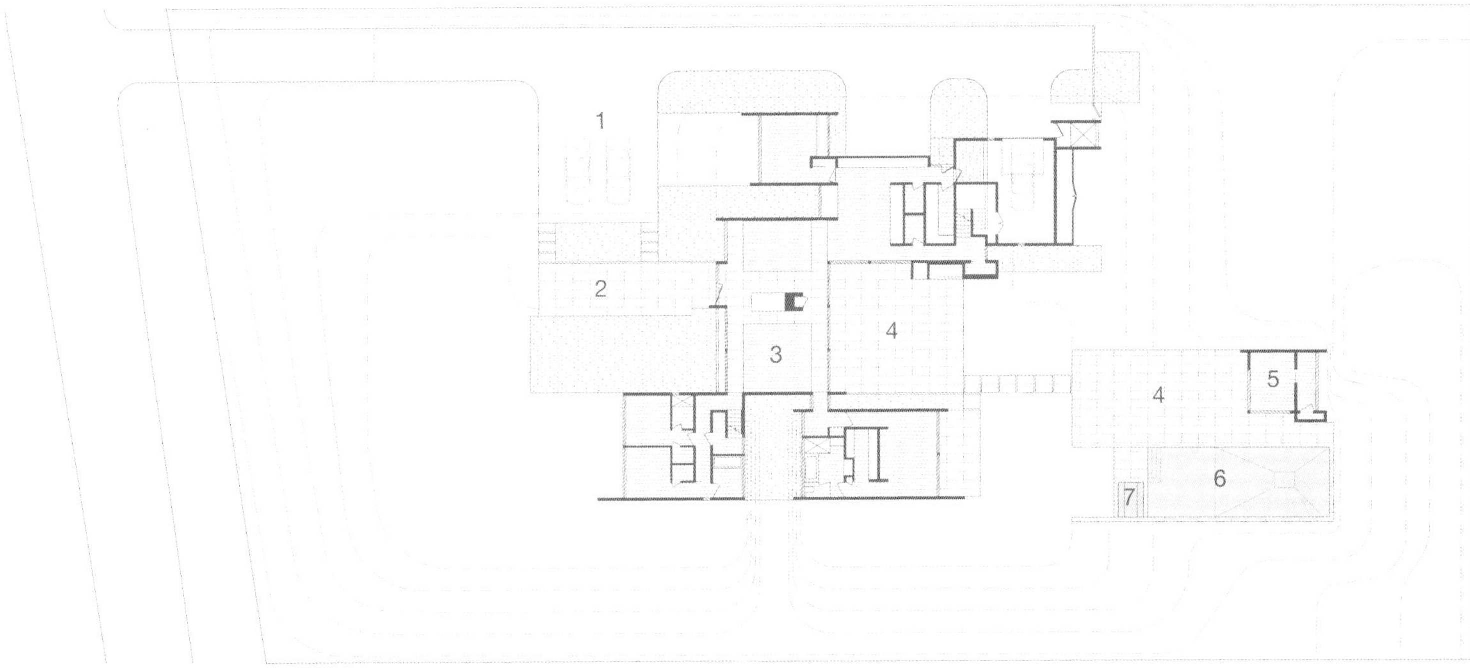

SITE PLAN

1. Parking
2. Entry
3. Main House
4. Patio
5. Pool House
6. Pool
7. Spa

SAGAPONACK
2012

Located between the Atlantic Ocean and a freshwater pond, this residence is for an adventurous couple and their four sons. They wanted a house for their large family and numerous guests with a lawn, swimming pool, pool house, garage, and sports courts on a site with a limited building envelope due to coastal and wetland zoning. The large program, relatively small footprint, and daunting regulations dictated a building envelope densely packed with program that stood as a barrier between the ocean and the pond. Thus, the design process was one of subtraction rather than addition: carving away at the solid mass of the house to reconnect site features and views and to distill the experience of the place.

Spaces run the full width of the house, with floor-to-ceiling sliding doors on both sides that create apertures through which views, light, and air completely penetrate the house and dissolve its mass. With the sliding doors open and recessed into the adjacent walls, interior spaces are transformed from formal rooms to open pavilions, merging seamlessly with the site.

The plinth of the elevated house is carved into a series of stepped planters that are further sculpted into the entry steps, mediating the different grades required by flood control regulations. Aside from dictating the minimum first-floor height, regulations also set the roof height. To maximize the ceiling heights within those limits, the house utilizes a steel moment frame to pare down the thicknesses of the floors and roof to the absolute minimum.

The design strategy to accommodate the extensive program is to nest spaces within one another. Operable partitions pull out from the walls of the living room, carving out a media room within the living room when privacy is desired. Conversely, with the partitions open, the media room merges with the living room for large gatherings. The thickness of the wall separating the dining room and kitchen is also cut away, utilizing its depth to accommodate a wine rack that also functions as a light fixture.

The process of carving is applied at the material and detail levels as well. The 5/8" weathering steel plate that clads the base of the house is water-jet cut into a delicate pattern that defies its mass. Inside, Corian is employed for the ease with which it can be milled. Corian countertops are cut to form towel bars, bunk bed frames are carved to create ladders, cabinet doors are recessed to form handles, and wainscoting is subtly etched with meaningful words chosen by the clients.

Materials were chosen not only for their workability, but also for their durability in the harsh coastal environment. Heavy-gauge weathering steel siding is zero-maintenance in spite of being relentlessly sandblasted by the wind. Cedar siding and screens are finished using a Victorian technique in which iron sulfate, in a blend of white vinegar and iron filings, reacts with the tannins in wood, creating an ebony finish that penetrates through the material and will not require refinishing. The lack of harsh stains or finishes reduces the ecological footprint of the house. Geothermal heating and cooling, as well as vegetated roofs, further reduce the environmental impact.

Using the design approach of sculpting away rather than building up, the house is pared down until the experience of the extraordinary site is dominant.

Carved steel sculpture

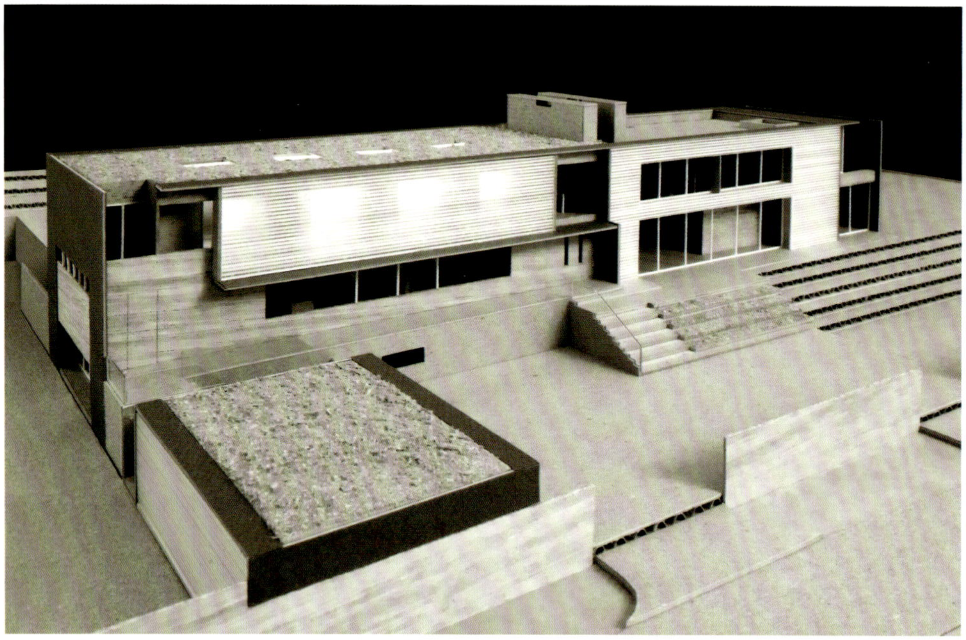

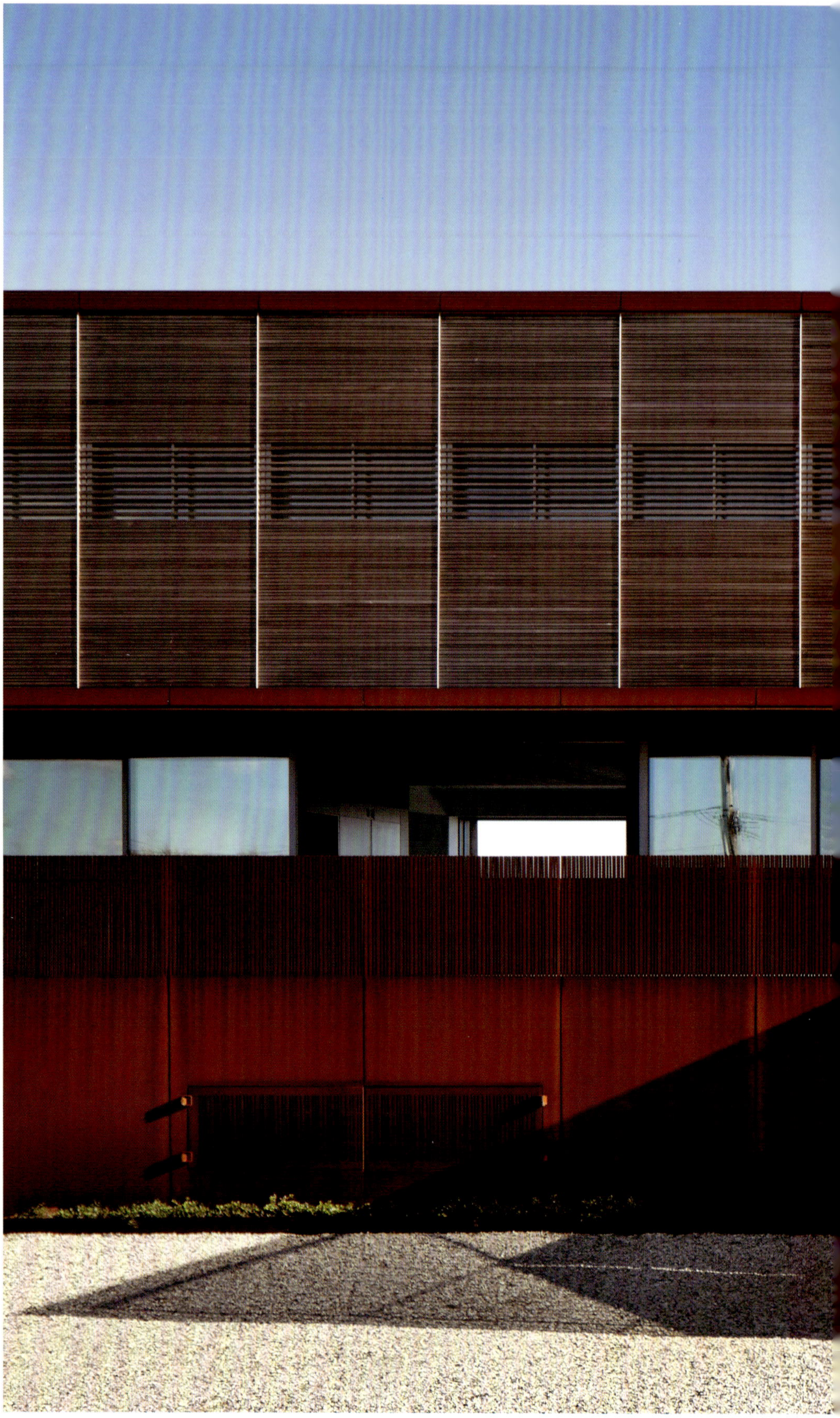

Weathering steel plate installation

CNC-milled ceiling panel studies

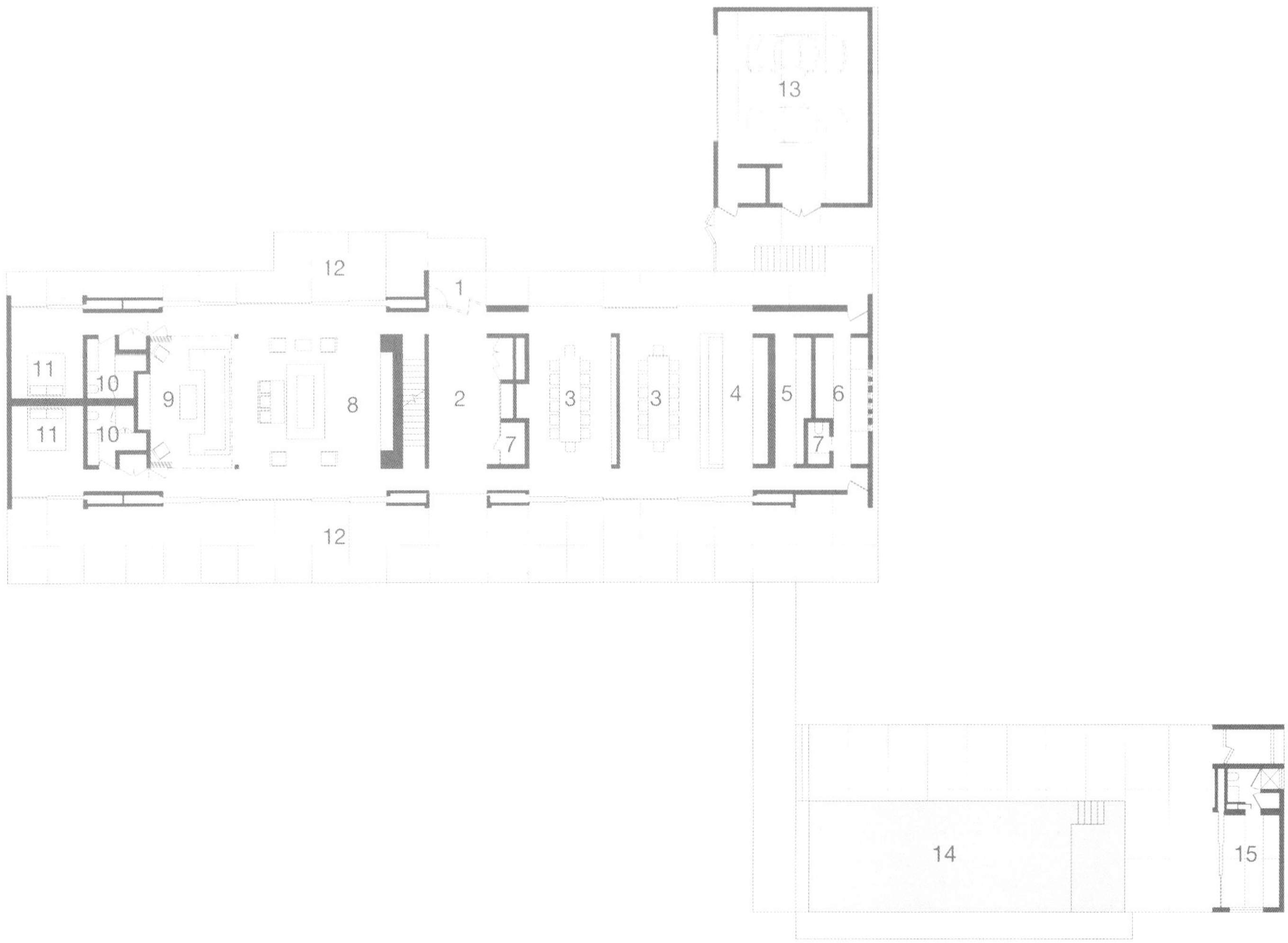

GROUND LEVEL PLAN

1. Entry Patio
2. Entry Hall
3. Dining
4. Kitchen
5. Pantry
6. Laundry
7. Powder
8. Living
9. Family
10. Guest Bath
11. Guest Bed
12. Patio
13. Garage
14. Pool
15. Pool House

OCEAN

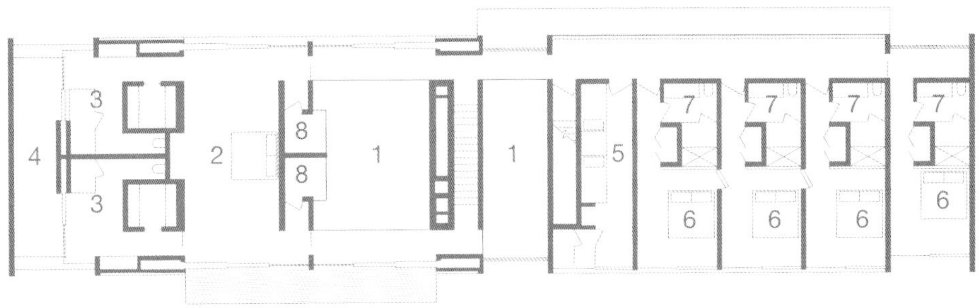

UPPER LEVEL PLAN

1. Open to Below
2. Master Bed
3. Master Bath
4. Spa Deck
5. Bunk Room
6. Kid's Bed
7. Kid's Bath
8. Office

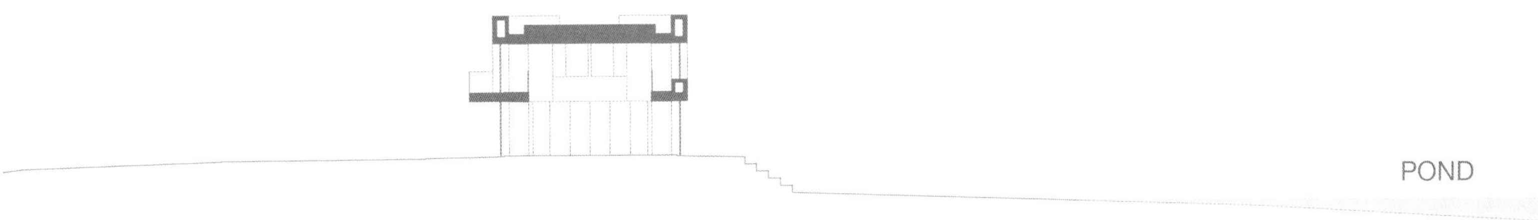

NORTHWEST HARBOR

2013

Straddling freshwater wetlands and a tidal estuary just six feet above sea level, this house's site demands extraordinary sensitivity to environmental concerns. Local zoning restricts the structure's maximum coverage and proximity to wetland areas, while FEMA requirements set the first floor structure above the base flood elevation. The house's basic massing is therefore predetermined, limited to a one-story, 1,900-square-foot design, raised eight feet above the ground. The spaces within this envelope are arranged, articulated, and fenestrated based on an innovative structural system that infuses the house's inner areas with light and circulating air.

Whereas most waterfront construction uses pilings to establish an artificial ground plane upon which a conventional house is built, these structural members are integral in this project: sixteen exposed, glue-laminated piles stake out the enclosing walls for each of the three bedrooms and extend continuously from the ground through the roof. The spaces between these piles house "utility" functions: closet, desk, laundry, pantry, and shower compartment. In addition to these conventional utilities, three vertical voids are opened between the piles to serve the spaces around them.

Without occupying any of the limited allowed coverage, these open areas add considerable value by improving the house's interior environmental quality and diminishing its impact on the local environment. The benefit is threefold: each opening draws light though the interior spaces to the carport below, conducts rainwater from the roof deck to the ground via integral downspouts carved into the piles, and ventilates by siphoning air through the middle of the structure.

At the roof, the projecting piles divide the space between a deck directly coinciding with the living areas below and a modular planting system installed above each bedroom to reduce runoff. The projecting piles also serve as supports for photovoltaics that power geothermal pumps, utilizing the abundance of high ground water to heat and cool the house. At the ground level, the space below the house is utilized for parking and storage to minimize the footprint on the site.

By allowing voids to permeate through the house, the owners have multiple visual connections to the landscape from below, within, and above, encouraging a sense of place.

Structure in nearby flood plain

Installation of pile structure

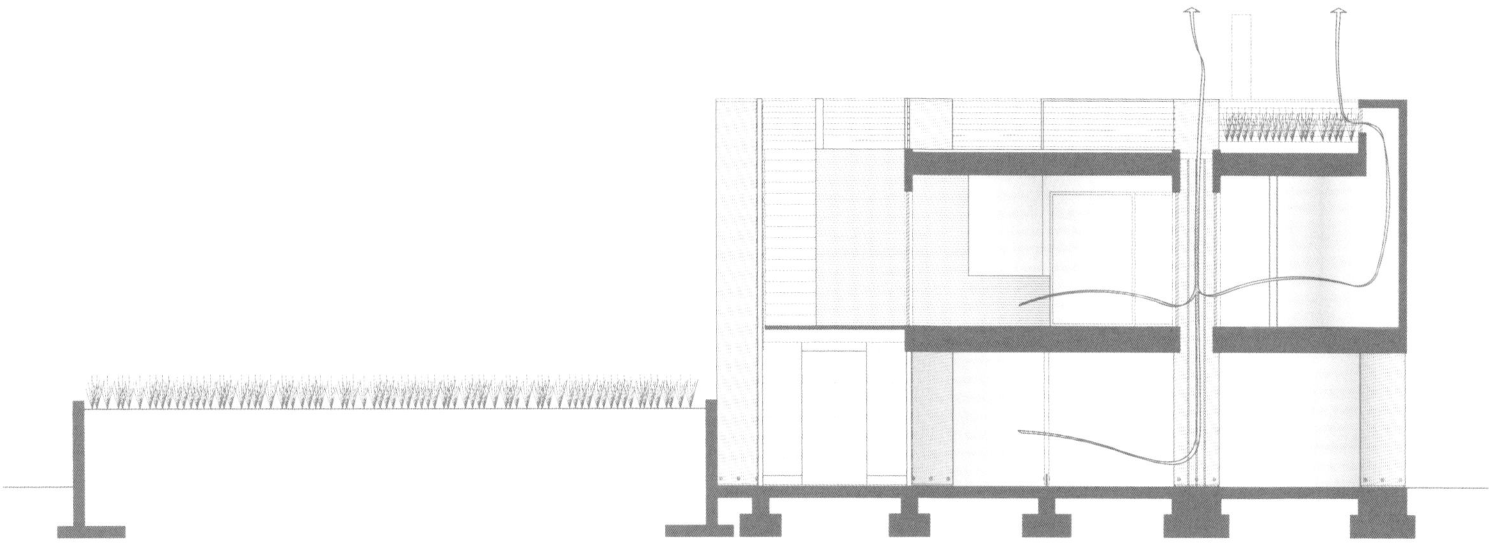

Building section illustrating air circulation

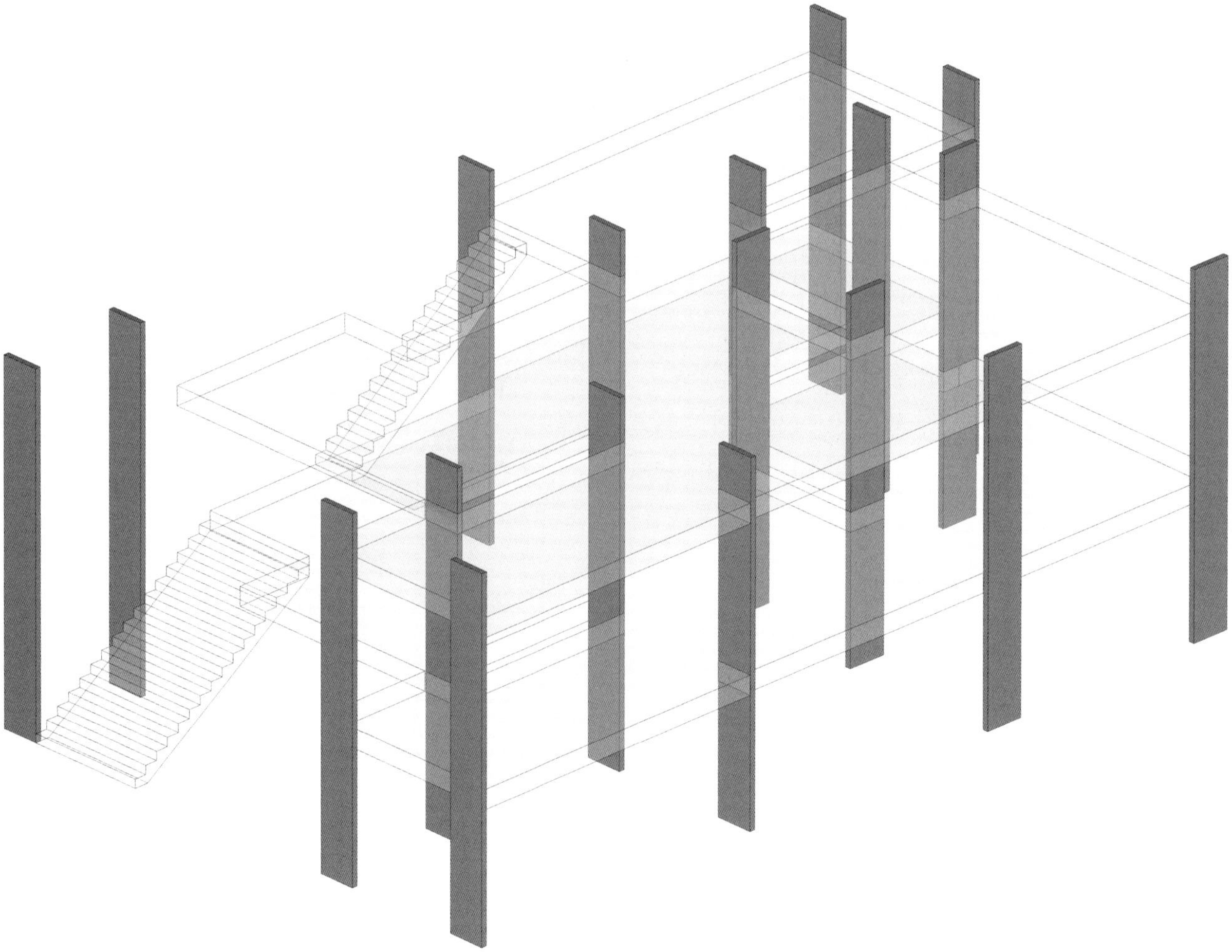

Structural diagram

UPPER LEVEL PLAN

1. Entry
2. Dining
3. Kitchen
4. Living
5. Grill
6. Guest Bed
7. Guest Bath
8. Master Bed
9. Master Bath
10. Office
11. Kid's Bed
12. Kid's Bath
13. Balcony
14. Light Well

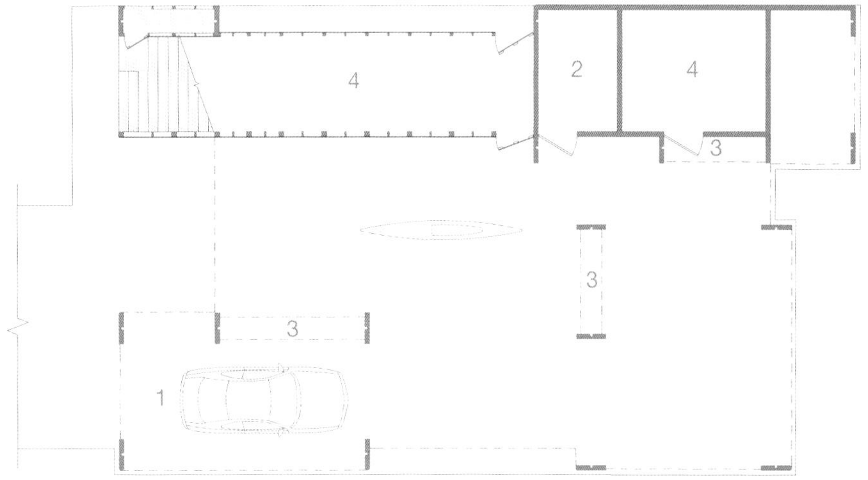

GROUND LEVEL PLAN

1. Parking
2. Mechanical
3. Light Well Above
4. Storage

MOTHERSILL
2013

Elevated, wooden boardwalks extending into the beachscape are a common occurrence in the dunes of eastern Long Island. Hovering slightly over the ground, this simple device is a pathway to the beach that carefully negotiates a constantly changing terrain. Their simple construction challenges the extreme natural elements found at the intersection of land and sea. In beachfront construction, the boardwalk provides a unifying accessibility that connects disparate elements of building and landscape; it is an extension of building that is knit within the landscape. This design for a vacation home in Water Mill, New York, utilizes a boardwalk as an architectural device for weaving together multiple portions of a historic site with new building and landscape elements.

Located on a creek-front property, the site contains two culturally significant structures designed by architect Andrew Geller and a diversity of landscape plantings. The two Geller structures, a small house and studio, were built in 1962. Common in Geller's architecture, a boardwalk extends from the structures to provide a connection between the two. A varied collection of botanically significant plantings populates the property, including a rare specimen Yew garden, serpentine Yew hedge, and more than 400,000 Siberian Irises. The western edge of the property slopes downward to a low-lying wetland bordering the creek. A conservation easement on the property protects the two Geller structures, Yew garden, and irises, while allowing for the addition of a new main house. The owners of the property requested a design that seamlessly incorporated the protected Geller structures, Yew garden, and new residence. To achieve this objective, a constructed path traverses the site to link visual and spatial relationships between these elements. The path takes the form of a raised, wooden surface that recalls the boardwalks of Geller's architecture.

Similar to the way the boardwalks in nearby dunes engage an undulating landscape, this low, horizontal path engages distinct site features with the historic Geller structures and new house. Building and wetland setbacks, existing landscape features, site access, and conservation easement restrictions overlap to create the parameters of a meandering path across the site. The path originates from the relocated Geller House in the Yew garden and winds around the serpentine hedge to a new swimming pool. Like the historic arrangement of the Geller House and Studio, the new boardwalk physically connects the two historic structures. As the path continues it passes the Geller Studio, now reprogrammed as a pool house, and connects to shaded outdoor living spaces. A new central lawn is defined as the boardwalk wraps to extend through the main house. A cantilevered deck wraps the end of the main house at the termination of the path, providing views of the sloping wetland and creek. The surface of the path folds up and over to become the enclosure of the main house, simultaneously functioning as floor, wall, and roof. All surfaces of this enclosure are constructed with the same wood decking as the boardwalk, and their uniformity gives the effect of a single envelope containing a variety of parts, which reflect the influence of design in Geller's work. In these ways, the physical, material, and spatial qualities of the path facilitate an architectural dialogue between the Geller structures and the new house that is interwoven with the existing landscape, collecting the once-individual elements into a unified whole.

Andrew Geller, George House, 1963

Siding detail

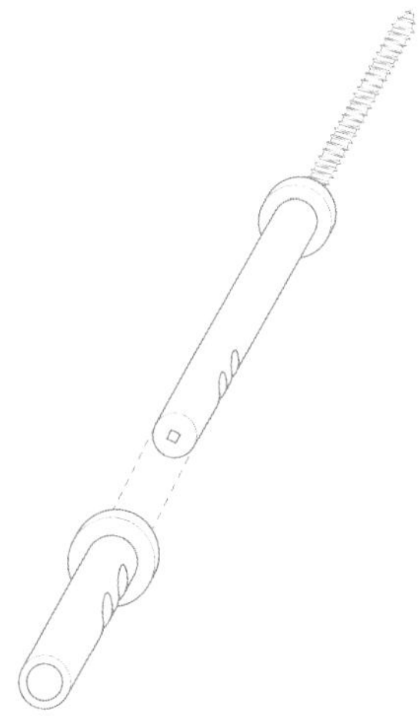

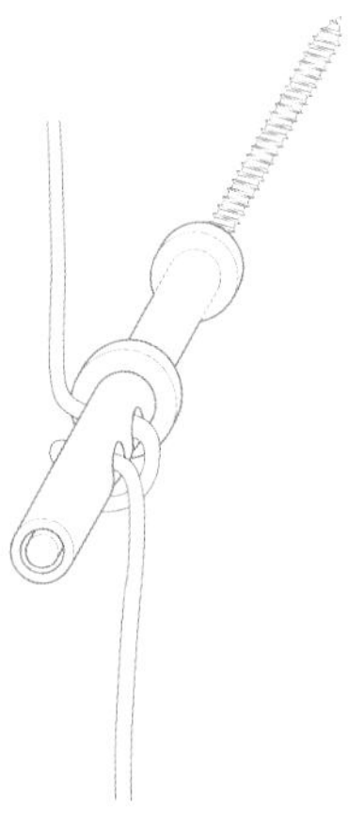

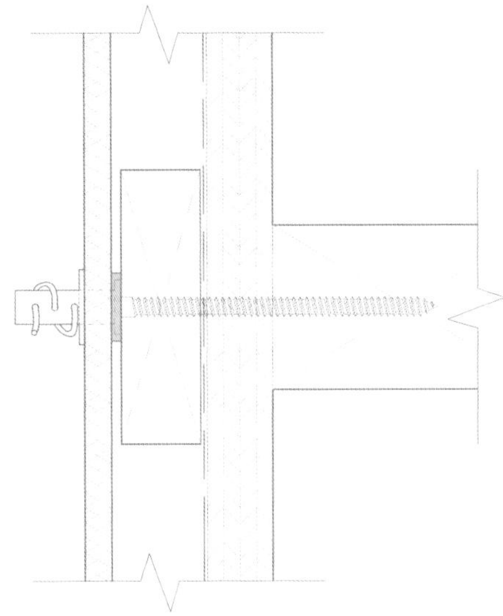

Custom siding fastener

GROUND LEVEL PLAN

1. Entry
2. Living
3. Outdoor Dining
4. Deck
5. Powder
6. Dining
7. Kitchen
8. Pantry
9. Family
10. Master Bed
11. Master Closet
12. Master Bath
13. Kid's Bed
14. Kid's Bath
15. Office
16. Pool
17. Pool House (Geller)
18. Outdoor Living

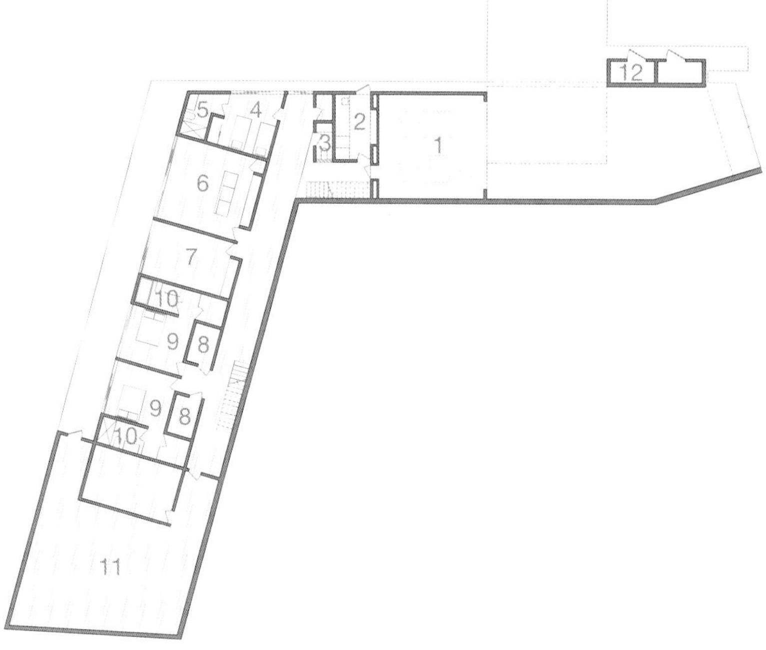

LOWER LEVEL PLAN

1. Garage
2. Laundry
3. Powder
4. Maid's Bed
5. Maid's Bath
6. Recreation
7. Gym
8. Wine
9. Guest Bed
10. Guest Bath
11. Storage
12. Outdoor Shower

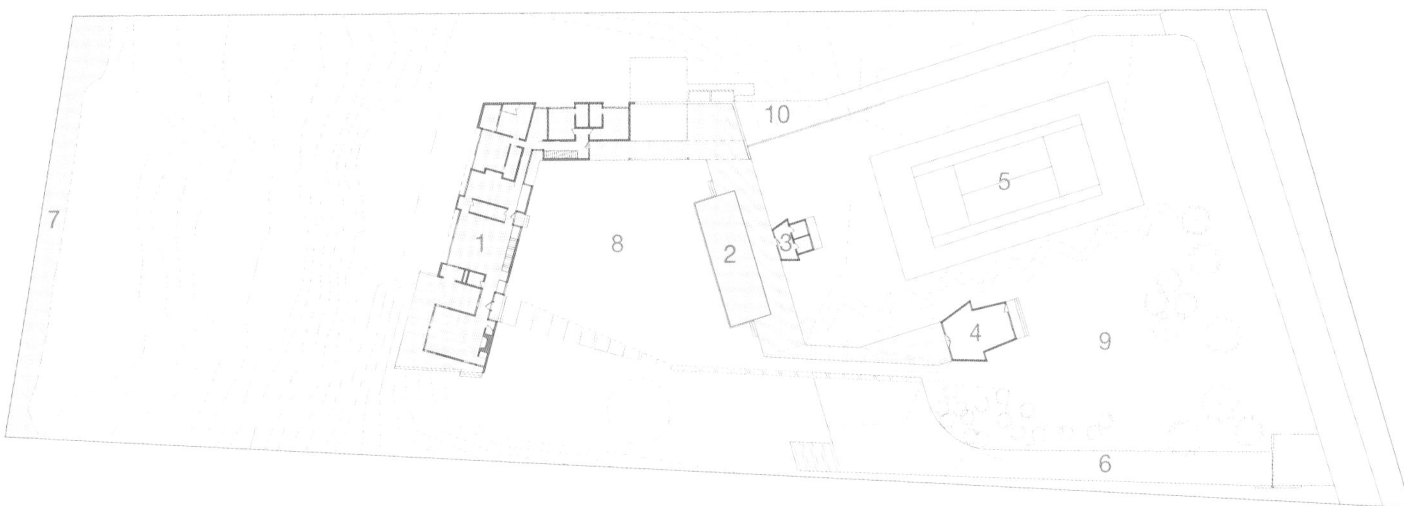

SITE PLAN

1. Main House
2. Pool
3. Pool House (Geller)
4. Guest House (Geller)
5. Tennis Court
6. Driveway
7. Pond
8. Center Lawn
9. Yew Garden
10. Service Driveway

PIERSON'S WAY

2013

Located within a private oceanfront community established in the nineteeth century, this residence is for a young couple looking for a home that would accommodate their growing family and reflect their modern lifestyle. Due to its history, most houses in the neighborhood are more conservative in design and scale than surrounding contemporary oceanfront communities. As a result, the clients desired a modern home that would fit within its historic context while embracing the modest scale of the property.

The design meets these goals by referencing the nearby agrarian vernacular buildings, specifically gabled potato barns embedded in the ground. A unique structural system was employed to create a false ground plane that slopes up from grade to the second floor, masking the scale of the house when viewed from the street. The structure consists of seven-inch-thick, glue-laminated wood panels supported by steel girders and columns. This structure eliminates the necessity for traditional wood framing and structural elements and is exposed as the finished ceiling surface throughout the ground-level spaces.

The structure allows for a number of design opportunities: the material transitions seamlessly from inside to outside as a 12' X 90'-long cantilever, stair treads are cut from the same material to express its thickness, and cylindrical recesses are carved out of the wood ceiling to transform surface-mounted fixtures into lighting elements. This method of carving continues throughout the design as casework and custom furniture. Most notably, the family room sofa is fabricated from the massive, glue-laminated wood beams and carved out to create side tables and drink rails.

While the first floor is dedicated to guests and entertaining, the second floor is reserved for the family. The elevated ground plane that surrounds the family bedrooms is planted with native grasses. Within the plantings, intimate outdoor spaces are created for small gatherings, including a fire pit and spa with views of the ocean. Sloping portions of the elevated ground plane include paths to connect the family areas with the more public entertaining areas at grade.

Materials traditionally used on agricultural buildings are selected for their low maintenance, durability, and ability to gracefully weather over time; here, cedar and weathering steel are executed in nontraditional ways. Alaskan yellow shakes monolithically clad the roof and sidewalls, with the coursing exposure four times larger than the typical coursing, in order to reduce the apparent scale of the house. The weathering steel references the corrugated steel often used on barn roofs and self-seals to create a durable, low-maintenance cladding. The warm, earthy tones of these materials blend with the weathered landscape that surrounds them.

Contemporary oceanfront communities are becoming known for their overdevelopment and disconnect from their surrounding environments. By referencing the local vernacular and elevating the ground plane, this large house is rooted within the landscape and becomes a cohesive addition to the neighborhood.

Local potato barn

de Kooning

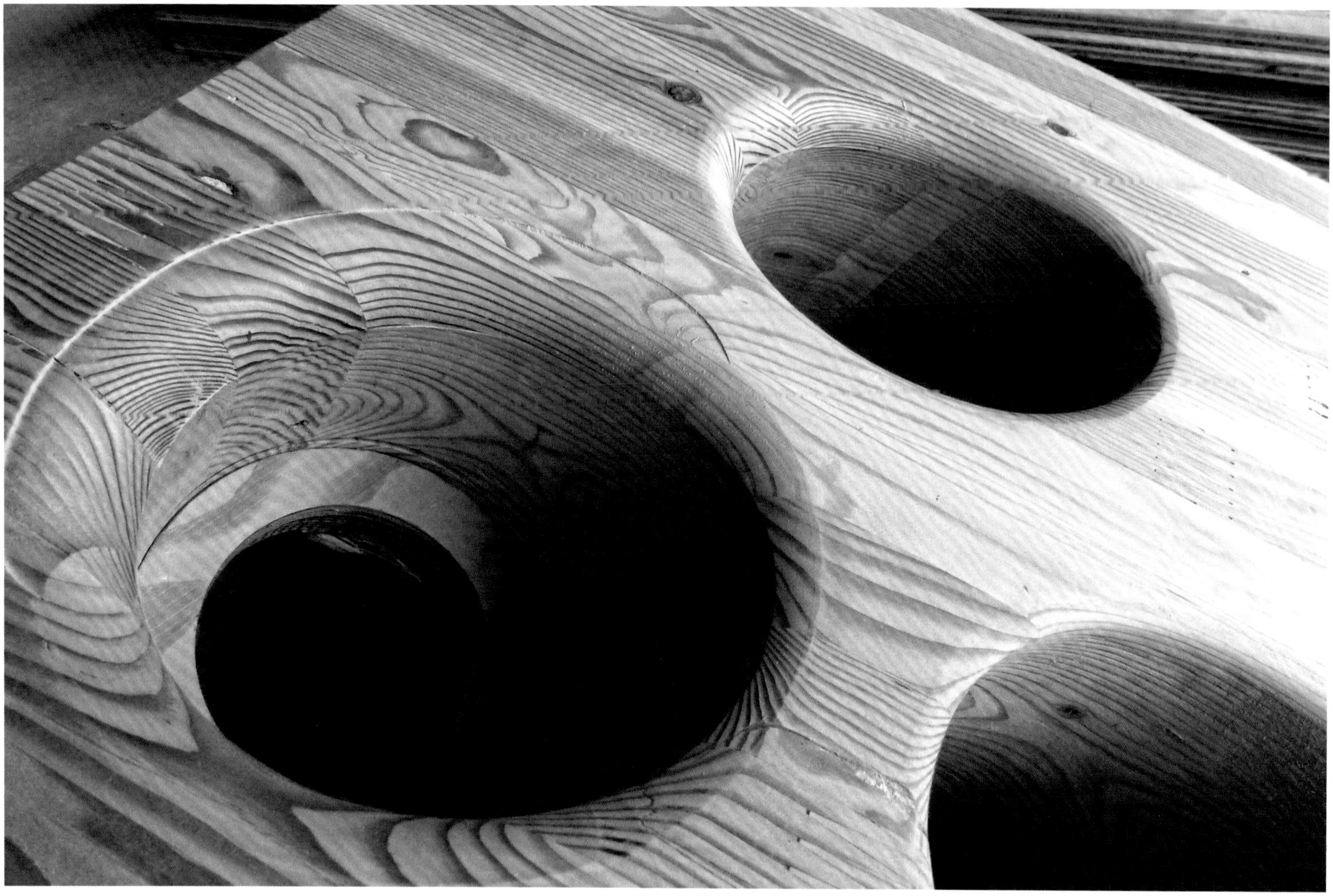

Top: Light fixture mockup
Bottom: Installation of glue-laminated structure

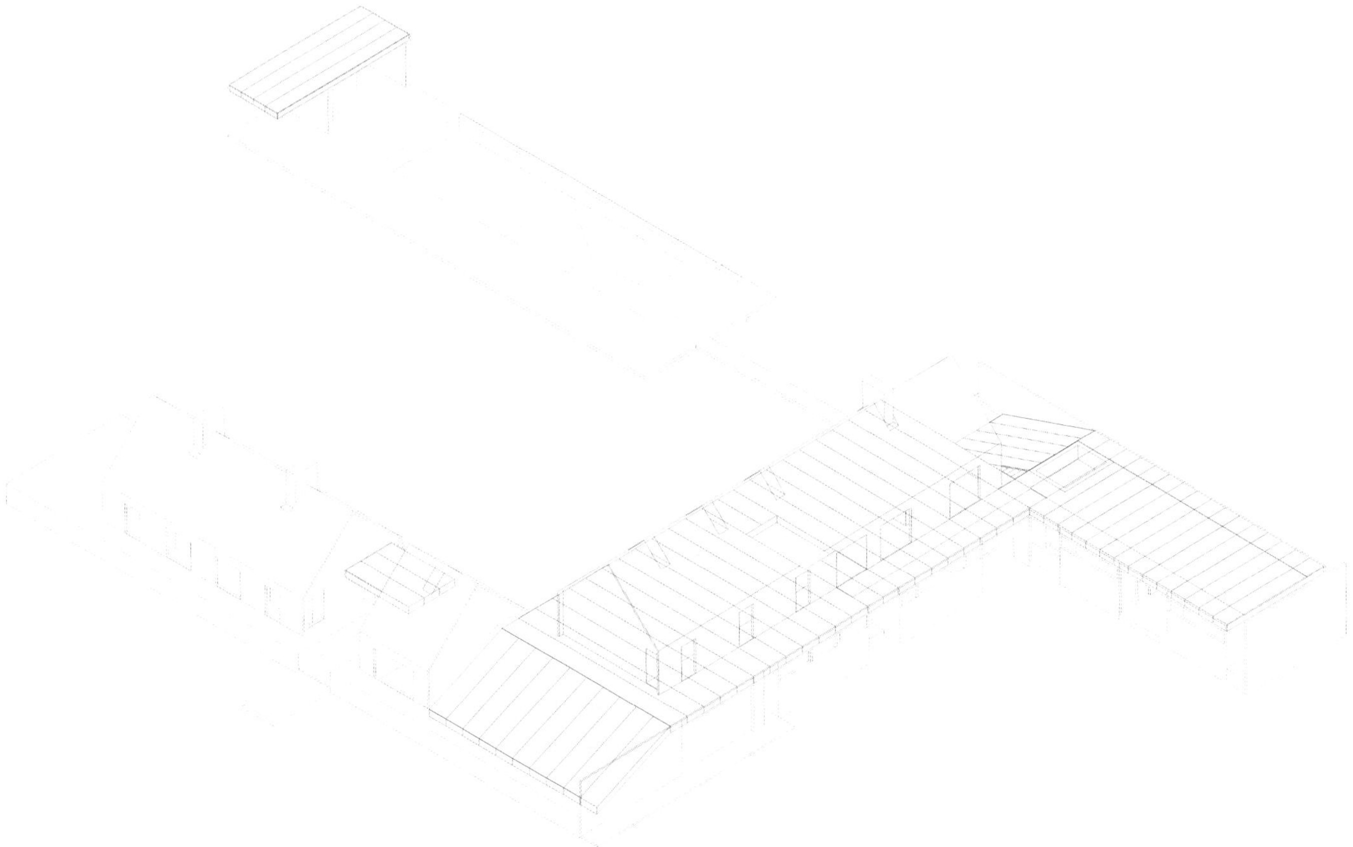

Glue-laminated structural diagram

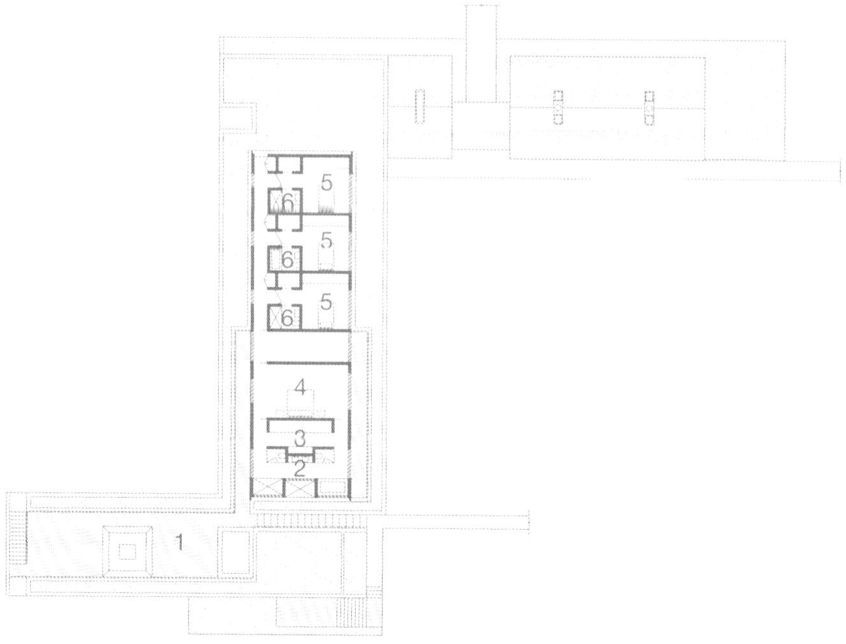

UPPER LEVEL PLAN

1. Deck with Spa and Fire Pit
2. Master Bath
3. Master Closet
4. Master Bed
5. Kid's Bed
6. Kid's Bath

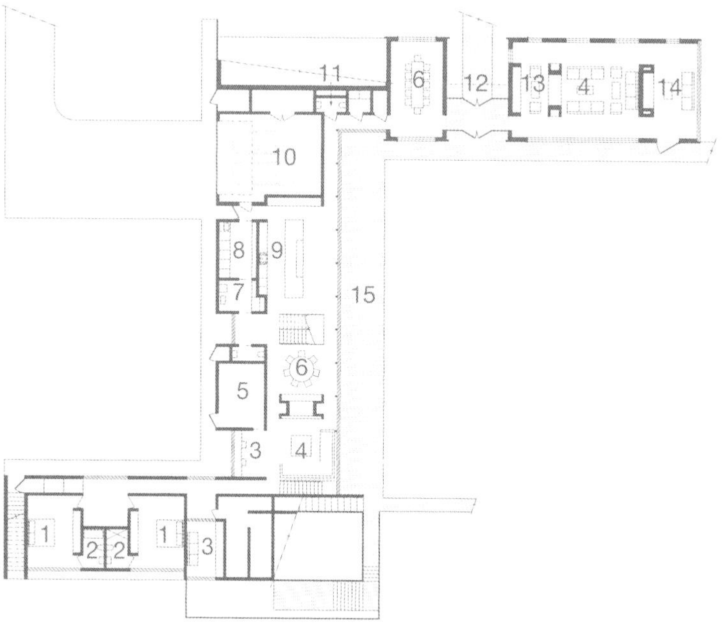

GROUND LEVEL PLAN

1. Guest Bed
2. Guest Bath
3. Study
4. Living
5. Recreation
6. Dining
7. Pantry
8. Laundry
9. Kitchen
10. Garage
11. Powder
12. Entry
13. Den
14. Screened Porch
15. Covered Terrace

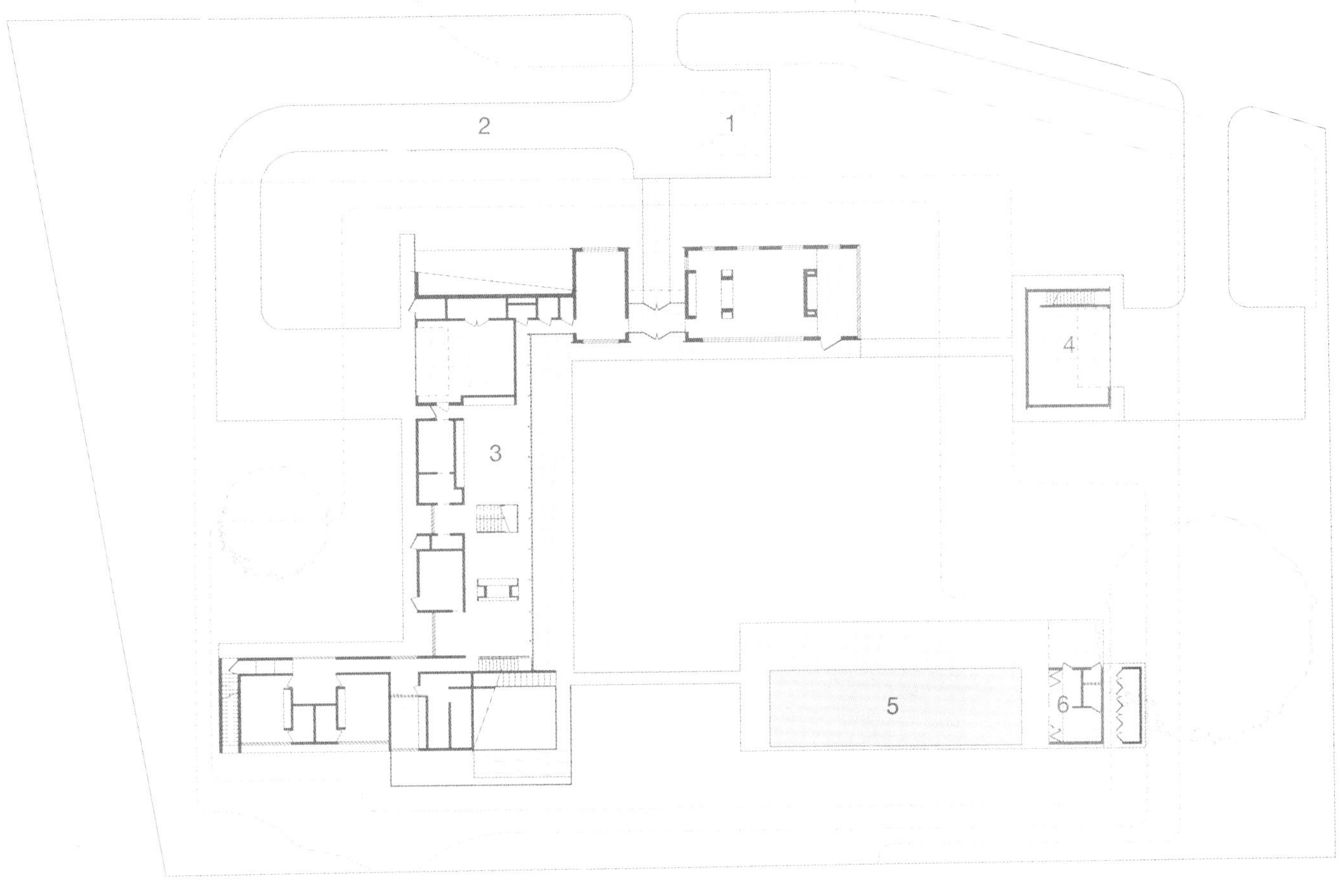

SITE PLAN

1. Parking
2. Driveway
3. Main House
4. Garage/Guest House
5. Pool
6. Pool House

ELIZABETH II

2014

Too often, architecture fixates on the visual sense, with little regard for other faculties of perception. The location of this house, in the heart of a bustling resort town, demanded special consideration of the acoustic sense. Research in architectural acoustics drove the form, materials, and detail of the house, not only shielding the property from the sound of the village, but also manipulating interior details to create a unique acoustic character for the house, one that will instill lasting memories for the family and their guests.

The house is comprised of a series of parallel walls that provide layers of privacy and insulation from the sound of the village. The walls project beyond the living spaces and ascend in height, building from a human-scale wall at the entry to a high wall along the center of the house. The walls diffract the sound waves moving past them, casting an acoustic shadow over the property to create a quiet outdoor gathering area.

The walls are built with insulated concrete forms: a wall assembly nearly twenty inches thick, comprised of a poured concrete core, continuous from footing to roof, wrapped in insulating foam, that also serves as formwork during construction. These walls provide excellent thermal insulation and an extremely low sound transmission coefficient. Due to the strength of their concrete cores, the walls act as structural beams, enabling them to span over the gathering space at the center of the house and the covered deck.

The custom stainless steel clips that attach the wide cedar board siding to the walls were designed to prolong the life of the siding. Traditional wood siding eventually fails because the natural expansion and contraction of the wood is constricted by the screws or nails that rigidly fasten it in place, slowly pulling out the fasteners or splitting the wood. The spring-like clips, however, hold the boards in tension against the house while allowing freedom for the natural movement of the wood.

Inside, variations on the clips are utilized as robe hooks, cabinet pulls, and hinges for an adjustable sound baffle in the central gathering space. The hinges hang cedar boards in front of a felt panel with spaces between them. Sound waves pass through the gaps between the boards, are trapped behind them, and absorbed by the felt. The hinges allow the spacing of the boards to be adjusted so the room can be acoustically tuned for intimate gatherings or boisterous parties. The stair is also tuned to create a subtle acoustic experience. The stair treads taper in thickness, changing the pitch of footfalls as one ascends from the woodshop in the basement, past the main floor with public spaces, guest room, and master bedroom, and up to the childrens' rooms on the upper floor.

The research of sound and how it affects our perception of space informed the details, materials, and form of the project. This approach to the design led to a richer and more meaningful home for the family.

Local precedent for siding fasteners

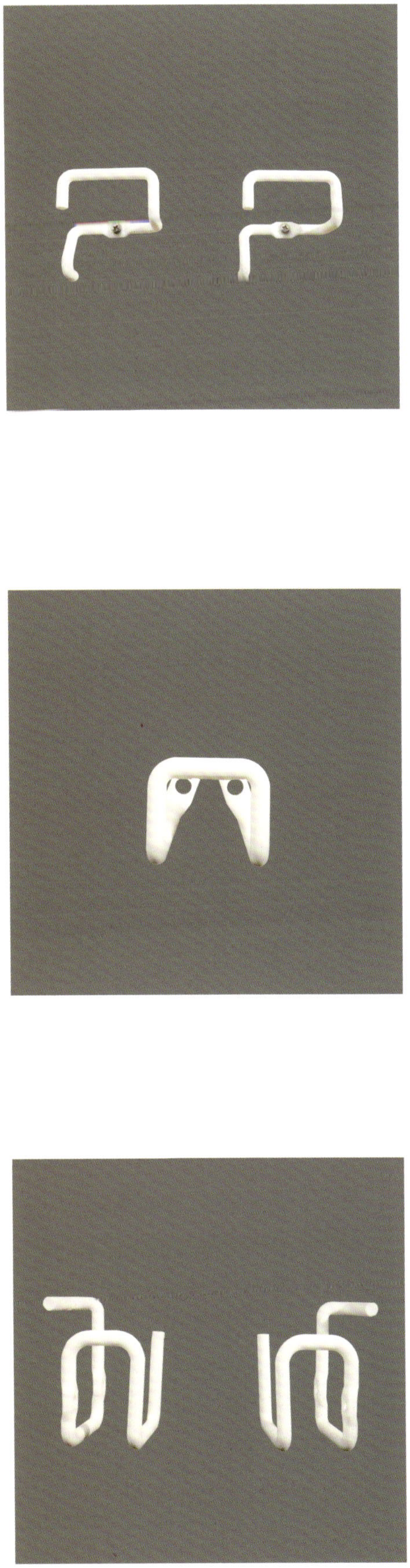

Clip studies

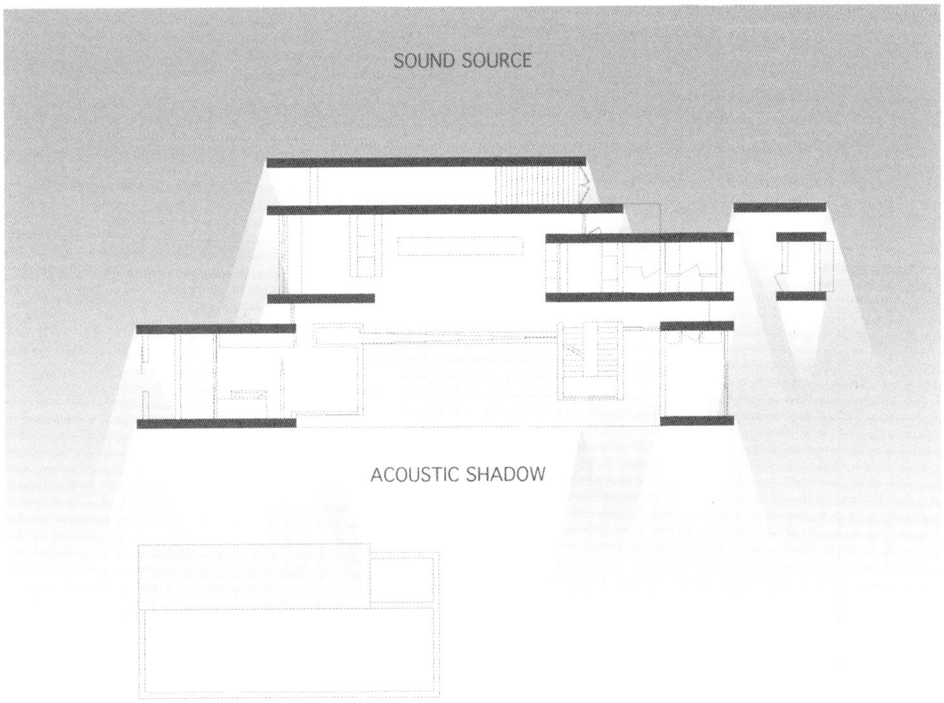

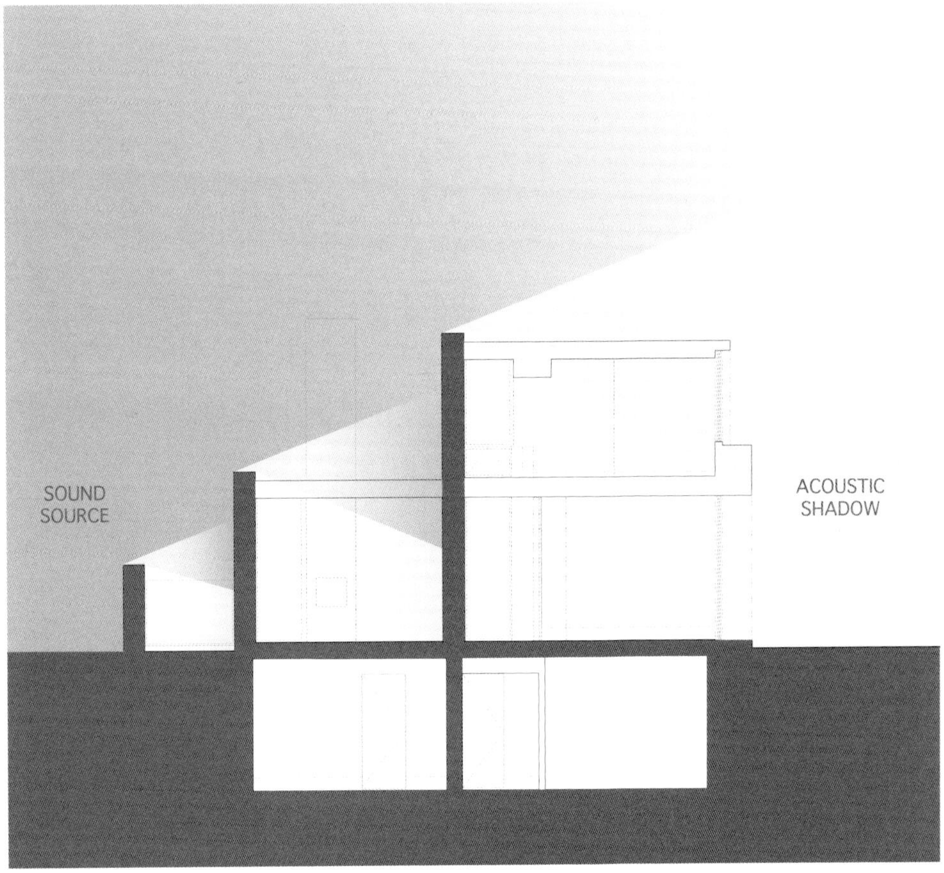

Plan and section diagrams

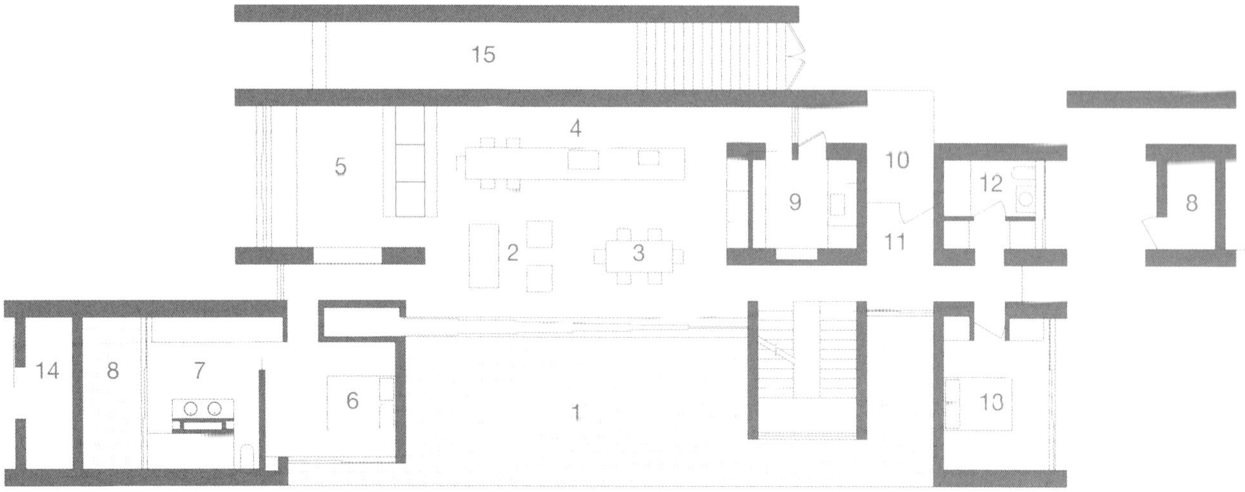

GROUND LEVEL PLAN

1. Covered Deck
2. Living
3. Dining
4. Kitchen
5. Family
6. Master Bed
7. Master Bath
8. Outdoor Shower
9. Laundry
10. Entry Deck
11. Entry
12. Guest Bath
13. Guest Bed
14. Storage
15. Light Well

UPPER LEVEL PLAN

1. Kid's Bed
2. Kid's Bath

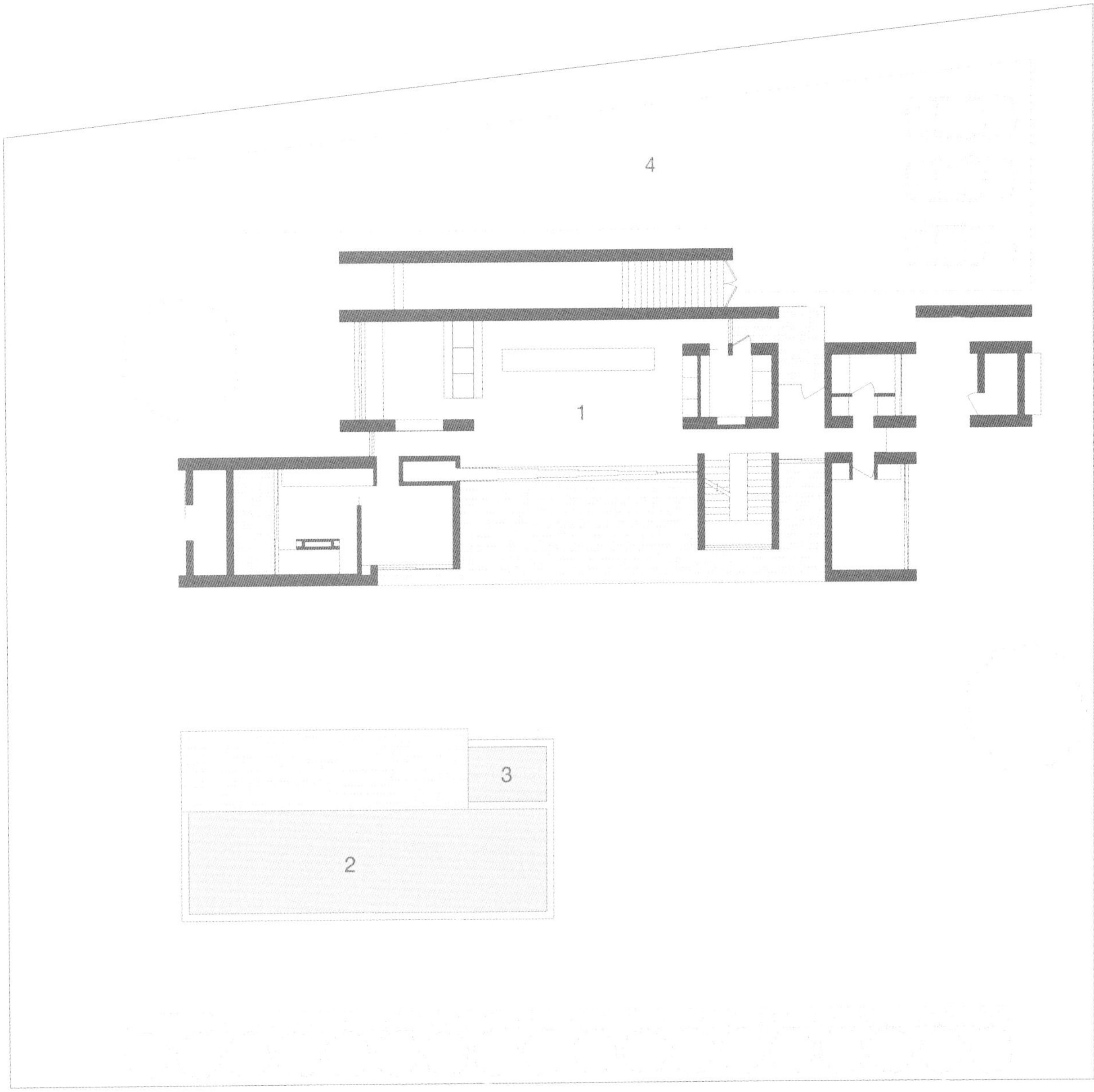

SITE PLAN

1. House
2. Pool
3. Spa
4. Driveway

SELECTED TIMELINE

BATES MASI + ARCHITECTS

2014 Smithsonian's Cooper-Hewitt Nomination

2013 Interior Design Hall of Fame Inductee

2013 Best of Houzz - Design

2010 Residential Architect "Architects We Love"

TREE HOUSE

1967

Bates Architects

RECOVER

1968 + 2006

2009 Wood Design & Building Merit Award

2008 AIA Peconic Honor Award

Bates Architects & Basi Masi + Architects

KAMEN

1968

Bates Architects

MADSEN

1969

Bates Architects

SALTAIRE

1971

Bates + Booher Architects

GEORGICA POND

1989

Bates, Booher + Lund Architects

STAR TOP

1997

BUZZARDS BAY II

1999

FRIEDMAN

2000

HERC

2002, *unbuilt*

CDCH

2003

2004 AIA Long Island ArchiAward

2005 Metal Architecture Awards

2007 AIA Peconic Awards

ELIZABETH-H

2003

2003 AIA Long Island ArchiAward

MONTAUKET

2004

CULLODEN POINT

2004, *unbuilt*

UPCHER

2005

2005 AIA NY State Award of Merit

2005 AIA Long Island ArchiAward

2006 Residential Architect Magazine Award

2007 AIA Peconic Honor Award

CHERRY POINT

2005, *unbuilt*

LANDFALL

2006

MONTE BRISAS

2006, *unbuilt*

MAKO

2007

SILVER HOLLOW

2007, *unbuilt*

2007 AIA NY State Award of Excellence

2007 AIA Long Island ArchiAward

2007 AIA Long Island Commendation

2007 AIA Long Island Sustainable Design

2008 Peconic Honor Award

ROAMAN

2008

2008 AIA Peconic Merit Award

NORTHWEST PEACH FARM

2008

2008 AIA Long Island ArchiAward

2013 Crittall Prize

TWIN POND

2008, *unbuilt*

PRYOR

2008

2009 AIA Long Island ArchiAward

2010 AIA NY State Award of Merit

2010 AIA Peconic Honor Award

2010 Int'l Design Awards Honorable Mention

SPINNER

2009, *unbuilt*

NOYACK CREEK

2009

2010 AIA NY State Citation of Design Award

2010 AIA Peconic Honor Award

2013 Houzz Best of Design Award

LIONS HEAD

2009

2010 AIA Long Island ArchiAward Commendation

SALT CAY

2010, *unbuilt*

2010 AIA Peconic Merit Award

ROBINS WAY

2010

2011 AIA Long Island ArchiAward Commendation

2011 AIA Long Island ArchiAward Lighting Award

2011 AIA Peconic Juror's Award

2012 Interior Design Best of Year Honoree

2013 Watermark Award

2014 Remodeling Magazine Grand Award

QUAIL HILL

2010

2010 AIA Peconic Honor Award

2010 AIA Long Island ArchiAward Commendation

GENIUS LOCI

2011

2011 Int'l Design Awards Gold Award

2011 CWC Residential Wood Design Award

2011 AIA Long Island ArchiAward

2011 AIA Peconic Honor Award

2012 AIA NY State Citation Award

2012 Architectural Record House

2012 Residential Architect Mag. Design Award

SAM'S CREEK

2011

2011 Int'l Design Awards Gold Award

2011 Int'l Design Awards Architecture of the Year

2012 Interior Design Best of Year Winner

2012 AIA NY State Award of Merit

2012 Metalmag Awards Honorable Mention

2013 Watermark Award

TWENTY SEVEN

2012, *unbuilt*

SAGAPONACK

2012

2012 Int'l Design Awards 1st Place

2013 Interior Design Best of Year Honoree

2013 AIA Peconic Merit Award

2013 AIA Long Island ArchiAward

2013 Builder's Choice Custom Home Award

2013 AIA NY State Citation Award

2013 Residential Architect Mag. Merit Award

2014 Watermark Award

FAR POND

2012

2013 AIA Long Island Best of the Best

2013 AIA Long Island ArchiAward

2013 HC&G Innovation Award–Kitchen Design

2014 Remodeling Best of the Year Design Award

2014 Watermark Award

2014 Architectural Record–Record Kitchen

432 PARK

2012, *in progress*

NORTHWEST HARBOR

2013

2008 AIA NY State Award of Merit

2008 AIA Peconic Merit Award

2013 Canadian Wood Council Award

2014 Int'l Design Awards Honorable Mention

MOTHERSILL

2013

2011 AIA Peconic Merit Award

2013 Interior Design Best of Year Winner

2013 AIA Peconic Honor Award

2013 AIA Long Island ArchiAward

2014 AIA NY State Merit Award

2014 Int'l Design Awards Gold Award

2014 HC&G Innovation Award –Architecture

2014 Builder's Choice Custom Home Award

PIERSON'S WAY

2013

2014 Residential Architect Mag. Design Award

2014 Int'l Design Awards Silver Award

2014 Int'l Design Awards Honorable Mention

2014 Builder's Choice Custom Home Award

2014 AIA Long Island ArchiAward Commendation

2014 AIA Peconic Juror's Award

STAR RANCH

2013, *unbuilt*

TESSA NYC

2014

2014 Interior Design Best of the Year Honoree

ELIZABETH II

2014

2014 AIA ArchiAward

2014 AIA Peconic Merit Award

BEACH HAMPTON

2014

AMAGANSETT DUNES

2014, *in progress*

PROMISED LAND

2014, *in progress*

HITHER HILLS

2014, *in progress*

UNDERHILL

2014, *in progress*

GEORGICA CLOSE

2015, *in progress*

132 NORTH MAIN

2015, *in progress*

2008 AIA Peconic Merit Award

2008 US Green Building Council Award

ACTON COVE

2016, *in progress*

GEORGICA COVE

2016, *in progress*

SHINNECOCK

2016, *in progress*

SEBONAC CREEK

2016, *in progress*

SAG HARBOR SANCTUARY

2016, *in progress*

1810 Church conversion to residence

SAGG FARM

2017, *in progress*

CREDITS

TREE HOUSE
Fire Island, NY
1967

Photographer: Courtesy of the owner
Contractor: William A. Lynch
Contributors: Harry Bates

SAM'S CREEK
Bridgehampton, NY
2011

Photographer: Bates Masi + Architects
Contractor: Breitenbach Builders
Structural Engineer: Steven L. Maresca
Landscape: Bates Masi + Architects
Contributors: Harry Bates, Paul Masi, Robert Couch, Kerry Sandoval, Clay Coffey

RECOVER
Amagansett, NY
1968 + 2006

Photographer: Christopher Wesnofske
Contractor: Paul Cassidy
Structural Engineer: Steven L. Maresca
Contributors: Harry Bates, Paul Masi, Lou Boza, S. Flavio Espinoza

SAGAPONACK
Sagaponack, NY
2012

Photographer: Michael Moran
Contractor: Wright & Co. Construction
Structural Engineer: Gilsanz Murray Steficek
Landscape: Stephen Stimson Associates
Interiors: Bates Masi + Architects with Victoria Pryor
Contributors: Harry Bates, Paul Masi, Aaron Weil, Satoshi Ohkami, Kerry Sandoval, Nathan Rittgarn
Photo Credit: Eduardo Chillida, La casa del poeta, Estela VII Corten steel, 1991

PRYOR
Montauk, NY
2008

Photographer: Bates Masi + Architects
Structural Engineer: Steven L. Maresca
Landscape: Coen + Partners
Contributors: Harry Bates, Paul Masi, Satoshi Ohkami

NORTHWEST HARBOR
East Hampton, NY
2013

Photographer: Bates Masi + Architects
Contractor: Brian Mannix Builder
Structural Engineer: Steven L. Maresca
Contributors: Harry Bates, Paul Masi, Aaron Zalneraitis, Adam Jordan

NORTHWEST PEACH FARM
East Hampton, NY
2008

Photographer: Michael Moran
Contractor: Robert Padden
Structural Engineer: Steven L. Maresca
Landscape: Coen + Partners
Contributors: Harry Bates, Paul Masi, Aaron Zalneraitis, Aaron Weil

MOTHERSILL
Watermill, NY
2013

Photographer: Bates Masi + Architects
Contractor: Keith Romeo
Structural Engineer: Steven L. Maresca
Landscape: dL Studio Inc.
Interiors: Damon Liss
Contributors: Harry Bates, Paul Masi, Robert Couch, Peter Storey, Doug Farrell
Photo Credit: The Andrew Geller Architectural Archive

NOYACK CREEK
Noyack, NY
2009

Photographer: Bates Masi + Architects
Contractor: Brian Mannix Builder
Structural Engineer: Steven L. Maresca
Contributors: Harry Bates, Paul Masi, Aaron Zalneraitis, Katherine Dalene Weil

PIERSON'S WAY
East Hampton, NY
2013

Photographer: Michael Moran
Contractor: Men at Work Construction Corp.
Structural Engineer: Steven L. Maresca
Landscape: Bates Masi + Architects
Interiors: Damon Liss Inc.
Contributors: Harry Bates, Paul Masi, Adam Jordan, Peter Storey

GENIUS LOCI
Montauk, NY
2011

Photographer: Michael Moran
Contractor: Davis Builders
Structural Engineer: Steven L. Maresca
Landscape: Bates Masi + Architects
Interiors: Bates Masi + Architects with Victoria Pryor + Alicia Scanlon
Contributors: Harry Bates, Paul Masi, Katherine Dalene Weil, Antonio Rodriguez

ELIZABETH II
Amagansett, NY
2014

Photographer: Bates Masi + Architects
Contractor: Bates Masi + Architects
Structural Engineer: Steven L. Maresca
Landscape: Bates Masi + Architects
Interiors: Bates Masi + Architects
Contributors: Harry Bates, Paul Masi, Doug Farrell, Peter Storey, Robert Couch

ORO
EDITIONS

Publishers of Architecture, Art, and Design
Gordon Goff: Publisher

www.oroeditions.com
info@oroeditions.com

Published by ORO Editions

Graphic Design: Bates Masi + Architects
Production Assistance: Meghan Martin
Project Coordinator: Alana Leland

Edited by: Bates Masi + Architects
Proofread by: Ryan Buresh

10 9 8 7 6 5 First Edition

Library of Congress data available upon request. World Rights: Available

ISBN: 978-1-941806-39-5

Color Separations and Printing: ORO Editions Inc.
Printed in Hong Kong.

International Distribution: www.oroeditions.com/distribution

ORO Editions makes a continuous effort to minimize the overall carbon footprint of its publications. As part of this goal, ORO Editions, in association with Global ReLeaf, arranges to plant trees to replace those used in the manufacturing of the paper produced for its books. Global ReLeaf is an international campaign run by American Forests, one of the world's oldest nonprofit conservation organizations. Global ReLeaf is American Forests' education and action program that helps individuals, organizations, agencies, and corporations improve the local and global environment by planting and caring for trees.

bates
masi+
ARCHITECTS
www.batesmasi.com

Falling Times, 2006-09, data-driven installation. Installation view, ZKM | Karlsruhe, 2007.

Falling Times, 2005–2010, data-driven immersive projection. Public installation views, Avenida Paulista, São Paulo, 2008.

Falling Times, 2006-09, data-driven

Falling Times, 2006-09, data-driven installation. Installation views, Czech Centre, New York, 2009.

Falling Times, 2006–09, data-driven installation. Installation view, Czech Centre, New York, 2009

Garden of Error and Decay, 2009–19, data-driven installation. Installation views, Wuhan Museum of Art, 2010.

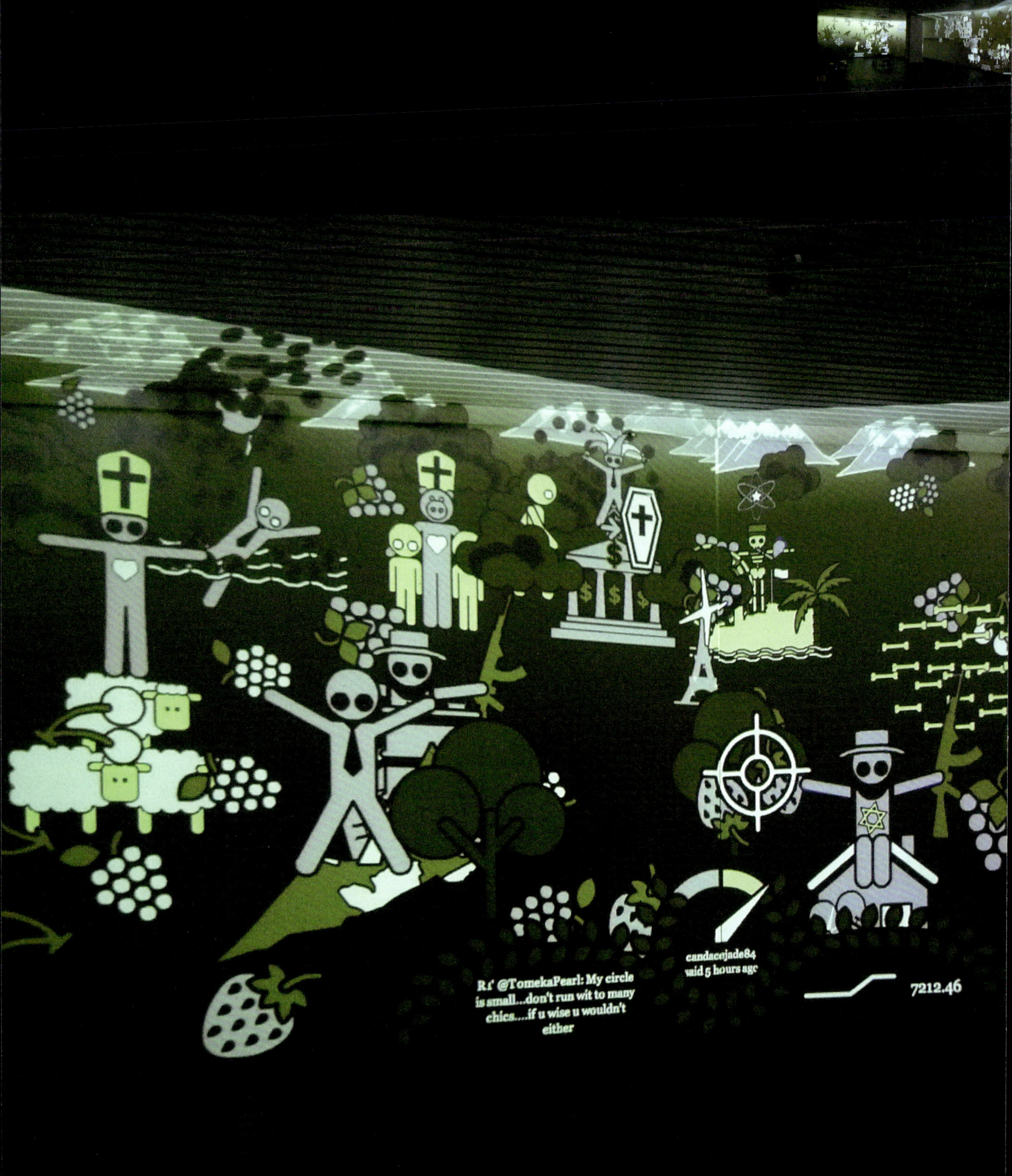

Garden of Error and Decay, 2009–19, data-driven installation. Installation views, Czech Centre, Berlin, 2011.

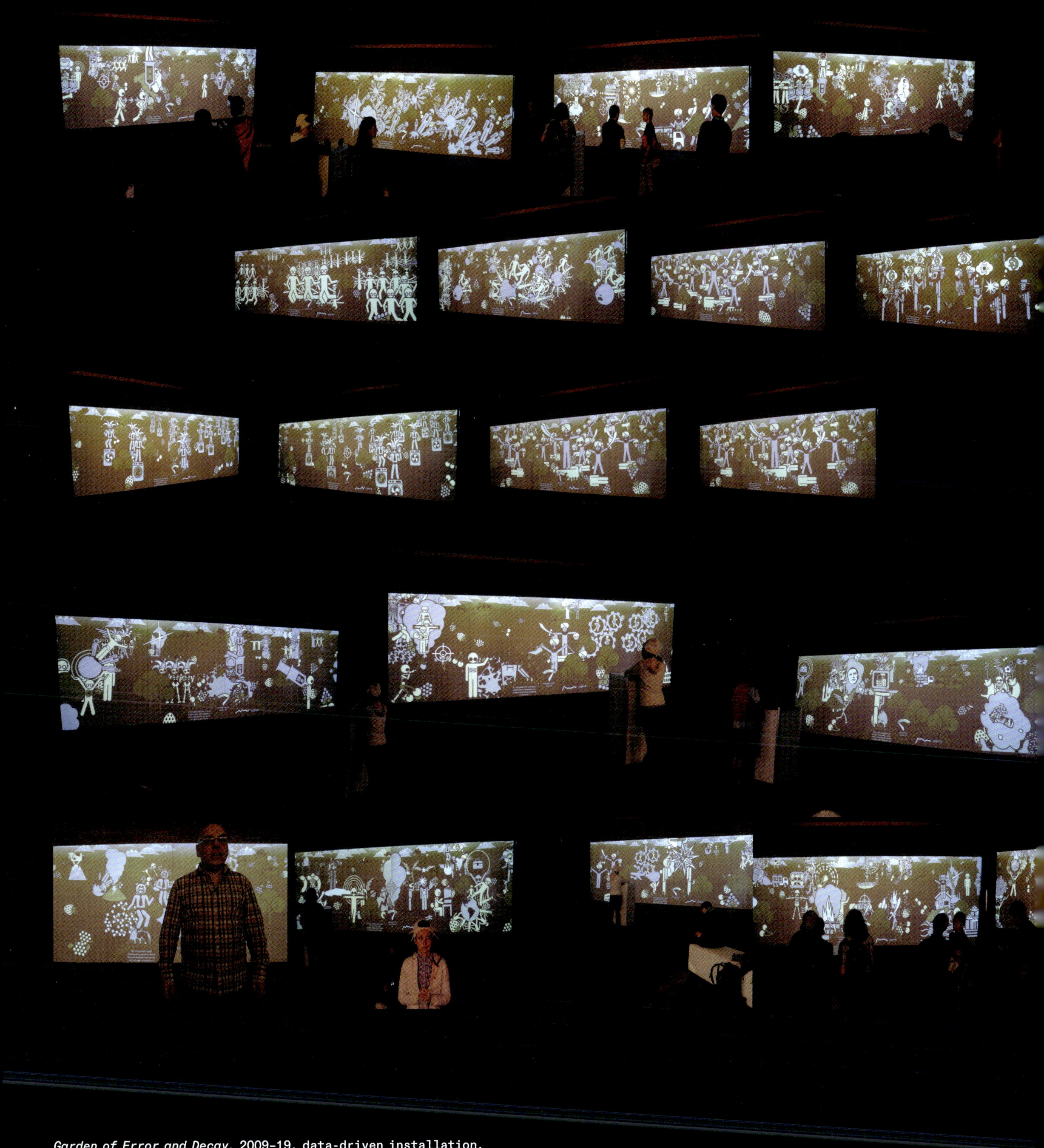

Garden of Error and Decay, 2009–19, data-driven installation.
Installation views, Siggraph 2011, Vancouver, 2011.

Garden of Error and Decay, 2009–19, data-driven installation.
Installation views, Palazzo Strozzi, Florence, 2011

Garden of Error and Decay, 2009–19, data-driven installation. Installation views, 4th Moscow Biennale, 2011.

Garden of Error and Decay, 2009–19, data-driven installation.
Installation views, 4th Moscow Biennale, 2011.

Sarkozy: "Fukushima was not a problem of nuclear energy; it was a tsunami problem." Guns don't kill people, people kill
Yascha_Mounk said 7 days ago

Garden of Error and Decay, 2009-19, data-driven installation. Installation views, 11th Havana Biennial, 2012.

Garden of Error and Decay, 2009–19, animated film. Installation views, Art Center Nabi, Seoul, 2013.

DIVE

STARBUCKS COFFEE

Garden of Error and Decay, 2009–19, animated film. Installation views, Art Center Nabi, Seoul, 2013.

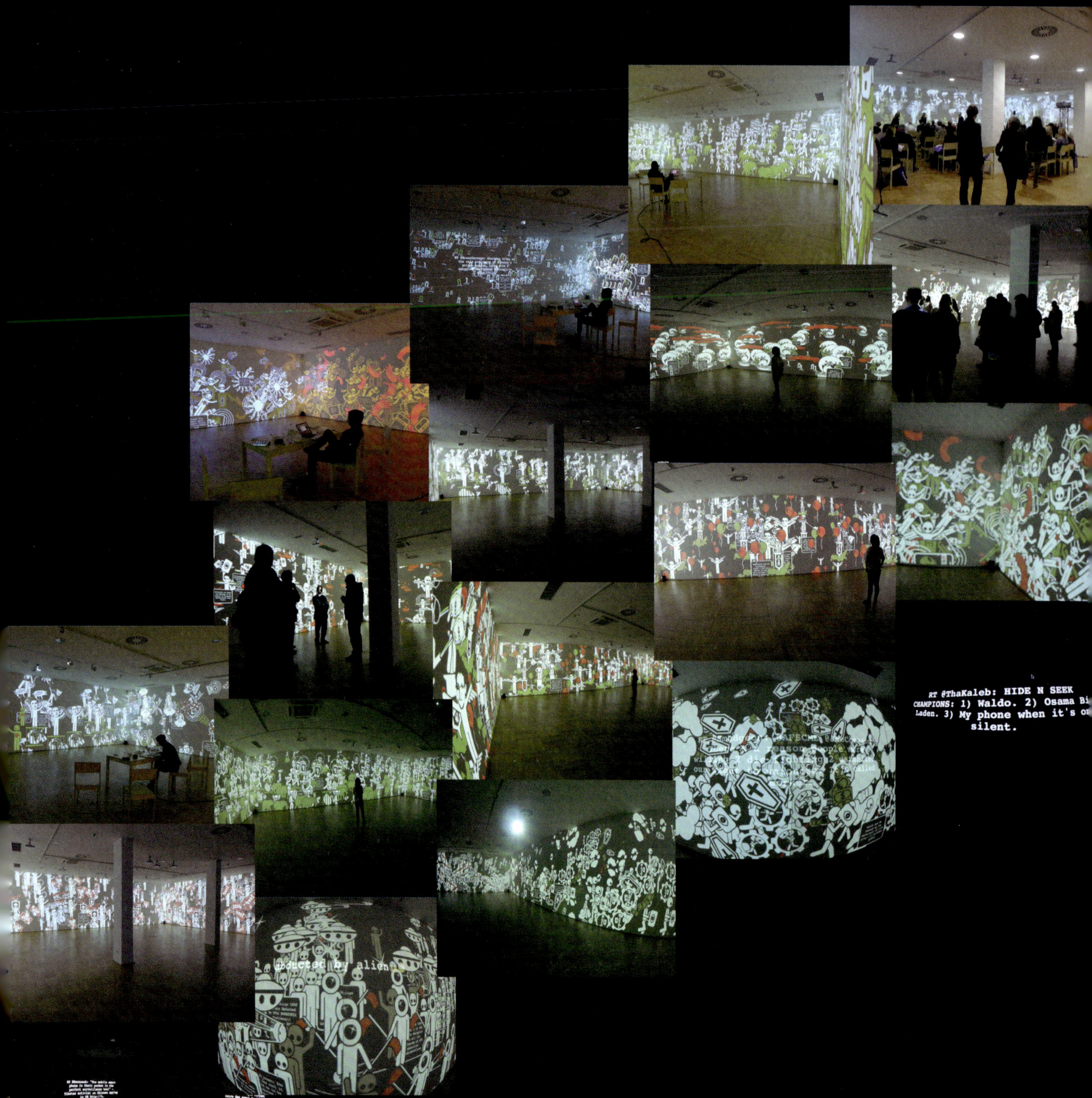

Why Don't We, 2013–17, data-driven installation. Installation views, IMAE – Inter Media Art Institute, Düsseldorf, 2014.

Data Driven Pictograms – *Why Don't We* (Düsseldorf)
Custom-made Flash software, Twitter data stream, projector: Vector graphics of pictograms are animated using the object-oriented scripting language ActionScript and played in the Flash Player along the Twitter messages in the form of a custom made Flash projector, an executable file.

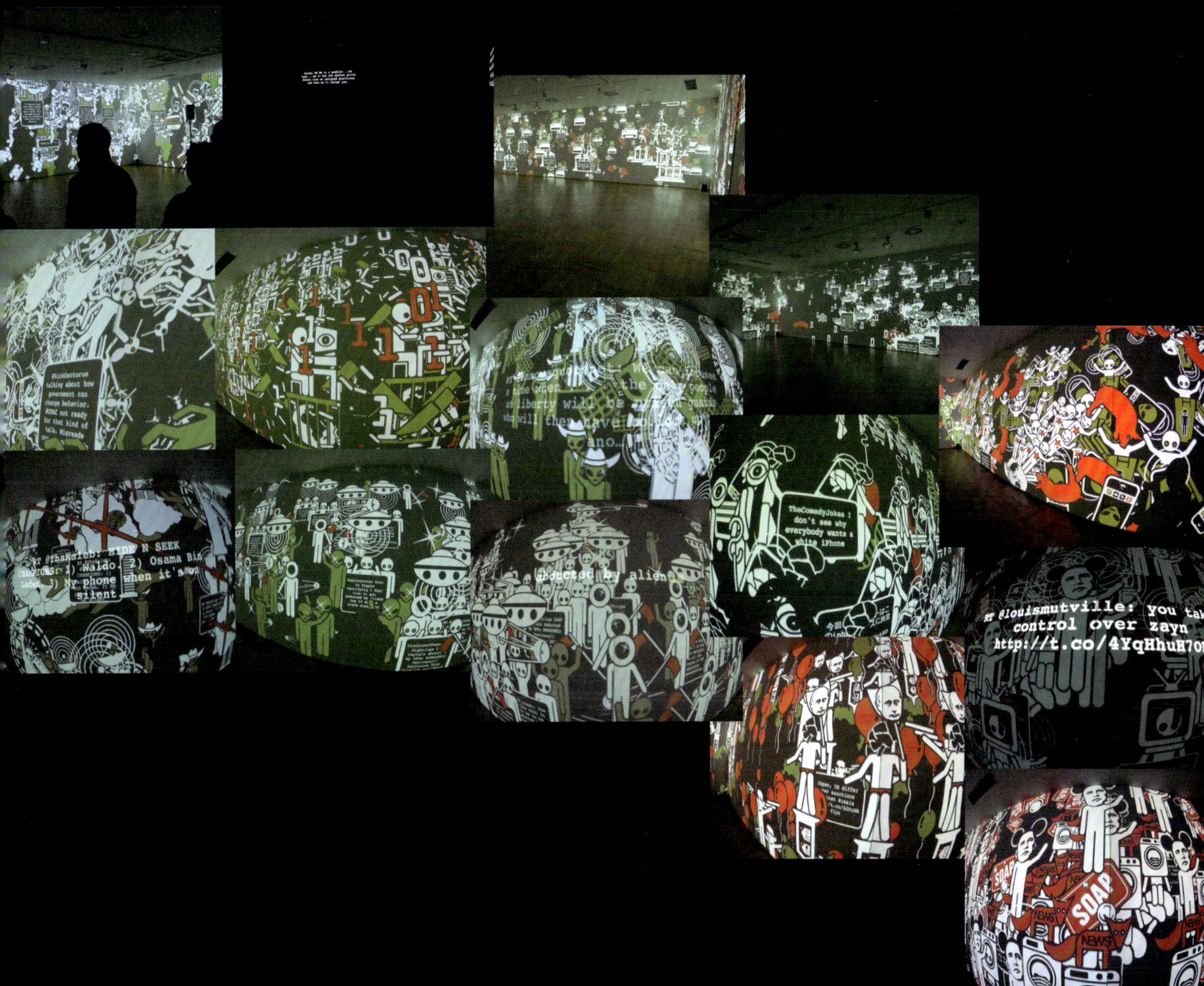
TheComedyJokes I don't see why everybody wants a white iPhone
control over zayn
SOAP
NEWS

RT @ThaKaleb: HIDE N SEEK
CHAMPIONS: 1) Waldo. 2) Osama Bin
Laden. 3) My phone when it's on
silent.

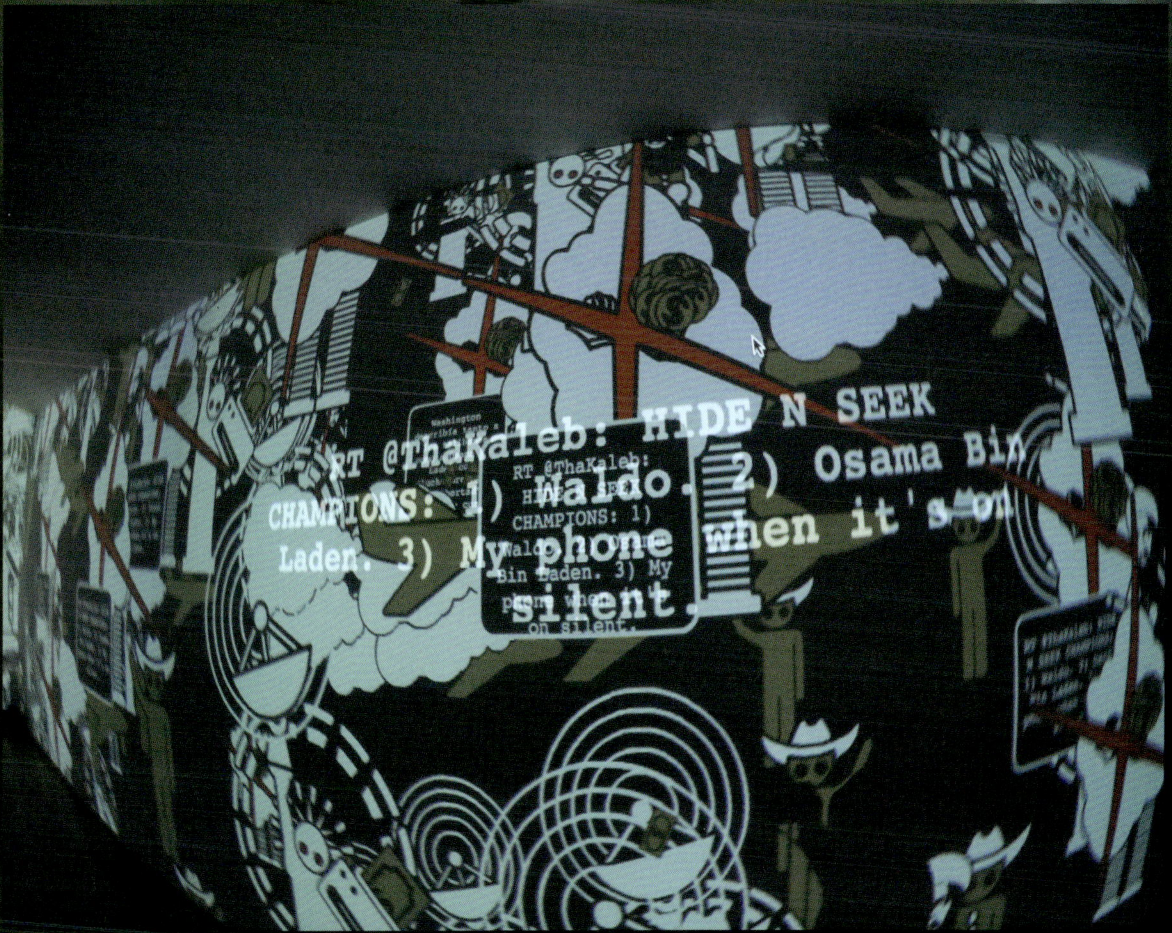

Why Don't We, 2013–17, data-driven installation. Installation views, IMAF – Inter Media Art Institute, Düsseldorf, 2014

Why Don't We, 2013–17, data-driven installation. Poster, Anna Klinkhammer Gallery, Düsseldorf, 2013.

NEWS

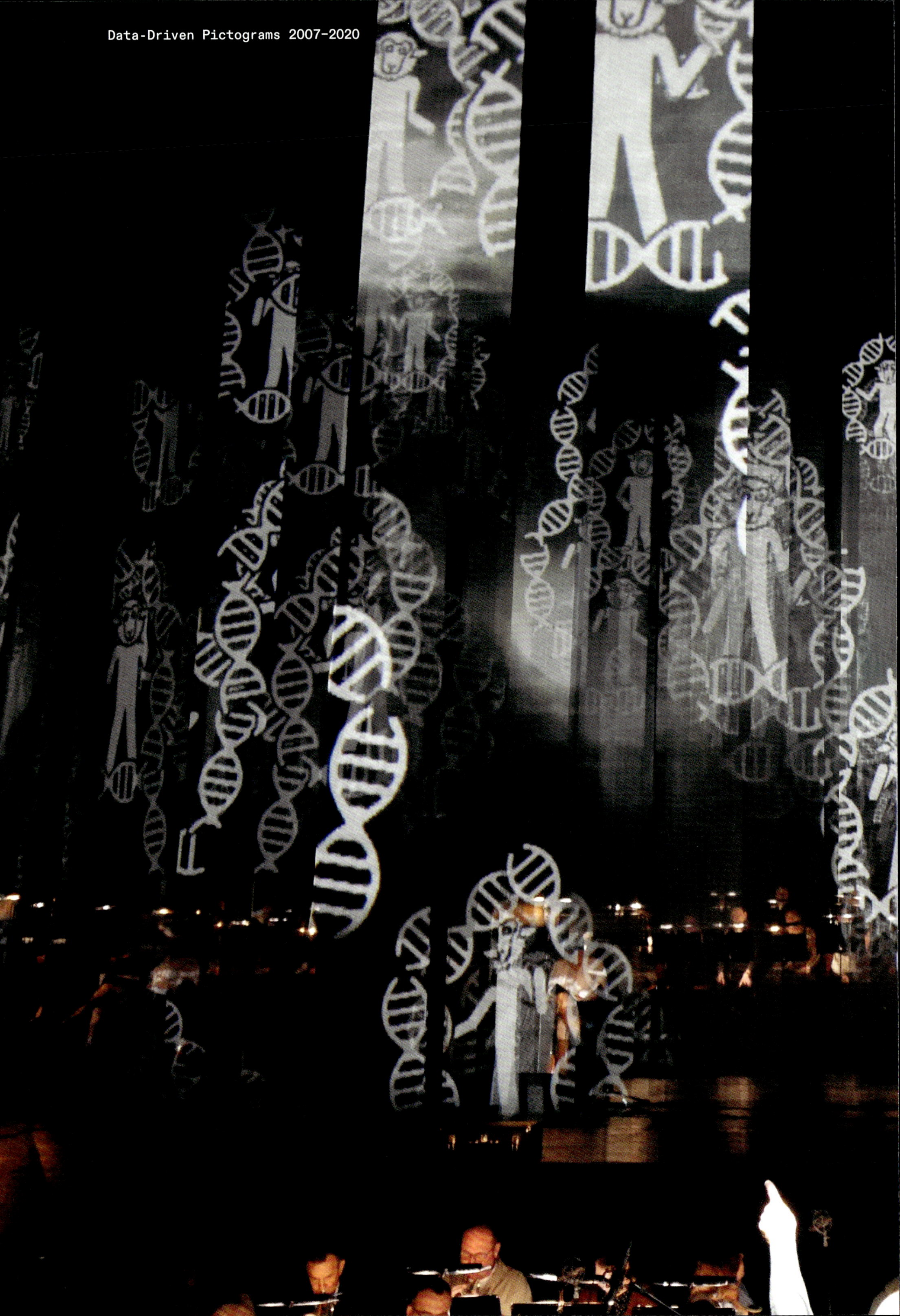

Lost Objects, 2015, data driven immersive postminimalist opera. Installation view, National Theatre, Prague, 2015.

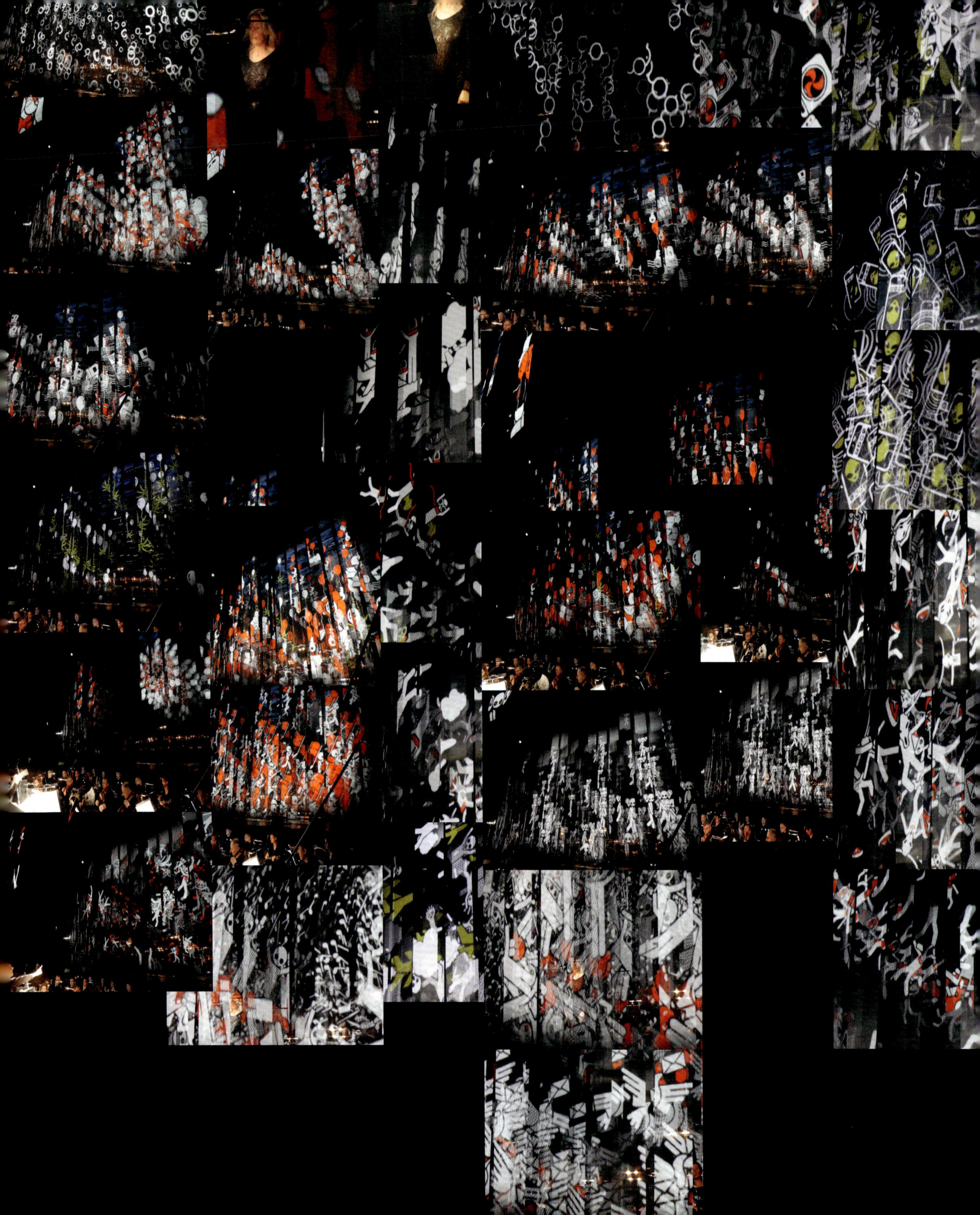

Lost Objects, 2015, data-driven immersive postminimalist opera. Installation views, National Theatre, Prague, 2015.

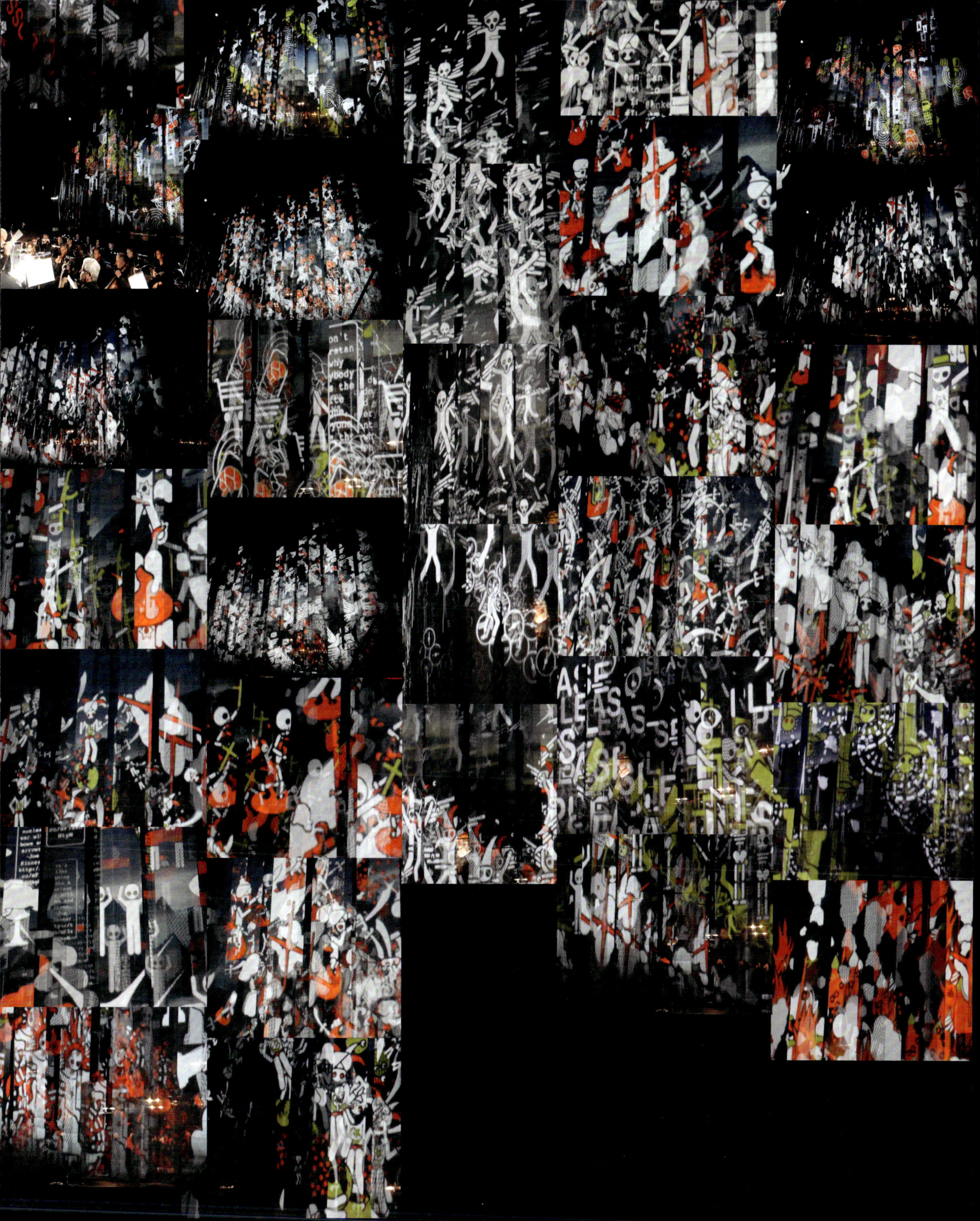

SOAP
NEWS

Why Don't We, 2013–17, data-driven installation. Poster, Anna Klinkhammer Gallery, Düsseldorf, 2013.

The Inner Observer, 1992, video sculpture.
Installation view Ars Electronica, Linz, 1992.

On Business Angels and Mentors

Peter Weibel in conversation with Michael Bielicky

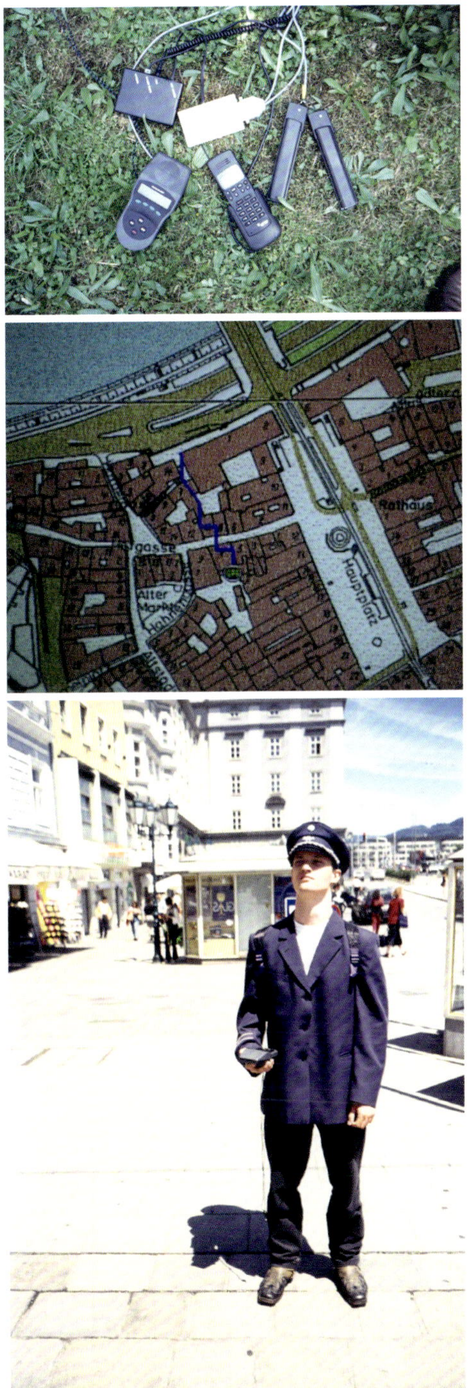

Intelligent Mailman, 1994, GPS-driven telematic performance. Ars Electronica, Linz, 1994.

Michael Bielicky: It is a bit strange to be sitting here with you, Peter, to be doing an interview with you about me – an absurdity, but also perhaps not. We have known each other for a quarter of a century now, from the days when you had just "invented" the fantastic Institute for New Media in Frankfurt am Main, an institution that was unique then within the European context. And I was a silent witness of this act. This, as I recall, was our first meeting. What year was it founded?

Peter Weibel: That was in 1992. On that occasion, we not only met for the first time – we didn't just cross paths, we launched straight away into our first project: the publication of Zdeněk Pešánek's book *Kinetismus* [Kinetism, originally published in Czech, in 1941]. At that time, we assigned Mr. Spiegelmann with the translation into German, which still exists, and we still have the project in the pipeline. I think it has not been translated into German yet?

Bielicky: No. Actually, it has not yet been translated – it is astonishing that you mention Pešánek, that you remember our first encounter was an instant collaboration.

Weibel: I remember it, of course, because it was very important collaboration, as because Pešánek's work mediates between cinema and fine art. And that was an important advice you gave me then – it is remarkable that you are very well versed in the history of Czech art, kinetics, and cinematography; and that, for your work, you draw not only on Czech media history, but also on the deep time of Czech spirituality – and we will publish, we still *must* publish the abovementioned book. My point is: we began our collaboration not as an artistic encounter, but in the form of a scientific project. Our following encounter was an artistic one at Ars Electronica '92: the exhibition *Endo and Nano. The World from Within* – "nano" in the sense of nanotechnology, which at the time was still a very new term. Back then, nobody believed in nanotechnology, plus the notion of endophysics, the physics of the inner observer. That was the context, as I recall, for our first artistic cooperation.

Bielicky: Exactly, that work was derived from a piece of mine that, at that point, had made the greatest media impact, *Menorah* [1989]; but instead of the religious symbolism, I had chosen a more sober, more scientific basic structure: it was consequently called *The Inner Observer* [1992] and consisted of seven iron balls, a candelabra of seven televisions – each built into one of the spheres and an external infrared camera that transmitted – wirelessly – out of the dark, the word "light" onto the TV sets. That was my reference to the inner observer, the overriding theme of that Ars Electronica. And I know that you were a bit perplexed when these rusty, huge balls were unpacked, because all we had at our disposal was a small opera house, Brucknerhaus, which was not designed for exhibitions, of course. That was our artistic beginning: yours as a curator and mine as an artist. And I'm very happy that, back then, you trusted my artistic idea. We were then able to continue that in 1994 at the Ars Electronica, where I was able to show my work *Intelligent Mailman* [1994].

Weibel: Yes, the exhibition was named *Intelligente Ambiente / Intelligent Environment …*

Bielicky: For that work, I had a man in a uniform walk around the city of Linz with a GPS device for four days. At that time, GPS was brand new technology. I dare to say that I was the first artist to use GPS in an artistic context. At any rate, this mailman walked around the city with an analog telephone – it was so large you could hardly call it a mobile phone. And the visitors were able to see his tour simultaneously, slightly delayed, in the museum – they were literally able to watch him all day. I like to say: The visitors were able to monitor him. It was a vision of decentralized surveillance – an everyday phenomenon today – and that was back in 1994. *Intelligent Mailman* was an anachronism, juxtaposing a traditional conveyor of information, in the form of letters, with an emerging information technology, the evolving internet.

Weibel: It was a telematic project.

Bielicky: It was a very early telematic project, yes. I presented the data from the GPS tracking – this constant identification of a living being's location – as an abstract line in the museum. So, as a "byproduct," the mailman drew an image, which could be watched at the museum.

Weibel: And then, the very next year, there was the world's first exhibition about the internet.

Bielicky: Right, like so often, you once again had the longest antennas and suddenly dared –moreover during the first year of the existence of the World Wide Web – to launch the first artistic reflection of this new socio-technological phenomenon.

Weibel: And back then everyone still believed the World Wide Web was a temporary phenomenon.

Bielicky: Everyone thought it was a fad, a fad that would soon pass.

Weibel: And then there was the briefly equivalent second term coined by your teacher Nam June Paik: "electronic highway." That was the one the American president, for example, liked to use.

Bielicky: Yes, Bill Clinton, right, and Nam June Paik then accused him of stealing the idea.

Weibel: During the preparations and even right up to the opening, all the nonexperts and experts, all the way up to the major German museum directors, said there was no need to do this exhibition; it was just a common fashion phenomenon. But I said, no, we're taking the word "highway" seriously. *Autobahnen* [highways] have durability, and the electronic highways likewise will have durability; they will last, just like the *Autobahnen* – and that is just how things turned out.

Bielicky: And there, at a really early point, you had a keen intuition, linguistically, scientifically, in comprehending the electronic highways as a kind of cultural space. We must bear in mind: this early, when hardly anyone was using the World Wide Web! I was certainly very disappointed, years later, as I was doing some internet research on the history of the WWW, to find no mention of your Ars Electronica *Mythos Information – Welcome to the Wired World* [1995]. I made a correction, at least, on Wikipedia – and it is still there today – as it had named other, later exhibitions on this topic as being first. When I entered the *Mythos Information*, they had to acknowledge its pioneering character. Not for the first time, history was falsified.

Pipilotti Rist and Michael Bielicky at the exhibition *Schirm-Herrschaft*, Städtische Galerie Villingen-Schwenningen, 1993.

Weibel: And that is the interesting thing about you: a media artist must also always think epistemically, that is, produce knowledge. A media artist must always search for images, produce images that explain the world, like a scientist, because they are epistemic. In other words, he must be technically trained, he must have faith in technology. That is why we spoke in detail about your work *Intelligent Mailman*, as you were the first artist to use GPS technology. Media artists are artists who are also up-to-date on technology, as I always say: at the forefront of research. Secondly, it must always be philosophically justifiable as well, whatever a media artist does. He shouldn't just address technology as a gimmick. In you, I found a type of artist who to me is the exemplary media artist – you recognized that the image, as we know it from painting, only has representative character and, even if it is abstract, it still just remains a representation.

Bielicky: Precisely.

Weibel: What people always hold against media art is not right. While there are artists who just produce technical gimmicks, most of them do not understand technology and many do not even want to understand it – so it remains a gadget, just playing around. That is why it is important to promote artists who are both technically versed, always up-to-date, but who beyond that are able to philosophically elevate and justify their own work. Those are media artists; everything else is no longer art. Then it is either cinema or painting, carried on by technological means. So, I would say: the darlings of art reviewers are the very ones who do not advance media art, but harm it – harm it in that they carry on in cinema and painting. One example is Pipilotti Rist. Anyone can make this sort of technical image, so her work cannot be philosophically elevated. It has no epistemic value. But because she makes colorful images, psychedelic painting, accompanied by pretty, colorful pop sounds, this approach is so popular with the art review supplement and the museums. But actually, it's nothing more than bad pop art with electronic images. Whereas such professional institutions as Ars Electronica or ZKM | Karlsruhe have the important task of showing what is the true core of media art. That is why I have not shown Pipilotti Rist again in recent decades. Back then I kept having to tell the managers of [Austrian public TV broadcaster] ORF's Upper Austrian Studio, one of the hosts and co-decision makers for Ars Electronica: we are not some Ars Pyromanica, and as such we don't have a keen interest in fireworks; nor are we the Ars Metallica, and so neither are we into crude robotics. No, I had to keep emphasizing: we *are* Ars Electronica *or* Ars Digitalis. For that is precisely what needs to be promoted. And, Michael, from the very beginning you fulfilled these criteria, and what is even more important: you have endured, meaning that you are still at it, twenty years later – and are still at the forefront of the research, with your internet projections. In brief, many other artists in the late 1990s managed to find this or that artistic approach to the internet, but then repeated it ad infinitum. First, they made video art, then video stations, and today are still doing video stations. So, even if the content may be different, it remains film, photography, carried out by technological means. They have not been able to develop further and are stuck as a result, artistically as well as philosophically. But since we are living in the media age and mediatization is on the increase rather than decrease – and with the internet of Things, we are even working on the mediatization of things – we all the more need artists who are adequately equipped to react, artistically and philosophically, to these problems of the media age. And you have held up to these demands that I am posing to media artists.

Bielicky: That is naturally why I am so spiritually kindred with you, Peter, because I have always been concerned precisely with this matter. My work was always tightly interlaced, I have always been focused on basic research, on the question of what technology can do and how this technology is embedded in society – I am not interested in experimenting superficially with technology, in improving it. For that I often have people who are much more versed *in* it. I am primarily interested in the essence of technology and how it can be applied in social, in philosophical, and other contexts; and only in those contexts does it make sense to me. This constant basic research also means I need to always re-invent myself. I always say, I would be long dead if I had to do repetitive projects, ones that are always the same. I do not understand artists who constantly do the same thing all their lives, because they have been understood and co-opted by the institutions. I thought being an artist means to research, sometimes playfully, sometimes wittily, sometimes technically; but always with the instruments of philosophy or idea history, and even more importantly: with curiosity. And that is where we, Peter, are very kindred; and Pipilotti Rist is, to me as well, with all due respect to her success in the art business, a very conservative artistic position. That is an artistic gesture that belongs back in the twentieth century; meanwhile we are living in totally different times.

Weibel: And the reason for your justified skepticism is that media art comes from photography. From the beginning, the stimulus was that a painter paints a picture, always wants to paint another picture, considers that his task. Since William Henry Fox Talbot, the photograph, or more precisely, the negative has created – and this is the crucial point – the technology and possibility to create hundreds of prints of images. Already here we have a multiplication of images, meaning we are no longer dealing with the production of *one* image; we are already dealing with the distribution of *many* images, which Vilém Flusser also very pointedly describes, in *Towards a Philosophy of Photography* [originally published in German, in 1983]. What you, Michael are doing, for example, in your current work, is precisely this: on the internet, there are yay many sources, yay many texts, yay many images, yay many facts and data. That is a distribution of information; and within this aesthetics of distribution, I take something out and, in turn, can distribute that onto an image or within an installation; and can then even take what I have redistributed, within a framework I have chosen, and exhibit it on the internet. The entire approach that you have, Michael, and have kept adapting over the course of decades, is to understand deep structure – how technology alters our perception, our perception of the world. That has a significant advantage and is the actual mission of media art. It is not simply film, nor is it painting. When we ask ourselves, which disciplines explain and change the world, unfortunately there's no getting around politics, which changes the world drastically; there's unfortunately no more getting around religion, and then science and technology. And the latter two change the world most drastically. And, in the process, we notice that art has really withdrawn, decades ago; for today, when a pictorial surface itself is portrayed, in color, then this approach, this discipline is merely an explanation of the artist's chosen means or of the approach, but it no longer relates to the world. It is ...

Bielicky: ... self-referential ...

Weibel: ... self-referential. And media artists do not act like that. First of all, media artists aspire to make their art the true alternative to politics, to technology, and to science. That is why it is important to emphasize that media art is always simultaneously media research, which means: art is once again claiming its ability to explain world, unlike politics, science, and technology – but *with the aid* of science and *with the aid* of technology, art is trying out a *new* way of explaining the world and changing the world. Neither greater nor smaller, this is the claim of media art; and it is a huge claim. The other artists' approach, or to stick with our example, the approach taken by Pipilotti Rist – and here already something is obvious: this sort of name, it doesn't even begin to strive to be taken seriously – the approach of Pipilotti Rist is merely to create beautiful pictures. That is the world of consumption. It is not enlightenment, it is not change, it is not learning, it is not epistemic. And here, people find it difficult to first of all understand this art, and secondly, to describe it critically – not to speak of elevating it. Most critics, most museum people, art people, do not even have the craft to install it. After all, most of them cannot even switch on a video recorder or camera, much less operate one. They are lucky if they can even switch on the TV set at home. And that, in most cases, is the extent of their technical knowledge – we cannot demand of them to have a better grasp of it. But lovely images – lovely images à la Bill Viola, for example, which moreover are repetitions, reminiscences, and echoes of historical paintings, of portrait painting or religious painting – this they understand: this is as it is with painting. These people are, especially in our increasingly mediatized cultural phase, the actual pall-bearers of media art.

Bielicky: They are regressive towards other media, are distinguished by an ignorance and unawareness stemming out of fear. The result is often an ignorance toward entire fields.

Weibel: With regard to ignorance what also seems particularly important, what I also never get tired of repeating: the artists who have a future, that is, those who are attuned to the future are also the ones who never deny their origins. That means they know they are dwarfs on the shoulders of giants, but also know that the dwarf on the shoulders of a giant can see much further than the giant himself, which is to say one can learn from history. Due to your rootedness in history, in Czech cultural history – based on the above-mentioned deep time of Czech spirituality – you have always wanted to learn

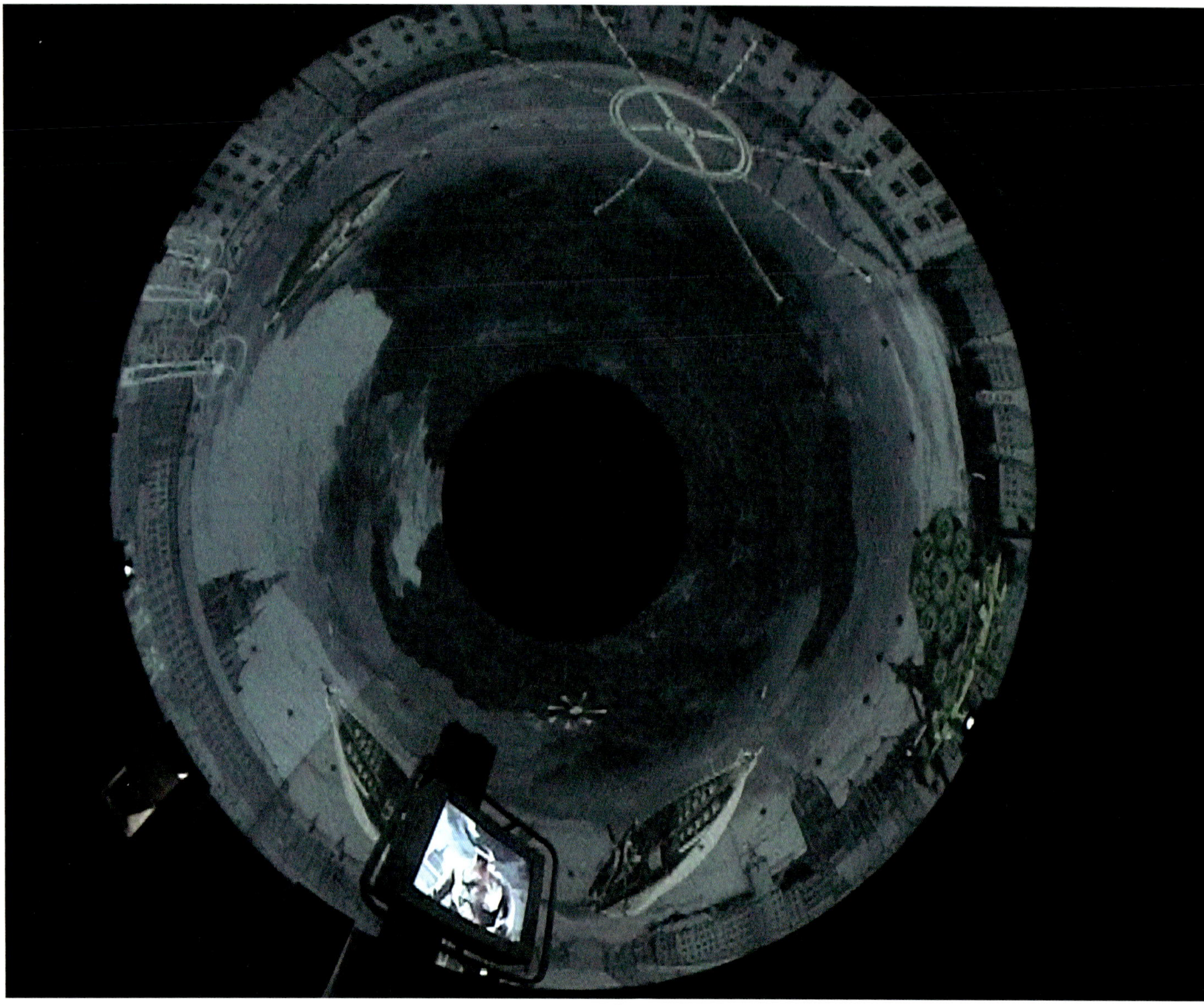

Room with a View, 2000, immersive interactive installation with 360 degree dome projection. Installation views, ŠKODA Pavilion, Autostadt, Wolfsburg, 2000.

Stage designer: Josef Svoboda, directors: Radúz Činčera, Ján Roháč, Vladimír Svitáček, *Kinoautomat*, program: *A Person and His House*, 1967, interactive film with live performance on stage, 35mm, b/w, sound, Czech Pavillion, Expo 67, Montreal, ČTV, Czech Television. Video stills.

Josef Svoboda, *Polyekran*, *Creation of the World of Man*, 1967, 112 moveable cubes with slide projections, 15.000 slides, color, sound, 11 min, Expo 67, Montreal.

and you are still prepared to learn from that today. We have also done many related exhibitions and had discussions. I'm thinking, for example, of the 1960s, that is the late 1950s; and of machine aesthetics in cinema.

Bielicky: You mean the projects *Kinoautomat* [1967] and *laterna magica* [1958]?

Stage designer: Josef Svoboda, directors: Alfred Radok, Vladimír Sviták̆ek, Jan Rohac; co-screenwriter: Miloš Forman; *Laterna Magica*,1958, multi-genre theater performance, Czech Pavillion, Expo 58, Brussels, ČTV, Czech Television. Video stills.

Weibel: Exactly, meaning the projection at the Brussels Expo 1958, *polyekran*; all those stories, with or without screens. The fact is: everything that came later, what became famous then, in the kinetic era, the Czechs did it all first. I am thinking of artists like Woody Vasulka, or the idea of the robot – and thereby robotics – the robot being indeed Czech, and the golem is a Czech invention, meaning the idea of artificial life and artificial intelligence – has its origins in Czech culture. From golem to robotics, just imagine: those are the essential Creation ideas. There, for the first time, they said: not nature, not evolution – the human being can now play creator. The human being can create life; he can artificially create life, he can create artificial intelligence. These are all Czech inventions. That is the measure of artists, whether they are also able to advance such historic missions. Most artists haven't a clue about their situation, even often haven't a clue about the setting in which they grew up, and have no interest in it either – and if it did interest them, they still couldn't advance these historic missions. And that is also one of the criteria, when I evaluate art: can this artist to elaborate on the text of a cultural evolution? And with you, Michael, more than in the case of others, the answer can only be: yes, you are able to do that. Or more so: yes, you're doing it. You can add to this text, for if an artist does not elaborate on the text of cultural evolution, then he is not historical; then he is arbitrary, he is insignificant. So, we must demand this of the artist. Ergo, cultural work involves elaborate on the text of other artists and not just the own.

Bielicky: Precisely. And somehow engaging oneself along that line. Only then does it make sense, otherwise it is pointless.

Weibel: This is culture.

Bielicky: This is culture. And today, unfortunately, many artists have often not internalized this – a great, perhaps *the* misunderstanding of art in our society.

Weibel: It is a public misinterpretation, the belief that it is about expression, the individual freedom of the artist. It is a misinterpretation, even an abuse – the prescription of a false mission of art – an abuse that has become commonplace, and which creates confusion.

Bielicky: Definitely. I'm trying to think one step ahead: I was at Ars Electronica four times; we've mentioned three times, plus with Bernd Lintermann from ZKM, with the Škoda Pavilion *Room with a View* [2000].

Weibel: It was an interactive, epistemological computer projection. And that was in 1999: a projected, interactive Wikipedia entry on Czech cultural history.

Bielicky: Exactly, and in 1999, you were suddenly, as I perceived it, the director of ZKM. I had no awareness of the preceding process – one minute we were collaborating at Ars, then you were here at ZKM, in Karlsruhe. To me it was such a logical continuum that I was not at all amazed that you were suddenly sitting on this chair and not in Linz. And it may have been largely because our dialog continued seamlessly, and we were already tackling the next huge project, with Škoda and Jeffrey Shaw. Then, however, I was off your radar for a couple of years. Our dialog continued, but during the year 2000 I had a change of location as well: I went to Prague.

Weibel: Yes, true, for a while our dialog became partially instrumental, because Jiří Ševčík had asked me whom I would recommend as founding professor for the newly established New Media Department at the Prague Academy of Fine Arts (AVU) – and I instantly recommended you for that professorship.

Bielicky: Yes, exactly, that's another thing I wanted to convey here in this conversation: you are a joker. In life, we may not need many jokers, but a good one. And you were not just my joker, you were above all my mentor, taking your place alongside Vilém Flusser and Nam June Paik. In my life, there have always been six people who provided firm direction; aside from my youth in Prague, six people who have had a lasting impression on my life, not just in the context of media art. In the context of media art, it was primarily, above all, Nam June Paik and you, Peter Weibel, then Vilém Flusser, and naturally Woody Vasulka and Mel Alexenberg. Those are my five icons, and naturally now, during these late years – though not so strongly in the context of media art, but nevertheless in a strong intellectual context – Peter Sloterdijk.

Weibel: Today they call this "business angels," one used to call them mentors.

Bielicky: Those are business angels. That is an interesting phrase. I probably also looked for such mentoring personalities. It is not the case that you fell in my lap. But there were also many coincidences, and in my professional media development these very people come to my attention, each in his own way. I mean, Vilém Flusser and you, you have an insane lot in common, overlaps; but your natures are nevertheless totally different, for sure also different in certain ways of thinking, but definitely also with an insane number of congruences. And so, it was no coincidence that you and Flusser were spiritually kindred.

Weibel: I was the first in Europe to invite Flusser, to participate in my symposium *Erweiterte Philosophie* [Expanded Philosophy]. That was in 1981. He came to my attention, because he had done one, two publications or texts in the magazine *European Photography*. And when I read them, I thought to myself: this is a very keen thinker, you have to invite him.

Bielicky: Amazing – in 1981? He was still a nobody then.

Weibel: He was still a nobody then, yes; living in Southern France. And then he became my lifelong companion, and that evolved into a close friendship, like with you. He was at the Ars Electronica, together with Jean Baudrillard and Friedrich Kittler – and then, when I gave lectures at the Institute for New Media, he was also there. And then, when I sat on the jury for the Siemens Media Arts Prize, I put it up for discussion to give Flusser the prize; and after some heated discussion that's what happened. Like with you, the initial exchange of theoretical discussion evolved into lifelong companionship and friendship.

Bielicky: For many people, your contribution was essential in enabling them to follow their path, and the same naturally applies to me too. But the experience at the Institute for New Media, where I encountered Zlavoj Žižek for the first time, stands out especially in my memory. Back then he was still totally unknown, too. Sitting in that lecture with my jaw dropping, I thought, how does Peter pick up such a phenomenon? All that remained in my mind was "modern archeology," because back then he was also totally unknown, Žižek.

Weibel: Absolutely. At that time, we put out an Institute publication with Merve Verlag: the publication series "Perspectives of Technoculture," in which Žižek published his first book, *Enjoy Your Symptom! Jacques Lacan in Hollywood and Out* [1991].[1] His first English book did not come until later. Indeed, through the publisher, Merve Verlag, we collaborated on the publication of his very first book; only after that did he start this huge global career. But you described it just as I remember it, when I heard him the first time, I was astounded.

Bielicky: I couldn't believe my ears – it didn't fit any category. He was such a strong individual: original, witty, smart.

Weibel: Although he was talking about the German philosophy of idealism.

Bielicky: Precisely, how boring, really, when one remembers the general graveyard mood in philosophical academia back then.

Weibel: With him also a lifelong friendship has grown. Today, when I organize symposia – like at ARCO in Madrid, for example – he doesn't need to be begged; or when I do a publication, like *Art in Europe 1945–1968* [2016], for which he wrote the epilogue "What Does Europe Want?".

Bielicky: You really have a gene, plus a radar that always recognizes things extremely early, before others, particularly talents. You promote them, you pave their way; as you've done with Flusser, you've done with Žižek, and probably many others where you recognized a fertile source before anyone else.

Weibel: And one of them is you: I do indeed have a gene that lets me discover art very early – even Pipilotti Rist, whom I criticized earlier, I exhibited years before anyone else.

Bielicky: Did you?

Weibel: Her too, that was the exhibition *Video Cult/ures: Multimedia Installations from the 90s*, which I did in 1999 at ZKM. At the end of the

1990s, I also exhibited the famous, today globally renowned Olafur Eliasson …

Bielicky: He was also still a nobody then …

Weibel: That was 1996. It was the group exhibition *Remote Connections*, held at the Steirischer Herbst festival, where I showed his first room-sized projection: *Die organische and kristalline Beschreibung* [The Organic and Crystalline Description]. Those were the 1990s. Then later at the Kunsthalle Basel, he also had his first solo exhibition, *The curious garden* [1997], an installation occupying several spaces. Then – with Christa Steinle and me –his first solo exhibition in Graz, with (re-)exhibited older works, such as *Doughnut projection* [2000] and *Room for one colour* [1997], about a dozen works in total. And then, at ZKM, just a year later, in 2001, *Surroundings Surrounded*, his first solo exhibition: a survey of his oeuvre with more than twenty works, including *Models* [2000–01], which dealt for the first time with his collaboration with architect and mathematician Einar Thorsteinn. For the exhibition, we published a sizeable book under the same title, with MIT Press. It quickly sold out. It wasn't until 2003 that his *The weather project* was shown at the Tate.

Bielicky: That was the leap.

Weibel: That was the leap, before that he was – to use your words – a nobody. So, one of these discoveries is definitely you, because I just can't help discovering talents very early. While there are criteria, and I have already named them: for starters, technical versatility, which does not mean we can do everything, but we must understand it.

Bielicky: How it came about, in what direction culture is moving in order to serve it is secondary …

Weibel: Like a composer. A composer need not play the piano perfectly, but he must know how to compose – how to get the most out of a piano as an instrument, what the instrument can do. And aside from this technical versatility, the mentioned talent must also include, secondly, the skill of interpretation; meaning, an artistically engaged talent must be able to elaborate on the others' cultural texts, to embed themselves in the cultural evolution, in which they are growing up, and drive it forward. So, to me – beyond whatever perhaps even genetic aptitude to respond to that notion – there are also certain criteria that I always have as a map in my head, criteria that I check and according to which I take note: this artist also has the potential to hold a place in cultural history. She or he is no flash in the pan, but one can expect her or him, over decades, to create and develop an oeuvre – and that was simply the case with you, Michael. Then, I believe, there was also your appointment to the Karlsruhe University of Arts and Design [HfG], which I also took note of within my endosphere.

Bielicky: I was also quite aware that I need someone there as an advocate, and, I mean there you …

Weibel: … turned some screws.

Bielicky: In the final analysis, at such a closely connected institution, only those who have the competence to make this decision should decide on a professorship for media art – it is certainly also in the interest of the institution that people come together who have a certain spiritual vision, a common understanding of art and media art.

Weibel: Especially since, at that time, there were no longer any media artists at HfG.

Bielicky: Because the world of media art to HfG did not exist, although it was the actual purpose, to establish long overdue media-oriented basic research or media research that is also up-to-date.

Bielicky: So now we have got to the new century, 2000, when you were already at ZKM. I was appointed in 2006 and immediately had the privilege of experiencing and co-designing a visionary exhibition: *You_ser 2.0*, subtitled *The Century of the Consumer*. In the context of this exhibition you gave me another idea, and I made a kind of translation machine to turn news into pictographs in real time, and called it *Falling Times* [2006–09]. In it, real-time news from the internet simply fell from the sky; which involved converting the news texts,

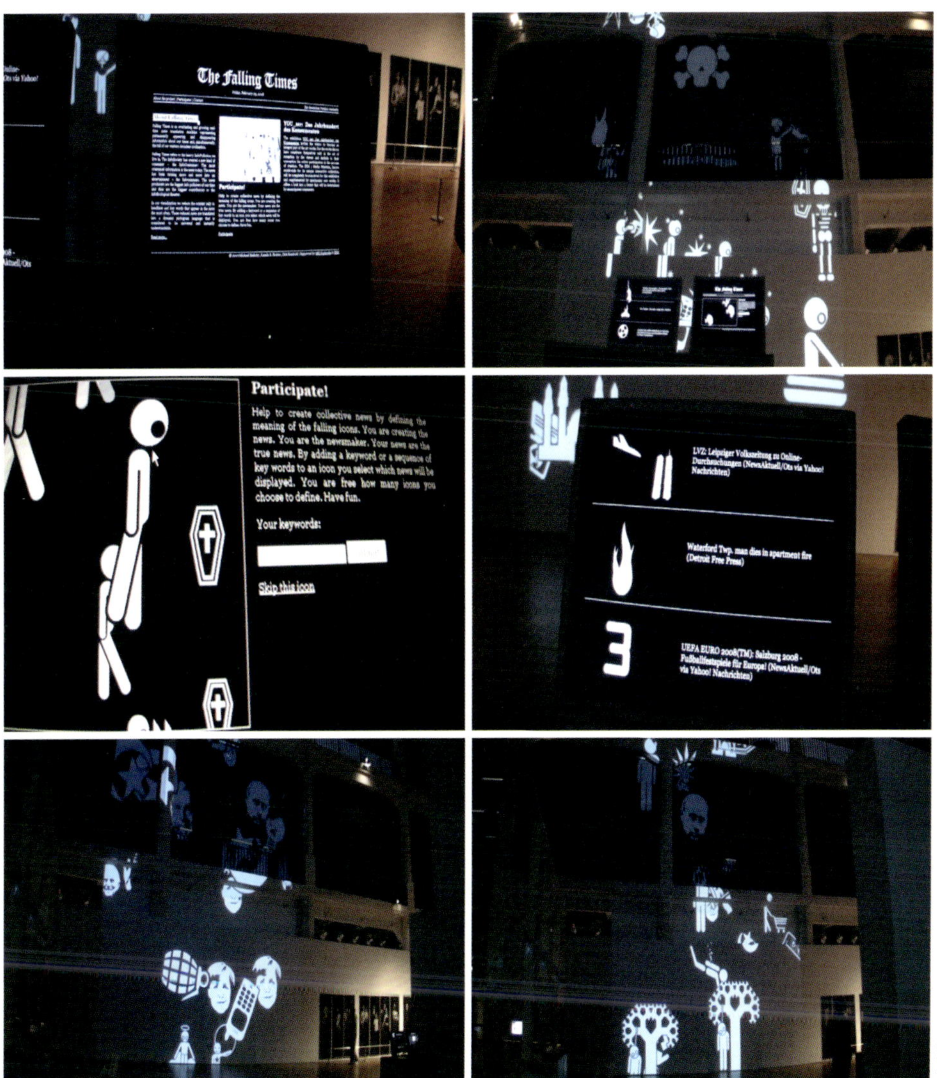

Falling Times, 2006–09, data-driven installation. Installation views and details, ZKM | Karlsruhe, 2007.

algorithmically, into pictographic representations of news. It was an algorithmic projection, algorithmically translated into pictograms, but the dramatic structure was also controlled by means of internet data and algorithms. This exhibition was again visionary – perhaps you could say a couple of sentences about it.

Weibel: This brings us right back to my two criteria. Firstly, the pictographic concept was coined in the *k. & k.* [Habsburg Dual Monarchy] realm, and it was invented by the famed Otto Neurath. For the development of Isotype [International System of Typographic Picture Education], Neurath, Gerd Arntz, and their team of scientists – and this is precisely the point – examined the question: "How can I present knowledge visually, find a pictorial hybrid that explains the world?" Today we only need to take the data – for example, how many cars are produced, how many workers there are, how many jobless, etc. – and feed it into a visualization tool, and can visualize, for example, statistics on unemployment that instantly gives people "Aha!" moments, regardless of their educational backgrounds. This entire amount of data is available on the internet, free of charge; we *simply* need to express it in a visual language that explains: this is what the world is like – in actual fact, with no major additional translation efforts. And this approach originated in the Austrian-Czech area, the k. & k realm. And this was precisely what you revived or, as we said, added onto, with new features ...

Bielicky: ... and with new technology.

Weibel: With new technology, exactly. Neurath, after all, used drawings on paper, and you did it in real time; meaning the internet text-to-pictograph conversion took place live, in the exhibition space. Your *Falling Times* [2006–09] is a work that is a must for any exhibition about the emancipated consumer, to whom nothing is actually explained in everyday life. Television is certainly a dedicated distraction machine, which simply does not explain, simply does not even intend to explain coherently. From this nexus, the idea evolved to express through the exhibition *You_ser 2.0* [2009]: no, we *do* have the possibility, with the aid of technology, for the consumer to emancipate himself. And that's why we need a visual strategy, to make news visual, for example through pictographs; to make connections explicable. In other words, in your work, the news is – we of course we have to add – made accessible and understandable. That, as a response to my exhibition concept, impressed me so much that I said: "We're doing it," we're doing the Biennial of Sevilla [BIACS 3, 2008/09]. There we also found a historical origin, in the harbor, in the *porto*, through seafaring. And you did not disappoint, on the contrary, there you created a very wonderful piece of work ...

Bielicky: ... *Columbus 2.0* ...

Weibel: ... a tremendous piece, with an interface.

Bielicky: With a very old interface, one that, through its history, is accessible to everyone: the old steering wheel of a ship. With this steering wheel, visitors could gain access to a digital ocean – through an analogy with the era in the seventeenth century. This analogy was naturally a reference to Christopher Columbus and the discovery and exploration of space. Today, in the twenty-first century, we have once more embarked on a journey of discovery; on the journey of discovery and exploration of data space, in the form of a digital ocean that is being moved back and forth on our screens. We no longer navigate in physical space, but in a virtual space of information. And in this space of information, people were able to navigate with the steering wheel, in all languages: Arabic, Chinese, and so on. And due the fact that the interface was so clearly recognizable, it also automatically attracted people. Due to its universal validity, visitors did not need to first learn how to operate it. Even children quasi naturally turned it, setting in motion the data space beyond it.

Weibel: A very important, one of your best works, because it makes the consumer visible within cultural history and, moreover, enables the consumer to perceive themselves as just that. That they are able to do by perceiving themselves as an emancipated consumer, who can navigate themselves. He is not the sailor, the galley slave; he is not, in the artist's case, the gallery slave who rows, but the helmsman. He is the helmsman, the captain, not the slave, who rows: he controls the volume of data, or that which can be seen in the galleries and museums. The consumer can go on experiencing himself as emancipated, when you show him that he can go on controlling the volume of data. As you correctly stated, Columbus conquered physical space, while today we are conquering virtual data space, which tends toward infinity. We have charted the seas; we will find a visual language that is capable of condensing the internet. What I found especially lovely about the work was that the news making up the data ocean was transmitted in real time to the installation: all languages actually being waves; they have been produced, and that also applies to every news or wave in *Columbus 2.0* [2007–19]. In that respect, it *is* an ocean of data. That is not just a metaphor.

Bielicky: Precisely.

Weibel: And then it is necessary to emphasize the notion of navigation. Indeed, one says today, I'm navigating the internet. And that is actually very interesting, that it basically should be clear to everyone that it is the same thing: just as a boat was used to navigate an ocean, today, in your work, we navigate with the instrument of a steering wheel through the data ocean. You in fact also talk about data streams, about data flows, not just about the data ocean.

Bielicky: Of course, yes. And what interests me about media art anyway, getting back to that interface, what interests me about media art is that one can also manage – because we, with our bodies, are indeed fundamentally analog beings and are bound to these bodies – to also offer analog explanations of the world. These world explanations are then conveyed through a high-tech medium, but are nevertheless analog ...

Weibel: Apparently!

Bielicky: Apparently. Yes, apparently is the right word.

Weibel: Precisely, the steering wheel, or analog technology in general, is the interface between old and new. Analog technology is the historical interface to culture, one can even go so far back as the first navigation aid being the stars. After all, back then one could not have moved across the sea, if it had not been gauged; and it was gauged by means of the stars. That is to say, the stars were the first alphabet. And today, instead of the stars, we use words, which is all the better, as the alphabet itself is the better steering device. Letters are the better stars. With the help of letters, I always navigate myself through the volumes of text, through the desert; initially across a wasteland of print, and today across the news space and, thus ...

Bielicky: ... information ...

Weibel: ... the information space, quite right, with letters I can navigate across data space. And this has finally become even more important than just navigation by means of the stars, for today anyone who does not manage – as a consumer, with the help of letters – to shape the data noise for himself ...

Bielicky: ... is lost.

Weibel: He is lost, exactly; he will drown. Then the consumer goes down, suffers shipwreck.

Bielicky: So, the consumer can in fact be compared with a ship.

Weibel: We see, *Columbus 2.0* is a highly complex work – an important work.

Columbus 2.0, 2007–19, immersive interactive installation. Installation views, Bienal Internacional de Arte Contemporáneo de Sevilla, 2008.

Bielicky: And this certainly also involves it being perceivable very superficially – those who only want to play, also get their "money's worth". It could even be offered in an amusement park; I even envision this work in Disneyland. It is definitely multi-layered.

Weibel: While one can elevate it philosophically ...

Bielicky: ... it doesn't always get ...

Weibel: ... across.

Weibel: It just meets all the criteria of technical innovation: it is an internet work, operated in real time, with great effort in programming, complex algorithms, and simultaneously clear visualization. Add to this the transcription of old technology by means of its analog interface, the steering wheel; the overwriting of old culture into new culture – so everything we spoke of before applies here. Plus being projected onto an old fortress wall, if I recall correctly ...

Bielicky: ... it was an Arab quarter: Alcazar!

Weibel: Yes, that was it: Alcazar, a medieval wall in an Arab quarter, quite right. Plus Sevilla is, indeed, the place where Ferdinand Magellan, the first person to sail around the world, landed. He landed in Sevilla, with the remains of his crew, now reduced to only a tenth, in rags and starved, having circumnavigated the world. So, in Sevilla we find the beginning of globalization: that was the beginning of what we have termed data space.
Columbus set sail from Sevilla. Yes, we see: Sevilla is a very historic place, a historically rich place, a very contextualized place, which made *Columbus 2.0* an ideal work, because its contextualization is at least as complex. And then we have also showed your installation several times here at ZKM.

Bielicky: For example, on the facade of ZKM and ...

Weibel: ... and then, the following year, your latest work in the exhibition *Global Control and Censorship* [2015].

Bielicky: The slightly mystifying name of the work is *Data Dybbuk* [2015]. *Dybbuk* is Hebrew, and can be roughly translated as "spirit." The work was derived from the consideration that we encounter a build-up and exponential growth of data information not only on the internet, but also around us and by us and through ourselves. In a word, they surround us, at diverse frequencies, from various sources – here too, in this space, now in the air; the transmissions from you to the microphone and so forth – so this work was derived from the consideration that we are not even aware of this data's effect on us. This simultaneous invisibility and efficacy of data is the topic I wanted to raise – the data streams' enormous, enormous influence on our existence. And by that, I mean not only the informative influence, as information about something else, but also in a very immediate manner, such as brainwaves. It's important to realize: even in this very moment, data streams are racing through our brain. All these reflections combined, indeed, *through* these reflections, I suddenly thought, to me they are *dybbuks*, spirits. Because the Hebrew term conveys something in addition to our term "spirits." *Dybbuks* come from the world of the dead, and not from the ether – similar to the Greek gods, they are almost organic beings. They are living beings that accompany us in life, which we cannot get rid of either. And these spirits are simply *dybbuks* – these data spirits come from a world that is not graspable, but is still there. At the time, in connection with the exhibition *Global Control and Censorship* at ZKM, with *Data Dybbuk* I primarily wanted to show that it took these spirits to make controlling people possible in the first place. Furthermore, I wanted to show that this control was made possible stealthily over the last ten, twenty years, as well as that these spirits were around us and in us. In my opinion, this could only be visualized through mathematical formulas, and so I explained my vision to two young KIT [Karlsruhe Institute of Technology] students, who with the aid of my idea developed a totally new program. So then this Java program realized by technical experts is also only controlled with numbers, which delimit certain tolerances and radiuses within which the texts then come to life. One can also *only* feed the program with texts, whether with real-time texts or static news texts. And then, in real time, these are geometrically formed and visualized, through diverse mathematical processes. These *dybbuks*, which we can then see, these bizarre waves, we then projected into the space in such a way that when people, visitors, walk through the space, they become part of these spirits – and thus even projected beings themselves. They become art objects, because the data on their bodies dances in the folds of their clothing. The visitor walks through this data field and suddenly becomes an object and visualizes the data through their body – like at the opening event, where, by the way, I shot a rare photo of you, Peter, where you yourself are in this ...

Exodus, 1995, telematic performance. Documentary photographs.

Weibel: ... data ocean ...

Bielicky: ... are looking around in this data ocean. And only once people see, when they see the others, who look like themselves, they suddenly see: that person is standing in this ocean of data – if they are just standing in it alone, they don't notice it.

Weibel: That is a nice image that you just drew with words: everyone has an invisible data dress. Everyone is a data hunter and a data carrier. And there are sensors and detectors that respond to precisely that; that, for example, filter the data that you take in; and then there are other sensors and detectors that filter or register the data that you transmit and that you again take in. That means the subject, the individual is subjected to a profound change, whose consequences the individual human being is also utterly unable to explain.

Bielicky: That describes a beginning that we cannot recognize as such.

Weibel: We would not even recognize the signs alone: to what degree the data from the – I always call it the infosphere – how this infosphere or data industry will alter our status as a subject. There is, after all, the genetic version of information, from which we have slowly learned to what degree we

Data Dybbuk, 2015, data-driven installation.
Installation view, ZKM | Karlsruhe, 2015.

human beings are determined by clinical pictures and similar biological programs, including even our mental abilities. That is the genetic information, the natural information – but your topic here is social information.

Bielicky: And that is such a quantum leap. What just occurred to me, we indeed much earlier examined the origins of this quantum leap, in an exhibition; in another work, similar to my work on the origins of globalization, which we've already discussed: *Columbus 2.0* in Sevilla. That was in 1995, so about twenty years before *Data Dybbuk* and *Global Control and Censorship*. In 1995, as we discussed at the beginning, you had the right intuition and the daring to invite me and many others to the first exhibition on the internet, the earlier mentioned Ars Electronica *Mythos Information: Welcome to The Wired World*, to which I wanted to contribute a bizarre project: *Exodus* [1995]. Following the trail of Moses, the project examined the biblical Exodus, the Exodus of Moses and his people from slavery in Egypt. Here I was again using an analogy, in this particular case a historical analogy, by extracting this key moment of human history, the Exodus itself, as a structure. Then I took the liberty of projecting, once the internet had arrived, this Exodus structure, as a cultural shift, formalized onto general human existence. I projected the Exodus onto all planes: the social, political, in fact onto the existential plane itself. This historic moment, which however on a microlevel has already lasted for several decades – the constant wish to leave physical space and emigrate to an info-space; this wish I called Exodus. We are not in the middle of upheaval, we are in the middle of an outbreak. We have been, we were and are – this feeling was strong back then and is even stronger today – we have been, for a quarter of a century now, on a journey on the internet. And for me this is just as fascinating today as twenty years ago; it is still totally new, and yet familiar. Just the fact that I took the liberty back then of doing this somewhat gestural transfer – in the desert, on the trail of Moses, using GPS technology to record on the internet 3D objects gathered from the desert – seems to me no less revolutionary today. Because this recording took place linearly, digitally tracing the original, analog Exodus, using the blueprint of the evolution of history. I wanted – to return to this notion – to add to the text of history, although everything was new: the technology, but also the internet. I wanted to elaborate on history, but I could do so only by simultaneously asking many people at universities for help – at ours in Prague, but also in Tel Aviv. In Israel, I even got some partial aid from military research – back then it was Motorola, they helped me build this first GPS device. They were just so enthusiastic that they made everything available to me free of charge. And you saw this enthusiasm too and let it rub off on you – at the beginning there was that feeling, but the end brought the realization: someday people will probably say – like today people say "before Christ, after Christ" – "before the internet."

Weibel: "After the internet." Precisely. What you are describing, the entering of the Internet Age; you are totally right, it can be compared with the biblical Exodus.

Exodus, 1995, telematic performance. Technical equipment.

Bielicky: And that's also why the internet interests me to this day. We mentioned *Falling Times* and Otto Neurath as the beginning of my work with the algorithmic visualization of news. After that I did the second algorithmic work, *Garden of Error and Decay* [2010–19], which led to the next stage in this project, *Why Don't We* [2013–17]. Those works, shown in variations around the world, again used pictographs as their visualization language or – in another recursion – as a "navigation alphabet," as well as real-time data from the internet that suddenly became part of the narrative. These works are no longer like paintings or films, they are not a sealed-can product, which begins here, ends there, and remains unchanged. Rather the narrative through the data is more variable, the story becomes more variable: that's why I introduced the term "data-driven narratives," out of a need to explain our being suddenly able to tell stories that derive their variability from the choice of metadata. And that is yet another cultural leap.

Weibel: I'm going to also jump backward, not just historically, but also with regard to media theory, before I resume this point later. I'd like to jump back to the religious references that you keep making in your work. These religious references, beginning with the seven-branched candelabrum right through to the Exodus, are very important to me as a theoretician, because I always say: all technology is initially tele-technology. In Greek, *tele* means distant, so it is distance technology, which is why we also say "television," "telefax," "telephone," everything that is technical: television, telefax, telephone, telegraphy, telex, and so forth – all technology, at its core, is tele-technology, technology to overcome temporal and spatial distances.

Bielicky: Right, right, yes.

Weibel: And that is also the media historical reason why we were talking about angels before– they can overcome space and time, after all they are *dybbuks* – there we have your analysis again. So, angels are the first primitive sons of communication engineering. God, on the other hand, is everywhere anyway. He was invented as the Supreme Being, Your Eminence, etc., and his eyes see everything – viewed in this light, God is the ideal of communication engineering, and so every technological development is designed to replicate divine capabilities. Those are all technical visions, except back then they could only formulate them religiously. People had technical visions then, just as today, only back then they did not consider that technology functions slightly differently than wish fulfillment. It is just not merely the fulfillment of these wishes – it changes us and our wishes, as we seem to be technically approaching our visions. They were very spiritual wishes, like, for example, the wish, perhaps the most godlike wish of all, namely the one for omnipresence: "We want to be everywhere." Yet we started small and first wanted to hear voices. God calls out, speaks to me. Sloterdijk always jokingly gave pause for thought: if I speak to God, which indeed is already rather strange, then it is called praying. If God speaks to me, then I am a psychiatric case. Something must be amiss here. (laughs)

Bielicky: (laughs) Wonderful, wonderful.

Weibel: Because if I'm speaking to God, it's just as much a psychiatric disturbance as it is a psychiatric disturbance if God is speaking to me.

Bielicky: Precisely, precisely – naturally.

Weibel: And then there are the people who firmly believe that God has spoken to them. The most convincing among them are known today as founders of religions, which is even more intense. But the bottom line is that time confirms our shared theory: that religious experiences involved the early prefabrication of technical wishes. Sigmund Freud even said, in his famous work *Civilization and Its Discontents* [1930], he basically predicted that technology makes us more godlike, making man what he called "a kind of prosthetic God"[2], he literally called him that. That is grand, truly grand media theory: with the media, from the telescope on, we're becoming more godlike. That is always overlooked, because the gallerists either do not even read it, or, if they read it, then they only read it as a cliché, without seeing ...

Bielicky: ... this dimension.

Weibel: And those who decide what is interesting have not read it attentively enough and have certainly missed the clou, namely: what makes us feel discontented in civilization is that we want to be similar to God, but not with prosthetics. Yes, we wish to fly, but not in an airplane. We wish to hear everything, but not spend our whole life on the phone. Having attached our divine abilities to ourselves as a prosthesis initially makes us happy, but in the long run it causes our discontent with civilization.

Bielicky: That is incredible.

Weibel: That's why I always say, technology always exists in two condensation states: all technology is initially tele-technology and all tele-technology is, in itself, a theo-technology. This can vary according to the description and perspective, but it is always simultaneously both.

Bielicky: I understand.

Weibel: So, tele-technology is also theo-technology, meaning technology makes more out of God. And that is why it is incredibly important for me what you are always doing in your works, from *Data Dybbuk* to *Exodus*: in your work art becomes religious, but in a profane way ...

Bielicky: ... almost spiritual even.

Weibel: Spiritual, yes. But in a technical way. Some people are contented, while others are more discontented. Semi-real, virtual, expanded reality – all these terms, they are just auxiliary concepts, empty notions. We have always had a state of mixed reality. Some are contented with the prostheses, and the others are not. It is therefore also consistent, as a technology artist, to illuminate these religious references. Because they are after all based on religious needs; and the whole motor, the motivation of art is religious, which means: constantly the same archaic wishes, to become more similar to God – that is the real drive behind technology.

Bielicky: Interesting. Yes, that is true.

Weibel: We have the psychic reality, we have the material reality, we have the immaterial; but we also had "psychic travel". As an alternative to this prosthetic development, during all these past centuries, such religious writers as Karl May were sitting at home, thinking up things. And they used to call this, literally, "psychic travel," as the pinnacle of literary thinking. Just imagine this for a moment: sitting at home, they said to themselves, now I am in Jerusalem. They then precisely imagined how their roamings would be. They talked to themselves – basically, a psychiatric case. Religious, spiritual experiences from the home. They simply wrote this down, and those were then the famous psychic journeys, an entire literary genre. So, in that sense, it is right: technology is always religious in a particular manner, while also demystified. It only repeats religious wishes; it imitates religious wishes.

Bielicky: In a relatively miserable manner.

Weibel: But in a popular manner, most people would say the technical manner of repeating religious wishes is right, more so than the original religious manner. And this can come to mind when we look at your works; it can occur to us that technology only imitates religion – especially when one recalls, in this context, your seven-branched candelabrum.

Bielicky: Yes, *The Inner Observer*, which we mentioned at the outset, indeed had a predecessor, which we also briefly mentioned, a video sculpture named *Menorah/Inventory* [1989], which was also acquired for the permanent collection at ZKM – significantly, under the inventory number 001/90L. For this work, my first video sculpture, I built a steel replica of the said seven-branched candelabrum, one of the most important religious symbols in Judaism. And instead of the candles, I mounted TV sets showing the transmitted signal of a burning flame. What evolved between *Menorah/Inventory* to *The Inner Observer* – which is why this fits also so well here – was the replacement of religious symbolism with the technical. The outwardly visible, religious symbol becomes the content of my installations, instead of their carrier ...

Weibel: And this obviously has something to do with the Judeo-Christian system – those are indeed all religions of redemption, and technology is basically ...

Bielicky: ... a material aid.

Weibel: A material aid. Yes: redemption. This also has to do with – and this is even more profound – it has to do with the ancient knowledge that the name of the Greek goddess of helplessness is Amechania, which conversely means, mechanics is the opposite of helplessness. Helplessness is *a-mechania*, the negation of mechanics; and mechanics basically means to help – we attempt, with the aid of technology, to existentially gain the most.

Bielicky: Sometimes better, sometimes worse.

Weibel: Sometimes better, sometimes worse. But as I always say: when one is ill, it is quite okay to pray to God – it can help, but there is no harm in also taking medicine. (laughs)

Bielicky: (laughs) That's a good one. That is once again the technical approach.

Weibel: That is the technical approach, yes. Here, on the plane of technology, one has the same wish for redemption: one would like the illness to be healed. And, indeed, that same wish I used to direct to God. Only God was much shyer; later, in his light version, he at the most would lay on hands; and then it was a matter of faith, whether one actually got rid of the illness. Nor does faith necessarily make it worse; it can be really good. The difference is, it does not always help, it is not reproducible, unlike technical, chemical solutions.

Bielicky: With respect to reproducibility, science can help – basically, medicine is the true wish fulfillment, made available by science.

Weibel: Medicine is basically globalized technical religion, a wish-bearer formatted for and thus compatible with the era of globalization. And it can even be dispatched well too. The humanization of existence is attended by the mechanization of need. And this makes it important to see: this is high tech, and simultaneously, I do indeed hope – this simultaneity, this is what matters.

Bielicky: It is both things together.

Weibel: Precisely, one should be aware of both, and not forget human will either. For only our will can bear this discontent between high-tech and faith, the humanization of existence and the mechanization of need. And as you have just said several times: sometimes worse, sometimes better. Those who cannot bear it, and those who keep on investigating, at the limit where they can still bear it, at the bow wave of what is bearable, those are then the real media artists, like you. Many try to bear it more within the group. For how else do you think you can bear it; they think: after all, you're not alone in the world.

Bielicky: Yes, pseudo-movements, slacktivism, they claim to be spiritual. But that is rather embarrassing. And there is no big supply there, it is quickly drowned out by the data noise.

Weibel: Precisely, it is consumer culture, pseudo-culture. Pseudo-cultures make it easier for those without a strong will to bear their discontent with civilization. Basically, they are distributed discontent.

Bielicky: Phenomenal, I think what we have heard, what we have produced here, together, is chock full of so many highly interesting insights; that is, insights that are totally new to me – whereas today we're not even talking about these things for the first time. Perhaps it is time for a symposium.

Weibel: Right, exactly. The words distribution and symposia remind me: we still need to talk about the Flusser symposia and Prague.

Bielicky: Yes, we must not forget that, in 1993/94, meaning very early, you already took part in the Flusser symposia in Prague – thus turning our talk to the formative way my growing up in this unique city shaped me: you also had a special connection to Prague. I don't even know when, for the first time in your life, you were actually in Prague …

Weibel: You are indeed right – I was actually in Prague for the first time, physically, in the early 1990s. But before that, I had already had a close connection to Prague, for a long time. Also, because I translated the book by Czech Nobel laureate Jaroslav Seifert. I translated his best poetic, experimental work, *Télegraphie sans fil* [1925], his most famous work, better known as *TSF*. At that time, Eva H. Plattner did the rough translation. Then, from her literary scholarly version, or from the scientific data noise, to recourse to our terminology, I re-assembled a literary work. I knew the Czech culture, the concrete poetry; I knew Jiří Kolář, Josef Hiršal, and Ladislav Novák. Knowing these three Czech concrete poets made me aware that there is that tradition, which I then also duly portrayed, in the epilogue to *TSF*. That is, I summarized the Czech cultural text and elaborated on it, in a literary fashion. I also knew action artists, Czech ones, some of whom were also poets. One, Petr Štembera, subjected himself to a lot of torture; he also drank his own urine, cut himself – he had painted before, but became an action artist.

Bielicky: In the 1960s?

Weibel: 1960s, end of the 1960s. And through my discovery of this Czech tradition, especially through the interface of poetry and then the interface

Karel Schulz, *Sever - Jih - Zapad - Vychod*, 1923. Book cover by Karel Teige.

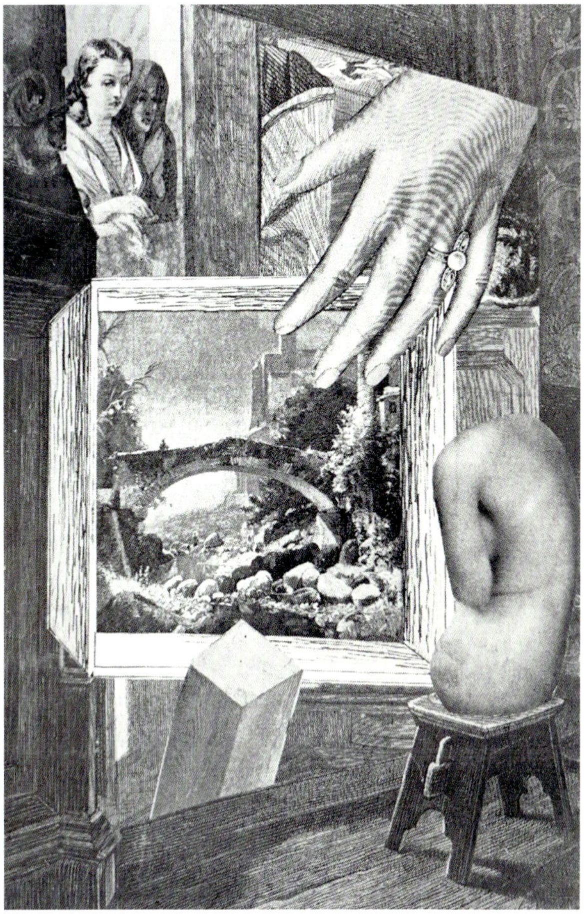

Illustration by Karel Teige in: Vitezslav Nezval, *Most*, 1937.

of action art, I started to deal with Czech history. Then I explored the wonderful Devětsil movement, within which Karel Teige, very early on, founded wonderful initiatives that extended the text of the avant-gardes in a much more convincing manner than anywhere else in Europe.

Bielicky: Surely you also discovered the famous dancer Milča Mayerová. I remember her, because she danced the alphabet, in a very idiosyncratic manner.

Weibel: The alphabet, or more precisely: she interpreted the individual letters. In a sense, she did a prototype of your *Data Dybbuk*. She explicitly did not want to represent anything in dance; she wanted to *be* the letter. At any rate, I dug into the history of the Czech avant-garde. And when Jaroslav Seifert was finished with his *TSF*, it was not easy for him to find a publisher.

Bielicky: Yes, that was even before his Nobel Prize. I believe he also received the prize rather late; I believe in 1984.

Weibel: Seifert received the Nobel Prize in 1984, yes. And before that, I translated him and then I wrote a long epilogue on the history of the Czech avant-garde. I elaborated on the cultural text of Europe.

Bielicky: That was your first project ...

Weibel: Yes, writing about Czech art, or rather modern Czech poetry, was my first concrete Czech project – and Karel Teige is indeed the interface between literature and art; then Josef Čapek – now everyone knows him. Then the entire Jewish Kabbalism, in Prague, was also of great interest to me; Kafka, it goes without saying – and then, what is also important, what goes even deeper, Michael, what is extremely important: physics. First Ernst Mach, and then Albert Einstein – what does he do, the great physicist who doesn't take himself seriously as such? Before becoming a professor in Vienna, he becomes a professor in Prague. Before they became famous, they were all professors in Prague. So, for a long time, around 1900, Prague was an important center for physics. Another great philosopher, a philosopher of the Vienna Circle, Philipp Frank, was then Einstein's successor in Prague. So, we can see: Prague was an important center for physical science, for mechanical science; and they were very, very productive; not only the literature that everyone knows, but also the attempts to overturn the dusty, traditional theories. Among them, for example, was one of my gods, Kurt Gödel, who is from Brünn. At the time, he was a kind of German immigrant.

Bielicky: There were indeed a lot of them in Prague. And finally, Ludwig Wittgenstein, too.

Weibel: Yes, that reminds of a special case of cultural connection: The father of the philosopher Wittgenstein was married to Leopoldine Wittgenstein, which was the reason that the steelworks of the patriarch – who was feared for denouncing competitors until he was able to buy them up – were truly called the "Poldi-Werke" ["Poldi" (short for Leopoldine) Works].[3] Once, when I was talking to Woody Vasulka, I explained this to him. He had always wondered how it was possible that, in Prague in 1909, the name of a woman stood for patriarchy, like almost no other expression – it was simply the name of the wife of Wittgenstein's father. Then he suddenly understood. And similar to these quite obscure but wonderful connections, there are really wonderful connections between ZKM and the Czech culture – not just the concrete ones, as the origin of artistic works, but in a great variety of media theoretical, and moreover, media historical forms.

Bielicky: Yes, there were literary figures, painters, action artists, theoreticians – it was a mecca. The entire region was a mecca and Prague also always had a close connection with Vienna.

Weibel: Yes, Prague and Vienna. There was always the debate, what actually is a typical person from Prague, such as Kafka – is he German, Austrian, or Czech?

Bielicky: None of that, but rather a mix of German, Jewish, Czech, and Austrian tradition – if Hitler had not appeared.

Weibel: It would have become the source of world culture, it would have been the Silicon Valley of our time.

Bielicky: Yes, Silicon Valley, but also with a strong intellectual tradition going back to the Middle Ages, which of course in America does not exist in this historical dimension.

Michael Bielicky and Peter Weibel in Karlsruhe, 2017.

Weibel: It would have become the capital of the world.

Bielicky: I think so too. People from Prague have always had a special relationship with those who wanted to assimilate them: Austro-Hungarians – the Czechs, the Czechs almost affectionately call Franz Joseph I. "František," a diminutive term of endearment.

Weibel: (laughs) And František was also the name of another important man: František Kupka.

Bielicky: František Kupka, yes, a visionary – above all, he was coming from a totally different place than Kandinsky.

Weibel: Kupka was no less than the inventor of abstraction, long before Wassily Kandinsky. Abstraction came from Kupka – that is also how my love for the Czech culture evolved. I kept being rejected, and therefore had to ask myself, why was I rejected; which then made me investigate into and discover my own sources. At some point, I realized that one should not just keep publishing the forgotten Greeks. Instead, we must, also in the area of curatorial practice and also in our role as publishers and authors, research and investigate: what has not been published yet, what has not been done yet ...

Bielicky: ... searching for parallels with our own interests ...

Weibel: ... kindreds, kindred spirits, yes. Kupka too, I discovered very early. My companion, Susanne Widl, had bought a Kupka very early on; back then it wasn't as hard to get one, but you had to recognize it, you had to know it. We still have an old Kupka, where I said back then: that's going to be a great man. We still have that at home. Indeed, meanwhile he is being rediscovered: from Paris to Berlin, all the way to Vienna, today everyone knows that he was a pioneer of abstraction.

Bielicky: Today he is unaffordable.

Weibel: And thus, we have, in the history of Austria and the Czech Republic, many, many intriguing connections, especially in Prague, as an important center for physics and philosophy. Around 1900, from about 1880 to 1930, so for fifty years, Prague was always a source of innovations of all kind. I even believe that the important philosophers – such as Bolzano – what all these people share is that they previously taught in Prague before they came to Vienna. They all had to take this path.

Bielicky: Yes, Prague has always been distinguished by its historically sedimentary character. There is this medievalism, we talked about Sevilla and Alcazar – but here the sedimentation is simultaneously more religious, though also more mystical and alchemical, along with the most modern history of ideas – a layering of sediments without which the golem, and thus the robot, would be unthinkable.

Weibel: There we have it, again: the deep time of Czech spirituality.

Bielicky: Yes, it is, after all, a city that has been growing slowly for a thousand years. And these sediments have also always exerted an influence on thinking in Prague. Vienna, on the other hand, was relatively new.

Weibel: What an interview!

Bielicky: Yes, a really lovely interview. Thank you ever so much.

Weibel: Long live friendship.

Bielicky: Long live friendship.

Weibel: And long live true affinity.

The interview was recorded on January 12, 2017 at ZKM | Karlsruhe.

1 Originally published in German, entitled *Liebe dein Symptom wie dich selbst! Jacques Lacans Psychoanalyse und die Medien* (Berlin: Merve, 1991).
2 Sigmund Freud, *Civilization and Its Discontents* (New York: W. W. Norton, 1989), 44.
3 Poldi s.r.o (also formerly known as Poldi-Hütte or as Huť Poldi), in Kladno (near Prague), was a company specialized in manufacturing high-alloy steels.

Michael Bielicky, Norman M. Klein, and Mel Alexenberg, Karlsruhe University of Arts and Design (HfG), 2014.

Michael Bielicky, Isaac Julien, Armin Linke, and Peter Weibel, Moscow, 2011.

Peter Weibel and Siegfried Zielinski, École polytechnique fédérale de Lausanne, 2018.

Michael Bielicky, DJ Spooky (Paul Dennis Miller), and Peter Weibel, ZKM | Karlsruhe, 2015.

Peter Weibel and Noam Chomsky, ZKM | Karlsruhe, 2014.

Unknown person, Bruno Latour, Peter Weibel, and Michael Bielicky, and unknown person ZKM | Karlsruhe, 2019.

Phill Niblock, Peter Weibel, and Michael Bielicky, ZKM | Karlsruhe, 2004.

Michael Bielicky (second from left) with his father, mother, and brother. Both photographs were taken in 1963 with one of the first color print Polaroid cameras on the American market.

Michael Bielicky (left) and his brother Peter.

Photography Has Long Lost Its Two-Dimensionality

Michael Bielicky

I advocate the following thesis: contemporary critical thinking is in a crisis because there are no criteria at its disposal that would allow it to criticize its own products.

Vilém Flusser

From today's perspective, it is impossible to talk about photography in the sense of single physical images. The mediatization and virtualization of our lives as well as our experiences with ubiquity have changed the idea of *image* (of photography) far and wide. With the advent of the digital image, a new era has dawned of image form and image perception. There are examples of the dematerialization of reality as early as during the Renaissance. The famous Rabbi Loew, who among other things aptly formulated the idea of artificial intelligence in his story of golem, created a virtual reality: once, as Emperor Rudolf II was visiting the simple house of the rabbi, Loew performed a "miracle": he turned his house into a castle by using his camera obscura to project images of the interior of Prague Castle onto the walls of his rooms. This gave the emperor the impression of being in a castle. This virtual room from back then has a lot in common with today's virtual rooms.

During my childhood in Prague, I played the following game with my neighborhood friend: we folded a camera with a slot out of paper and drew small portraits on paper with a pencil, which we then put into the slot. When someone came past us, we asked if we could take a picture of her or him. We pressed the shutter button of the "camera" and then pulled one of the portraits drawn out of the slot and handed over the "photo" to the person. That was around 1959. A few years later, the son of friends from New York visited us and showed us the first Polaroid camera. I was not surprised at all when the visitor gave us the finished picture about a minute after he had photographed us. In my Prague years, I had other "real-time image experiences," namely with the *laterna magika* and the *Kinoautomat*. Both types of image production were used at the Expo in Brussels in 1958 and in Montreal in 1967 as innovations in the conceptual, formal, but also technical handling of pictures. The laterna magika consisted of many film screens on which films were projected and actors who were at the same time on stage and in film on the screens, interacting with each other. The *Kinoautomat* was the first interactive cinema in the world, in which viewers had the opportunity to help shape the progress of the film by casting their votes. The nonlinearity and the intervention in the plot of the film were new qualities in dealing with technical images and their perception. Both the early and later real-time image experiences had a lasting impact on my own handling of images.

Years later I studied photography with Bernd Becher at the Düsseldorf Art Academy. The work I had submitted for the entrance exam at the time was created during a one-year stay in New York. I had a job as a horse-drawn carriage driver, doing portraits of "outsiders" from different social groups. The more I respected and admired the work of Bernd and Hilla Becher, the less I was able to understand the attitudes of my fellow students and the theoretical disputes they had about their pictures. The theorists used new terms, such as *distant objectivity*, in connection with the work of Becher's students. I felt that this kind of "student photography" had a retro character. According to me, those photos resonated with nineteenth-century painting rather than

Stage designer: Josef Svoboda, directors: Alfred Radok, Vladimír Svitáček, Ján Roháč; co-screenwriter: Miloš Forman; *Laterna Magica*,1958, multi-genre theater performance, Czech Pavillion, Expo 58, Brussels, ČTV, Czech Television. Video stills.

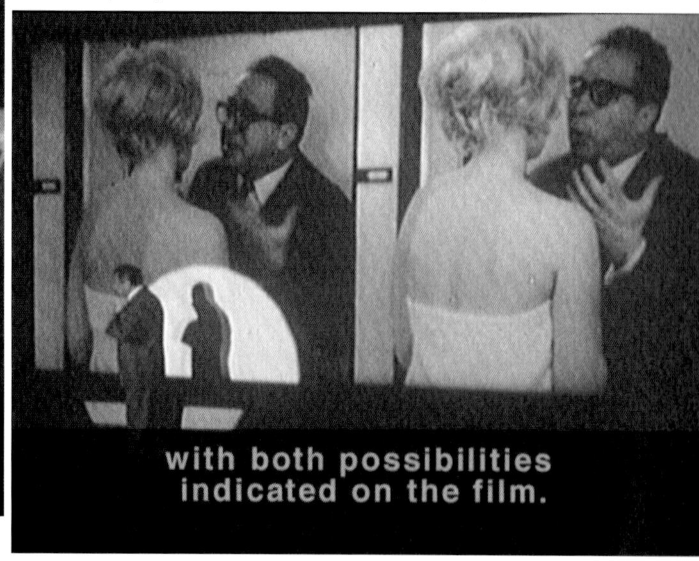

Stage designer: Josef Svoboda, directors: Radúz Činčera, Ján Roháč, Vladimír Svitáček, *Kinoautomat*, program: *A Person and His House*, 1967, interactive film with live performance on stage, 35 mm, b/w, sound, Czech Pavillion, Expo 67, Montreal, ČTV, Czech Television. Video stills.

"distant objectivity." I still remember well how art theorists introduced the term *Neue Wilde* (new savages) to contemporary painters and how a few years later, authors relativized or rejected the term. We know today very precisely that the peculiar alliance between certain theoreticians and the needs of the art market enabled the emergence of such new myths as that of the Neue Wilde.

During my studies, I switched to the Nam June Paik class. There we were confronted with the problem of time-based arts as well as with the emerging phenomenon of globalization. Paik's live satellite project *Good Morning, Mr. Orwell* (1984) was a milestone in addressing the ubiquity of images. The internet has radically changed how many artists work but has also expanded the field of presentation options. At the moment, there are two very unique problems for me: one is the question of the framework in which the new pictures are viewed. Hasn't the art business become a little too small a reference, and is the interdisciplinary context not completely missing? The other question relates to the pictures themselves: What pictures are we talking about today? Vilém Flusser says: "We are no longer the objects of a given objective world, but projects of alternative worlds. From the submissive position of subjection we have arisen into projection. We grow up. We know that we dream. [...] With us, the adventure of becoming human has entered a new phase. This becomes most apparent in the indistinguishability between truth and apparition, or between science and art."[1]

Today we can look at pictures from the outside and at the same time see ourselves in real time or even experience the three-dimensionality of the picture with virtual reality (VR). We no longer experience the images exclusively from the outside but merge with the images we have created. There are already images that we can change with our eyes by looking at them, and those that consist of living cells that can change through growth. But the dematerialization and ubiquity of the images are new dimensions of complex visual phenomena of our time. The perception of the pictures becomes multidimensional. It is as if someone had only experienced the world in black and white, two dimensionally, and then suddenly discovered unimagined dimensions of reality, such as color and space. It is not easy to find an adequate categorization and terminology for all these new phenomena. Photography seems to me to be the minimal art of our time. It is a tone in a large symphony. Just as we appreciate Steve Reich's minimal music, we will continue to appreciate two-dimensional, material photography. Computational artificial intelligence goes one step further. It not only addresses the visual process, but is also able to reconstruct it. VR is able to model not only all other media, but also those that do not yet exist. The changed framework conditions for artistic work in our world shaped by information and communication technologies cause completely new forms of art. Information technology produces not material objects but immaterial situations. Thus, the traditional idea of art – that only material art is permanent – is now questioned by art.

Deception is also an aesthetic-conceptual category of new technical images. Through Photoshop we can create all possible and impossible picture realities. It is no longer a question of whether what we see (for example, a photo) is true (if recorded from a subjective perspective) or not; it is more a question of being able to pinpoint the interdependencies between the illusions with which we are increasingly confronted. A lot of practice will be necessary to master this.

About four years ago I realized some projects using the CU-SeeMe program, a technology that can be used to organize videoconferences via the internet. When I received an invitation to take part in another artist's CU-SeeMe project, I had an incredible experience. Live images of eight different participants appeared on my screen, and you could talk to them using the keyboard. Up to this point I was familiar with the method. But when about ten minutes had passed, I had the impression that some of the participants who communicated with me were not personally present but were represented by a computer program. Another five minutes later, I realized that I was the only human being who was communicating with a machine here, and that the heads that I saw were not really there. I was alone; the other participants were only recorded. It was pretty irritating. Who can decide today whether, in the future, if there are such developed programs that can generate inspiration in us, for example, that we would not prefer to communicate with them rather than with a real "small talk person."

In addition to the aesthetic dimension, the technical images of today's artists also often have a social and political effectiveness, which is frequently caused by image-deception strategies. For example, the artist group ®mark

(Artmark) became a prime example of the *artist forger*, with fake web pages of the US president George W. Bush. The "false" Bush pages contain information about George Bush that does not convey a positive impression of the American president but is nevertheless true. The appearance of the wrong and the right websites about Bush are identical. But which Bush websites are actually fake, and which are correct? In Brian Springer's video work *Spin*, the American artist unmasked various personalities, especially from politics. He collected hundreds of hours of the so-called feed, which are TV breaks in which the television hosts and their guests wait until the advertising block is over. Knowing that they are not on air, they chat and often make racist or discriminatory statements. Brian Springer put these broadcast breaks together over many years. *Spin doctor* is now a frequently used technical term and is well paid as a job. Primarily politicians seek advice from a spin doctor.

"The skies of Baghdad are illuminated" – this sentence in combination with the green infrared images of antimissile lights from the Gulf War have become a new archetype of the modern media era, as have the images of the TV revolution on Romanian television. In 1992, my students and I participated in the *Piazza Virtuale* project (documenta IX) from Prague, an interactive TV model developed by the artist group Van Gogh TV. We decided to do the following experiment on a broadcast evening from our Prague broadcasting studio. The television picture was divided into two parts: Prague was in the lower part of the monitor and New York in the upper part. We faked a live connection between the two cities. In reality, the actors were in the same room. The next day we talked to viewers, and it turned out that no one had questioned the authenticity of the live broadcast. If it is becoming increasingly difficult to distinguish between real and false images, why couldn't images that theorists are writing about have a different meaning than they assume? Won't the real counterfeiters explain the fake images in the future?

Vilém Flusser believes that all revolutions are technical revolutions. This also applies to art, regardless of whether it was the invention of bronze casting, painting, photography, film, or the computer. These inventions have been recognized as new methods to create novel artifacts. The tool was always outside the user; it was a means of production. With the invention of the computer, the situation changed radically. We ourselves become part of the tool, the equipment, and suddenly find ourselves within a system in which we play a new role. This system is a universe full of dynamic processes in which interaction, ubiquity, virtuality, synchronicity, and telepresence enable the creation of an infinite number of realities. The aesthetics of communication are not concerned with the production of objects; they are not interested in concrete forms: their topic is space-time. There is no denying that both the framework, in which the new pictures are viewed, and the pictures themselves in a radical way represent a different context than before. Today the sciences, the sub- and pop culture, the hackers, the infinite cultural space of the internet, but the industry also, take on the innovative role. The new picture makers create their own platforms. The contemporary art world is becoming a lame duck. It owes its right to exist only to the mechanisms of the art market. The disappearance of the boundaries between high art and low art will provoke conservative counter-reactions. The extended time space from which the new images come is a laboratory that some perceive as a threat, and that poses an unprecedented challenge for others. The dynamic nature of this development and the resulting willingness to reorient oneself again and again will have the consequence that some will hide behind old values while others will be charged by this state with unexpected energy.

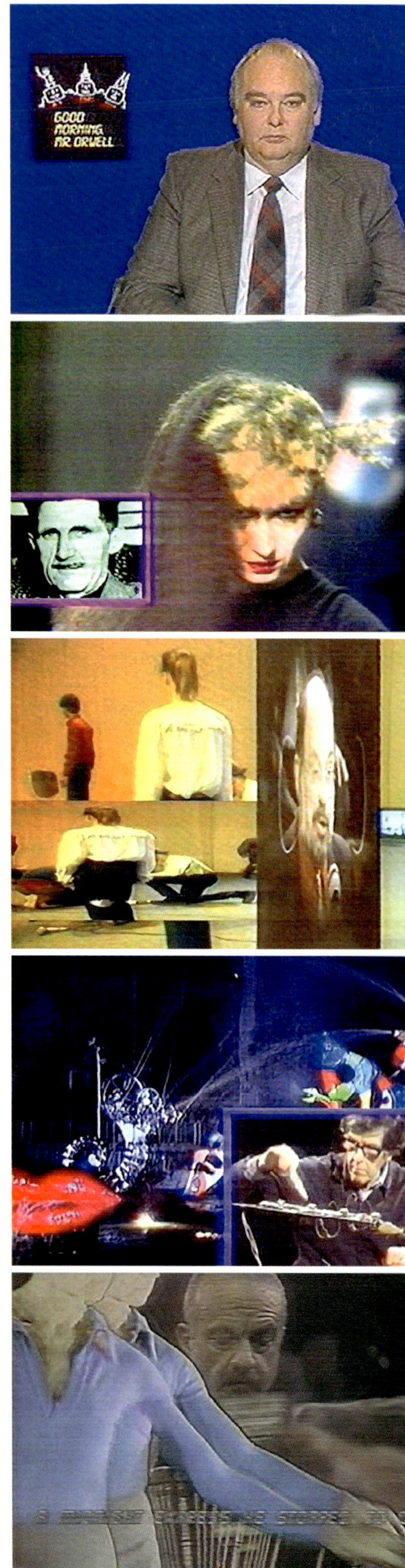

Nam June Paik, *Good Morning Mr. Orwell*, 1984. Video stills.

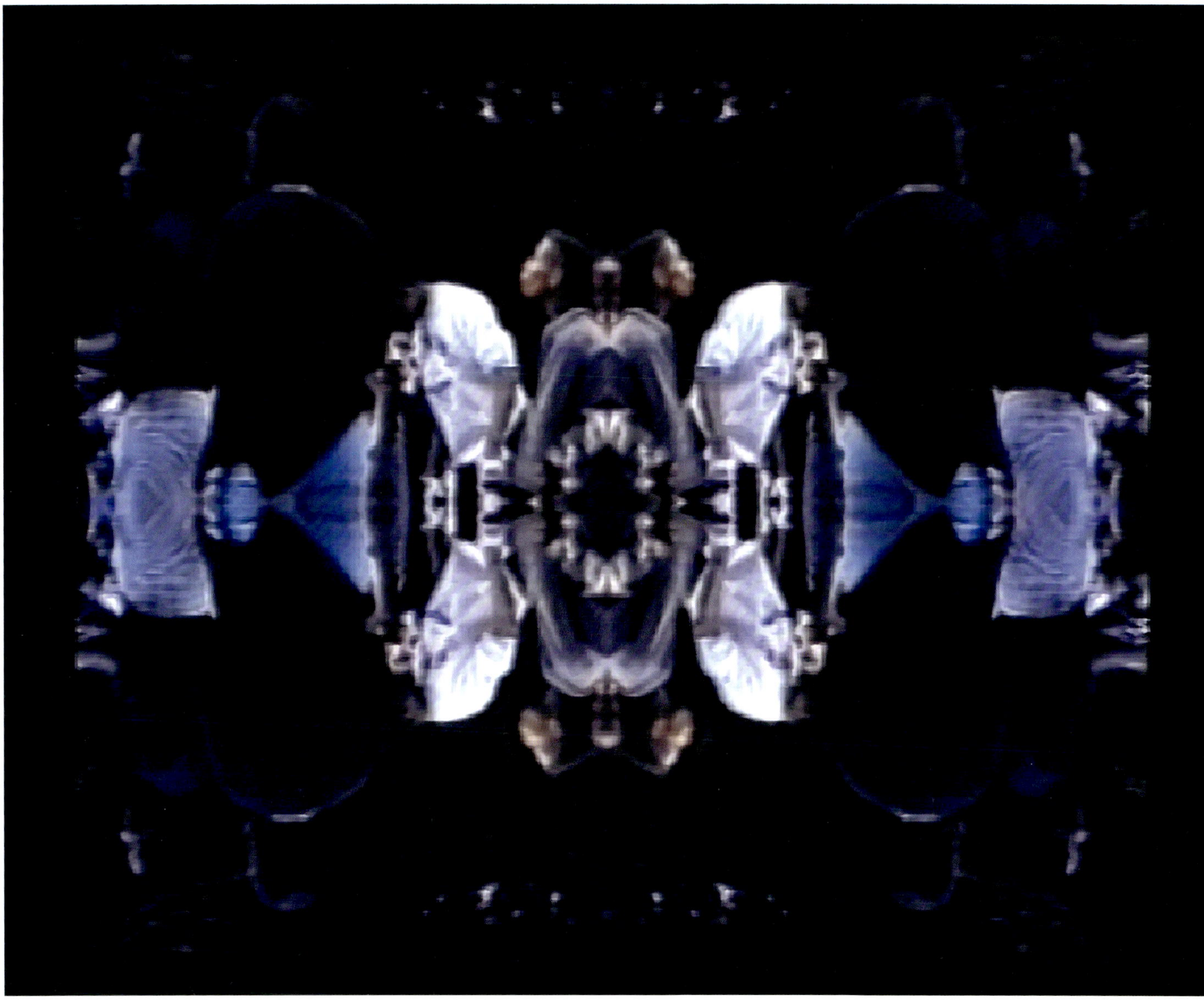

Perpetuum Mobile II, 1990, single-channel video. Screenshot.

Piazzetta Prague – Piazza Virtuale/Van Gogh TV, 1992, New Media Art studio, Prague Academy of Fine Arts (AVU). Video stills.

Lost, 2017, data-driven installation. Installation views, Centro de Arte Contemporáneo Wifredo Lam, Havana. Installation view.

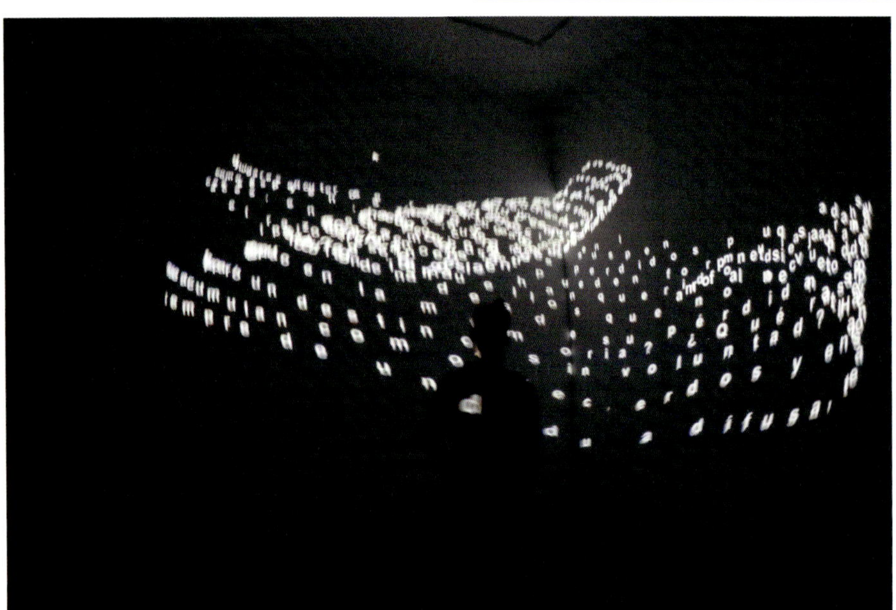

Data Dybbuk, 2015, data-driven installation. Installation view, Centro de Arte Contemporáneo Wifredo Lam, Havana, 2017.

Today, the image poet can be an engineer, social worker, hacker, biologist, and creative director at the same time. He or she no longer acts out of the art business but surfs between the disciplines and searches for new strategies and ways to find a language relevant to our time. The *aesthetics of disappearance* – dealing with genetic and digital codes, subversive strategies, telepresence, and so forth – should be taught as new subjects in art schools. The stereotype of the artist as a lonely individual, who creates relevant images in his studio, has long since survived. As part of the Ars Electronica held in Linz in 1995 with the topic "Welcome to the Wired World," in the footsteps of Moses in the Negev desert, I realized the virtual teleperformance *Exodus*, equipped with military grade GPS, GSM, and internet technology. I had an inspiring experience. During our hike, which could be followed worldwide in real time and in the form of three-dimensional images, Israeli fighter jets flew over our heads again and again. Our companions explained to us that our group would probably be used as a kind of shooting target. A journalist present joked that pilots sometimes miss a target. He asked me what I feel when the jets suddenly begin to shoot with live ammunition. Despite the tragedy of such a hypothetical incident, I was thrilled by the idea that I would no longer exist physically but would still be present through the live images for the viewers in Linz. The fulfillment of man's eternal desire to extend his existence closes in. In conclusion, I would like to note the following: the more I learn about the effects of intangible media, genetic engineering, ubiquity and so on, the less I know about it. The only thing I know is how the master of the Bauhaus, László Moholy-Nagy, put it: "All the same, it seems to me indispensable that we, the creators of our own time, should go to work with up-to-date means."[2]

First published in Tamara Horakova, Ewald Maurer, Johanna Hofleitner, and Ruth Maurer-Horak, eds., *Image:/images: Positionen zur zeitgenössischen Fotografie* (Wien: Passagen Verlag, 2002), 277–85. Translated from the German by Paul Kenig.

1 Vilém Flusser, "Digital Apparition," in *Electronic Culture: Technology and Visual Representation*, ed. Timothy Druckrey (London: Aperture, 1996), 244f.
2 László Moholy-Nagy, *Painting, Photography, Film* (London: Lund Humphries, 1969), 9.

Analog Photography
1980–1985

1 See Andrew S. Dolkart, "The Greenwich Village Society for Historic Preservation," in *National Register of Historic Places Inventory: Westbeth* (New York: New York City Landmarks Preservation Commission, 2009), section 8, 1–2, 5–15.
2 See Robert A. M. Stern, Thomas Mellins, and David Fishman, *New York 1960: Architecture and Urbanism Between the Second World War and the Bicentennial* (New York: Monacelli Press, 1995), 263–70.
3 See James R. Hudson, *The Unanticipated City: Loft Conversions in Lower Manhattan* (Amherst: University of Massachusetts Press, 1987).
4 See Nadja Sayej, "Alvin Baltrop: Remembering New York's Forgotten Queer Photographer," *Guardian*, August 19, 2019, https://www.theguardian.com/artanddesign/2019/aug/18/alvin-baltrop-remembering-new-yorks-forgotten-queer-photographer.

Analog Photography 1980–1985

In December 1973, a highway repair truck totaled the structure of the West Side Elevated Highway, New York City, leading to the highway's closure and thereby severing the city area until 1988. Michael Bielicky had started living at the intersection of West Side Highway and Bethune Street in Westbeth housing complex, Greenwich Village, seven years after the disaster and stayed there from 1981 to 1982. Upon his arrival, the complex was bursting with utopian energy: it was the first time the United States government had attempted to solve the issue of artists' living conditions, by subsidizing renovation schemes and, most significantly, rezoning industrial sites between 1967 and 1970.[1] Westbeth typifies the growing trend toward institutionalization from the late 1950s, whereby artists illegally moved into the empty parts of industrial buildings large enough to house almost any size of canvas or sculpture, most commonly in the neighborhood south of Houston Street, more famously known as SoHo.[2] Government intervention in artists' living conditions was completely new in the United States at this time. Westbeth "remains a major pioneering effort – the spiritual father of all the commercial loft conversions that have created a whole new housing type for Lower Manhattan in the last decade."[3]

The Westbeth project entailed the conversion of the former Bell Telephone Laboratory site (where the "talkie," or sound film, was invented) into the nation's first subsidized housing complex for artists and was greatly influenced by Le Corbusier's *Unité d'habitation* in Marseilles, France. As Westbeth was the first significant project for the architect Richard Meier, the young Princeton graduate Tod Williams critically introduced Meier's team to ideas on utopian socialism and housing derived from European schools of thought.

To the right of Westbeth, floating on the waterfront just above the Hudson River, was Pier 51 – a huge decaying wooden structure long out of industrial use. Pier 51 was one of many abandoned ruins visible from Michael Bielicky's Westbeth apartment: the immediately facing West Side Elevated Highway and the crumbling industrial shacks adjacent along the piers, today known as the Christopher Street Pier, and the spanned piers 42, 45, 46, and 51. Their namesake was the vibrant gay scene, then thriving and reanimating the ghosted piers with social interactions of all kinds. This namesake, though, masks the reality that these piers were also unsafe sites of violence, theft, and homicide, especially at night.

Since then the area underwent drastic urban planning changes, was plastered with green spaces and playgrounds, and is now famously used for recreation by families, completely concealing its edgy past. In February 2020, the exhibition *The Life and Times of Alvin Baltrop* ended at the Bronx Museum of the Arts.[4] Baltrop's obsessive documentation of the West Side Highway area is today recognized as an invaluable, unmasked piece of New York documentary photography, showcasing this merciless paradise in all its aspects.

From this uniquely heterotopic New York landmark, where illustrious artists like photographer Diana Arbus and choreographer and dancer Merce Cunningham resided, Michael Bielicky embarked on his journey into media art by refining Fredrich Cantor's direct flash technique. Cantor, a New York photographer, became friends with Bielicky and visited him multiple times over the 1980s and 1990s in Prague and Düsseldorf.

Bernd Becher, who embodied the most documentary and technical approach to photography at the time, accepted Bielicky at the Kunstakademie in Düsseldorf in 1984. But Bielicky's heterotopic roots began to pull hard on him, and he grew increasingly alienated from Becher's approach. When Bielicky's orientation year came to an end the following year, he chose Nam June Paik's master class.

Untitled (Bielicky's first atelier,
New York), 1980, analog black-and-white

Untitled (view from Bielicky's first atelier on Pier 51, Westbeth, New York), 1980, analog black-and-white photograph.

Untitled (World Trade Center, New York),
1981, analog black-and-white photograph.

Untitled (Westbeth Housing, Westbeth, New York),
1981, analog black-and-white photograph.

Untitled (Christopher Street Day, New York),
1982, analog black-and-white photograph.

Untitled (Kecizate Atahualpa, New York), 1982,
analog black-and-white photograph.

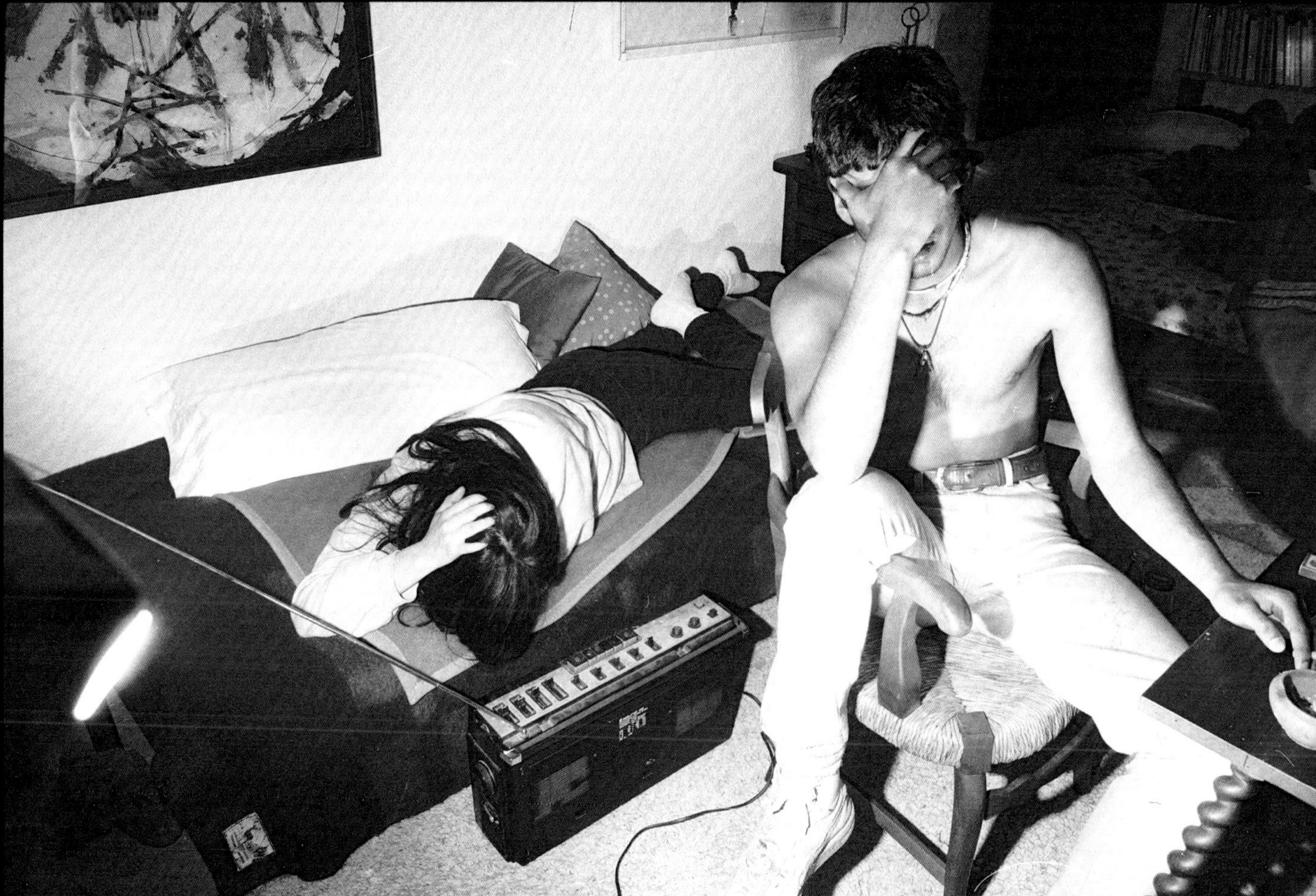

Untitled (Metro, Paris), 1982, analog black-and-white photograph.

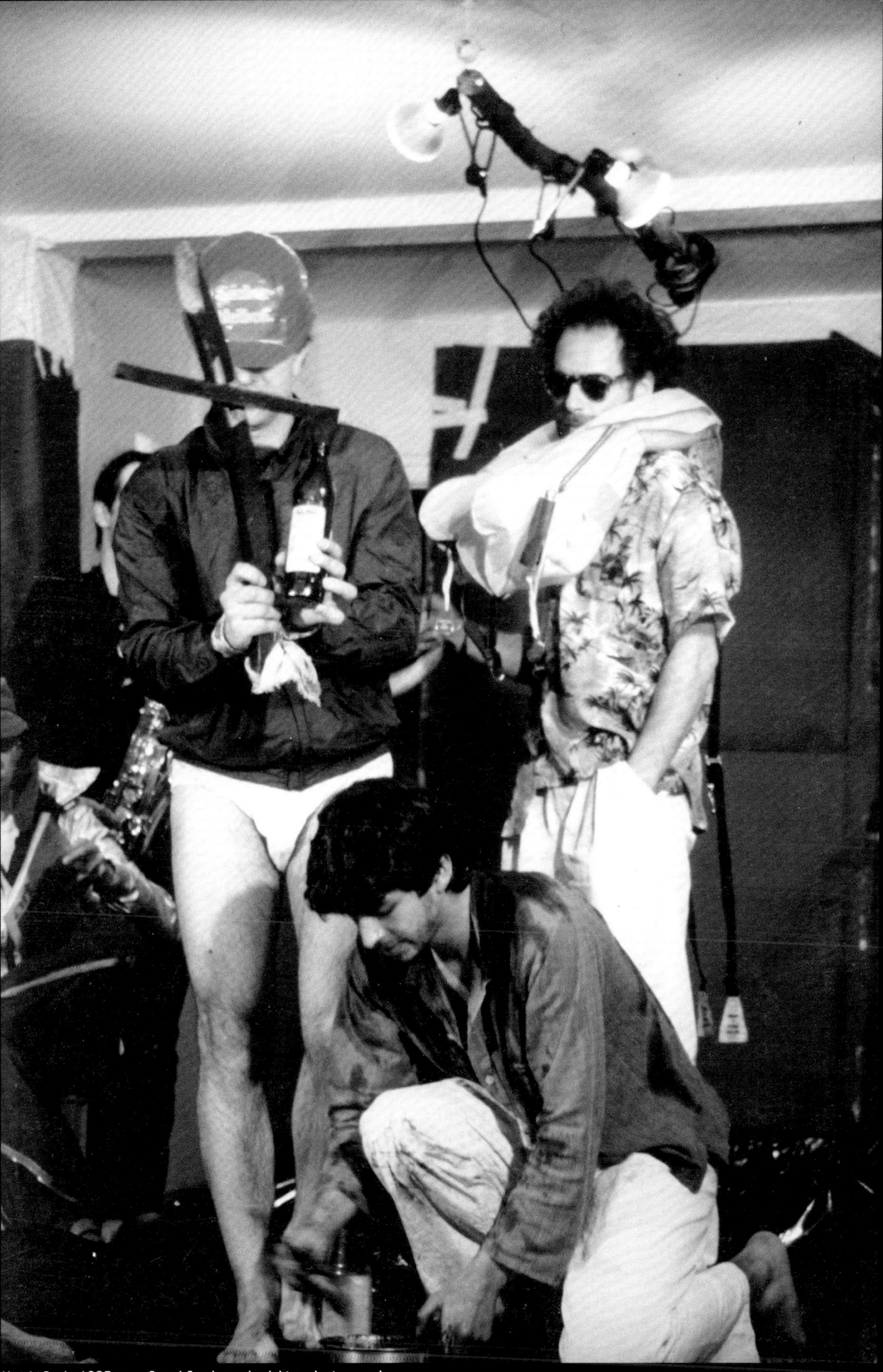

Untitled, 1985, analog black-and-white photograph.
On set of *Moorritual* performance by Ricardo Peredo,
Galerie Art d'Ameublement, Bielefeld.

SONY
Coke

ntitled (Nam June Paik, Düsseldorf Art Academy),
985, analog black-and-white photograph

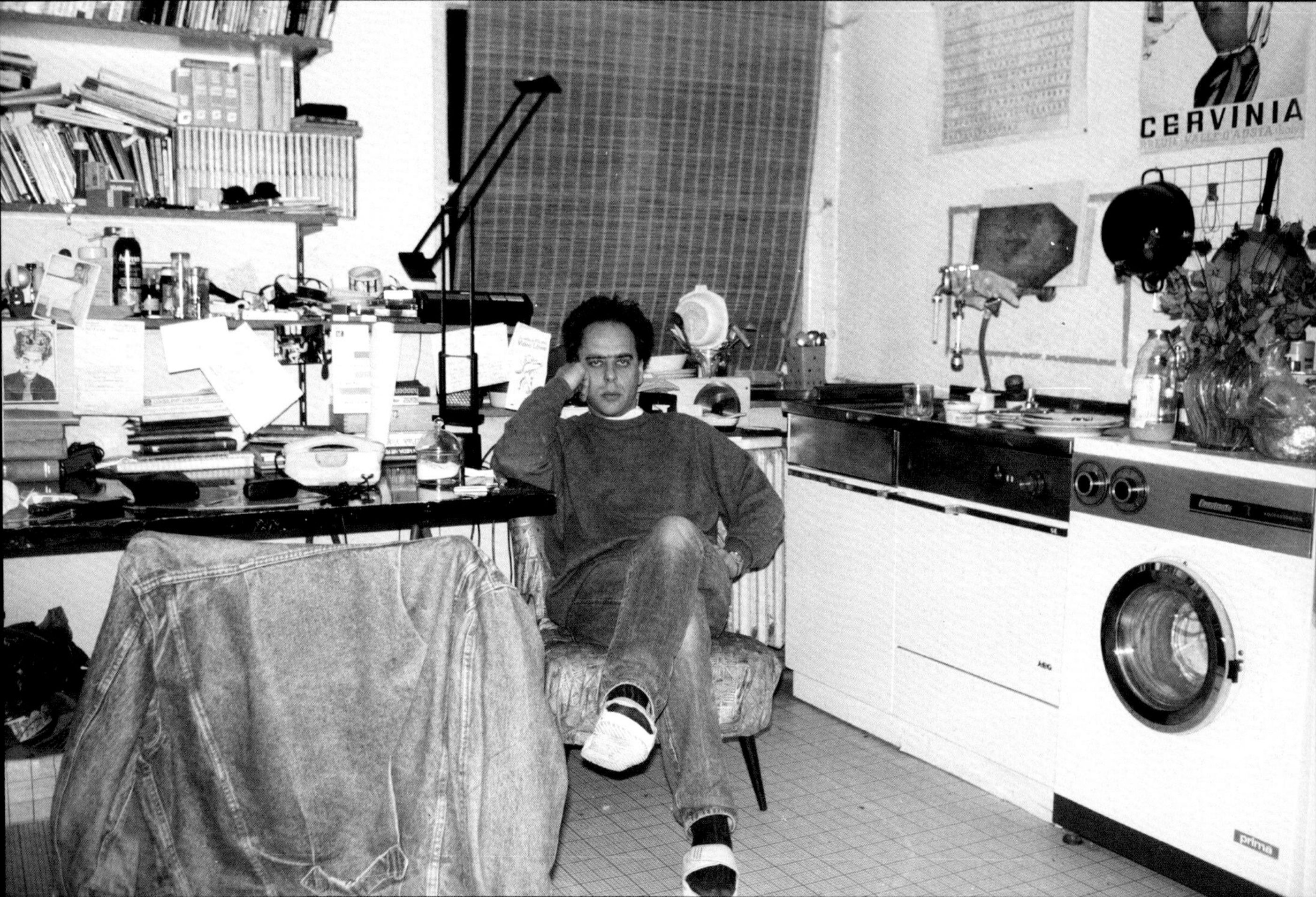
CERVINIA
prima

VINCENT VAN GOGH
UND DIE MODERNE

Patissier

Untitled (street in Paris), 1985, analog black-and-white photograph.

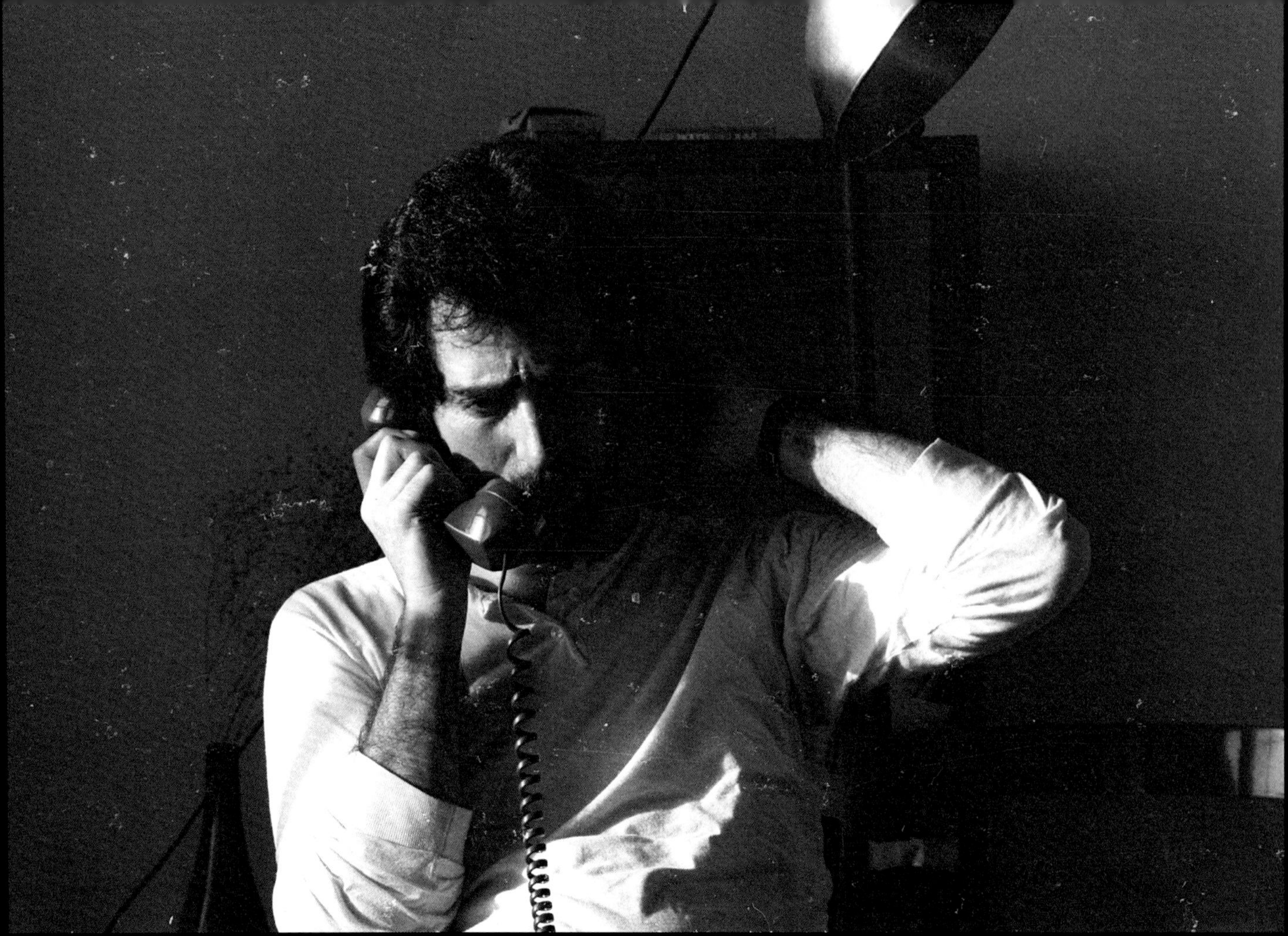

Untitled (Fredrich Cantor, New York), 1982,
analog black-and-white photograph.

Untitled (Pamela Goldblum and Fredrich Cantor, Paris), 1985, analog black-and-white photograph.

Untitled (Prague), 1991, analog black-and-white photograph.

Untitled (Bielicky's atelier, New York), 1989, analog black-and-white photograph.

Getty

Untitled (Prague), 1995, analog black-and-white photograph.

Untitled (Prague), 1995, analog black-and-white photograph.

Laurie Anderson and Michael Bielicky, Karlsruhe, 2019.

Jan Světlík and Peter Weibel, Karlsruhe, 2021

Ernesto Guevara (son of Che Guevara) and Michael Bielicky, Havana, Cuba, 2017.

Peter Sloterdijk and Michael Bielicky, Berlin, Germany, 2021.

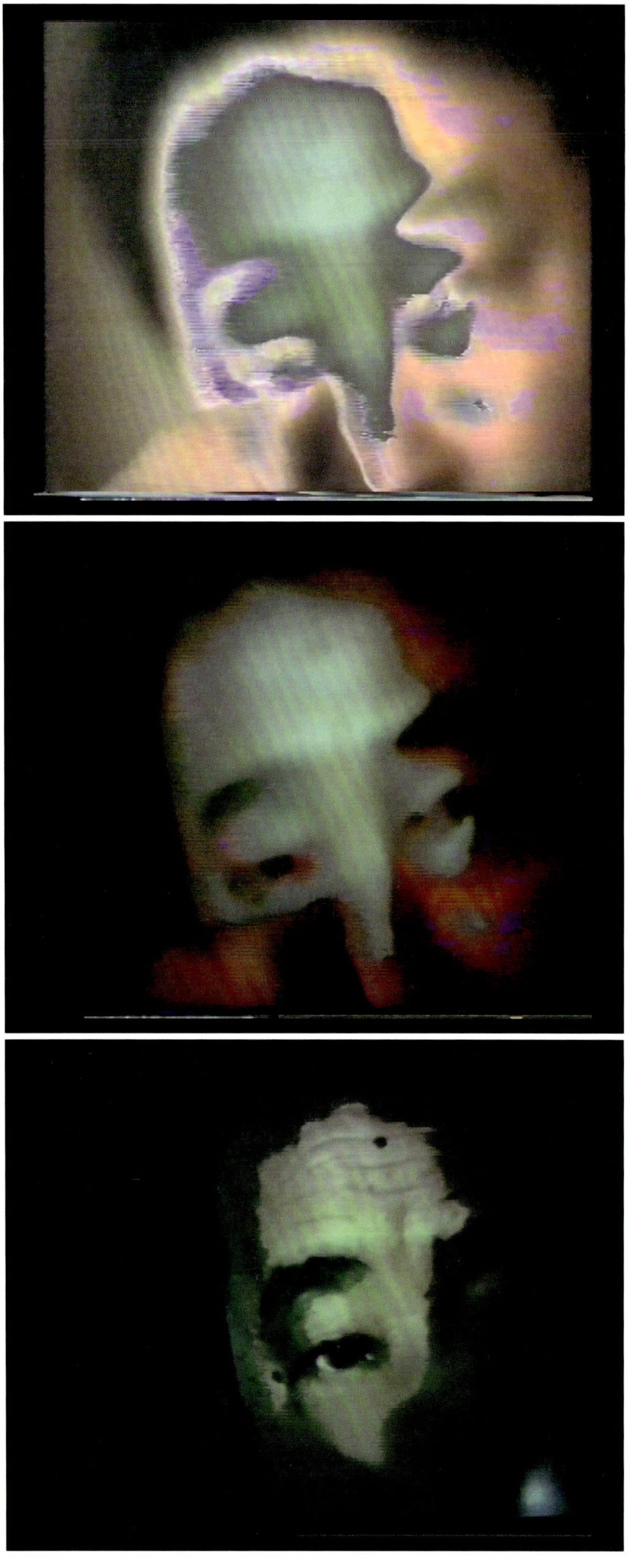

Paik – I'm an Experimentalist, 1987, single-channel video. Screenshots.

For Michael Bielicky,

who comes from the town where an Alchemists' Alley seems to have existed for ages and where, more than four hundred years ago, Rudolf II had already created the intellectual and material foundation for such fields of thought and action as bio-informatics, cryptology, instrument and laboratory-aided astrophysics, and the so-called life sciences – searching for the intelligible philosopher's stone, for the golem, who of course is still alive, even today, and in remembrance of his teacher Nam June Paik's self-perception: "[...] I am an experimentalist."

One loses one's knowledge,
when one loses one's purity of heart.

Nicholas Valois

Expanded Materiologies

Siegfried Zielinski

1.

European modernism sought to teach us to strictly separate the heterogenous realities of the material, on the one hand, and the spiritual, on the other. Albeit, several of their prominent protagonists enjoyed lingering over the treatises of the magicians and in the laboratories of sorcerers' apprentices, quacks, and early genetic manipulators. This was allowed only surreptitiously. Considering the latest research in bio-design, in bio-informatics, or other branches of algorithmically permeated life sciences, we should not repeat the mistake of separating what can only be thought about together. Let us approach the new hybrid realities between computable control mechanisms and the nervous, sensitive matter with an expanded hermeneutics, what I call "expanded materiologies." This is currently, in my opinion, a suitable method for addressing the challenges of artificial *ex*telligence, i.e., the transfer of intelligent materials from human bodies to another platform, specifically a machine one. Their most advanced versions are already operating as hermaphrodites of digital and analog electronic components, such as the neuromorphic computer BrainScaleS, built by Karlheinz Meier and his research team at the Kirchhoff Institute of Physics of the University of Heidelberg.

Let us accept the challenge and interpret the current trends in art and design as an update of archaic experimentation with the creation of experiences within particle and wave forms of the physical world. With this reference to physics, I am referring, on the one hand, to the quantum mechanical nature of a hyper-physics, with its blurred distinctions between the expanded and the thinking things, and also to the natural scientific understanding of such scientists as Johann Wilhelm Ritter (1776–1810), for whom there could be no such thing as dead matter. As a chemical physicist and early theoretician in electrics, he only accepted different resonance states of highly vital material circumstances. Ritter – whom Joseph Beuys revered above all others, and from whose experimental micro-universe he derived his selection of materials for his objects and installations (felt, fat, cardboard, etc.) – fundamentally considered himself a life scientist. To him, art and physics were one. And since, in his view, physics was filled with life, the equation "art = life" was naturally true for him. Two-and-a-half thousand years ago, the band of natural philosophical thinkers who viewed reality as resonating and streaming matter – or something like that – were called *atomists*. They conceived the spirit as being matter that was pulverized into the tiniest particles – ergo, a sort of *lapis philosophorum*.

And they invented a particular smallest thing, of an extraordinary nature: "The clinamen is an infinitesimal *swerve*, 'as small as possible'; 'no one knows where, or when, or how' it occurs [...] ," French philosopher Louis Althusser wrote in his essay "The Underground Current of the Materialism of the Encounter" (1982).[1] As a reference he cited a text from ancient Greek – *De rerum natura*, the unique natural philosophical poem by Lucretius (99 BC–ca. 55 BC), from the first century before our time. The effect of the *clinamen* was: "what causes an atom to 'swerve' from its vertical fall in the void, and, breaking the parallelism in an almost negligible way at one point, induce *an encounter* with the atom next to it, and, from encounter to encounter, a pile-up and the birth of a world – that is to say, of the agglomeration of atoms induced, in a chain reaction, by the initial swerve and encounter."[2] Along with natural philosopher Epicurus (341 BC–270 BC), Althusser was convinced that "the origin of every world, and therefore of all reality and all meaning, is due to a swerve, and that Swerve, not Reason or Cause, is the origin of the world [...] ."[3]

2.

In ancient Greece, *chēmeia* denoted any work with castable materials or, in technological terms, metallurgy. Europeans had adopted the methods for creating refined, shiny gold from ancient Egyptian civilization, where this knowledge existed already more than two thousand years before Christ. *Chēmeia*'s core concern was the project of converting a raw, but hardly base material into a more valuable form by initially heating it, and then, after this passage of liquification (*solutio*), hardening it into a solid form.

Metallurgy was complemented by dyeing techniques. *Chēmeia* also taught and practiced methods of immersed such material surfaces as woven fabrics in various colors, making them attractive for their lovely impression. Pharmacy served the same purpose – dealing with the production of medical substances and cosmetics, that is, with mediums designed to heal and beautify human bodies by means of plant bodies extract. Like tattooing, these were also early forms of interface techniques.

Particular alchemical ideas and practices go way back to the deep times of ancient Chinese, Egyptian, Byzantine, Indian, and Persian civilizations to ancient European times, and to the âge *d'or* of Arab-Islamic scientific advances between the eighth and thirteenth century of our time. The fourth century, one of its strongest periods in Europe, witnessed the alchemical shaping of the world, as hegemonial Christianity fought a ruthless battle against all that was non-Christian. The mysterious and subversive language of alchemical treatises, such as those of Zosimos of Panopolis (late third century BC–early fourth century BC), had its brutal origins in the historical violence of its context. Alchemy was the art of fallen angels, of multiplied Gabriels, who strove to equal or even surpass God and even trump him in the production of lovely lustre – an ideal and impressive world of mediums, which as such has still been far too poorly explored. Alchemy is one of those knowledge fields that were discarded before they were properly understood.

Those strong movements of the first post-Christian centuries were revived and reformulated during the eighth and ninth centuries in Arab-Islamic

Room with a View, 2000, immersive interactive installation with 360 degree dome projection. Installation views, ŠKODA Pavilion, Autostadt, Wolfsburg, 2000.

scholarly civilization. *Al-kimiyá* was the term used in the House of Wisdom in early ninth-century Bagdad to refer to the involved experiments and the written culture of idiosyncratic treatises, either arising from them or translated from other languages.

In medieval Europe, writings in the hermetic tradition of natural philosophy were imported to Spain and became established there as the program *alchimia*. During this period of its renewed success in Christianized Europe, alchemy acquired a strong imprint of the predominant deistic faith. Chemical conversion processes were analogized by a process in which a heathen or doubter becomes converted. It was during this period that the Jewish variant of alchemy, which was closely tied to the hermeneutic practices of the Kabbalah, brought forth the golem: that lump of clay that, by means of numbers and symbols, was brought to life and empowered to follow its creator's orders. Its most important task was to protect Prague's Jewish community.

During the early modern age, alchemical knowledge and experimental methods of the adept was increasingly diversified into every possible area of life, including medicine, agriculture, viniculture, and various crafts. One result was the popularization of alchemical treatises and communications in the form of recipes and all kinds of instructions for creating more or less inviting artificial paradises – an enhanced experience of reality, of a metaphysically charged reality, a *hyper-reality*, which, a few centuries later, would be called *augmented reality*.

With the emergence of an obscure avant-garde of world-changers into a broader public context, alchemy has become a more general intellectual model between applied natural science, technology, art, and magic. It has become an attempt to understand nature – internally and in its relational complexities with regard to the human mind – to grasp it in language and sound, and, above all, to visualize it. The linking of world complexity and relational obsession would become the characteristic feature of a long era, the achievements of which in media we are witnessing. The *nexus,* the chain that, as far as possible, connects everything with everything is today no longer imaginary. It has become a technological reality, proceeding as the temporally and spatially omnipresent telematic, correlative measure that we have learned to call the internet.

The "immense variety of things that 'are not, and cannot be; but that have been imagined and believed'"[4] was able to develop to an outrageous extent through the wild and wonderful world of imagination and natural experimentation, in what is possibly its final blossoming, before modern civilization began performing its relentless work of standardization and universalization. One might, thus, accentuate the cultural historical function of alchemy.

3.

Nature, turned back upon itself, transforms itself – the fundamental principle of alchemy has been frequently thus described. The dragonesque snake biting its own tail, embodied in ancient Egypt by the figure uroboros, is an expression of the principle of the oneness of the individual with the universe. In an old, only partially extant treatise entitled *Physika kai Mystika*,[5] attributed in alchemical literature to Pseudo-Democritus (ca. 60 BC), we find an elaboration of this: "*Nature delights in Nature / Nature conquers Nature / Nature masters Nature.*"[6] The alchemical process leads to the overcoming of nature, once it has been radically explored.

In its current design with its experimentation with data, algorithms, cells, molecules, and atoms, the process is reversed. The natural material is first analyzed and then *informed*. The data or algorithms are projected into the expanded body, thus sensitizing it to control from without and within. The body of the material frees itself, as it were, through the porous skin surrounding it, into the world. This creates an ideal interface, such as that described during the 1960s by the Austrian writer and artist Oswald Wiener, in an appendix to his experimental novel *Die Verbesserung von Mitteleuropa* [The Improvement of Central Europe] (1965/66)[7], as a "happy suit," in the bio-technological form of a full-body adapter.

The individual designs itself within the world, which in turn frees it, to ally it with itself, as an indissoluble hybrid reality. This is the world of tomorrow, in which individual humans feel thoroughly comfortable and gain insight through endless loops of visualization; hearing acousmatically, feeling in a sensual way, in artificial paradises, as a matter of course.

Media-machines and media-humans alike act, with their dualities, in an open, porous framework. This enables them to exchange their energies, both constructive and destructive; making contact with each other, to communicate with each other sympathetically, or to antipathetically destroy each other.

Uroboros – the mystical, dragon-like snake; biting its own tail, swallowing itself, and thus giving birth to itself, over and over. There is neither beginning nor end – like in the Great Work in alchemy. The color green stands for the beginning and the color red for the goal of the process.

4.

Alchemy was not invented in order to sharpen terms. Rather, it is a *poetic* practice, in the direct sense of the word, that is a manner of *making* and, thus, intimately connected to design. The colorful multiplicity of meanings in its semantic treatises and fragments is one of its characteristics. Alchemy is a specific form of expenditure, of wasting, in the sense of French philosopher Georges Bataille's "accursed economy". Alchemy is concerned with the processing of particulars, of individual matters, even in the texts that it has produced. Some alchemical treatises have still been read and understood only by a few adepts and later exegetes. These include, *Das Buch der Heiligen Dreifaltigkeit* [The Book of the Holy Trinity] by the Franciscan Ulmannus from the early fifteenth century – a prominent example of a hermetic text. The Viennese classical scholar and specialist for such treatises, Helmut Birkhan, deemed that the text had been understood by only a handful of scholars.[8] In this sense, alchemy is a thoroughly elitist theory and practice. It "is a dream one can only listen to and that, when told, one can only stammer. Once humans were no longer able to dream by their stoves and to listen to themselves in the materials, the dream of alchemy receded back into the night."[9]

Numerous alchemical treatises explicitly refer to the highest stage of transformation of base matter into the radiant, beautiful lustre of coveted refined material as *proiectio*. Depending on the specified architecture of the alchemical model, this is generally the seventh or twelfth stage of the transformation process. With regard to experimental practice, *proiectio* meant a process of throwing, or more precisely: of throwing forth. Precisely calculated quantities of pulverized *lapis philosophorum* (philosophers' stone) were coated with heated wax and cast onto the boiling base metal. In the event that the *lapis* actually possessed the transformative power attributed to it, the desired conversion was supposed to occur during the final amalgamation.

Etymologically, this attribution is quite unambiguous. The Latin verb *proicere* means that something is thrown forth, thrown down, or thrown forward; and it certainly denotes an active, generating, constructive activity. Projecting contains the meaning of turning out, in the sense of transforming shapes. The projector is not just an image-casting apparatus, but also the designer.

Neither in the history of the sciences and technology nor in the history of the arts and media do we have a homogenous idea of projection. The term denotes a heterogenous field of artifacts, technical object systems, and especially experimental or cultural visual practices for throwing excerpts of the perceivable or imagined world onto a two-dimensional surface. Projection oscillates between two extreme poles of meaning: spectacular proof – in the direct sense of the word – that something sent through the image machine was, or is, as we can see it in the semi-space of the projection surface; and the creation of a reality *as* an image that exists, in the form in which we see it, solely in the projection.

The *lapis philosophorum* was of course a promise, just as the digital realm today is an endlessly formulated promise that can be held holy and on high, but that cannot be kept. "The digital realm is the analog equivalent of the alchemical formula for gold"[10] – this was how I translated a text by Jean-Paul Fargiers about Nam June Paik's early video tape on Fluxus artist Allan Kaprow and the poet Allen Ginsberg. In the act of transformation everything depended on which substances were used for the transmutation, and which qualities were invested in the hyper-material that was supposed to cause the transformation. The higher substance can be generated only from something less base, but not from inferior material. What is true for profane culinary art is of greatest relevance to the alchemist's kitchen.

The great speculative rationalist of the late European Middle Ages, Roger Bacon, described in his alchemical treatise "The Mirror of Alchimy" (1597) – which in 1608 was awkwardly translated into German – a special paradigm of

Delvaux's Dream, 1998–99, immersive virtual reality environment. Installation views and screenshots, ZKM | Karlsruhe, 2010.

the theory and practice of the *opus magnum*. The material that was supposed to be projected, that is, the *lapis philosophorum*, itself had to contain abundant higher substances. To obtain the most splendid shine of the moon (silver) and the sun (gold) – in the text Bacons still considered with those reverse gender assignments, as they still apply today for the Romantic languages (as in the German: der Mond/die Sonne) – the philosopher's stone must contain plenty of that which is to be achieved. "Therefore we seek *proiection*, to the white or to the red work / then we shall take it from the gold [...]"[11] In his treatise on the philosopher's stone, Edward Kelly, the assistant of the great British mathematician and cartographer John Dee, proposes that the substance must certainly contain abundant mercury. "The tincture and the metal tinged must belong to the same root or genus; and as it is the imperfect metals upon which the Philosopher's Stone is to be *projected* [Kelly's italics], it follows that the powder of the Stone must be essentially Mercury."[12] One of the most beautiful reddish-gold, shining objects that the late Nam June Paik created was named *Mercury* (1991).

5.

In the early Modern age, theories and experimental practices of alchemy served the self-understanding of a yet unestablished, highly unsettled, cautiously prancing, rather empiric and possibly in the future thoroughly tentative subject, seeking to redefine its relation towards the Other, towards that which is not at all, or not yet accessible through the mind. The cosmos buzzed mightily; listening to it actively was perceived to give the listener a "buzz." It projected itself acoustically into the souls of the adept, who had decided to participate in the world and not to merely observe it or subserviently revere it as the creation of God. As an alternative and heretical model of world experience and world processing, alchemy, thus understood, shows the way, not backward into an equally mystical and magical past, but forward into possible futures, in which the connection between scientific analysis, philosophical hermeneutics, experimental practice and artistic design would be of importance. An esoteric kind of education evolved, such as is found again today in the fields of expanded but also esthetically applied information science: *This is about something that one learns and does before one really understands it.*

Translated from the German by Lonnie Legg.

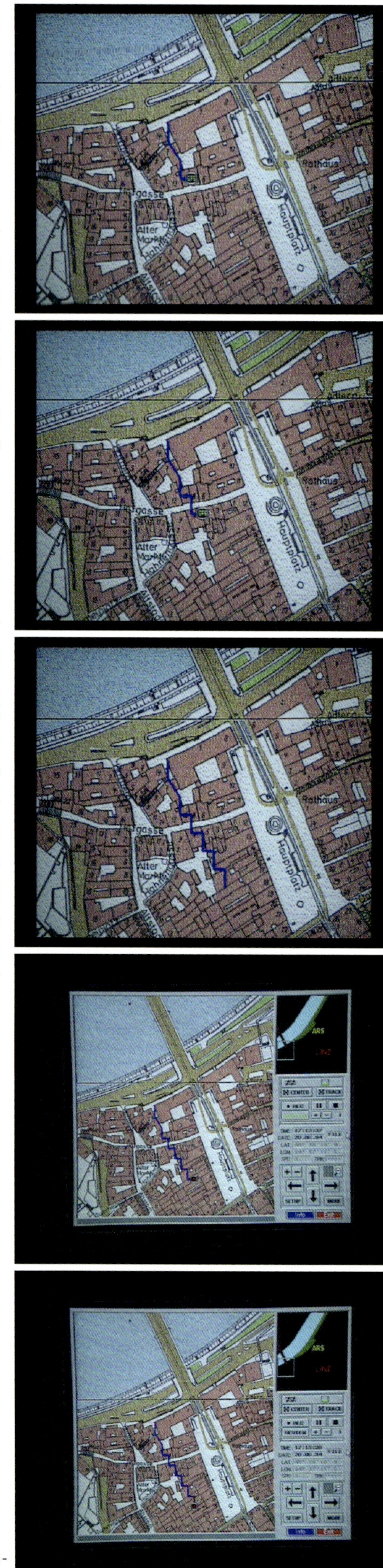

Intelligent Mailman, 1994, GPS-driven telematic performance. Screenshots.

1 Louis Althusser, “The Underground Current of the Materialism of the Encounter,” trans. G. M. Goshgarian, in *Philosophy of the Encounter: Later Writings 1978-1987* (London: Verso, 2006), 163-207, here 169.
2 Ibid., 169.
3 Ibid.
4 Charles Mackay, *Extraordinary Popular Delusions and the Madness of Crowds* 1841 (Hertfordshire: Wordsworth, 1995), 86.
5 Florian Ebeling, *Das Geheimnis des Hermes Trismegistos: Geschichte des Hermetismus von der Antike bis zur Neuzeit* The Secret of Hermes Trismegistus: History of Hermeticism from Ancient Times to the Modern Age (Munich: C.H. Beck, 2005), 47ff.
6 Quoted from Hans Eduard Fierz-David, *Die Entwicklungsgeschichte der Chemie: Eine Studie* The History of the Development of Chemistry: A Study (Basel: Springer, 1952), 45.
7 First published in 1965/66, the text was developed from 1963, during Wiener's years at Olivetti, as a manager in charge of data processing.
8 See Birkhan's contribution “Das alchemistische Zeichen. Allgemeines zur wissenschaftlichen Axiomatik der Alchemie und Spezielles zum Buch der heiligen Dreifaltigkeit” / The Alchemical Sign. General Thoughts on a Scientific System of Alchemical Axioms and Some Specifics on the *Book of the Holy Trinity*, in *Keith Griffiths: The Presence*, ed. Siegfried Zielinski with Angela Huemer (Graz: edition blimp 1993), 40-53.
9 Fierz-David, *Die Entwicklungsgeschichte der Chemie*, 132.
10 Jean-Paul Fargier, “Allan and Allen's Complaint' de Nam June Paik and Shigeko Kobuta,” *Cahiers du Cinéma*, no. 341 (1982): 28-34, here: 33. Translated from the German translation in: Siegfried Zielinski, ed., *Video: Apparat/Medium, Kunst, Kultur. Ein internationaler Reader* Video: Apparatus/ Medium, Art, Culture. An International Reader (Frankfurt: Lang, 1992).
11 Roger Bacon, *Vom Stein der Weisen / and von den vornembsten Tinkturen des Goldes* (Leipzig: Jacob Apel, 1608), 57. This bizarre treatise I discovered in 1992, in a former Jesuit library that had been endowed to the library of the University of Salzburg - tied up in a bundle with a contemporary version of the famous *Monas Hieroglyphica* (1564) by the English mathematician, physician, cartographer, and alchemist John Dee (1527-1608).
12 Edward Kelly, “The Stone of the Philosophers” 1676, in *The Alchemical Writings of Edward Kelly* (London: James Elliott & Co., 1893), 15. Kelly dedicated the original manuscript, dated to 1676, “to the most potent Lord of the Holy Roman Empire, Rudolfus II, King of Hungary and Bohemia, etc., His Most Gracious Master” (page 3). See https://archive.org/details/TheAlchemicalWritingsOfEdwardKelly1893/page/n67.

Data-Driven Language Waves
2008–2020

1 See Davina Jackson, *SuperLux: Smart Light Art, Design and Architecture for Cities* (London: Thames and Hudson, 2015), 92–93.
2 See *Global Control and Censorship*, exhib. booklet (Karlsruhe: ZKM | Center for Art and Media, 2015), 22.
3 See Mel Alexenberg's essay "From the Golem of Prague to Waze from Israel," in this volume.

Data-Driven Language Waves 2008–2020

Since 2005 – in cooperation with Kamila B. Richter – Michael Bielicky has developed web-based, often interactive projects controlled by real-time data fed from the internet. Market and stock exchange data, news, Twitter, and other information streams guide their animated stories, often in an uncanny and counterintuitive way. This work series can be described by four major setups. The earliest web-based project with Richter is *Columbus 2.0* (2007–19).

Columbus 2.0 was displayed in Wuhan (2007), Sevilla (2008), and Thessaloniki (2009), and Karlsruhe (2008 and 2019).[1] The work is essentially an interactive wave animation of Twitter messages; the masses of pictograms have yet to populate the data waves. Being one of the most successful works by Bielicky to this day, it stems from its simplicity, resembling Bielicky's early video sculptures more than the complex and somewhat chaotic *Garden of Error and Decay* (2010–19) and *Why Don't We* (2013–17) series, which are more akin to his video works. The latter could be understood as chock full of cultural criticism and for some even held considerable potential for cultural pessimism. *Columbus 2.0*, though, is one of Bielicky's most positive works and the onset of a series that can even be cautiously called abstract. Whereas *Columbus 2.0* utilizes one of the oldest interfaces – the ship steering wheel – and encourages the cultural optimism that even a boundless immaterial ocean of data can be navigated, *Data Dybbuk* (2015) seems to leap right back to cultural criticism.[2] It consists of immaterial projections that engulf the subject in data, uniform in a genial and indiscernible way that only becomes visible through, or quite literally *on*, others, but not by oneself. Only at this mirror stage with other subjects, through the uniformity of visualized language waves glimmering on the subjects, one begins to fathom the great leveler of the digital age: the dissolution of *the subject* into fragmented, dissociated interest groups on the internet. While wandering through the seeming uniformity of *Data Dybbuk*, the fragmented society becomes apparent, vibrating loudly in their respective digital irrelevance. We seem to be happier shored up on a vaguely familiar island, bobbing up and down rhythmically with the other shipwrecks, than inventing new ships to set out for new frontiers.

On an exhibition label during the exhibition *Dia-Logos: Ramon Llull and the ars combinatoria* at ZKM | Karlsruhe, Bielicky explains his next abstract work series iteration, *The Names* (2018): "The information always appears in the same form in space and time. It has the shape of a spiral. The genetic code for example is stored in the double helix spiral in the same way as the information is written down in the Torah scrolls. The audio waves of spoken language move through space just as the solar system moves through the universe. The names of the gods of the monotheistic religions make the universal principle visible in an installation of a dematerialized, dynamic spiral of light. The endless waves of the names of God in Latin, Arabic and Hebrew language put the visitor in a complementary state of perception."

In an innocuous way, the oscillating language waves in *The Names* intermingle the words for the one and only monotheistic God in the respective Arabic, Hebrew, and Latin version, where they coexist in peaceful plurality, vibrating maniacally in silence, waiting for those who care enough to hotwire them for another ideological war.

Our competence to decipher pictograms is relatively old and for the most part primitive – even very experienced curators and art connoisseurs assess the *Garden of Error and Decay* and the *Why Don't We* series in superficial ways and are quick to judge them as comical, not serious enough, or downright absurd. They fall prey to a principle that Bielicky proved to be more aware of than many of his contemporaries, in fact, as a member of "the People of the Scroll," what he even grew up to be aware of: if the medium really is the message, we need to look behind.[3] Hiding (technical) behavioral pattern manipulators behind language art that is sublime, often abstract, and difficult to decipher really should not be a thing anymore.

Columbus 2.0, 2008, data-driven interactive installation.
Installation views, ZKM | Karlsruhe, 2008.

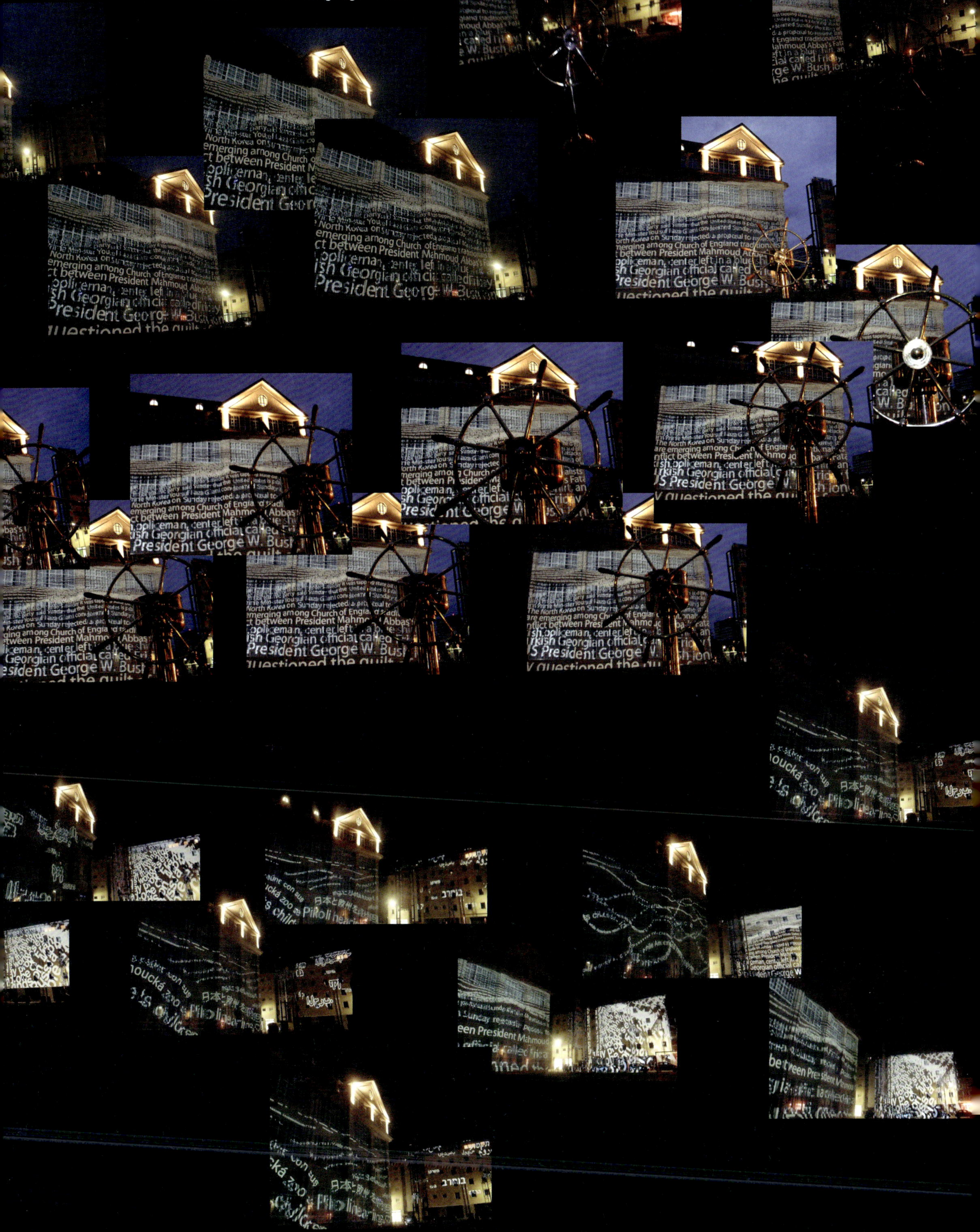

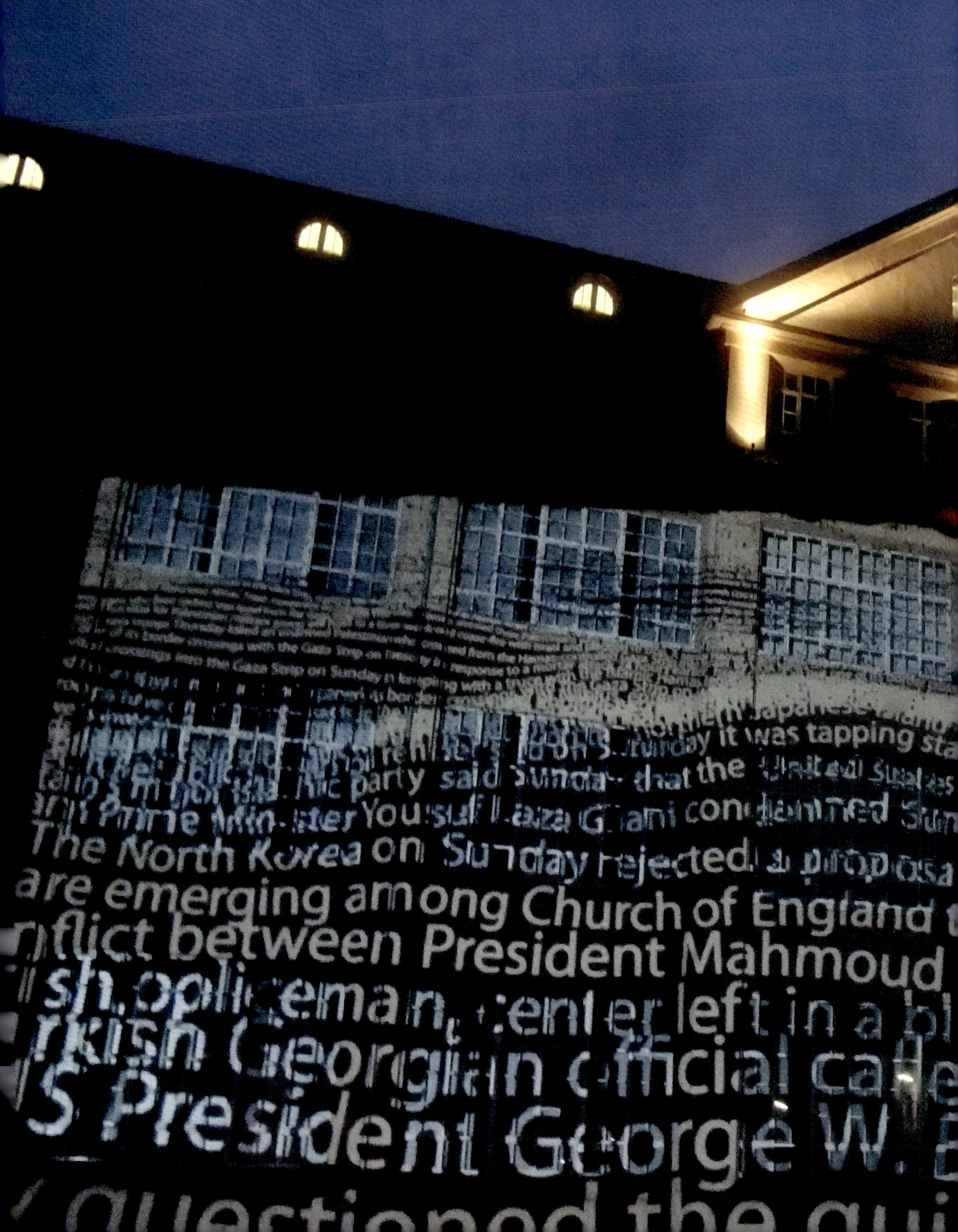
it was tapping
The North Korea on Sunday rejected
are emerging among Church of England
nflict between President Mahmoud
President George W.

Data Driven Language Waves – *Columbus 2.0* (2007–19)

Computer, projector, software, steering wheel: a specially programmed custom-made Java-based text editor of just over 0.4 MB generates language waves in an endless loop, whereby the angles of the movements, the vectors of the movements, their speeds and many other settings can be programmed seamlessly in the decimal range. The text that appears is also entered in the editor.

The gears of the steering wheel are provided with an adhesive tape so that they set a (trackball-based) computer mouse in motion and thus result in the unreal and jerky-smooth control movements on screen.

Columbus 2.0, 2008, data-driven interactive installation. Installation views, BIAC3: International Contemporary Art Biennale Seville, 2008.

encapuchados
Europas Steuer
componente
complicado
am Steuer

Columbus 2.0, 2008, data-driven interactive installation. Installation view, BIAC3: International Contemporary Art Biennale Seville, 2008

Columbus 2.0, 2008, data-driven interactive installation.
Installation views, Musee Historique, Strasbourg, 2009.

MUSEE HISTORIQUE
DE LA VILLE DE STRASBOURG

Riding the Mind, 2009, data-driven installation.
Installation views, ZKM | Karlsruhe, 2009.

Riding the Mind, 2009, data-driven installation.
Installation views, ZKM | Karlsruhe, 2008.

Vatan
自由時報
引爆雙
社區

Columbus 2.0, 2011, data-driven interactive installation. Installation views, State Museum of Contemporary Art, Thessaloniki, 2011.

Haringey
sur une

Data Driven Language Waves – *Data Steel* (2015)

Computer, projector, software: a specially programmed custom-made Java-based text editor of just over 0.4 MB generates language waves in an infinite loop, whereby the angles of the movements, the vectors of the movements, and many other settings can be programmed seamlessly in the decimal range. The text that appears is also entered in the editor.

Data Steel, 2015, data-driven immersive installation. Installation views, presented by Galerie Zdeněk Sklenář at Bolt Tower, Dolní Vítkovice during the Colours of Ostrava Festival, Ostrava, 2015.

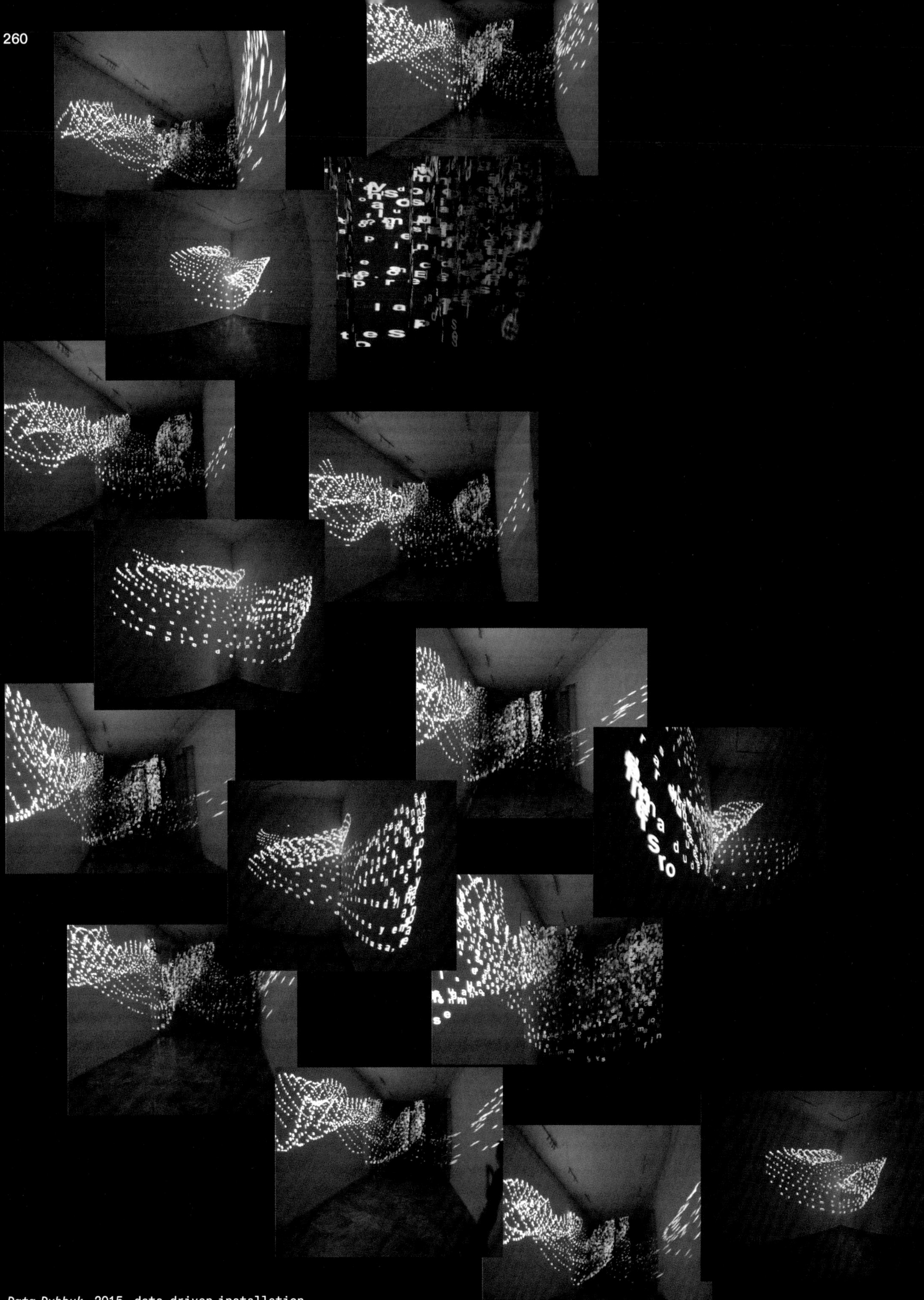

Data Dybbuk, 2015, data-driven installation.
Installation views, Centro de Arte Contemporáneo
Wifredo Lam, Havana, 2017.

Data Driven Language Waves – *Data Dybbuk* (2015)

Computer, projector, software: a specially programmed custom-made Java-based text editor of just over 0.4 MB generates language waves in an infinite loop, whereby the angles of the movements, the vectors of the movements, their speeds and many other settings can be programmed seamlessly in the decimal range. The text that appears is also entered in the editor.

Data Dybbuk, 2015, data-driven installation. Installation views, Apollonia, Strassbourg, 2016.

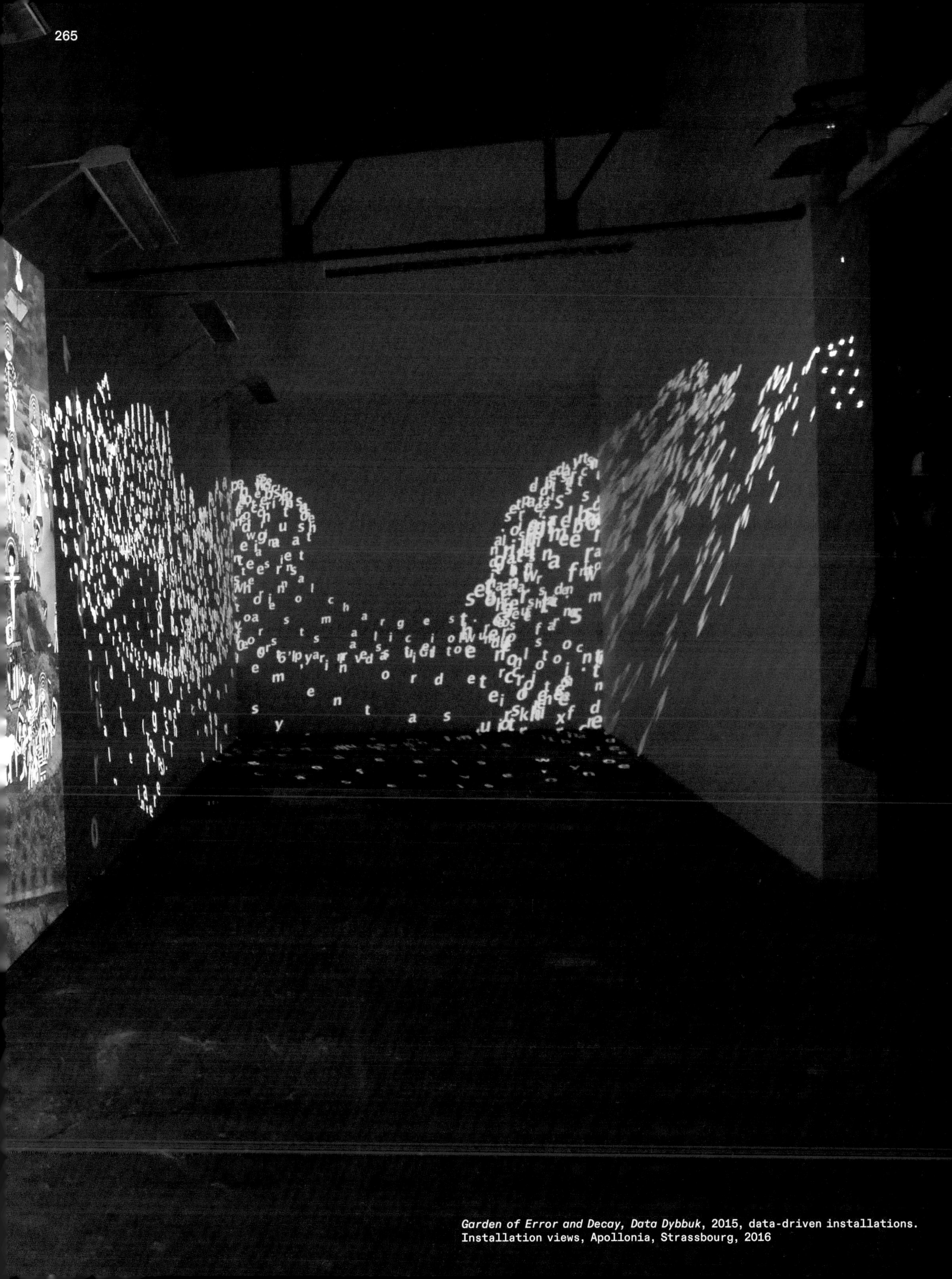

Garden of Error and Decay, Data Dybbuk, 2015, data-driven installations.
Installation views, Apollonia, Strassbourg, 2016

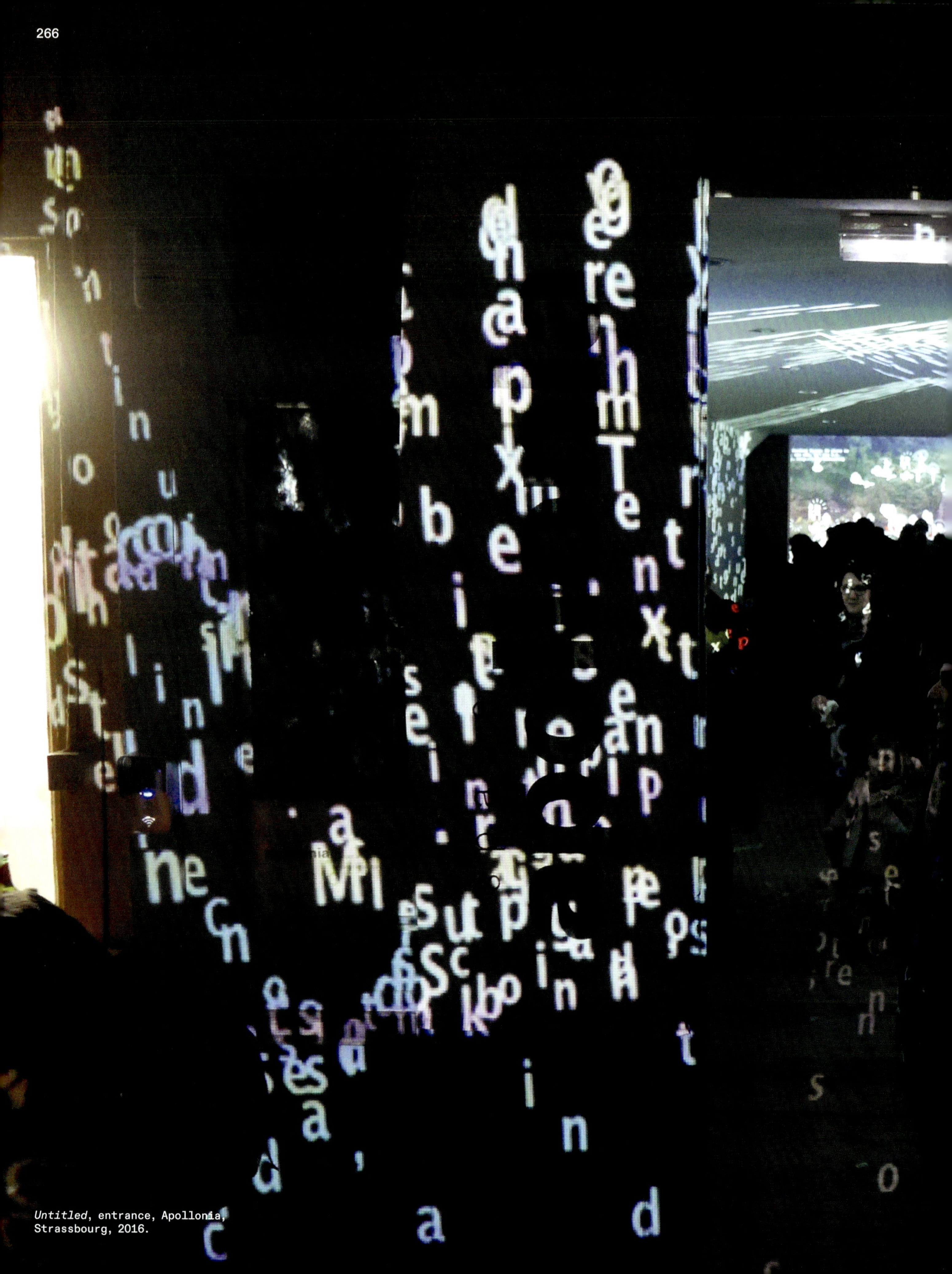

Untitled, entrance, Apollonia, Strassbourg, 2016.

Data Driven Language Waves – *The Names* (2018)

Computer, projector, software: a specially programmed custom-made Java-based text editor of just over 0.4 MB generates language waves in an infinite loop, whereby the angles of the movements, the vectors of the movements, their speeds and many other settings can be programmed seamlessly in the decimal range. The text that appears is also entered in the editor.

The Names, 2018, immersive data-driven installation.
Installation views, ZKM | Karlsruhe, 2018.

The Names, 2018, data-driven installation.
Installation views, ZKM | Karlsruhe, 2018.

The Names, 2018, data-driven installation. Installation views, Ècole polytechnique fédérale de Lausanne – EPFL, Lausanne, 2018.

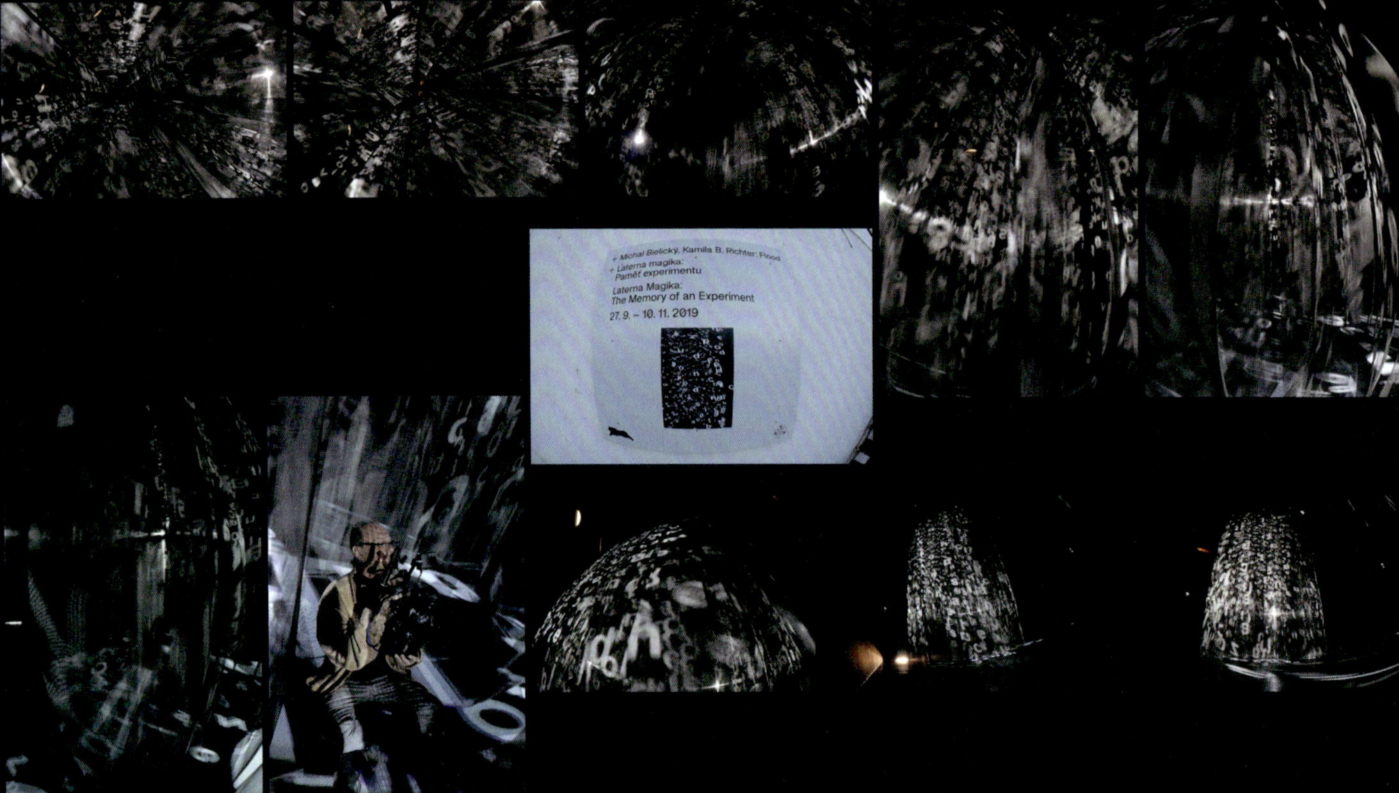

Kostka, 2019, immersive data-driven installation.
Installation views, Meetfactory/Kostka Gallery, Prague, 2019.

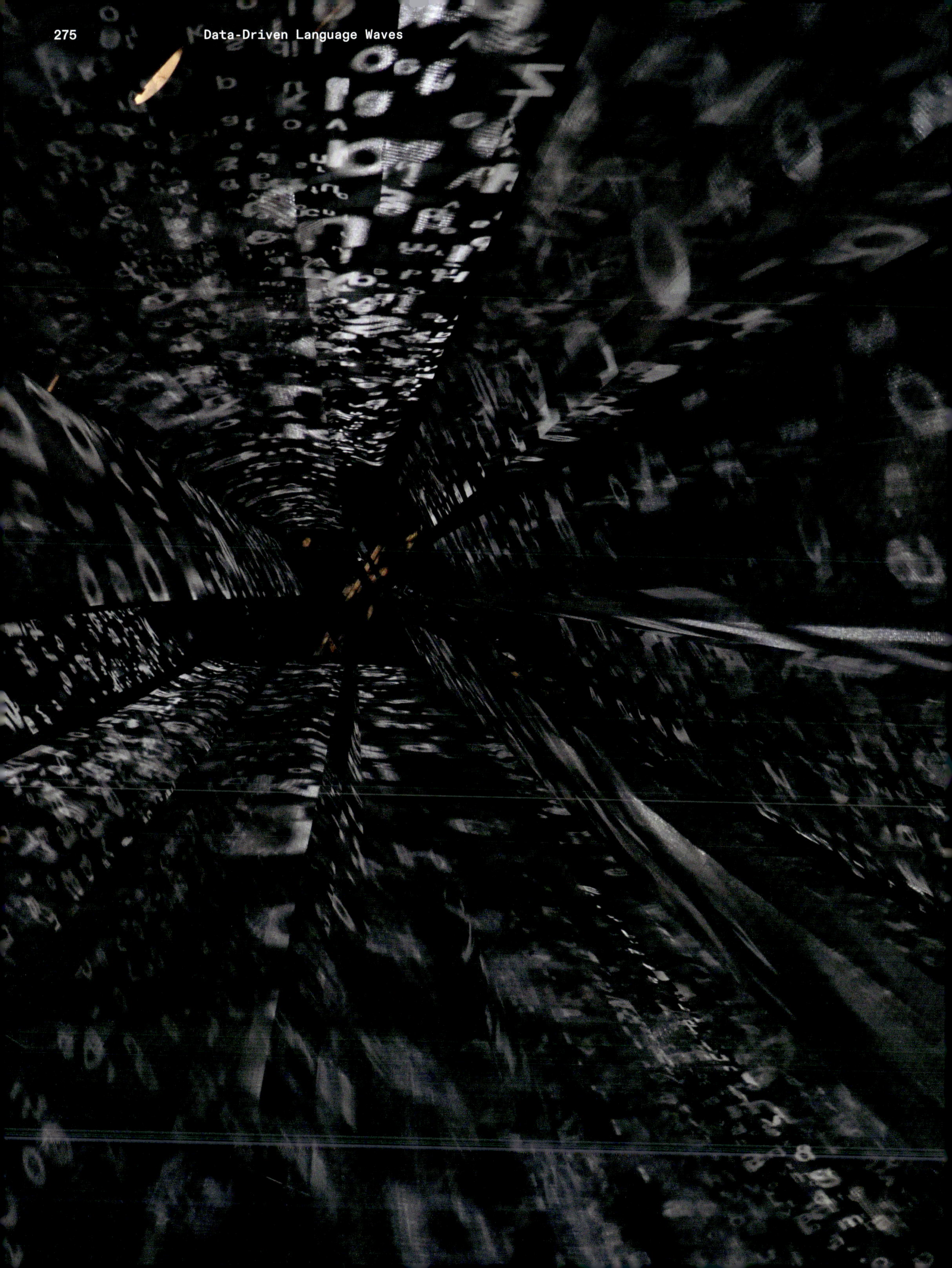

Karel Malich's students Lubomír Čermák, Tomáš Mašín, Tomáš Veškrna, Janka Žáčková, Martin Škarda, and Tomáš Hejtmánek. Michael Bielicky's first media art class at the Prague Academy of Fine Arts (AVU), 1991.

Beyond Number Crunching

Anne Renahan

"What do you see?" Petr Svarosky, a thirty-two-year-old student artist at the Prague Academy of Fine Arts (AVU), asks. "For some people it's an angel; for some it's rockets. For some it's not a real art project at all, but more like a hallucination or the flashes you get behind your eyelids when you close your eyes."

Surrounded by the bright light streaming through the huge windows of the top-floor atelier of the academy, Svarosky stares into the sunshine and insists he has a vision of the future. On the screen in front of him is his video art form *Cradle*. Intense flashes of yellow ebb and flow to a background accompaniment of low-level white noise, creating a futuristic atmosphere in sharp contrast to the peeling walls of the studio.

He is a leading student in one of the newest and most controversial departments at the traditional one hundred-year-old academy. The institution is now being thrust into the last decade of the twentieth century by the charismatic Michael Bielicky, age forty-one. He founded the media department at AVU in 1990, when he returned to Prague after twenty-two years in Germany.

Media art is created with the aid of computers. It involves video, sound, lights, lasers, and virtual reality, ranging from the simple to the bewilderingly complex, the banal to the esoteric.

"Art is changing completely," says Bielicky dramatically. Media art has a higher profile in the United States because the computer is rapidly becoming more acceptable there as an art tool. But it is still rarely employed here.

The AVU department was the country's first academic department dedicated to media art; a second was later opened in Brno. But interest in the subject has existed since the seventies, fueled by TV, says Keiko Sei, a writer on and curator of media art who has been researching the field in this region since 1988.

Bielicky has just returned from Israel, where he says his project *Exodus* was a success. "It is a virtual teleperformance on the internet," says Bielicky. He traveled through the deserts of Israel by jeep in an attempt to recreate the biblical journey of Moses. Using a cellular phone attached to a modem, he transmitted his movements to a tracking satellite, which then beamed images to a computer. Now anyone anywhere in the world can log on to the internet via computer and "see" Bielicky's journey.

The internet has its roots in military technology. In simple terms, it is a network of computer networks. There are at least eighteen thousand networks, with millions of computers on each network, so the system is vast. The president of the Internet Society suggests that the internet might reach 1 billion people in the not-too-distant future.

It hasn't quite reached those proportions here yet. "In the States, the internet is in common usage, but here it is still a very rare thing. Anyone who has access to a university can use the internet for free, but the private sector here is shamelessly expensive," says Bielicky. "In the U.S.A., it is twenty dollars a month to use; here it is forty dollars. So university people, Americans, and companies are really the only users of the internet here in Prague. Regular people cannot afford it."

But the cost hasn't prevented a burgeoning new art scene in Prague. Andreas Strohl, coordinator of the cultural program at the Goethe-Institut, says that the development of the new media in this country has been astonishing, considering the long absence of modern technology here. "I've seen one very interesting thing here in the four years I have been here. There is a wonderful scene of new artists developing, and this is due to Michael Bielicky." The number of people becoming interested in media art may be increasing in Prague, but it doesn't mean that everyone is embracing the computer as the next great art movement. Bielicky sighs as he talks about the skepticism of the more traditional departments at AVU. "There is still the concept of the traditional nineteenth-century art school that exists throughout Europe, but times are changing, and art schools must change, too. I believe even traditional artists can be inspired by new media."

"It follows a well-worn historical pattern," says Svarosky, speaking of some people's reactions to his art. "The same thing was said about cubism or impressionism; there's always opposition to anything new."

Svarosky says the new art form can be compared to music. "I'm in a group called Silver. There are three of us, a software engineer, sound engineer, and me. So, it's like a rock group of film producing. One of us on the bass, one singing. If you did it by yourself, it wouldn't be the same."

He's done two sound installations, which require a complex synthesis of ideas, philosophy, and technical expertise. His 1994 project *Amnesty* consisted of eight infrared sensors connected to loudspeakers and computers. As people moved into the hall, they activated the sensors, which in turn activated the computers, which were programmed with the sounds of twelve bells recorded in Prague churches.

"The point is that the music has really no beginning and no end. I'm exploring how man moves within the structure of sound. If you go to a classical music concert, it ends after two hours, but this is unlimited," explains Svarosky.

Media art is not just a highbrow version of MTV. Svarosky insists that his current project – a virtual creature that will respond to the human voice – is very complex. He will create an image of a creature on the computer and place it in a container with a window. The image will respond to the human voice as if it were actually alive. "It's complex," smiles Svarosky. "It involves a lot of math."

"There are certain parallels to Renaissance painting, certainly," says Strohl. "The Renaissance was a paradigm shift in the visual arts because of perspective. It was the first time people wanted to look at their own heads. They were challenging God. There's something very similar about media art."

This philosophical attitude is what distinguishes media art from MTV. Bielicky has close ties to the Goethe-Institut and the Soros Center for Contemporary Art. They will jointly organize a December symposium and exhibition dubbed *The New Media and Visual Arts*. Representatives from the Goethe and Soros organizations say that these activities demonstrate that Prague is becoming an important center for the discussion of the new media.

Bielicky says that the anonymity of the internet offers the freedom to be or do anything you want. "It's an anarchist construction," says Bielicky.

And it is this element of fantasy that makes media art so attractive to Czech artists and gives it its unique flavor, explains Keiko Sei. Whereas in the United States, the medium is largely political, here that element is almost entirely absent. "It's an escape from reality," Sei says.

First published in *Prague Post*, July 12, 1995.

Michael Bielicky and Kamila B. Richter, Wuhan, 2009.

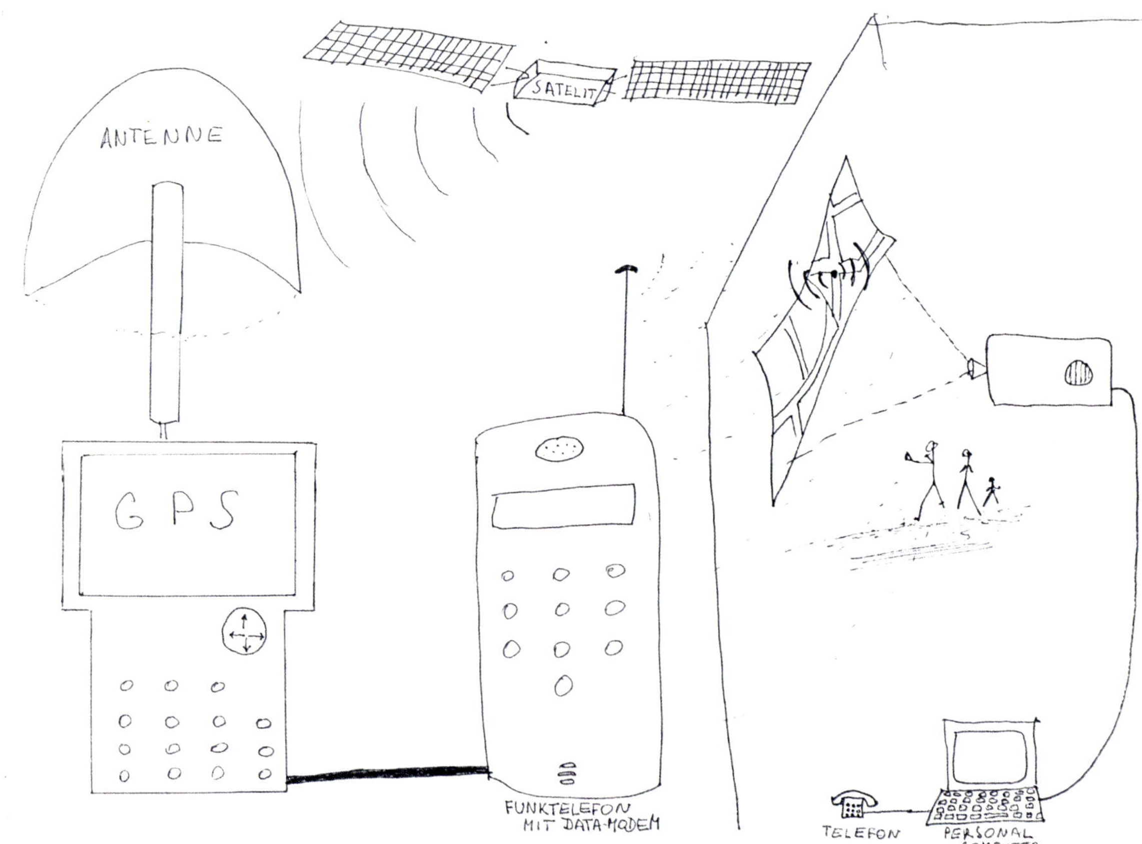

Intelligent Mailman, 1994, GPS-driven telematic performance.
Conceptual sketches.

Hypertext

Michael Bielicky

> You have to hurry
> if you want to see something.
> Everything's disappearing.
>
> Paul Cezanne

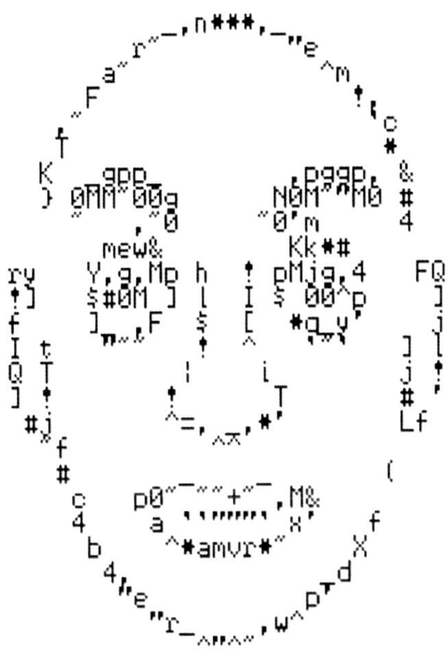

Kamila B. Richter, *Michael Bielicky*, 2009, ASCII-portrait.

Ladies and Gentlemen,

I actually shouldn't present this paper in a linear text form if I am to use a mode of expression that is fitting to the age. Rather, I should be giving you a *hypertext*. This is a text that the members of the audience read themselves as a nonlinear electronic book in the form of a digital code stored on disk and read from a monitor screen with the help of a mouse. You would then have the opportunity to move through the text individually, following your own interests, and see pictures and hear sounds with it. Each reader would have his or her very own experience, and each of these experiences would have their own quality and veracity. In fact, I shouldn't even be standing here in front of you in person, but rather should be somewhere else in the world and speak to you from an image on a projection screen here in the room transmitted over the "data highway." And this should be not just a video image of me being played from tape, but rather a synthetic, digital, artificial Bielicky speaking to you. Perhaps this experience would be more effective at making the issues of the new media clearer than this that I am now reading from.

And while I am writing these lines, I am logging on through the telephone to the world's largest computer network, known as the internet, and looking at the new pictures presented there by various artists. These artists may be in Siberia, New York, Tokyo, Berlin, or elsewhere, and they all are parts of an organism that is constantly developing its own unique dynamics, and that has its own effect on their creative efforts. Information technology does not produce material objects anymore, only immaterial ones. Thus the traditional concept of art is put into question, as art usually appears to be lasting only in a material form. The experience of electronic media, and not necessarily in an artistic context, but also in day-to-day life (with taxes, television, telephones, computers, virtual reality, networks, etc.) will doubtlessly change around our perception of reality and our system of values so radically that we are able to only vaguely evaluate and classify this revolution. Electronic media have altered our relationship to time and space so deeply that we now have only the choice either to link up to this most vital of organisms and thus participate in an adventure – the dimension of which nobody can describe or predict from today's perspective – or to stay back in a romantic longing for individual realization that has little to do with today's reality.

The age of electronic poetry has been with us for a long time. Global networks offer an endless time space in which we meet ubiquity, a continual presence everywhere at the same time, anew again and again, and that has us experience not just one reality, but a selection of realities. We become nodes in an enormous network, in whose connections (whether material or of energy) flows information. In this context, concepts such as *soul*, *spirit*, *identity*, *ego*, and *self* must be reexamined.

Because of the character of media art and the way it is understood, it is utterly inappropriate to display such works in a museum. Despite this inappropriateness, many media artists make an effort to fit this immaterial form of media works into the standard art system of museums, galleries, and such. The paradoxical nature of such a setting is made particularly clear when media artwork is seen in a gallery by eighty visitors but simultaneously can be observed through the computer network by thousands in all corners of the world all at the same time. For the media artwork, the museum becomes superfluous. A new type of immaterial museum, such as the recently established ICC (NTT InterCommunication Center) in Tokyo, or the Ars Electronica Center being built now in Linz (both should be opened in 1996), are intended to display a new sort of object as pure information. But to me, even these new forms of museums seem questionable, as the museum of the future will be able to be everywhere: at home, at the North Pole, in the desert, in a dance club, in prison, or at one's deathbed. All we will need to visit the museum of the future will be a portable computer and connection via telephone, perhaps through radio or satellite. One has recently begun to observe and discuss the transfer or the migration of urban life onto the computer networks. It seems as if what is far is coming closer and what is close is becoming more distant. This spatial exchange will introduce people to an utterly new reality.

Dominique Allard, Zaza Barisch, Yvette Pistor and Marcela Snaselova (curators), *Media Circus*, 2010, media art department presentation during the annual exhibition *Sommerloch* of the Karlsruhe University of Arts and Design (HfG). With works by Jan Cordes, Philipp Engelhardt, Eva Franz, Andy Goralczyk, Kilian Kretschmer, Marianne Schmidt, Jens Stober and others.

Similarly, time has become a new experience: it can expand; it can run forward but also backward. But above all, the experience of simultaneousness is making us into a new species. The televised revolution, which we experienced in Romania, changed our consciousness. The live coverage of the Gulf War by CNN changed our perception and interpretation of historical events. The speed with which information flows around the world is breathtaking, and we are the first generation that has to learn how to deal with this phenomenon. In my most recent project *Intelligent Mailman*, I attempt to describe the anachronism in which the mail*man* finds him or herself. On the one hand, mail carriers still deliver information in the form of (material) letters, a method that is many centuries old; that is, from place to place by hand. On the other hand, they can, with navigation technology such as GPS, transmit information about their location and movements in many different places on Earth simultaneously in real time, and make it all visible in virtual form. Presence in absence becomes possible! Leonardo da Vinci, the artist-engineer, strived to realize this synthesis of art and technology. The futurists recognized that one understands its forces, its rhythm, and the endlessly numerous analogies that the machine suggests as the essence of the machine. And they also understood that the machine so understood becomes the source of inspiration for the unfolding and development of the visual arts. When the Gutenberg press was invented, nobody dreamed that this meant the beginning of a totally new era for humankind. This invention made the reproduction of human thought possible. Society was divided into the literate and illiterate.

This division was closely associated with the contemporary power structures. Through the availability of information, the literate had an enormous advantage. Today we find ourselves in a similar situation. There are people who can manipulate digital code and thus experience a world with far more numerous levels than that of someone who cannot work with digital code. This affects not just the amount of information but also the fact that we become part of the machine and the machine becomes a part of us, through which we can pass into any as yet unknown reception experience. The philosopher Vilém Flusser says that revolutions are technical revolutions. This has its effects on art, whether it is the invention of bronze, paint, photography, film, or even the computer. But the main difference between then and now

Circulus Viciosus X (Gulf War coverage), 1991, single-channel video. Video stills.

Władysław Starewicz, *The Cameraman's Revenge*, 1912, stop-motion animated short film. Video stills.

is that the earlier inventions were recognized as new tools with which one can produce new artifacts. This new tool was outside of us, however. It was a means of production. We could never become a part of it. This situation changed radically with the invention of the computer. We become a part of the tool, the machine, and thus we are now inside of a system in which we play a wholly new role.

A prime example of this is the experience of virtual reality. We enter artificial worlds and in them integrate with other humans. We meet friends in a "bar." All these friends come from other places to this bar: one from Leningrad, another from San Francisco, another from São Paulo, that one from Jerusalem, this one from Tokyo, and so on. We drink, we dance, we tell jokes, and we talk about death, love, art, and the meaning of life. And after a while we forget that we are thousands of kilometers away from each other in different time zones. The idea that everything we experience in the real world we can experience as a simulation strikes us as both a challenge and a threat at the same time. Intercultural communication that leaves behind time and space has become real. And while I formulate these thoughts here, I am again linked up to the network, and a colleague who is sitting far away is asking me to write a contribution for a new hypertext book, which he is sending me over the network. And while I write my contribution to their book, it is being read in real time by the other authors all over the world. And, as I mentioned in my introduction, the hypertext in the form of an electronic book has no linear form, that is, the text has no beginning and no ending. You can enter it anywhere and exit it anywhere. It branches out like a tree, and because it is always on the internet, anybody with access to the book can expand it with text and pictures. Thus this book grows from day to day, over years, ever taking on new forms.

Since Leonardo's rationalization of visual impressions, much has happened in the visual arts. The many metamorphoses they have undergone have exerted different influences. First, one was freed from the ethic of visual duplication, which then freed color, which then turned around and freed it from itself; then it freed material, then finally freed itself from traditional media, like the two-dimensional surface. At some point, the visual arts became reflexive, its own meta-field, which made itself into the subject. This was an important moment. Artists such as Cezanne, Chirico, Albers, Magritte, Escher, and others contributed to this important step. The visual arts discovered itself as a social process, and they made their materials and media into the subjects. In one of the first animated films by the Russian director Ladislas Starevitch, in 1912, he animated dead insects to make a film. It was the first time in film history when the film medium reflected itself. The artificial intelligence of the computer is taking a step further, not just in that it turns the visual process into a subject, but in that it is in a position to reinvent it. Virtual reality is able to model not simply all other media, but also those that don't even exist. One can, for example, look at a landscape picture in a virtual museum and be able to run around in that very landscape, and a virtual painter can disappear into his own picture and turn up again as something else. Reality seems to become more and more virtual, while the virtual world becomes more and more real. So why shouldn't it be like this? We take the three-dimensional world for granted, even though to understand it fully we have to perceive a four-dimensional world. But because we have no sense for experiencing four dimensions – we have no way of directly perceiving curved space – we have to be satisfied with a partial reality that we see as real. It is by all means possible that at some point in the future, with the help of virtual reality, we will obtain and experience a more complete view of the world than the one we have now.

The material space of art expanded from the painter's canvas into the landscape – land art – and more recently from geographic space to network space. The philosopher Jean-François Lyotard says that the media arts create a connection with the observer without resulting in materialized works in the form of objects. These works are composed from the "immaterial." And the philosopher Paul Virilio says that after the age of "representation" comes the age of "presentation."

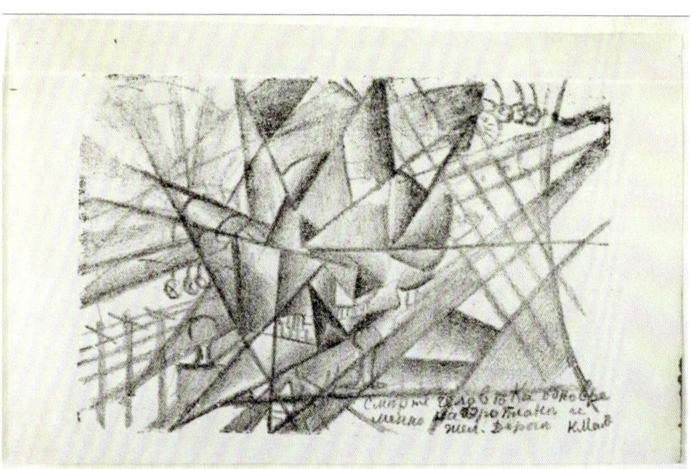

Kazimir Malevich, *Simultaneous Death in an Airplane and at the Railyway*, 1913, drawing.

International Painting Interactive, 1992. Booklet cover.

The communication aesthetic concerns itself not with the production of objects; nor is it interested in concrete forms. Its subject is space-time. The 1913 painting by Kazimir Malevich, *Simultaneous Death in an Airplane and at the Railway*, is a prophetic vision that is freed from time and space.

The interactive teleproject *IPI* (*International Painting Interactive*), which our Department of New Media at the Academy of Art here in Prague participated in two years ago during the Siggraph in Chicago, was an attempt to experience space-time in a new way. Artists in all parts of the globe, with the help of high-performance graphics computers (SGI) could create a collective work of art in real time over telephone lines. The dematerialization of art was present also in events that took place here in Prague even in the Middle Ages. The famed Rabbi Loew, who also wonderfully captured the idea of AI in the tale of the golem, created a virtual reality situation. During a visit of Emperor Rudolph to the rabbi's humble house, the rabbi performed a miracle: he changed the house into a castle by projecting pictures of the interior of Prague Castle onto the wall of his house with the help of his camera obscura. The emperor had the impression of being in a castle. The virtual space of then has something in common with the virtual spaces of today.

During a recent visit to Prague by the media artist Jeffrey Shaw, the idea came up to create the absolute vulgarization of the writer Franz Kafka. He suggested setting up a room in one of the places where Kafka had lived where the visitor could, with the help of virtual reality, transform into an insect (as described in the short story "The Metamorphosis"). Thus, this double metaphor would reach a new dimension. One could actually materialize the Kafkaesque idea with the help of an immaterial medium of virtual reality, and so have an absolutely real experience. This apparent contradiction is a fact we will have to learn to live with. To close one's eyes to it would lead to fatal results. We are in the middle of an adventure, of which all earlier generations could be envious. The American magazine *Newsweek* announces the theme of the week on the cover: the differing relationships of men and women to the computer and their consequences. Vilém Flusser says, "We are no longer the subjects of a given objective world, but projections of alternative worlds. From a subservient subjective position, we have set ourselves up as projections. We became grownups. We know that we dream. The adventure of becoming a person has entered a new phase with us. This is shown most clearly by the fact that we can no longer make a difference between truth and image, science and art."

I am not alone in that the more I learn of the effects of immaterial media, the less I know about it. The only thing I do know is the thought that Bauhaus leader László Moholy-Nagy came up with: "It seems impracticable to work on the shaping of one's own time in contemporary ways."

First published in Olga Shishko and Irina Alpatova, eds., *Newmediatopia, newmedialogia* (Moscow: Soros Center for Contemporary Arts, 1996), 171–73.

TerrorAttackBerlin, 2007, inverted pictograms, part of Michael Bielicky's and Kamila B. Richter's pictogram library. Software screenshots.

The Passage between Worlds in Michael Bielicky's Installations

Norman M. Klein

(Including a Walk across the Street to Kafka's Apartment from 1914)

Michael Bielicky has said that his work often centers on the "ephemerality" in how information is delivered. The word "ephemeral" comes from the Greek, meaning one day only, like a 24-hour news cycle. "Ephemeral" can also suggest evanescence, a fine mist, a brilliantly immediate atmosphere. Most of all, the ephemeral is trapped in the present. As Charles Baudelaire famously explained, modernity is "the ephemeral, the fugitive, the contingent, the half of art whose other half is eternal and the immutable."[1]

But there is a deeply personal element as well. Michael's personal journey was often consumed by the politics of the ephemeral. It is the story of Middle Europeans being caught in between. We can start at practically any time in the twentieth century. The year 1969 suits this essay well: a year after the ephemeral struck deeply throughout Europe. During World War II, Bielicky's parents managed to survive the Holocaust. After 1945, they migrated across the melted aftermath of Middle Europe, finally settling in Prague. However, they arrived at the beginning of the Soviet occupation.

The cultural ironies of Prague at this time – especially in the sixties – are so often overlooked. Bielicky especially remembers the echoes he spotted during his early teenage years. Prague had become a haven for media experiments. The range was extraordinary. In Karel Zeman's film montages, live-action was embedded inside animation. Throughout Czechoslovakia, Baroque puppetry was being applied to modernism, notably in plays staged by Josef Krofta. Even more crucial for Bielicky were unusual media installations developed in Prague. These were surely ephemeral in the Baudelairan sense (featured at the Montreal World's Fair in 1967). They were theatrical machines "imagining" what the computer might someday become. They were devices for a modernist Baroque theater, built utterly in analog, rigged like ships. Yet they "imagined" the algorithmic as a ghostly fiction just around the corner. The algorithm was solid, but like a golem in waiting.

All this prepared Bielicky for a post-1968 world, but in a subjunctive tense. The Russians invaded Prague. The troops destroyed analog computer machines, because they suggested anti-Soviet voting and elections. Michael emigrated to West Germany in 1969. At first, he studied medicine. Then he entered the gig economy for a few years. One of his favorite odd-jobs was driving a horse cab. And for a dose of Western consumer madness, in 1978, he visited New York and crossed the United States. By 1984, the aesthetics of media had absorbed him entirely. He received a master's degree under Nam June Paik at the Düsseldorf Art Academy. That introduced him to the rarified Fluxus universe of media aesthetics. He exhibited media sculptures and installations throughout the eighties, and experimented in real-time interactive telematics.

Finally, in 1991, he returned to Prague as Professor at the Academy of Fine Arts (AVU). Typical of the nineties, he continued his peripatetic travels, one emergent globalization hot spot after another. These were mostly museums, in which the media arts tended to be sponsored the most. He showed widely. By the time he and I met in 2005 (in Los Angeles), he had thoroughly absorbed the intercontinental styles thoroughly, had even exceeded them, because the romance of the algorithm was being replaced by the paradoxes of the ephemeral, by the corruptions.

TerrorAttackLondon, 2007, inverted pictograms, part of Michael Bielicky's and Kamila B. Richter's pictogram library. Software screenshots.

He immediately sensed my thick Hungarian immigrant childhood, what I call medieval Brooklyn, or growing up inside a Breughel painting. The ludic ironies of our antique, comic histories were plain to us. We shared many of the same fascinations, saw post-structuralism as a Middle European picaresque. Michael was after all, an immigrant as much as I was, but without leaving his own country. America meanwhile was being colonized by its own economy, growing more neo-feudal and foreign week by week.

Most of all, our Middle European "dialects" had been updated through TV, urbanism, and the vapors of high consumer taste. The universe was sweetly warped, like faces stretched into each other on the shallow display mode of a grainy fifties TV. We talked about Zeman flying ships, styled for Baron Munchausen or Jules Verne. We imagined the virtual as a two-and-a-half dimensional pop-up book of the world – of its half-truths made of glyphs and ideograms; inside vanishing twenties' cityscapes.

In reviewing Bielicky's preferred canon of master texts and cultural heroes, I noticed a recurrent theme. Among the names are Nam June Paik, Karel Zeman, Dziga Vertov, Joseph Beuys, Mel Alexenberg, and Vilém Flusser. As we chatted about these, I pointed out that almost all of them entered the cultural debates around entropy and on the randomizing effect of media. This is connected, but not at all the same as cybernetics. Nor is it the same as chance techniques. It is about the perverse decay of meaning, and memory. Let me explain:

In 1991, Michael Bielicky interviewed Flusser right before his death (in a tragic road accident). The two men had been close friends. Flusser's concepts deeply influenced Bielicky's work throughout the nineties, particularly on the fragility of all communication, how the real lays hidden in plain sight whenever media speaks. By media, Flusser meant any mode of speech, any time-based transmission, through whatever device.

Flusser believed that media (especially the digital) communicates in a circular way. Its messages continually dissolve when received, in a downward spiral. Its reception follows the laws of entropy in the universe, a cooling down of meaning. The message that returns is less. The wheels of cognition – and reception – have somehow ground it down. We are cognitive machines that cannot receive the present directly. Something gets in the way. That something was often compared to entropy in the universe, in debates going back to the fifties: Norbert Wiener on cybernetics, and Claude Lévi-Strauss on structural anthropology. In a lecture in Kyoto in 1998, Paik compared the irony to the schizo-mechanics of some of his work, for instance, the "Cagean" pieces he entitled "playable music [...] since most of my musical compositions are not playable."[2] Paik relies on Wiener's summary of the slippery dynamics involved: "Just as entropy is a measure of disorganization, the information carried by a set of messages is a measure of organization."[3] One erases while communicating.

In Middle Europe, this debate echoed the decay of the Cold War, and the fall of the Soviet regime. By the nineties, it had fully entered media theory and practice. Can the growing indeterminacy of Flow in data and capitalism still generate meaning?

Flusser compares the problem to digital images. Digital pictures, after all, are not the same as light through glass. They are closer to moths caught in a windstorm. Their pixels are worn away by the wind. They are like Cro-Magnon petroglyphs: pictographs. On the walls of the cave, we see faded traces, irregular bits of syntax. They float through our mind like ideograms. For an instant, their pale lines make sense, like part of a lost alphabet, or a word.

TerrorAttackMoscow, 2007, inverted pictograms, part of Michael Bielicky's and Kamila B. Richter's pictogram library. Software screenshots.

TerrorAttackMosque, 2007, inverted pictograms, part of Michael Bielicky's and Kamila B. Richter's pictogram library. Software screenshots.

Then just as quickly, they scatter again, become aesthetic ciphers. According to Flusser, this coming and going represents "a different vision of time."[4] Meaning fluctuates until "time a tendency which goes from the past into the future without stopping in the present. Nothing is, everything becomes. Everything is a process, nothing ever can repeat itself. Every lost moment is an opportunity definitely lost."[5] One might summarize the argument in this way: entropy is a law of nature. But its negation – a more positive result known as negentropy – is also a law of nature. Media is speeding up the two at once. It is the simultaneity of erasure and revelation at the blistering speed of light. As a result, we are increasingly becoming a cognitive mess in a collective low-grade nervous breakdown. Our plight is funny, and clearly terrifying; but most of all, it is a mad, comic picaresque that Bielicky enjoys capturing through projection, like (Plato's) moth caught in a wind – not in a cave. His work proceeds from the utopianism of the nineties to the dystopic ironies after 2000, but he never falls prey to the hyper glamor associated with digital capitalism in the nineties. He was too much of a Middle European for that.

In 1990, Bielicky exhibited a choreographed dance video named *Perpetuum Mobile II*. Two halves of the frame seemed to rhythmically crowd into each other. Each writhed in synch to dance music. Rubbery bodies stretched as if in a funhouse mirror, or inside a warped TV signal. They were an "elementary manifestation of nature and of the human being."[6] "Without this permanent movement (this micro-kinesis deep in every living thing), our existence would be in a static condition: death."[7]

It is micro-kinesis. Instead of gears and cams, there are false memories and logos. That is what remains of our cosmic law of nature. There was something both hopeful and desperate about the dance. 1990 was precisely the year when the Soviet occupation was ending. An incommensurate thrill spread throughout Middle Europe. It was difficult not to imagine the computer as part of this emerging utopia. Of course, as it turned out, the carnival was brief, filled with an almost drunken sense of possibilities, but over by the year 2000 or so. As the nineties carnival wore down (in very different ways from one region to another) what remained was a sense of *memento mori*. After all, carnivals are mostly a celebration of mortality, not immortality. Neoliberalism and globalization had been a false friend, but a friend nonetheless (sometimes with deep pockets). Had we all made a devil's bargain somehow? Within the enthusiasms of the nineties carnival, media experimentation had seemed to flourish. The coming of the internet in 1994 was heralded as a new Genesis.

At the Ars Electronica in 1994, Bielicky tested how dystopic the dreamy futures of GPS might become. In a performance piece, *Intelligent Mailman* (1994), an actor was dressed as a mailman. He walked through Linz, while carrying a primitive GPS device (like a Christmas fruit cake). Clearly, the mailman was "an anachronism," bringing "information by hand from place to place."[8] At the same time, the mailman was transmitting his movements and location, as an act of surveillance, or as the victim of surveillance. In fact, would surveillance really be the problem, in the end? There was something so twentieth century about a Big Brother narrative.

I am reminded of Bielicky's video sculpture *The Name* (1990) as ideogrammatic. TV monitors are attached to a metal spiral. Like a spider's mind, the spiral delivers a "wireless transmission between objects."[9] Bielicky installs his ideograms like archipelagos, islands of shellfish trapped in a fishnet. Since 2008, these ideograms are featured often in huge projections. The projections are inhabited by a crowd of playfully familiar imagos (designed by media artist, Kamila B. Richter). The faces look familiar, images from the news, and are whimsically naughty. They perform like medieval *zannies* (updates from Hieronymus Bosch). Crazy wormlike animations (portraits, bodies, logos) stream from room to room, or across long buildings. The walls are bulging with ideograms, an AI sales staff proudly delivering nothing that quite makes sense (and of course, from the internet). Their story – and anti-story – anxiously unwinds, but never finishes. And yet, certain conjunctions, for a moment, stop you cold. The reception and squirming suddenly captures a news event. A dark moment is suddenly clear. Then, like a circus train, the parade takes off again – an agit-prop that both leaves and arrives at the same time. That would be our strange world after 2008 in particular, that stillness that is now cracking.

Over the past decade, Michael and I have endlessly discussed how this post-2008 *interregnum* might conclude. At first, before 2008 certainly, it seemed like a precise repetition of fascism was coming. But then, so much autocratic noise that was not simply fascism interceded. We looked for through twenties and thirties Productivist art for extra templates. We imagined the data interface turning into bizarre modes of fiction.

One fact was clear: the period from 1994 to 2008 had launched an age of criminalized data privacy: of money laundering, analytical piracies, financial swindling. Michael had been tracking GPS software since the early nineties. He never presumed that GPS was merely about surveillance. Other granular and odd forces were in play. We agreed that GPS might be granular, might suggest the dissolution of the vertical nation-state throughout the world. George W. Bush and Dick Cheney were symptoms. Then came Brexit and Trumpismo. The corruption of electoral politics seemed to be overwhelming the developed and developing worlds everywhere you looked (as of 2019). New modes of authoritarianism are now wrapped and ready on every continent; and they are often very atavistic in their populist rage. And yet, they are clearly not Spenglerian meltdowns. We need a new set of myths. Much of Bielicky's visual aporias (like anti-operas) suggest a ship of state ready to shipwreck, but doing something else instead.

Imagine streaming protoplasm. This liquid flesh is inhabited: by text, animal shapes, consumer products, corporate logos, portraits of political figures. The whole formula sounds like a recipe for a new kind of golem. But what does the golem of Flow want? Mel Alexenberg (a gentler voice) might call it an agent of post-digital humanism, a Talmudic body without organs. I am a paranoid utopian; I imagine the golem of Flow as deregulation itself, a sociopathic parasite colonizing the American economy. Bielicky sees it as the failure of digital culture to thoroughly escape from the centripetal forces of earlier centuries. But in all three examples, Bielicky's experience of Middle Europe may be perfect training for the new *Game of Thrones*.

In our chats, Bielicky and I agree that 2008 was a transition, not just a pendulum swing. Aspects of this transition are getting clearer. For example, our arts culture since 2008 has been showing infernal signs of weariness, despite more big money at biennials and big-box events. Something about late globalism both grows and eats away at our cultural institutions.

2008 accelerated a populist wave throughout the Americas, Europe, Turkey, and the Near East. It is changing labor relations toward even greater precarity. We observe the creatures invented by Bielicky (and Richter) grazing through precarity. The stomachs of these creatures are getting bloated with new parasites. What do the parasites "want"? Above the creature, like a fading cabala on a weak battery, the sun appears to be frozen at twilight.

TerrorAttackPisa, 2007, inverted pictograms, part of Michael Bielicky's and Kamila B. Richter's pictogram library. Software screenshots.

TerrorAttackRome, 2007, inverted pictograms, part of Michael Bielicky's and Kamila B. Richter's pictogram library. Software screenshots.

This is essentially the Bielicky (and Richter) carnival style since 2008. Their creatures sink underneath an algorithmic Flow. This Flow symbolizes our growing underdevelopment worldwide (entropy). This mythic anti-story is especially clear in their cycle entitled *Garden of Error and Decay* (2010–19). Imagine a nineteenth century novel (a Bildungsroman) that is forever stuck on chapter two; its subplots remain curled up like a snake. And yet the stream of its anti-story never stops. Randomized plot points just flow. They express what he calls "Falling Times," like an electrical brownout rather than a blackout. This brownout is a less hopeful message than his Genesis of media studies from the nineties. It has media spiraling into an underworld (or a black well) bubbling over with dark data. "Why don't we," he asks, then never stops.[10] I like to jump into similar kinds of media picaresques, but as an historian. We both love to twist facts into a sword dance. Where is the "true measure"? His journeys continue to inform me. They are trails through misplaced intentions. His Middle European voice adjust easily to newly perverse media (like cyber weapons), appears to be as much at home now as ever.

Entropy and Piracy: Kafkaesque Capitalism

Michael Bielicky grew up across the street from 48 Nerudova Street (now Polski Street). That is the address where Franz Kafka (1883–1924) lived from September 1914 to February 1915, in his sister Elli's (1889–1942) apartment. It was empty because she had just returned to their father's large suite of rooms: that tormenting place, according to Kafka's diaries. Elli needed to feel more protected, because her husband had just left for the war. Thus, over the period of five months, Franz Kafka (not yet sick with tuberculosis, always fighting depression; yet still at a hopeful stage in his new relationship with Felice Bauer) had found a quiet space alone. At 11 p.m. every night, after his relentless job at the Workers Accident Insurance Institute, he wrote much of *The Trial* (published in 1925, translated to English in 1937). I believe his Josef K. lived some of the time, while awaiting trial, in that apartment: "K. said nothing, he knew what was coming, but, suddenly relieved from the effort of the work he had been doing, he gave way to a pleasant lassitude and looked out the window at the other side of the street. From where he sat, he could see just a small, triangular section of it, part of the empty walls of houses between two shop windows. 'You're staring out the window!' called out his [stern, fatherlike] uncle, raising his arms, 'For God's sake, Josef, give me an answer! Is it true, can it really be true?' 'Uncle Karl,' said K., wrenching himself back from his daydreaming, 'I really don't know what it is you want of me.' 'Josef,' said his uncle in a warning tone, 'as far as I know, you've always told the truth. Am I to take what you've just said as a bad sign?'

'I think I know what it is you want,' said K. obediently, 'I expect you've heard about my trial.'"[11]

I can easily imagine Josef K. at work in software today. He has been arrested due to volatility of his job contract. His industry is run by inept kleptocrats. In their callousness, they surround themselves with precariats like K. They inject a neoliberal, nihilistic flavor to K.'s job at the bank. The more economic inequality, the more they flourish, like pirates on an entropic Hobbesian freeport. In my research on the years 1973 to the present, I identify the growth of inequality in the West since 1973. That is standard across hundreds of studies. The cause of this inequality is an emergent urban industrial feudalism, a dissolve brought on by globalization. This feudalism is a condition more than a system. It strikes economies internally like an autoimmune disease. The mood it creates is certainly Kafkaesque, a slow-moving polarizing depression. The safety valves (so much an interest of Kafka's in his day job) continue to worsen, relentlessly. Statistics today indicate that economic inequalities are now as extreme as a century ago, according to economists, such as Thomas Piketty or Joseph Stiglitz. Many labor protections as old as Kafka in 1914 are steadily dissolving, certainly in the United States. The twentieth century, in that sense, has begun to lapse, as if it has nothing left to teach us. As a result of worsening policies, we find more child urchins lost on the street. Their anger is frantic, but carnivalesque. They play noisily outside the painter Titorelli's apartment, in Kafka's *The Trial*.

Most of all, Kafkaesque capitalism is volatile, ever on trial. Bureaucratic disregard steadily enhances the inequalities. The protections of labor are literally arrested, but now algorithmically at the speed of light. We are trolled, erased, remaindered. As entropy increases, more pirates appear. The internet accelerates the Kafkaesque. It compresses our identity like a Middle European madness from 1968, or 1988, but also from 1914. The dead hand of Cold War logic has returned. This logic was more about a dissolving nation-state than totalitarianism. The center has lost its sight, rather like Kafka's vision of late Habsburg Prague. We are stuck in a rather Middle European corruption of modernity. It is a joke on us. Kafka saw his worlds also as deeply comical. Our present is very much a picaresque comedy. It is hard not to laugh at our monstrous Trumpian mannerisms.

Michael Bielicky and I got to talking about Kafkaesque capitalism. His projections suggest half-remembered news cycles, like a picaresque entropy, choking on its mindless secrecies. We are literally inside Kafka's garden of decay, even more than Bosch's. Kafka's ship of fools operates stochastically, by dead reckoning. Michael feels that capitalism is a ship of fools operated increasingly by a new breed of apparatchiks. Michael and I agree that 2019 is just an interregnum, not unlike 1914; but for how long? The public mood reminds him of Prague in the 1980s. Its gaudy style relies on a Gilded-Age brittle madness. An ebb tide has returned.

We agree that all frontiers grow harder to cross. As contrast, he remembers travels in 1978 across the United States. "America was to me, from where I came from, a utopia," he said. "Everything worked. The people were so open." But that is clearly no longer true. The US has split into three separate countries: the Eastern kingdom, the greater West, and old Confederate South. A cultural civil war is fully underway. So many small towns I knew are now too angry to visit anymore. Petty racist atavisms, and vigilante madness, have returned, even from a century ago, like a chronic allergy. Premonitions of more violence are increasing throughout the US, in so many parts of the world. However, Michael and I are both convinced that something positive must emerge, however imperfectly. We as teachers, writers, and artists must not reinforce nihilism. So, we need to resist the nihilistic reading of Kafka as well. That does not summarize his Middle Europe. There is also a humanist comic picaresque in its story.

The growth of the American frontier is often compared to an Exodus. Kafka himself was fascinated by America's perverse blitheness, its city-on-the-hill imaginary. Now for Americans that Exodus is essentially frozen. But it is 2019. The last act is far from being told yet. The cost is not thoroughly clear yet; nor was the future of Kafka's Middle Europe. He died before the full madness took over. Thus, Kafkaesque capitalism is a premonition, an allegory about capitalist futures more than the future. We do not yet know which catastrophe is about to unfold. So many risks lie in waiting. But I am convinced that we have a choice, even though the crisis today feels as daunt-

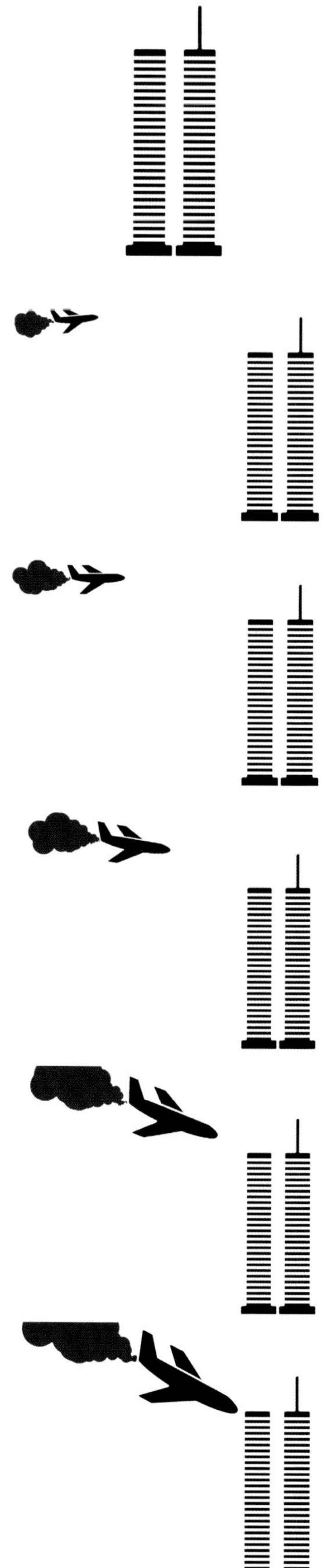

TerrorAttackTwinTowers, 2007, inverted pictograms, part of Michael Bielicky's and Kamila B. Richter's pictogram library. Software screenshots.

ing as 1914 must have felt in Prague; or the final decades of the Cold War, before the false spring of the 1990s.

So, I will close briefly with a quote from Kafka's unfinished novel from 1922, *The Castle*. In it, Kafka imagines the law that governs desire, and the will to enact desire. This law unfolds from the dark matter of the *scheinbare Leere*, or illusory emptiness, that lies within *The Castle*, which is an ever-dissolving un-seat of power.

He compares citizens serving this law to chambermaids; (what a symbol for the gig economy, like the voice-over for a Pasolini movie about Uber drivers): "When you're a chambermaid you feel forgotten and forlorn, it's like working down the mine, or at least it is in the corridor where the secretaries stay, you don't see a soul for days on end except for a few members of the public flitting back and forth, never venturing to look up, no one but the two or three other chambermaids who feel just as bitter about their lot. You can't leave your room in the morning, the secretaries want to be on their own, the servants bring their food from the kitchen, the chambermaids don't usually have anything to do with that, and you can't show yourself in the corridor at mealtimes either. It's only while the gentlemen are working that the chambermaids are allowed to tidy up, not of course in the rooms that are occupied but in those that happen to be empty, and the housework has to be done very quietly so as not to disturb the gentlemen at their work. But how can anyone clean and tidy quietly if the gentlemen stay in their rooms day after day, and then there are the servants going around, dirty riffraff that they are, and when a room is finally free for the chambermaid to go in, it's in such a state that not even a deluge could wash it clean?"[12]

The final draft of *The Castle* was reassembled by Max Brod in 1926. Kafka never even completed the last sentence, nor the last third of the book. Its unfinish speaks to all middle passages. We must be resolved. There is an old union cry that activist Studs Terkel (1912–2008) always repeated, to close each of his radio shows, back in 1970s Chicago. "Take it easy," he would say, then pause, "but take it."

"The living-room in Gerstäcker's house was only dimly lit by the fire on the hearth and a candle-end. By the light of the latter someone could be seen stooped in a niche under the sloping rafters that stuck out there, reading a book. It was Gerstäcker's mother. She gave K. her trembling hand and made him sit down beside her. She spoke with difficulty, it was hard to understand her, but what she said"[13]

1 Charles Baudelaire, *The Painter of Modern Life and other Essays*, ed. and trans. Jonathan Mayne (London: Phaidon Press, 1964), 1–35, here 13.
2 Nam June Paik, "Norbert Wiener and Marshall McLuhan," in *The Inamori Foundation: Kyoto Prizes and Inamori Grants* (Kyoto: The Inamori Foundation, 1999), 178–88, here 179.
3 Norbert Wiener, *The Human Use of Human Being: Cybernetics and Society* [1950] (Boston: DaCapo Press, 1988), 21.
4 Baruch Gottlieb, "Translations and Transcriptions from Bielicky's Recordings with Flusser in Summer 1991," *Flusser Studies* 17 (2014): 10, http://www.flusserstudies.net/archive/flusser-studies-17-double-issue.
5 Steffi Winkler, "Vilém Flussers Fluß: Transkript der Videodokumentation von Gesprächen mit Vilém Flusser im Sommer 1991," *Flusser Studies* 17 (2014): 11, http://www.flusserstudies.net/archive/flusser-studies-17-double-issue.
6 Michael Bielicky, *Perpetuum Mobile,* audiovisual file, 1986, https://www.bielicky.net/projects/perpetuum-mobile-1986.
7 Ibid.
8 Michael Bielicky, *Intelligent Mailman*, audiovisual file, 1994, http://bielicky.net/projects/intelligent-mailman-linz-1994.
9 Michael Bielicky, *The Name*, audiovisual file, 1990, https://www.bielicky.net/projects/name-1990.
10 *Falling Times* is an installation by Bielicky and Richter from 2006, and *Why Don't We* is a digital installation from 2013.
11 Franz Kafka, *The Trial*, trans. Breon Mitchell (New York City: Schocken Books, 1999), chapter 6. Originally written in German from 1914 to 1915, it was published only in 1925 by Kafka's friend and editor Max Brod (original German title: *Der Process*). The first English translation was published in 1937 by Willa and Edwin Muir.
12 Franz Kafka, *The Castle*, trans. Anthea Bell (New York: Oxford University Press Inc., 2009), 254ff. Originally written in German in 1922, it was published only in 1926 by Kafka's friend and editor Max Brod (original German title: *Das Schloss*).
13 Ibid., 275.

Amy Dolin, Michael Bielicky, and unknown person, Prague, 1995.

Susanne Widl, unknown person, Steina Vasulka, Michael Bielicky, Sevilla, Spain, 2008.

Gerd Stern, New York, USA, 2012.

Michael Bielicky, Düsseldorf, 1971.

Photographic Research 1946–2020

Bielicky took a sudden break from his vocation for photography and video editing that would last twenty years. Throughout that long hiatus, however, he researched and creatively misused the first digital video editing techniques continually – stop motion via U-Matic, time-base correction, and drop-out compensator (DOC) – after his obsessive mission to provoke and document the aesthetic errors of the specter in the machine. After these twenty years, and with the help of digital photography storage apps, he finally started to accumulate photographs again. Starting with 900 images in 2005, he produced more than 3,900 in 2007, and 7,500 in 2009: roughly 4,600 images a year over the course of fifteen years, which he neatly stored in a daily folder structure. The *Falling* series (2004–09) alone was depicted with 2,640 images, *Columbus 2.0* (2007–19) with 2,160, the *Garden of Error and Decay* (2010–19) with 1,410, and the *Why Don't We* series (2013–17) with 2,650.

Also stored are photographs of the following people visiting various exhibitions, in heated café and restaurant talks, or presenting in lecture halls all over the world over the last sixty years: Marina Abramović, Mel Alexenberg, Jean Baudrillard, Hans Belting, Joseph Beuys, David Blair, James Lee Byars, Fredrich Cantor, Mike Hentz, Hiroshi Kawano, Jule Kewenig, Norman M .Klein, Heinrich Klotz, Kasper König, Lev Manovich, Jonas Mekas, Frieder Nake, Howard Rheingold, Jeffrey Shaw, Margit Rosen, Peter Sloterdijk, Klaus Staeck, Howard Stern, Andreas Ströhl, Nam June Paik, Steina Vasulka, Woody Vasulka, Lino Ventura, Wolf Vostell, Peter Weibel, and Siegfried Zielinski.

Bielicky today owns one of the most refined collections in the rapidly evolving, vibrant media artist social scene, which only began to gain critical public exposure in 1982, just two years before Bielicky chose Paik's master class at Düsseldorf Art Academy.[1]

1 See Wulf Herzogenrath, "Versuche, die verdammte Kiste abzuschaffen – oder: die Anfänge eines Kunstmediums in Europa mit Fluxus," in *Videokunst in Deutschland 1963-1982: Videobänder, Installationen, Objekte, Performances* (Stuttgart: Hatje Cantz, 1982), 26-29.

Mimi Bielicky and Tibor Bielicky, Prague, 1946.

Michael Bielicky, Prague, 1956.

Michael Bielicky, around Prague, 1964.

Michael Bielicky, Düsseldorf, 1971.

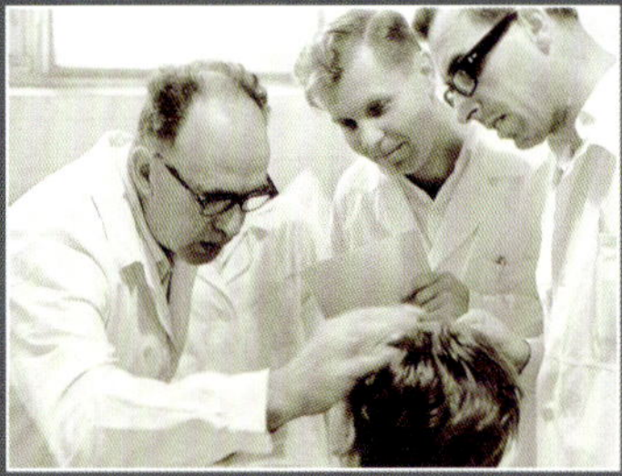

Tibor Bielicky, Düsseldorf, 1972.

Michael Bielicky, Marianne Mikat-Stevens, Christel Hohagen-Ahring, and Christoph Ahring, Düsseldorf, 1977.

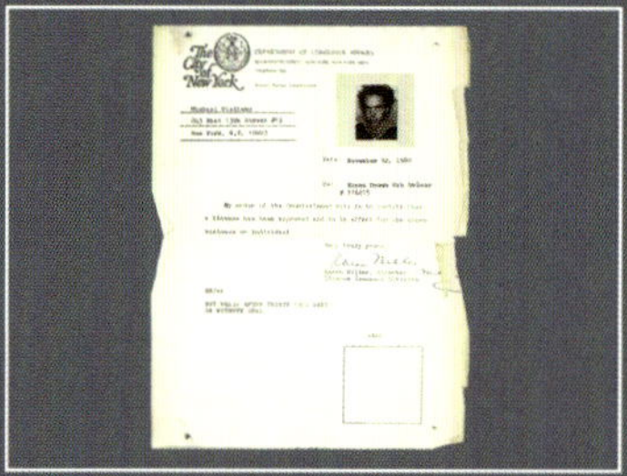

Horse Drawn Cab Driver license, New York, 1980.

Naty, Düsseldorf, 1980.

Ricardo Peredo and unknown person, Düsseldorf, 1980.

Westbeth Housing, Westbeth, New York, 1980.

Fredrich Cantor, New York, 1981.

Dieter Eikelpoth Atelier, Düsseldorf, 1982-83.

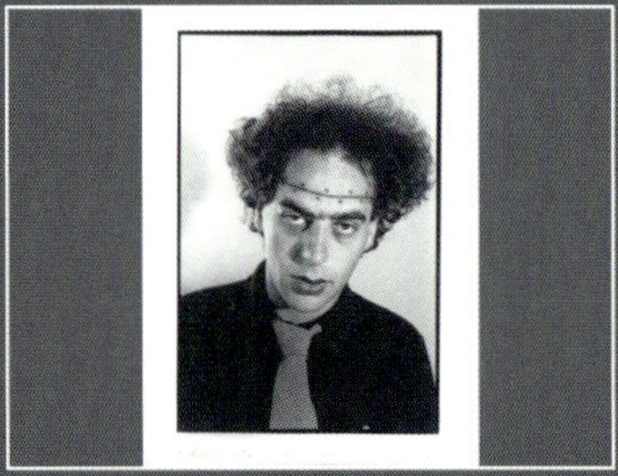

Fredrich Cantor, *Atomic Brain*, portrait of Michael Bielicky, 1982.

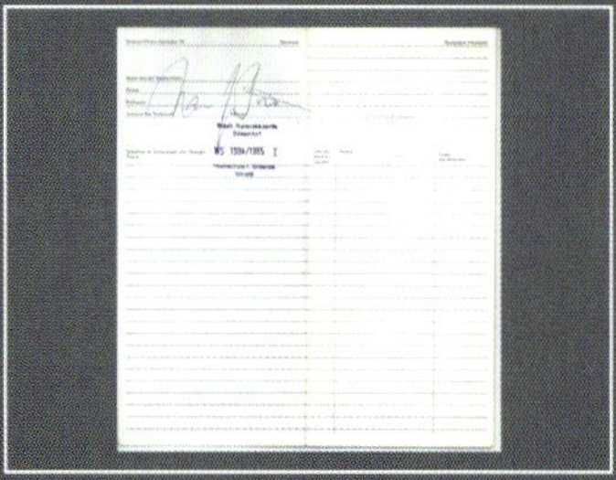

Kunstakademie study record, Nam June Paik signature, Düsseldorf, 1984/85.

Burned hats, Düsseldorf, 1986.

Michael Bielicky and Nam June Paik, Düsseldorf, 1986.

Michael Bielicky and Nam June Paik, Düsseldorf, 1986.

Michael Bielicky, Düsseldorf, 1986.

Nam June Paik, École nationale supérieure des arts décoratifs (EnsAD), Paris, 1986.

Nam June Paik and Wulf Herzogenrath, Düsseldorf, 1986.

Michael Bielicky, Nam June Paik, and Ricardo Peredo, Düsseldorf Rundgang, 1987.

Ricardo Peredo, Johannes Stüttgen, Klaus Staeck, Harald Naegeli, and Michael Bielicky, Rundgang, Düsseldorf Art Academy, 1987.

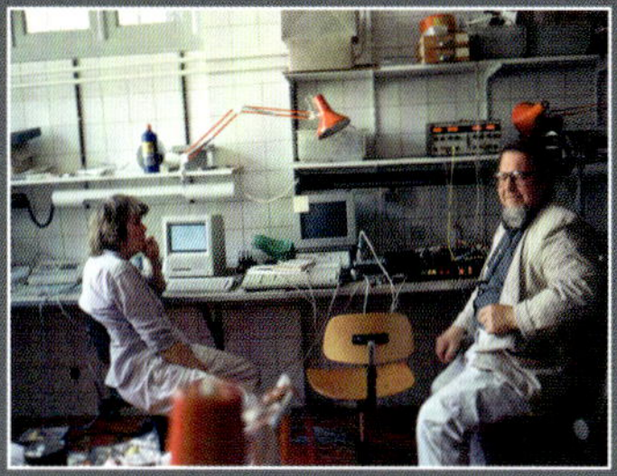

Steina and Woody Vasulka, Studio for Electro-Instrumental Music (STEIM), Amsterdam, 1987.

Woody Vasulka, Michael Bielicky, and Nam June Paik, Hotel Metropol, Düsseldorf, 1987.

Michael Bielicky and Alf Bold, Arsenal 2 Filminstitut, Berlin, 1987.

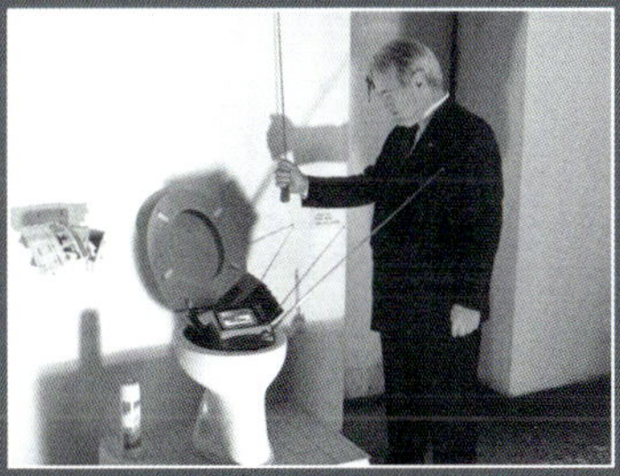

Johannes Rau, Düsseldorf Art Academy, 1988.

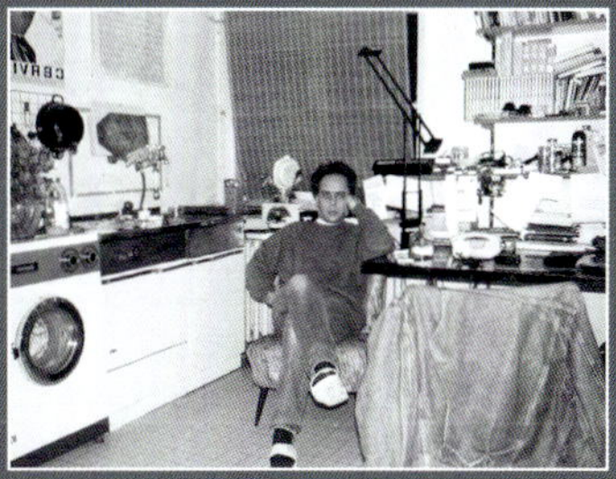

Michael Bielicky, Düsseldorf, 1988.

Ratinger Straße, Düsseldorf, 1988.

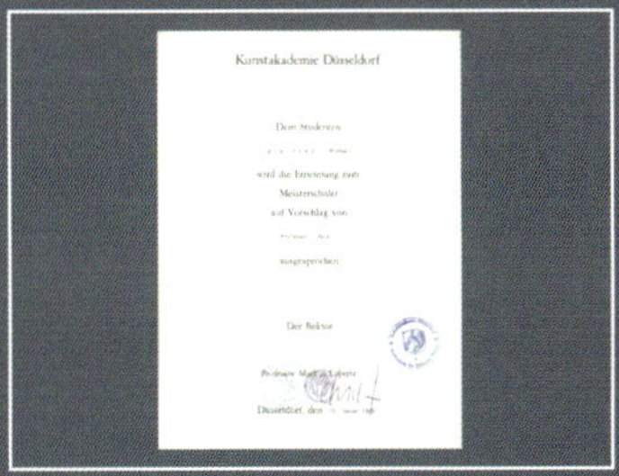

Michael Bielicky, Master class diploma, class of Markus Lüpertz, Düsseldorf, 1989.

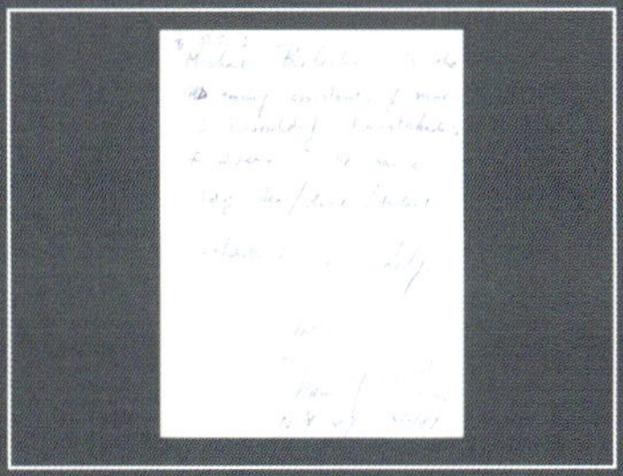

Nam June Paik, „Michael Bielicky is teaching assistant of mine in Düsseldorf Art Academy for 2 years. He has a lot of idea/Drive/talent. Thanks for your help. Your Nam June Paik, NY 30/2/89," handwritten certificate, 1989.

Class of Nam June Paik, New York, 1990.

Nam June Paik at the exhibition opening of *Discover European Video*, Anthology Video Archives, New York 1990.

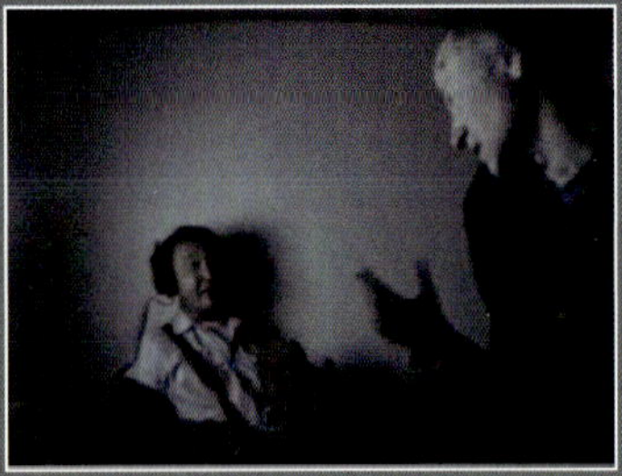

Nam June Paik and Jonas Mekas at the exhibition opening of *Discover European Video*, Anthology Video Archives, New York 1990.

Nam June Paik's atelier, New York, 1990.

Bill post by Michael Bielicky and Ricardo Peredo, New York, 1990.

Fredrich Cantor and Cathy Weiss, New York, 1990.

Ken Feingold and Fredrich Cantor, New York, 1990.

Woody Vasulka, Film and TV School of the Academy of Performing Arts, Prague, 1990s.

Unknown person, Woody Vasulka, and Rene Coelho, Prague, 1990s.

Wolf Vostell and Heinrich Klotz, Karlsruhe, 1991.

Wolf Vostell, ***MultiMediale 2***, ZKM | Karlsruhe, 1991.

Nam June Paik, unknown person, Wolf Vostell, and Mercedes Vostell, ***MultiMediale 2***, ZKM | Karlsruhe, 1991.

Peter Bielicky and Mimi Bielicky, ***MultiMediale 2***, ZKM | Karlsruhe, 1991.

Rene Coelho and Nam June Paik, ***MultiMediale 2***, ZKM | Karlsruhe, 1991.

Woody Vasulka, Rene Coelho, Nam June Paik, and Wolf Vostell, ***MultiMediale 2***, ZKM | Karlsruhe, 1991.

Woody Vasulka and Rene Coelho, ***MultiMediale 2***, ZKM | Karlsruhe, 1991.

Vilém Flusser, Edith Flusser, and Michael Bielicky, in Robion, France, 1991.

Peter Weibel, Ars Electronica, Linz, 1992.

Woody Vasulka and Peter Weibel, Ars Electronica, Linz, 1992.

Steina Vasulka, Ars Electronica, Linz, 1992.

Woody Vasulka and Peter Weibel, Ars Electronica, Linz, 1992.

David Flusser, International Vilém Flusser Symposion, Prague, 1992.

Jochen Bloss, Andreas Ströhl, and David Flusser, International Vilém Flusser Symposion, Prague, 1992.

Michael Bielicky, Prague Academy of Fine Arts (AVU), 1992.

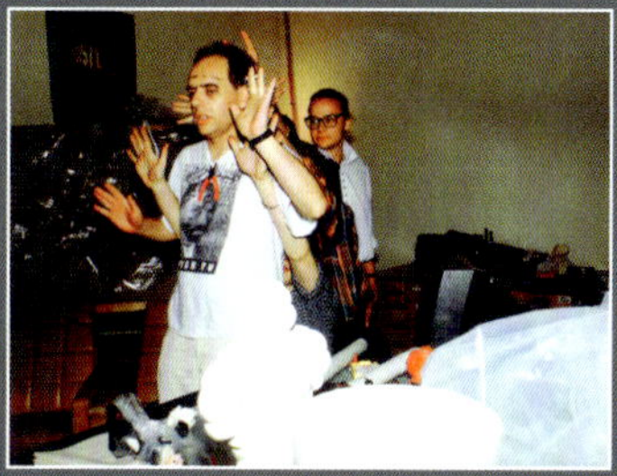

Michael Bielicky, Prague Academy of Fine Arts (AVU), 1992.

Mike Hentz and Milan Knížák, Prague Academy of Fine Arts (AVU), 1992.

Péter Vrana, Milan Kunc, Michael Bielicky, and Karel Dudesek, documenta IX, Kassel, 1992.

Piazza Virtuale/Van Gogh TV, documenta IX, Kassel, 1992.

Michael Bielicky, Zdeněk Sýkora and Lenka Sýkorava, 1992.

Steina and Woody Vasulka, European Media Art Festival, Osnabrück, 1992.

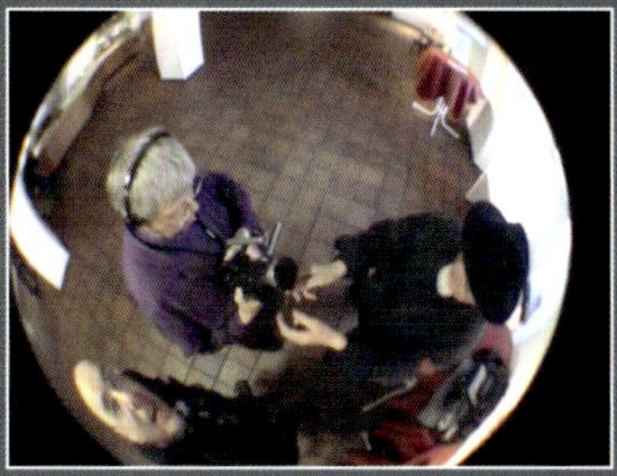

Michael Bielicky, Steina and Woody Vasulka, European Media Art Festival, Osnabrück, 1992.

Fredrich Cantor (photographer), Bielicky brothers at Peter Bielicky's doctor's office, Düsseldorf, 1992.

Boris Mikhailov, Kiev, 1993.

Oleksandr Roytdurd, Sofia Usoeva, unknown person, Lesja Zajac, and unknown person, Kiev, 1993.

Martin Skarda and Clemens Golf, Prague Academy of Fine Arts (AVU), 1993.

Michael Bielicky, Herbert Wentscher, and Pipilotti Rist, Villingen-Schwennigen, 1993.

Michael Bielicky and Ricardo Peredo, Prague, 1993.

Jeffrey Shaw, Ars Electronica, Linz, 1994.

Michael Bielicky, Alma Ata (Almaty), Kasachtsan, 1994.

Jaron Lanier, Ars Electronica, Linz, 1995.

Jaron Lanier, Ars Electronica, Linz, 1995.

Marina Abramović, ICG Studio, 1995.

Tony Oursler, ICG Studio, 1995.

Aleš Veselý and Milan Knížák, Prague Academy of Fine Arts (AVU), 1995.

Amy Dolin, Michael Bielicky, and unknown person, Prague, 1995.

Arnold Dreyblatt, unkown person, and Amy Dolin, Prague, 1995.

Howard Rheingold, Ars Electronica, Linz, 1995.

Unknown person, Vladimír Kokolia, unknown person, Michael Bielicky, and Jiří Sopko, Prague Academy of Fine Arts (AVU), 1995.

Jaroslav Anděl and Steina Vasulka, National Gallery, Prague, 1996.

Jiří Skála, National Gallery, Prague, 1996.

Michael Bielicky, Ars Electronica Center, Linz, 1996.

Virtual reality apparatus, Ars Electronica Center, Linz, 1996.

Jaroslav Borovička and Michael Bielicky, Düsseldorf, 1996.

Jennifer Miller and Cathy Weiss, Prague, 1996.

Zdeněk Sýkora, Peter Bielicky, and Fredrich Cantor, restaurant, 1996.

David Larcher, European Media Art Festival, Osnabrück, 1988.

Fredrich Cantor and Michael Bielicky, Prague, 1998.

Fredrich Cantor (photographer), unknown person, Kamila Richterova, and Michael Bielicky, Villa Richter, Prague, 1998.

Oleksandr Roytdurd, Henry Zemel, and Ira Dratva, New York, 1998.

Michael Bielicky and Jeffrey Shaw, inside the blue screen of *Delvaux's Dream*, ZKM | Karlsruhe, 1999.

Lucia de Leon, Michael Bielicky, Miloš Vojtěchovský, unknown person, Konstantyn Akynša, and unknown person, Kiev, 1999.

Woody Vasulka and Karel Vachek, Film and TV School of the Academy of Performing Arts, Prague, 2000.

Steina and Woody Vasulka, and unknown person, New Media Atelier, Prague Academy of Fine Arts, 2000.

Steina Vasulka, New Media Atelier, Prague Academy of Fine Arts, 2000.

Adam Michnik, Konstantyn Akynša, and Michael Bielicky, Barcelona, 2002.

Unknown person, Bernd Witte, Konstantyn Akynša, unknown person and Michael Bielicky, Barcelona, 2002.

Peter Weibel, Boris Groys, Konstantyn Akynša, and Natasha Groys, on the train, 2002.

Unknown person, Peter Weibel, and Stéphane Hessel, Portbou, 2002.

Stéphane Hessel, Konstantyn Akynša, and unknown person, University of Barcelona, 2002.

Woody Vasulka, Espace Electra, Paris, 2002.

Maxim Biller, Michael Bielicky, and Peter Green, Saint Ivan's Cave, 2002.

Jeffrey Shaw and Peter Weibel, ZKM | Karlsruhe, 2003.

Jean Baudrillard and Peter Weibel, ZKM | Karlsruhe, 2004.

Jean Baudrillard, ZKM | Karlsruhe, 2004.

Peter Bielicky, Zdeněk Sýkora, and Michael Bielicky, Prague, 2004.

Kamila B. Richter and Maxim Biller, Brandenburg Gate, Berlin, 2005.

Lev Manovich, South Bohemia, Czech Republic, 2005.

Maxim Biller and Kamila B. Richter, Berlin, 2005.

Peter Sloterdijk, introductory speech for Michael Bielicky, Karlsruhe University of Arts and Design (HfG), 2006.

Enrique Rivera, Roy Ascott, and Woody Vasulka, Prague Townhall, 2007.

Kamila B. Richter, Herbert W. Franke, and Woody Vasulka, New City Hall, Prague, 2007.

Michael Bielicky and Herbert W. Franke, New City Hall Prague, 2007.

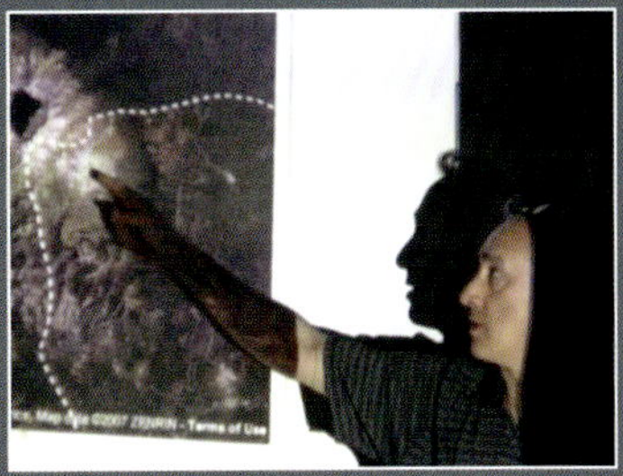
David Blair, Karlsruhe University of Arts and Design (HfG), 2007.

David Blair, Woody Vasulka, and Steina Vasulka, Karlsruhe University of Arts and Design (HfG), 2007.

Gerald O'Grady, ZKM | Karlsruhe, 2007.

Gideon Bachmann, Karlsruhe, 2007.

Michael Bielicky, Woody Vasulka, and Tomas Ruler, Karlsruhe, 2007.

Michael Bielicky, Jeffrey Shaw, Stephan Doesinger, and Norman M. Klein, ZKM | Karlsruhe, 2007.

Michael Bielicky and Lev Manovich, ZKM | Karlsruhe, 2007.

Norman M. Klein, Lev Manovich and Sabine Himmelsbach, ZKM | Karlsruhe, 2007.

Victor Flusser, Edith Flusser, Mischa Flusser, unknown persons, and Louis Bec, Prague Townhall, 2007.

Arnold Dreyblatt, Karlsruhe University of Arts and Design (HfG), 2007.

Christophe Charles, Karlsruhe University of Arts and Design (HfG), 2007.

Maxim Biller and Michael Bielicky, Karlsruhe, 2007.

Mel Alexenberg, lecture, Karlsruhe University of Arts and Design (HfG), 2007.

Mel Alexenberg, lecture, ZKM | Karlsruhe, 2007.

Michael Bielicky, Barbara London, and Henry Zemel, Karlsruhe, 2007.

Michael Bielicky, Steina Vasulka, Woody Vasulka, Tony Conrad, and Margit Rosen, Karlsruhe University of Arts and Design (HfG), Karlsruhe, 2007.

Norman M. Klein and Peter Weibel, ZKM | Karlsruhe, 2007.

Tony Conrad and Steina Vasulka, Karlsruhe, 2007.

Unknown person, Woody Vasulka, Don Foresta, Hans H. Diebner, and Keiko Courdy, Prague, 2007.

Lothar Späth, unknown person, ZKM | Karlsruhe, 2008.

Dirk Reinbold, Kamila B. Richter, Andreas Siewerdt, Peter Weibel, and Michael Bielicky, Bienal Internacional de Arte Contemporáneo de Sevilla, 2008.

Peter Weibel and Paul DeMarinis, Bienal Internacional de Arte Contemporáneo de Sevilla, Sevilla, 2008.

Henry Zemel and Stephan Doesinger, Karlsruhe University of Arts and Design (HfG), 2008.

Nira Pereg, Mel Alexenberg, and Kamila B. Richter, Karlsruhe, 2008.

Phill Niblock, Karlsruhe University of Arts and Design (HfG), 2008.

Susanne Widl, unknown person, Steina Vasulka, and Michael Bielicky, Bienal Internacional de Arte Contemporáneo de Sevilla, 2008.

Won-il Rhee and Mel Alexenberg, ZKM | Karlsruhe, 2008.

Boris Groys and unknown person, Karlsruhe University of Arts and Design (HfG), Karlsruhe, 2009.

Michael Bielicky, Forum on Sustainable Development, Wuhan 2009.

Jeffrey Shaw and Michael Bielicky, ZKM | Karlsruhe, 2009.

Kamila B. Richter and Won-il Rhee, Songdo International City, Incheon Meropolitan City, Korea, 2009.

Michael Bielicky and Kamila B. Richter, Wuhan, 2009.

Michael Bielicky and Norman M. Klein, Hollywood, Los Angeles, 2009.

Peter Weibel, Robert Wilson, and Vadim Fiškin, ZKM | Karlsruhe, 2010.

Robert Wilson, ZKM | Karlsruhe, 2010.

Robert Wilson, Won-il Rhee, and Kamila B. Richter, ZKM | Karlsruhe, 2010.

Won-il Rhee, Andreas Beitin, Peter Weibel, Michael Bielicky, Robert Wilson, and Vadim Fiškin, ZKM | Karlsruhe, 2010.

Margo Bistis, Mel Alexenberg, Norman M. Klein, Adam Rafinski, Michael Bielicky, Kamila B. Richter, Timothy Druckrey, Jens Stober, and Michail Rybakov, Karlsruhe, 2010.

Wulf Herzogenrath and Shigeko Kubota, Museum Kunstpalast, Düsseldorf, 2010.

Hans Belting and Peter Weibel, Médiathèque André Malraux, Strasbourg, 2011.

Elisabeth Walther-Bense, unknown person, Hiroshi Kawano, and unknown person, ZKM | Karlsruhe, 2011.

Hiroshi Kawano and Peter Weibel, ZKM | Karlsruhe, 2011.

Peter Weibel and Joseph Bachstein, 4th Moscow Biennale, Moscow, 2011.

Peter Weibel and Kamila B. Richter, Universalmuseum Joanneum, Graz, 2011.

Peter Weibel, Gerhard Johann Lischka, Susanne Widl, and Michael Bielicky, Wichtrach/Bern, 2011.

Woody and Steina Vasulka, David Blair, and Michael Bielicky, Karlsruhe, 2011.

Michael Bielicky and Frieder Nake, ZKM | Karlsruhe, 2011.

Gerald O'Grady, Karlsruhe University of Arts and Design (HfG), 2011.

Gideon Bachmann, unknown person, Kamila B. Richter, Mel Alexenberg, and Nira Pereg, Karlsruhe, 2011.

Mel Alexenberg and Gerald O'Grady, Karlsruhe University of Arts and Design (HfG), 2011.

Michael Bielicky, Gerald O'Grady and Steina Vasulka, Karlsruhe University of Arts and Design (HfG), 2011.

Michael Bielicky, Isaac Julien, Armin Linke, and Peter Weibel, Moscow, 2011.

Michael Bielicky, Steina Vasulka, Mel Alexenberg, and Woody Vasulka, Karlsruhe University of Arts and Design (HfG), 2011.

Péter Vrana, unknown person, Woody Vasulka, and Michael Bielicky, Prague, 2011.

David Amram, Teri C. McLuhan, and Michael Bielicky, ZKM | Karlsruhe, 2012.

Gerd Stern and Michael Bielicky, Karlsruhe, 2012.

Peter Sloterdijk and Bazon Brock, Karlsruhe University of Arts and Design (HfG), 2012.

Peter Weibel, Teri C. McLuhan, David Amram, and Gerd Stern, ZKM | Karlsruhe, 2012.

Gerd Stern, New Jersey, USA, 2012.

Manfred Wolff-Plottegg, Michael Bielicky, and Stephan Templ, Vienna Künstlerhaus, 2012.

Peter Weibel and Hans Belting, ZKM | Karlsruhe, 2012.

Michael Bielicky and Karel Malich, Prague, 2013.

Peter Sloterdijk, Michael Bielicky, and Peter Weibel, Karlsruhe, 2013.

Jean-Jacques Lebel and Ira Schneider, ZKM | Karlsruhe, 2014.

Jean-Jacques Lebel, Jonas Mekas, an Gideon Bachmann, Karlsruhe, 2014.

Jonas Mekas, Gideon Bachmann, and Egon Bunne, ZKM | Karlsruhe, 2014.

Jean-Jacques Lebel, unknown persons, Jonas Mekas, Michael Bielicky, and Gideon Bachmann, Karlsruhe, 2014.

Michael Bielicky, Norman M. Klein, and Mel Alexenberg, Karlsruhe University of Arts and Design (HfG), 2014.

Michael Bielicky, Norman M. Klein, and Mel Alexenberg, Karlsruhe University of Arts and Design (HfG), 2014.

Michael Bielicky, Joseph Cohen, Peter Sloterdijk, and Peter Weibel, Karlsruhe, 2014.

Peter Weibel and Noam Chomsky, ZKM | Karlsruhe, 2014.

Peter Weibel, Joseph Cohen, and Antonio Negri, ZKM | Karlsruhe, 2015.

Antonio Negri, ZKM | Karlsruhe, 2015.

Saskia Sassen, ZKM | Karlsruhe, 2015.

Pavel Smetana, Louis Bec, Michael Bielicky, and Andreas Ströhl, ZKM | Karlsruhe, 2015.

Michael Bielicky and Louis Bec, ZKM | Karlsruhe, 2015.

George Legrady, Timothy Druckrey, and Gerald O'Grady, ZKM | Karlsruhe, 2015.

Gideon Bachmann, Michael Bielicky, unknown persons, and Gerd Stern, ZKM | Karlsruhe, 2015.

Ingo Günther and Elisabeth Klotz, ZKM | Karlsruhe, 2015.

Margo Bistis, Norman M. Klein, Alice Cavoukdjian dite Galli, and Kamila B. Richter, Karlsruhe, 2015.

Michael Bielicky, DJ Spooky (Paul Dennis Miller), and Peter Weibel, ZKM | Karlsruhe, 2015.

Peter Weibel, Marianne Milani, and Gerhard Johann Lischka infront of Erwin Wurm's *Truck*, 2006/11, Karlsruhe, 2015.

Peter Weibel and Zdeněk Sklenář, ZKM | Karlsruhe, 2015.

Peter Weibel, Jiří Ševčík, and Zdeněk Sklenář, Prague, 2016.

Woody Vasulka and Zdeněk Sklenář, Prague, 2016.

Peter Sloterdijk, Beatrice Sloterdijk, Monika Theilmann, Martina Kaltenbrunner, and Siegfried Zielinski, Karlsruhe University of Arts and Design (HFG), 2016.

Peter Weibel, ZKM | Karlsruhe, 2016.

Milan Grygar, Zdeněk Sklenář, Noemi Smolik, Kamila B. Richter, and Pavel Cink, ZKM | Karlsruhe, 2016.

Jana Chytilová, Michael Bielicky, Markus Lüpertz, and Peter Weibel, ZKM | Karlsruhe, 2017.

Peter Weibel, Markus Lüpertz, and Michael Bielicky, ZKM | Karlsruhe, 2017.

Zdeněk Sklenář, Kamila B. Richter, Jana Chytilová, Michael Bielicky, Miroslav Vránek, Galleria Continua, Havana, 2017.

Ernesto Guevara and Michael Bielicky, Havana, Cuba, 2017.

Norman M. Klein, Peter Weibel, and Michael Bielicky, ZKM | Karlsruhe, 2017.

Frieder Nake and Michael Bielicky, ZKM | Karlsruhe, 2018.

Jorge Fernández Torres and Michael Bielicky, Prague, 2018.

Maxim Biller and Michael Bielicky, Heidelberg, 2018.

Michael Bielicky, Peter Weibel, and Frieder Nake, ZKM | Karlsruhe, 2018.

Peter Sloterdijk, Michael Bielicky, and Peter Weibel, Karlsruhe, 2018.

Peter Weibel, Herbert W. Franke, and Siegfried Zielinski, ZKM | Karlsruhe, 2018.

Peter Weibel and Siegfried Zielinski, École polytechnique fédérale de Lausanne, 2018.

Michael Bielicky, ZKM | Karlsruhe, 2019.

Zdeněk Sklenář, Jiří Fajt, and Peter Weibel, ZKM | Karlsruhe, 2019.

Exhibition banner for the exhibition *Michael Bielicky. Perpetuum Mobile*, ZKM | Karlsruhe, 2019.

Unknown person, Bruno Latour, Peter Weibel, Michael Bielicky, and unknown person, ZKM | Karlsruhe, 2019.

Laurie Anderson and Michael Bielicky, Karlsruhe, 2019.

Phill Niblock, Peter Weibel, and Michael Bielicky, ZKM | Karlsruhe, 2004.

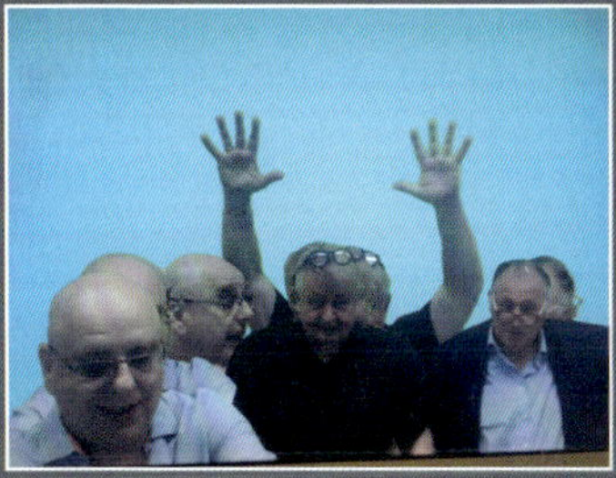

Michael Bielicky, Jan Světlík, and Peter Weibel, ZKM | Karlsruhe, 2019.

Michael Bielicky, Peter Weibel, and Peter Sloterdijk, ZKM | Karlsruhe, 2019.

Michael Bielicky, Peter Weibel, and Peter Sloterdijk, Karlsruhe, 2020.

Jan Svetlik and Peter Weibel, Karlsruhe, 2021

Pavlina Pudil and Petr Pudil, Karlsruhe, 2021

Peter Weibel, Michael Bielicky, Peter Sloterdijk, Baden Baden, 2022

DE MAATSCHAPPIJ VOOR OUDE EN NIEUWE MEDIA
SOCIETY FOR OLD AND NEW MEDIA
c/o Kleine Gartmanplantsoen 10, 1017 RR Amsterdam, The Netherlands
tel: +31-20-6233673, fax: +31-20-6384489, e-mail: society@dds.nl
terminal
dwlab
email: studio@terminal.cz
www.dlab.terminal.cz
web design studio
NETWORK!
RÜDIGER LIEDTKE
NATIONAL MUSEUM OF FINE ARTS
Adrian Bartolo
Assistant Curator
National Museum of Fine Arts
South Street, Valletta VLT 11
Malta
Tel: 356 - 233034
Fax: 356 - 239915
Timothy Druckrey
269 Union Street #2L
Brooklyn, New York 11231
718 237 9457
druckrey@interport.net
Rodney Wilson
14 Great Peter Street
London SW1P 3NQ
THE ARTS COUNCIL OF ENGLAND
EXPERIMENTAL INTERMEDIA
224 Centre Street New York N Y 10013
212 431 5127, 212 431 6430, Fax 212 431 4486
El v.z.w. Gent, Sassekaai 45, B 9000 Gent Belgium
pniblock@compuserve.com
Phill Niblock, Artist / Director
Frank Kunkel
http://www.icf.de
Maurice BENAYOUN
Z.A PRODUCTION
GALLERY DIRECTOR - PETER RÓNAI
ART COUNSELLOR - MILAN ADAMČIAK
EXPERT - JÚLIUS KOLLER
FLUX GALLERY
address: Hviezdna 5
82106 BRATISLAVA
CZECHOSLOVAKIA
88 Greenwood Road, London E8 1NE, UK
http://www.artonline.co.uk/artonline/faure.htm
Thomas Feibel
Journalist
TERMINALBAR
Internet Café s.r.o.
John-D.G. Hawkes
Ron Barack
Siemens Kultur Programm
Stefan Iglhaut
CYPRUS THEATRE ORGANISATION
Andy Bargilly
FRED FOREST
Université Nice Sophia Antipolis
Artiste-Professeur Titulaire
Christophe F. Maire
chief financial officer
business development
Velvet
Michael Wayne
Fredy CANTOR
edelmistmacher
Am Wald 44A 40667 Meerbusch
Tel: 02132 / 4005 Fax: 02132 / 6402
SiliconGraphics
Ivan Paderta
NAN HOOVER
M.V.B. BASTIAANSESTR. 75
1054 RT AMSTERDAM NEDERLAND
TEL: 31.20-6162397
FAX: 31.20-6890237
smikami@bionet.org
Ma'ariv Daily Newspaper
DAVID GORDON
Computer & Communications Editor
P.O.B. 20010 TEL AVIV 61200 ISRAEL
Godfrey Pye
chief executive officer
Mgr.Tomáš Fassati
http://www.ecn.cz/osf/scca/cz/kalendar/gvuben.htm
VIRTUAL
Stefania Garassini
VSTUPENKA
Peter Callas
c/o ZKM
Institut für Bildmedien
Gartenstr. 71
76049 Karlsruhe, Germany
name.space
a pgMedia company
11 east 4th street 2f new york, ny 10003 (212) 6774080
SEOS
Displays Limited
Sarah Minett
Corporate Development Manager
Christa SOMMERER
ATR Advanced Telecommunications Research Institute International
Invited Researcher & Artist
2-2 Hikaridai, Seika-cho, Soraku-gun, 619-02 Kyoto, Japan
E-mail: christa@hipatr.co.jp
Nesys Licht Systeme
für Foto, Film, TV und Bühne
Hartmut Schadt
Technische Leitung
Schadt & Co. oHG
Kirchplatz 35
82538 Geretsried
SOROS CENTER FOR CONTEMPORARY ARTS-SLOVAKIA
Mária Hlavajová
Director
Riečna 2, 811 02 Bratislava, Slovakia
E-mail: hlavajova@scca.sanet.sk
AGENTURA PP
penzijní připojištění
Georg Scalé
Andreas Braun
Kunsthistoriker
Schriftsteller
Brunnerstraße 41
80804 München
Telefon 089 / 300 99 11
ROBERT HORVITZ
International Coordinator
INTERNET PROGRAM
Open Society Institute
Motokov Building, Rm. 506
Na Strzi 63
140 62 Prague 4
Czech Republic
e-mail: HORVITZR@OMRI.CZ
VIRTUAL REALITY ASSOCIATION
CZECH REPUBLIC
Lubor Benda
research & development
MaXimac
V2_Organisatie
Andreas Broeckmann
Ing. Michal Cílek
sales manager
Expert Service s.r.o.
Alias
wavefront
Bart Nel
Regional Sales Manager
LES MUSÉES DE LA VILLE DE STRASBOURG
Friedemann Malsch
Chargé des collections contemporaines
au Musée d'Art Moderne et Contemporain
WERKSTATT KOLLERSCHLAG
HEINZ BAUMÜLLER

Collage of business cards Michael Bielicky collected over the years.

Lost, 2017, data-driven installation. Installation views, Centro de Arte Contemporáneo Wifredo Lam, Havana, 2017.

Lost in Cuba: Michael Bielicky and Kamila B. Richter

Jorge A. Fernández Torres

One of the most notable exhibitions to have taken place in Cuba in the last few years was, without a doubt, *Lost* by Michael Bielicky and Kamila B. Richter at the Centro de Arte Contemporáneo Wifredo Lam in Havana in 2017. The exhibition was presented in a country in which internet access still remains a limiting factor, a country where change runs through narrow streets that gradually try to approximate themselves to broad information highways. In 2015, right before the closing night of the Havana Biennial, the first public zones with Wi-Fi access – which could be used by all Cubans – were set up. From the position of the director and the leading curator, I knew that this situation could be the main issue for consideration when hosting the next year's Biennial. Experiments are currently being conducted in Cuba with various methods of accessing the *network of networks* via mobile phones. In this context, Peter Sloterdijk tells us that in order to understand negation, we must not only see the Hegelian fury of destruction, but also the fury of absence and the fury of escape and breakaway.

The thoughts of this German philosopher encourage us to contemplate the opposites in our reality. On one hand, many of those who come to Cuba from various parts of the world perceive the disconnection from the internet as creating a certain form of emptiness, an oppressive freezing of the virtual world. Time does not only occur in the concepts of *chronos*, *kairos*, or the one that we know exists at the speed of light; but it also manifests itself in a state of being without communication, in an isolation that generates a contrast to stress, and an isolation that turns into resignation and at the same time perversion due to experiencing the risk of temporary absence from the usual information environment.

Cubans who live their everyday life on the island, however, have adopted an entirely different attitude. The lack of internet access has given rise to different constructs here. Virtuality itself finds analog ways of circulating information through micro-environments and micro-communities. This offline intertwining creates new forms of association with characteristics similar to those that exist in the online world. This very fact that was the main topic of the latest Havana Biennial, which incorporated a certain form of ethics and relations between groups of videogame players, who created their own messenger. Some of the presented works were also a part of the so-called *Paquete Semanal* ["weekly packet"], which is a certain form of a virtual market and a means to commercialize mostly media content in the form of a USB device, which exists thanks to clandestine downloads from the internet. These downloads take place in workplaces that have the privilege of a broadband connection, or through satellite antennas that transfer large amounts of audiovisual content from places where data volumes exceeding one terabyte a week get downloaded for one reason or another.

Paquete Semanal stopped being a mere form of entertainment: it became a social phenomenon. Its community is created as a chain on multiple levels, where each of them fulfills certain functions. The first one, which is dedicated to the creation of matrixes, are people who structure the entire distribution process and design the contents. Large distributors then play the part of agencies that ensure the availability of *Paquete Semanal* in each of the country's provinces. By purchasing the product, consumers define the wide range of prices that are in line with a specific number of gigabytes they receive for their storage devices. Then there are also points of sale, which set up the payment systems and determine the supply and demand dynamics as well as the relations between the production, distribution and consumers. The final aspect worth mentioning is the possibility of renting data storage devices, and the overall method in which this system finds mechanisms to adapt to the material conditions of a clientele coming from various social classes.

Studies on how this entire process works have already been conducted in the environment of Cuban society. The content includes a wide range of media, in which audiovisual content plays the main role. We can find *telenovelas*, documents on science and technology, sports, movies of all genres, reality shows, advertisements by private companies and sections dedicated to art. These are promoted by young Cuban artists, as was the case a few years ago with Nestor Siré.

There are many causes behind the development of this phenomenon, among which are the objective difficulties with a large-scale installation of the internet at a required speed; the low attractiveness of television broadcasting for a population consisting of various age groups; and the taste of intellectual elites changing over time. It is these intellectual elites that, in some cases, take part in managing the content that has subsequent influence on forming primarily the youngest generation's taste. More pointedly in the abovementioned causes is the low credibility of informative programs that official channels broadcast. *Paquete Semanal* finds itself in a legal limbo – it is tolerated, but has no legal recognition.

An exhibition such as *Lost* by Bielicky and Richter is interesting because even though it was conceived in a different environment, it takes on a new meaning in Cuba. The context of the Cuban environment gives it new subject matter, enriches it, and transfers its successes and frustrations onto it. Cuba is a place of significant historical encounters, a place defined by the dispute and debate between being and the duty of being. The Cuban Revolution changed the history of the country and created a system of social equality, which has worked and is able to maintain the minimal guarantees for survival; however, there is a demand and scope of needs whereby satisfaction, for one reason or another, lags behind the expectations of the majority of the Cuban population. This situation has led to a necessary change in mentality: a step, which, to quote José Martí, a national hero of the island, must be taken "by everyone and for the good of everyone."[1]

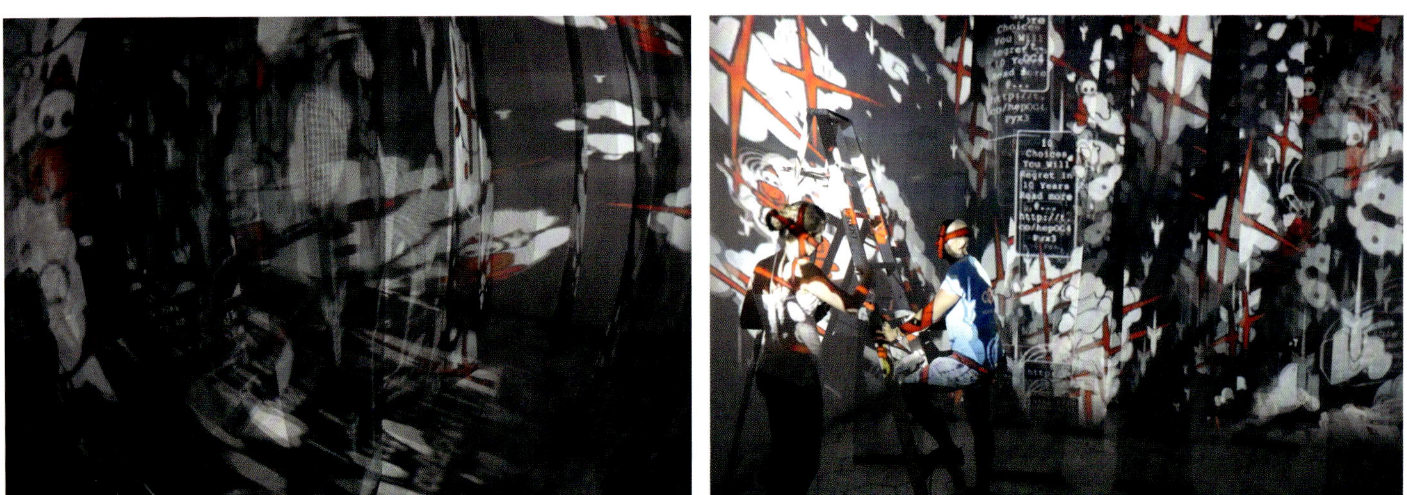

Lost, 2017, data-driven installation. Installation view, Centro de Arte Contemporáneo Wifredo Lam, Havana, 2017.

Lost, 2017, data-driven installation. Installation view, Centro de Arte Contemporáneo Wifredo Lam, Havana, 2017.

Lost manages to touch the Nirvana we wish to find. The work does not make use of technology in a particularly mesmerizing way, but it enters the apertures of social psychology that does not hide its platforms. There is an interchange that points to the humanity of what is happening. In terms of Michel Foucault's methodology, *Paquete Semanal* is not a dystopian space, but rather a heterotopic one. Society weaves its nets thanks to differences, thereby creating new spheres of influence in which experimental novelty and disagreement with the establishment find refuge. Lack makes way for a room to escape here, since new types of knowledge and skills arise and inspire each other within its scope. Being lost means, besides other things, to learn to prosper on the edge. It is a form of coexisting at the boundary of the possible, based on determining the possibility of going beyond it.

In his book, *New Essays on Human Understanding* (written in 1704 and first published in French language in 1765)[2], Gottfried Wilhelm Leibniz expands on the term apperception. Apperception takes place because there is consciousness of a perception that, on a spiritual level, simultaneously leads to reflection of a broader range. We are not able to perceive everything that is happening at the same time in every moment of our existence, which, however, does not lead to the deterioration of our spiritual consciousness. Verification of existence does not have to be proven on the level of perception. This type of thinking, based on the analyses conducted in the area of infinitesimal calculus, led the German philosopher to an ideological separation from his French followers. Leibniz considered it to be a useful method even though we cannot rationalize the discovery of this scope. The difference between Leibniz and John Locke then lies in Leibniz's precise definition of

Havana, Cuba, 2017.

Centro de Arte Contemporáneo Wifredo Lam, facade and exhibition poster, Havana, 2017.

Lost Objects, 2015, data-driven immersive postminimalist opera. Photographs of the performance at the National Theatre, Prague, 2015.

the fact that perception is not a product of divine guidance, since perception belongs to us, and with regard to physical emotions and affective character, we act with full autonomy.

On the other hand, current phenomenological studies define the discipline itself as the approach to the essence, as behavior that goes further than just the facts from the studies of humans and the world. It is based on the assumption that the world is always here. When looking for these elementary rules, the aim is to find what the foundation of philosophy is. For Edmund Husserl, it was essential to define a doctrine of sense, which was simultaneously the structure of existence. He calls it the genesis of sense, which is the last instance to show us what the message of the doctrine is. All confrontations, coincidental or not, unite in a convergence with reason. There is an effort to reduce history to a single drama, which renders the world confined to sense, and everything that is expressible must obtain its name in history. These arguments form the basis on which Maurice Merleau-Ponty credits phenomenology with the unification of subjectivism and objectivism into one ideology that includes the world or rationality. And rationality can be measured by the degree of experience in which it manifests itself.

None of these philosophers could have imagined the technological progress of the last few years. The dominance of visuality has overshadowed the traditional forms of expression. The user base of social networks switches from Facebook to Twitter, only to end up using the influence of Instagram. Extensive texts are reduced to a few characters, and visual depiction gains unprecedented autonomy. It is a revolution that requires new epistemological analyses, in which we can also find patterns of philosophical thought from Arthur Schopenhauer's work, in which he claims: "Of all the senses, that of sight is capable of the most delicate and diverse impressions from without, yet in itself it can give only sensation which first becomes intuitive perception through the application of the understanding to it. If anyone standing before a beautiful landscape could for a moment be deprived of all understanding, then for him nothing of the whole view would be left but the sensation of a very manifold affection of his retina, resembling the many blobs of different colours on an artist's palette. These are, so to speak, the raw material from which just a moment previously his understanding created that intuitive perception."[3] Johann Wolfgang von Goethe would add from his point of view that a visual image is not separate from its observer. Quite to the contrary, an image sinks into the personality of its observer and surrounds it.[4]

The fact that art can exist on the internet in the same environment as its audience leads to it leaving the traditional space and changes the dynamics of its consumption. It is impossible to calculate the number of internauts, who play the part of the receivers and are already fiefs, influential entities within which they become nontransferable among each other. The reception of art simultaneously leads to the creative process itself being influenced, which thereby takes the form of permanent transformation. This process related to cultural consumption was described by Néstor García Canclini as shared creation and led him to speak of the emergence of the so-called prosumers.[5]

With *Lost,* Bielicky and Richter comment on alienation and distraction in the expansion of late modernity in which we find ourselves. In his reflections on the gaps between impressionism and expressionism, Hermann Bahr stated that it is necessary to find a middle ground between both of these main artistic avant-garde movements of the twentieth century. From the point of view of this Viennese writer from the period around 1900, it was necessary to achieve a comprehensive way of seeing that would not violate nature through human existence, or human beings through nature. To Bahr, the direction of each artist depended on their education via these correlations.[6] Today's debate is not about the illustration of what is human and what is natural, but about the technological mediation of artefacts, which together allow for the same space to be shared between that which is artificial and that which is organic.

We are unable to break away from our computers, tablets, and mobile phones. They are the pillars upon which we construct our cosmo-vision of the world. There is a certain type of faith and religiosity that affects each decision or behavior due to which we cannot get by without these devices. Each activity in our life becomes reduced to one application. We thereby create a new unity of consciousness, which, obviously, has exceeded the scope that Leibniz imagined. The occurrence of new realities also means the emergence of experiences in which myths do not have to be supported by rituals, as they are carried over as one inseparable unit. The psychological and gnoseological mechanisms, apparatuses, and materials we consult and the actions we perform all come together in one all-encompassing unit. The fury of absence and escape creates a full circle, even though it might appear as an illusion in which a human stands in front of something seemingly endless. This is where despair stems from in *Lost*, in which characters – created with the help of the archetypal basis of pictograms – come and go, and where seriality, modern

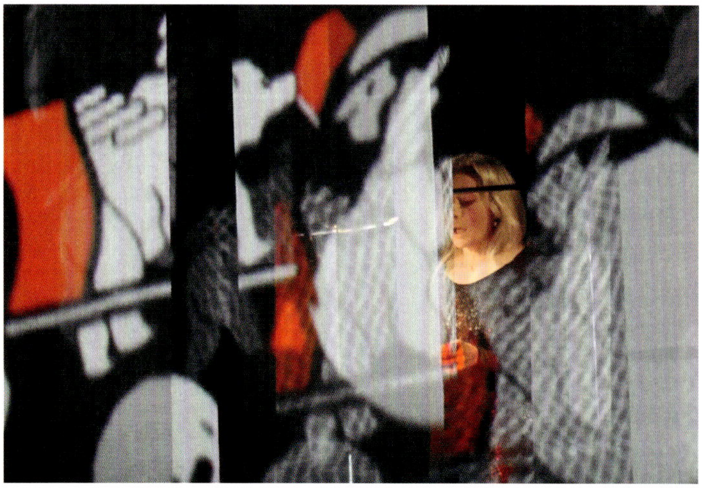

Lost Objects, 2015, data-driven immersive postminimalist opera. Photographs of the performance at the National Theatre, Prague, 2015.

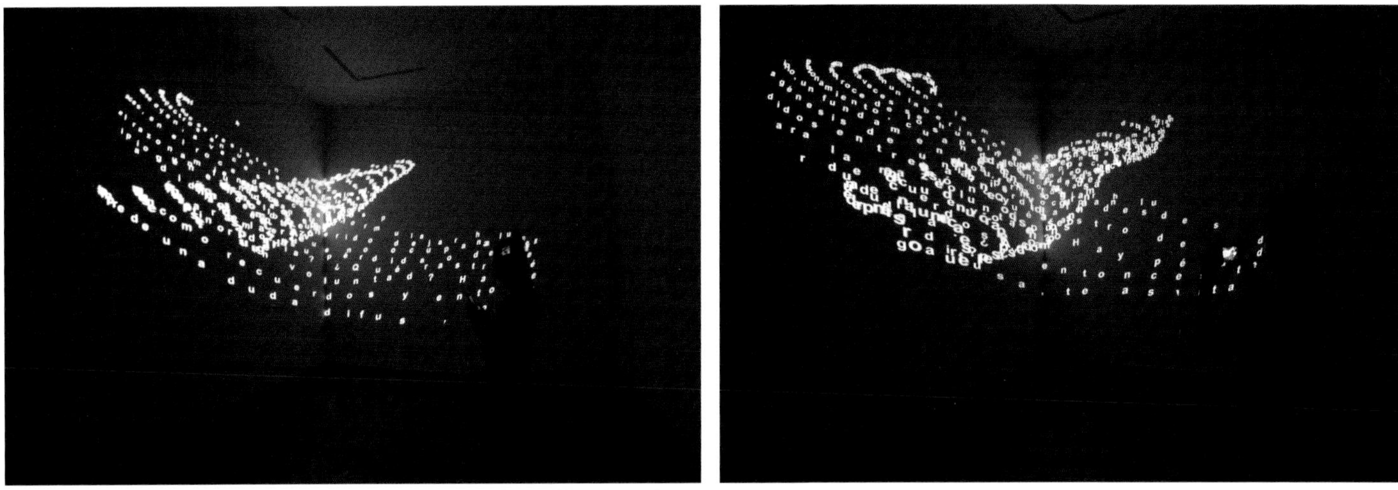

Data Dybbuk, 2015, data-driven installation. Installation views, Centro de Arte Contemporáneo Wifredo Lam, Havana, 2017.

appliances, and current artefacts play the role of actors captured by tragedy surrounding us on all sides.

When observing the infinity of paths that Bielicky and Richter open to us in *Lost*, I am still astonished by Paul Virilio's somewhat caustic statement. This thinker does not see any difference between secular and spiritual art, but instead sees the profanation of its forms over the course of the twentieth century. Virilio introduces one of his criticisms, the main question of which is the insignificance or pertinence of contemporary art, with a passion typical of his texts: "A contemporary art, yes, but contemporary with what?"[7]

Based on these assumptions, Virilio believes that the Nazis lost the war, but achieved peace and foresaw the aesthetics of disappearance as something that exists along with the present. This apocalyptic view persists in all of the forms of existence of all individuals in the present-day world. The need for new aesthetic points of view and the cancellation of miscellaneous approximations of humanism forces us to ponder the difficulties of the present day. And this is the reason why *Lost* presents itself as emptiness, or as a compass that does not display possible directions of memory because it is fragmented.

The main work that lends the name to Bielicky and Richter's entire exhibition in the Centro de Arte Contemporáneo Wifredo Lam in Havana has its predecessor in an opera entitled *Lost Objects*, which had its premiere on December 17, 2015 in the National Theatre in Prague, under the direction of both artists. The music for a soprano, two countertenors, a mixed chamber choir, and a baroque orchestra in a fusion with a rock band and DJ, was composed by Michael Gordon, David Lang, and Julia Wolfe. The libretto was written by Deborah Artman and the opera conducted by Petr Kofroň.

As the name *Lost Objects* indicates, the opera deals with lost objects and a crisis of culture that gets drawn into an emptiness of ownership as an intemperance exceeding the substance of the needs themselves. The work is outlined as a post-minimalistic oratorio, however, with a Wagneresque strength, Bachian contrapunto and a modernization of operatic structures, which were achieved by Philip Glass and Robert Wilson in the opera *Einstein on the Beach* (premiered July 25, 1976). Glass and Wilson, together with Lucinda Childs managed to convey in their work the brutality of war, the scars left on our memories by the Holocaust, and the uncertainty of the question of whether we can find ourselves on the edge of a tragedy of such proportions ever again. *Lost Objects* is a work that is no stranger to its time, and which follows a line that is more experimental than the aforementioned operatic one. The main role is assumed by scenography, which is based on a tangle of pictograms; the visibility of voices and music is not particularly enhanced. The images surface from a depth that we cannot see, and which is a sort of crack in the earth's surface where Biblical passages connect with the important figures from the history of humankind, which are remembered with the same veneration as prophets or apostles. This work owes a lot to the *Panopticon* (1791) designed by the English philosopher and social theorist Jeremy Bentham. We get lost, carried away by a spiritual flow, but all our assumed escapes are guarded and punished.

Another piece in the abovementioned exhibition is *Data Dybbuk* (2015). The title comes from an environment of Judaism, indeed, a sphere to which Michael is no stranger, being an artist of Jewish origin. In the interpretation of mythology, *dybbuk* is the embodiment of an evil ghost, which is generally connected with the terms *Gehenna* as hell and *kareth* as the possible reincarnation of a spirit. *Dybbuk* oscillates between the good and the bad, and it is also something to be eradicated. Bielicky and Richter take these routes in the work. By using operating systems for *big data*, they create an alphabetical loop in which we cannot distinguish a longer coherent text. Movement turns into chaos; the viewer gets attacked by it. Typography comes and goes in continuous movement, which evokes the feeling of a new skin in the viewer.

It is like a tattoo that covers everything; as well as the beginning and boundaries of *logos*, it is a statement of volatility during the futile attempts to show a text. We can no longer count on Michel Foucault's statement describing the painting *Las Meninas* (1656) by Diego Velázquez, in which he claims that an image functions like a text and a text like an image.[8] In *Data Dybbuk*, both the text and image have disappeared – they disperse in space where meaning is not what matters. What matters is the statement that it is not possible to grasp the boundlessness of its expansion. Bielicky and Richter know that language is present here, but that any word is circumstantial. The issue is in what way abstraction is used in order to be on a denotative and demonstrative level, on which, as was demonstrated very well by Husserl and Merleau-Ponty, it forces us to name.

Dybbuk, in Bielicky and Richter's version, is that which completely surrounds and encircles us: how to generate new words, how to rediscover communication at a time when we are swamped with immediacy, an avalanche of messages that we cannot react to. An evil spirit becomes an everyday part of life, it organizes our activities and rejoices maliciously in our behavior. This work appeals to us, whether it should happen in a latent or a clearly manifested way, to achieve introspection that would make us reconsider our individual thinking, and encourages us to sharpen our gaze with the aim of finding the true script, which might be yet to come.

The cycle of works in the exhibition *Lost* is concluded by *Garden of Error and Decay* (2017), which makes use of Donald Trump's tweets in terms of content. In a cynical way, Bielicky and Richter create a mixed environment here, which is a hybrid between the kindness of Asian cultures and the anarchy and disorder of the financial and political lobbies of the Western world. The Trump phenomenon has already become an ecstasy of power, resembling a reality show or some sort of a performance. Not a single US President in recent years could imagine a situation in which Trump would achieve great popularity, while having a substantial part of the media against him. Neither could anybody have imagined that the leading representative of present-day North America would, without any hesitation, support immigrant and racial ghettoes as well as misogynistic and xenophobic opinions. It is a situation

The Names, 2018, data-driven installation.
Installation view, ZKM | Karlsruhe, 2018.

which, if we were to view it through the lens of the present day, can appear to us as something that is not yet entirely known. Trump has been in the position of both subject and object on social networks, especially on Twitter. From this position, he is able to generate a theatre of media confrontation that oscillates at the intersection between Samuel Beckett's Theatre of the Absurd and the fabrication of new facts that corresponds with the unpredictable politicization of visuality.

The tweets in *Garden of Error and Decay* are both fictitious and documentary about a development bringing geopolitics into play. Events change into messages displayed in the form of tweets with comments, and pictographic figures roam around like machines controlled by artificial intelligence against the backdrop of a Japanese garden filled with greenery. Many of the depicted pictographic figures are holding mobile phones, which are like oracles leading them to an unknown place. An eye, which can be observed on each of these devices, is like some sort of a selfie pointing to figures that have been deprived of their souls.

This technological monotheism also produces its heroes and its villains. It is as if its creativity relied on the tools that the development of videogames left behind for us as its legacy. Osama bin Laden, Putin or Snowden can become a threat that this entire system, which logically also functions as a chronometer, will live off of. Once again, this is a work by Bielicky and Richer that relies on highly sophisticated algorithms with various options and probabilities that have been studied perfectly and which are not created at random. The spectator must also be a participant in the entire event, but they cannot transform it, since the work retains its autonomy without giving up the ability to draw the audience into what is happening. We are all a part of this mega surveillance, as privacy has never been this external and so easily violable as it is now. Nothing at all stands between what is public and what is private anymore, and the true creators of opinions and political "ecosystems" are therefore nowadays *hackers*. They are a part of today's cyberculture and this might be one of the reasons why they are, along with the new media, the subject of interest for so many artists and theoreticians, including Peter Weibel. In the present day, these people resemble great artists and ancient warriors in certain aspects. The consequences of one cyberattack can be as destructive as a nuclear war.

In 2018, the artistic duo of Bielicky and Richter created a work entitled *The Names* (2018) for one of the exhibitions at the ZKM | Center for Art and Media Karlsruhe called *DIA-LOGOS – Ramon Llull and the Ars Combinatoria*. The light and texts in it create an environment that adds emotion to the exhibition space. The names of gods in monotheistic religions, and including the Arabic and Hebrew languages, levitate, drawn by light. And Bielicky and Richter once again enter into a dialogue with the great thinkers of human history. Ramon Llull was a visionary, whose legacy follows the nature of his manuscripts even 700 years after his death – they are a riddle that we haven't fully solved yet. When it comes to religion, Llull was a layman, who was very close to the Franciscans. According to oral tradition, he passed away in 1316 when returning from Tunisia, disappointed after extensive debates with the Muslims he met there.

His book, *The Book of the Gentile and the Three Wise Men* (1274) is based on a polemic between a pagan, who is a scholar, does not follow any religion, and is convinced that there is nothing else after death, and three other scholars whom he meets when leaving a city full of springs and fruit trees. One of the scholars is a Christian, the second one a Muslim, and the third one a Jew. The polemic between these three highly educated men is of high quality and demonstrates Llull's excellent knowledge of all religions.

Llull is known in wider circles as the founder of the method of the graphic classification of knowledge, in which he unites elements of logic, geometry,

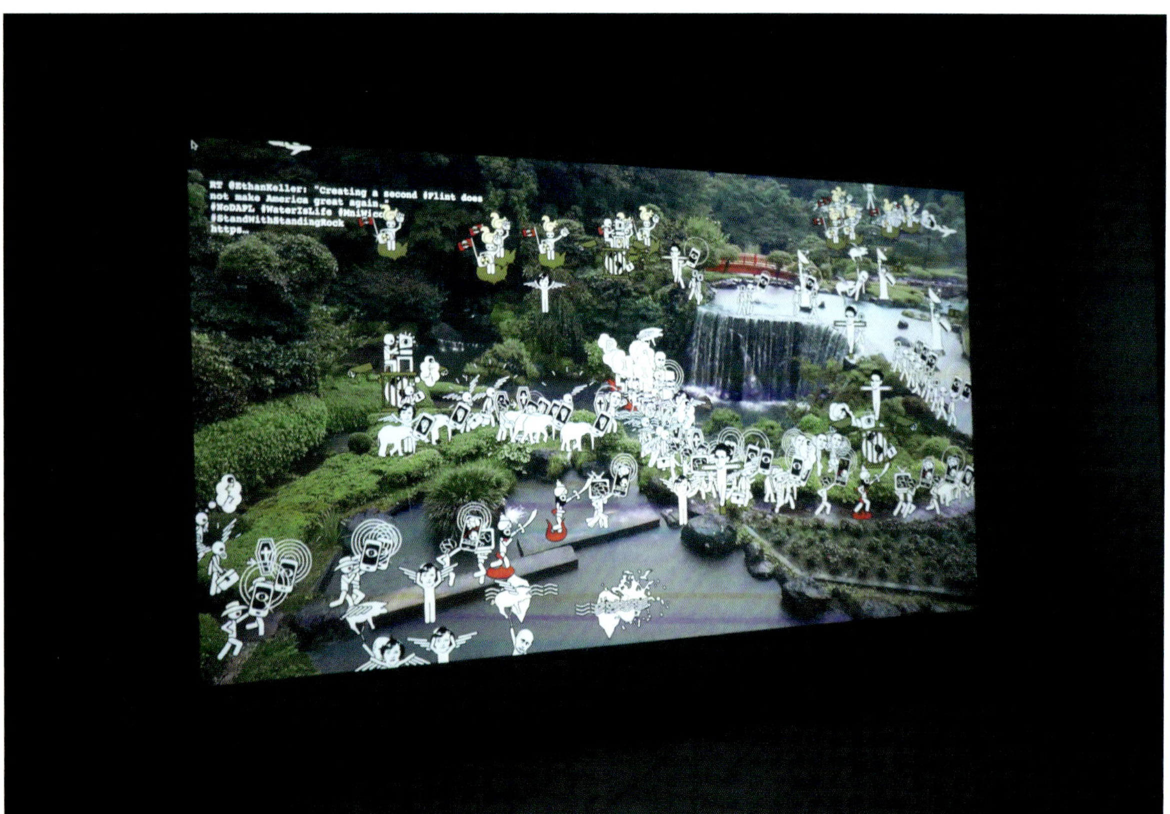

Garden of Error and Decay, 2009–19, data-driven installation.
Installation view, Centro de Arte Contemporáneo Wifredo Lam, Havana, 2017.

universal language, and various thought concepts. His thoughts on the universal language and combinations of expressions later became known as *ars combinatoria*. Llull used research to prove all of his theological philosophies. His research led him to mathematics, set theories, and structures based on algorithmic formulas. He did not abandon his devoutness, and fully devoted himself to a single God in the hands of divine providence. He also wanted faith to find support in educational, holistic, and integrating elements. *The Names* is, without a doubt, Bielicky and Richter's way of paying homage to Llull, a human, who predicted the probability theory in the Middle Ages and who thought in the form of algorithms in order to understand the depth of social systems. According to some experts, we can consider him to be the inspiration behind what we nowadays call the *network of networks*. An institution such as ZKM and a piece of work such as that by Bielicky and Richter could not exist had it not been for Llull.

The Names discusses the events of a single era, when it appeared that the Cold War was over after the fall of the Berlin Wall and the dissolution of the Soviet Union. At the time, Francis Fukuyama wrote his triumphalist book *The End of History and The Last Man*, which was first published in 1989. Seven years later, in 1996, Samuel Huntington's *Clash of Civilizations*, in which the author presents his image of a new map of the world, saw the light of the day. Huntington, a professor of political science at Harvard University provides this very illustrative commentary at the beginning of the book: "In the post-Cold War world flags count and so do other symbols of cultural identity, including crosses, crescents, and even head coverings, because culture counts, and cultural identity is what is most meaningful to most people. People are discovering new but often old identities and marching under new but often old flags which lead to wars with new but often old enemies."[9] He goes on to add: "The central theme of this book is that culture and cultural identities, which at the broadest level are civilization identities, are shaping the patterns of cohesion, disintegration, and conflict in the post-Cold War world."[10]

The concept of civilization as an act and the result of civilizing keep leading us to discussions: Who is the object of civilizing? Who is being civilized and with respect to what? These are questions of a deeply colonizing origin. However, in this context, Huntington's theories helped us meditate on an era that was just beginning and that was not too different to the one in which Llull lived. Demonstrations against the regime of Ben Ali in Tunisia, which started in December 2010 and later turned into a wave of happenings against the governments in Egypt, Yemen, Libya, and Syria, later started to be commonly referred to by certain experts as the *Arab Spring*. And the destabilization of this region is a phenomenon that still continues. The local events are still historically too recent to conduct a deeper analysis of their causes and consequences. However, this is where religious and political aspects as well as domestic interests and the interests of external powers all intersect. Llull could hardly imagine that the last country he visited to debate with Muslims – Tunisia – would set off the most radical political and social upheavals in recent memory.

These are all the things that *The Names* talks about. The way I see it, it functions as a genealogy of power. The predecessor of the State, the forms of control and supervision – constants in Bielicky and Richter's works – all have religion as their starting point.

The leading curator of the Seville Biennial in 2008 was Peter Weibel, who invited Bielicky and Richter to participate. They presented a piece of work

Susana Pilar, Nelson Han, María Teresa Álvarez, Jorge A. Fernández Torres, Kamila B. Richter, Helena Sklenářová, Miroslava Kubíková, and Zdeněk Sklenář (left to right), Centro de Arte Contemporáneo Wifredo Lam, Vernissage, Havana, 2017.

Zdeněk Sklenář and the Cultural Attaché of the German Embassy in Havana, Centro de Arte Contemporáneo Wifredo Lam, vernissage, Havana, 2017.

Centro de Arte Contemporáneo Wifredo Lam, vernissage, Havana, 2017.

Havana, Cuba, 2017.

Havana, Cuba, 2017.

entitled *Columbus 2.0* (2008), which was a system of interactive navigation working with large volumes of information. The visitors could interact with the work through a helm, which worked as a user interface. It is noteworthy that the term navigation, which originates from the ancient times of cartography from a vocabulary that was inherent to sailors and seafaring, also spread to the world of the internet as a term for the facilitation of travelling through all the data that can be found on it. This work also creates a certain blend of analog and digital universes. The internet environment is as opaque as the ocean, and due to its dense information network woven of emails, Twitter, WhatsApp, Facebook, Instagram, and many other services and applications that crush us with the amount of content, it is difficult for us to grasp. It is a statement of the finitude of human existence in contrast with the disproportionate infinity of any learning. Besides, in the context of Seville, this work also attains a special added value, because it is in this city that the General Archive of the Indies is located; it was founded in 1785 by Charles III of Spain and represents the largest existing collection of knowledge about the Spanish administration of the so-called New World. According to certain information, the scope of the archive is over 8 kilometers of documents and 80 million pages. In the case of Cuba, a significant portion of the collective memory from the colonial era is located right here. The documents were brought here by the Spanish after the Spanish-American War in 1898, that is, after the conflict in which Spain lost control over the island and which made way for the intervention by the United States of America.

These connections between the internet *big data* and the abovementioned archived documents lead to the creation of a certain dialogic mutation. Every historical era is in thrall to what it creates on a cultural level and in awe of the countless destinations of its own navigation. Reality becomes a construction and the truth is subjectivized by imaginaries that ceaselessly impose new rules and assign new meanings. If we want to ponder today's Cuba, we must go back to studying its colonial history. In the field of art, it is a period in which there is still a lot left to be discovered.

The chroniclers of this period were the first ones to publish their historical reflections on the native inhabitants. Reality was, thus, not born without bias, but through the first preconceived records in written form. It is now up to us, therefore, to give some thought to the pluralism of the *network of networks* and to a question, which has already been discussed for various reasons – and that first arose in the 1980s – the question of postmodernism. Bielicky and Richter do not reassure us that the direction of our voyage is correct; on the contrary, there is a tsunami that threatens us. We, the Cubans, are very well aware of the metaphorical mystique of Christopher Columbus's quote which he uttered not long before going ashore in Cuba: "[…] heard the bustle of a bird's wings and a fiery bouquet struck the sea."

The piece of work entitled *Garden of Error and Decay* (2010–19) is considered by critics to be comprehensive within the scope of Bielicky and Richter's work. Its various statements could possibly be in close agreement with the thoughts of Edgar Morin from his book *Introduction à la pensée complexe* [Introduction to Complex Thought] (1990). Here, it is necessary to point out some of the questions posed by this author: "Science causes an increasingly greater dominance of verification by means of empirical and logical methods and techniques. Myths and lack of clarity seem to be rejected from the depth of one's soul in the light of Reason, however, omnipresent mistakes, ignorance and blindness progress at the same pace as our cognition."[11] The author then claims that: "The deep cause of error is not error of fact (false perception), or error of logic (incoherence), but rather the way we organize our knowledge into a system of ideas (theorics, ideologies)"[12] and then goes on to add: "I would like to show that these mistakes, ignorances, blindnesses and dangers have a common nature that results from a limited way of organizing knowledge, when it is impossible to identify and understand the complexity of reality."[13]

Garden of Error and Decay was the work through which Bielicky and Richter presented themselves at the 11th Havana Biennial in 2012. The work was included in the *Open Score* project (2013) at USF Contemporary Art Museum in Tampa, Florida, whose curators were Luis Gómez and Dannys Montes de Oca, and which was the collective exhibition of the curators of that year's Biennial. It was necessary for us to show the relationship between art and technologies in a country where a global matter becomes an act of resistance and social challenge. When choosing the method of presenting these ideas, they could not be limited to a hedonistic reflection of the environment; it was necessary to start working at the semantic level that uncovers the opposites between both low and high technology.

This work by Bielicky and Richter creates an illusion that makes the spectator feel as though they are standing in front of a videogame. The spectators use a joystick and can therefore succumb to the illusion of controlling the content, that is, something that is not possible. *Garden of Error and Decay* is a certain chronicle of its time, wars, the creation of myths, and the chronicle of their self-destruction. It is activated through the movement of stock market indexes on the internet, and this artistic duo suggests that we take an apocalyptic walk with the aim of returning to the essence of being. Finally, we arrive at the conclusion that the modes in which we had been operating can no longer function.

Bielicky's career has come a long way since the time he studied at the Düsseldorf Art Academy, where he experienced its golden age. He was lucky to have the opportunity to lean on a team of professors that adopted changes to their teaching at the same pace as art was changing. Amongst his work, we can also find audiovisual works that were created separately while still retaining their transgressive character. They are some of the best works to have ever been created in this field. I am referring to the *Intelligent Mailman* (1994), *Exodus* (1995), or *Room with a View* (2000). Through his research and production, Michael also arrived at video sculptures and video installations. It is also necessary to emphasize the level of elaboration and innovation that the duo Bielicky and Richter achieves. Their works place us into the epicenter of an issue that warns us of the possible difficulties of contemporaneity, and while art or artists cannot change this world, they help us to understand it better.

Translated from the Spanish by Michal Petkov.

1 From the Resolutions adopted by the Cuban exile community, headed by Martí, in Tampa, Florida, November 28, 1891. Quoted from Frank O. Mora, Jeanne A. K. Hey, eds., *Latin American and Caribbean Foreign Policy* (Lanham: Rowman & Littlefield Publishers, 2003), 87.
2 See Gottfried Wilhelm Leibniz, *New Essays on Human Understanding* [1704/1765], trans. and eds. Peter Remnant and Jonathan Bennett (New York: Cambridge University Press, 1996). Originally written in French and finished in 1704, it was published in 1765 as *Nouveaux essais sur l'entendement humain*.
3 Arthur Schopenhauer, *On the Fourfold Root of the Principle of Sufficient Reason*, trans. E. F. J. Payne (LaSalle: Open Court, 1997), 240.
4 See Johann Wolfgang von Goethe, *Maxims and Reflections*, trans. Elisabeth Stopp (London: Penguin Classics, 2005), 144-66.
5 See Néstor García Canclini, *Consumers and Citizens: Globalization and Multicultural Conflicts*, trans. George Yúdice (Minneapolis: University of Minnesota Press, 2019).
6 See Hermann Bahr, *Expressionism*, trans. R. T. Gribble (London: Frank Henderson, 1925). Originally published in German as *Expressionismus* (Munich: Delphin, 1920).
7 Paul Virilio, *Art and Fear*, trans. J. Rose (London: Continuum, 2003), 27.
8 See Michel Foucault, *The Order of Things: An Archaeology of the Human Sciences* (London: Pantheon Books, 1970), 3-16.
9 Samuel P. Huntington, *The Clash of Civilizations and the Remaking of World Order* (New York: Penguin Books, 1997), 20.
10 Ibid.
11 Edgar Morin, *Introduction à la pensée complexe* (Paris: ESF éditeur, 1990), 15. Translated from the French.
12 Ibid., 15.
13 Ibid., 16.

Crispijn de Passe, *Opera Didactica Omnia*, 1657, title page, engraved by de Passe's pupil David Loggan for Jan Amos Comenius.

Prague – A Place of Illusionists

Michael Bielicky

Thanks to the techno-imagination, it is possible to decipher technical images and thus to unmask the intended deception which is a component of our contemporary image civilization.

Vilém Flusser

Prague does not have a consistent historical development of either old or new media; but for this very reason, the city should be proud of several events that are of singular importance for the history of visual techno-media. Examples of such modern-sounding phenomena as *electronic art*, *multimedia*, *virtual reality*, *interactive art*, and *artificial intelligence* can actually be found in past times, even as far back as the Middle Ages. Of course, these phenomena had different names then. These events almost always had a particular relation to the time and the atmosphere of the places in which they occurred. Not least, the special energy of the city of Prague always drove people to search for an interface into the beyond. Linguists claim that the name Prague stems from the Czech *prah*, which means "threshold." True to its name, there are places in Prague where, through various optical illusions, one has the curious sensation of finding oneself in a twilight zone. The visual impressions of my childhood were deeply influenced by experiences with the 360-degree panorama *The Battle of Lipany*, now over a hundred years old, and a Russian film panorama in a Prague amusement park. A very old mirror labyrinth left me with impressions just as deep as Karel Zeman's fantastic films. Likewise, the experience with the magic lantern had an enormous effect on me. When one speaks of Prague, one really must say that it has always been a mecca of optical illusions.

In 1658, the Czech theologian and pedagogue Jan Amos Comenius published one of his first illustrated books for children: *Obris Sensualium Pictus* (*The Visible World in Pictures*). This pioneer of media pedagogy is considered to be the forerunner of modern attempts at international cooperation in the fields of education, science, and culture. Many artists whose work was devoted to the experience of seeing and to the new pictorial arts were inspired by Comenius's ideas. Examples are Oskar Kokoschka's treatise *Das Bewußtsein des Bildes* and some of Roberto Rosselini's writings. Judah Loew ben Bezalel, famed as High Rabbi Loew, also lived in Prague in the seventeenth century. A great scholar and mystic, who possessed an encyclopedic knowledge, he was both the spiritual and the physical forefather of the great mathematician Theodor von Karman. Von Karman discerned in Rabbi Loew the first genius of applied mathematics. Rabbi Loew is credited not only with having invented the golem; his experiments with the camera obscura and with the magic lantern so impressed Emperor Rudolf II that he was invited to join a circle of alchemists, artists, and astronomers whose members included Giuseppe Arcimboldo, Johannes Kepler, and Tycho Brahe. Rabbi Loew is said to have accomplished a miracle when Rudolf II called upon him at home one night: the Rabbi transformed his house into a palace by using his magic lantern to project painted pictures of the interior of the Prague castle Hradschin onto his own walls. So it was that Rudolf II was given the impression that he was in a palace. One can, in this context, speak of medieval virtual reality.

In natural scientist Jan Evangelista Purkyně's dissertation, published in Prague in 1818, he was one of the first to realize that we continue to perceive objects for a fraction of a second after they have disappeared from our

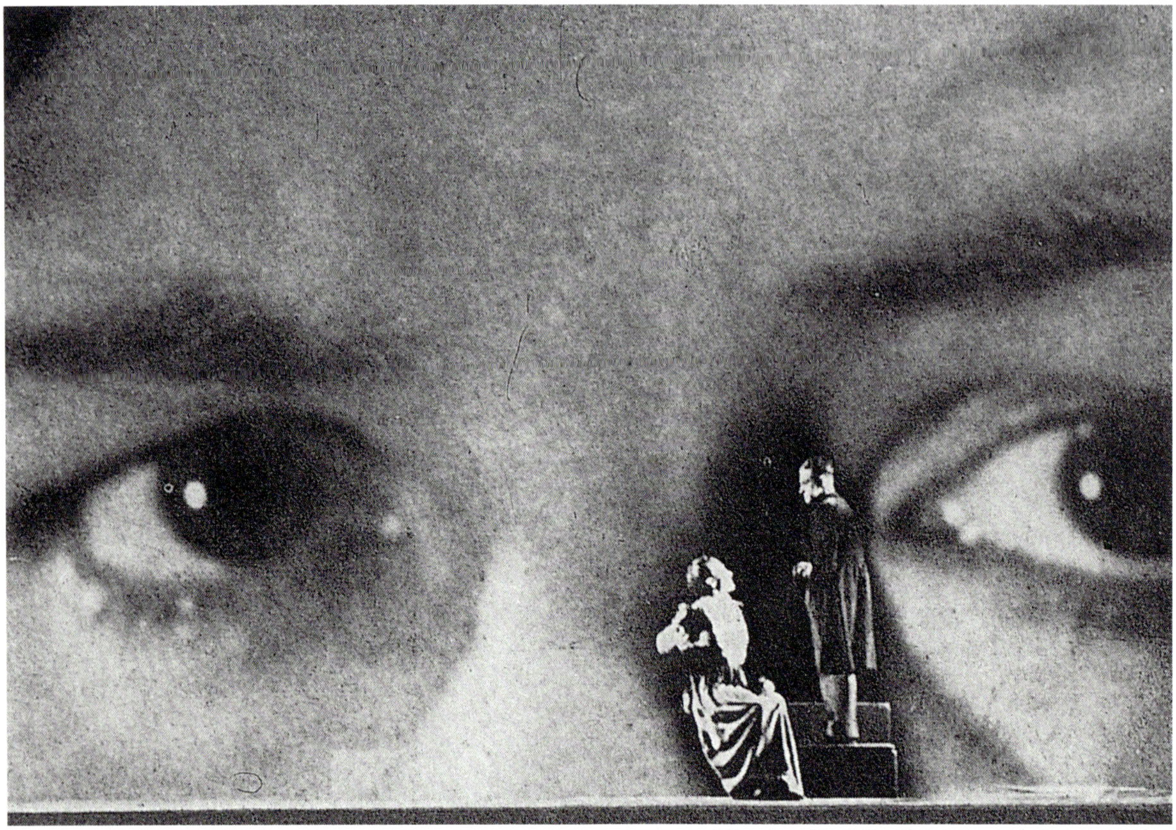

Miroslav Kouřil, Theatergraph presentation of Wedekind's *The Awakening of Spring*, 1936, theatrical stage with integrated projection slides, 35 mm film, b/w, sound.

Josef Svoboda, sketch for *Diakran*, 1958. Expo 58, Brussels.

Stage designer: Josef Svoboda, directors: Alfred Radok, Vladimír Svitáček, Jan Rohac; co-screenwriter: Miloš Forman; *Laterna Magica*,1958, multi-genre theater performance, Czech Pavillion, Expo 58, Brussels, ČTV, Czech Television. Video still.

field of vision. In 1824, Peter Mark Roget went on to give a more detailed description of this perceptual phenomenon, naming it "the persistence of visual impressions." The discovery of this perceptual phenomenon provided the basis for numerous technical inventions and new equipment that could turn still images into moving ones, which have transformed modern life, not only through cinema and television but also through digital and audiovisual techniques. Purkyně's insights make clear the fundamental relation between the birth of the neurological sciences and the triumph of technologies in the moving image. They serve as an important point of departure for reflections on the present-day development of electronic media and their influence on our lives. In 1865, Purkyně constructed the *kinesiscope*, an instrument by means of which one can observe a pulsing heart or even one's own portrait as animated photography. Purkyně predicted that the time would come in which it would be possible to tell entire stories with the help of moving pictures.

At the beginning of the twentieth century, Franz Kafka suggested that a cinema for the blind be established in Prague. Many Kafka specialists are convinced that much of his writing was influenced by his experiences with the then extremely young medium of film.

Even before World War I, the Czech cabaret performer Karel Hasler had a film projected on the stage that showed him running through the city, approaching the cabaret, and going through the door. At the end, the scene continues uninterrupted as he himself runs onto the stage.

In 1930, Alexander Hackenschmidt set new standards for cinematic expression with his experimental film *Aimless Walk*. The filmmaker, who had emigrated to the United States before the war (he had changed his name to Sasha Hammit), not only influenced his later wife Maya Deren, but also inspired an entire generation of American experimental filmmakers who came together to form a new film movement.

In collaboration with Miroslav Kouril, the theater director Emil František Burian developed the Theatergraph, a theatrical stage with integrated projection screens, on which films and slides directly relating to the events on the stage were projected during a theatrical performance. This technology was first put into practice for a production of Frank Wedekind's *The Awakening of Spring* in 1936 and then later for Alexander Pushkin's *Eugen Onegin*. Denis Bablet, in his book *Revolutions in Stage Design in the 20th Century*, confirms that Burian and Kouril's experiments, along with Erwin Piscator's and Traugott Müller's research, were instrumental in paving the way for the development of new theatrical forms. Set design, which had been characterized by screen and color up until then, was being replaced by architectural structures, light, and projected images. A new civilization of audiovisual communication had come into being.

In the 1930s, Prague-based artist Zdeněk Pešánek wrote his book *Kinetismus*, in which he investigated the potential of multimedia performance as a new form of visual expression – regardless of whether it involved an installation, a film, a fireworks display, or the aesthetics of antiaircraft defense. He built light kinetic objects that had multimedia qualities. They moved, they changed color, they produced sounds.

Karel Zeman was a great poet of the new cinematic expression. This master of special effects developed a kind of physical "virtual set" for his films of the 1950s. A unique animated-film technique enabled actors to be placed in unreal surroundings that roused associations with old etchings, for instance.

In the period after World War II, Czech film experimentation attained a phenomenal and unique dimension. Josef Svoboda, the master of set design,

Josef Svoboda, *Polyekran*, *Creation of the World of Man*, 1967, 112 moveable cubes with slide projections, 15.000 slides, color, sound, 11 min. Expo 67, Montreal.

set completely new standards with inventions like *laterna magika* as well as polyscreen and polyvision techniques. Moreover, Radúz Činčera, the father of the first interactive film, made a quantum leap with his *Kinoautomat* (automatic cinema) project. It is considered groundbreaking both because of its use of the new nonlinear narrative form and because of its inclusion of the spectator as an active participant in the film action. Although these inventors lived under a totalitarian regime, they enjoyed more freedom of experimentation than they would have in some Western countries. In his long and international career, Svoboda created more than seven hundred sets, most of which contained multiple projections of film and slides in combination with architecture and light.

In 1951, Svoboda began to deploy several sets at once in his theatrical productions. Through the development of his concept for Expo '58 in Brussels, his idea for a polyphonic theater became reality. This is how his laterna magika project came into being – a synthesis of theater and film. By then, he was already wondering whether the spectator was even capable of simultaneously perceiving parallel film projections. The director Alfréd Radok, collaborator on the laterna magika for the past fifteen years and, in the ensuing decades, chief writer of the film narratives in Svoboda's laterna magika, made a crucial contribution to the realization of this interface between theater and cinema. Other film directors, like Miloš Forman or Jan Švankmajer, were also involved in laterna magika productions. The magical moment of this system is above all the fluid transition between the stage and the projected film: the action begun on stage continues in the film, and vice versa. Actors from several projection screens appear on stage, then disappear again into the film projection. It was not always easy for the spectator to distinguish between the real action on stage and the virtual action in the film. Real and filmic worlds combine with each other to form a unity.

The technical principle is based on three projection cabins, more than twenty light projectors, and a back projection over an anamorphic lens. If necessary, the projection screens could be moved. Given that films could be projected onto any conceivable form, a further dimension was added to the dynamic of the on-stage action. The variability of space (dynamic architecture of the screen), of time (the film editing), and of the actor's identity on stage and in film allowed for the development of a convincing optical illusion. In addition, the sound was designed in such a way as to produce a highly spatial experience for the spectators. This flowing movement between the material and the immaterial worlds, the back and forth between reality and dream, has continued to enchant Prague audiences up until the present day.

Polyvision, another Svoboda invention, presented a panorama of Czech industrial life in an eight-minute film that used twenty slide projectors, ten ordinary motion picture screens, and five rotating projection screens. While the subjects were usual industrial operations, such as hydroelectric power plants, steel rolling mills, and textile mills, the visual material was presented in an unusual way. The screens were unconventional, in that during the show they would move around: backward, forward, even sideways. Then there were other projection surfaces formed by steel hoops that spun around so rapidly that they seemed to constitute solid spheres, and yet they were not solid. One could partially look through the image at what was in the room beyond. The presentation was completely controlled by electronic memory circuits that controlled the projectors and moved the screens around in a cinematic ballet.

Svoboda's *polyekran* was a fascinating audiovisual experience presented during the Expo '67 in Montreal. One entered a large room and sat on the

Josef Svoboda, Jaroslav Fric, *Polyvision*, 1967, multi-projection cinema set-up, 35 mm film and slides projected on moveable geometrical objects, projection screen color, sound, 8 min., Expo 67, Montreal.

Jaroslav Erik Frič, *Vertical Cinemascope*, 1970. British Columbia Pavilion, Expo 70, Osaka.

Jaroslav Erik Frič, *Rondovision,* 1984. Expo 1984, New Orleans.

carpeted floor to watch a wall of 112 cubes whose ever shifting and changing images moved backward and forward. Inside each cube were two Kodak Carousel slide projectors that projected stills onto the front of the cubes. In all, there were fifteen thousand slides in the eleven-minute show. Since each cube could slide into three separate positions within a two-foot range, the cubes produced the effect of a flat surface turning into a three-dimensional surface and back again. It was completely controlled by 240 miles of memory circuitry, which was encoded onto a filmstrip with 756,000 separate instructions.

The show was *The Creation of the World of Man*. On the 112-part screen, planet Earth came awake, flowers bloomed, tigers suddenly appeared, the first men walked the Earth, then machinery was invented. Sometimes the image sequences would appear complete at first, then be broken up into an abstract modern-art composition. It was pure multivisual technique that enchanted the viewer.

Radúz Činčera's *Kinoautomat* was introduced at Expo '67 in Montreal. Among Činčera's team members were the directors Ján Roháč and Vladimír Svitáček, the set designer Josef Svoboda, as well as Jaroslav Frič and Bohumil Mika, the technical masterminds behind the system. The world's first interactive cinema, the *Kinoautomat* confronted spectators with a film that would keep stopping. Two principal actors in the film appeared on stage and asked the audience how the film should be continued. The spectators voted, using either of the two buttons that had been installed in their seats. Afterward, the version that received more votes was played. The film narrated extremely turbulent relationships between the inhabitants of a "completely normal house." In one of the scenes, a young inhabitant slams the door shut upon seeing who is ringing. Since she has come directly out of the bath, she appears wrapped only in a towel. In her panic, she rings her neighbor's doorbell and asks for help. There the film stops, and the spectators are asked if the neighbor should let her into his apartment. The audience inevitably voted "Yes," apart from once, at the Expo, when the "No" vote was due to the presence of a large group of nuns.

The inclusion of the spectators in the film action represented a completely novel situation. Through their participation, the spectators were actively involved in a nonlinear film narrative. After the Expo, the *Kinoautomat* was presented in Prague. In 1968, however, shortly after the invasion of the Warsaw Pact troops, the unique venture was closed down. Perhaps the powers of the time were afraid that the *Kinoautomat* might heighten democratic awareness. After all, during the performance, votes were cast according to democratic principles.

In the years following, Činčera developed different cinema systems that had a nonlinear, and often also interactive, character. In 1990, the Cinelabyrinth was introduced in Osaka. In this ambitious project, the spectators could follow the action in the film by moving through various spaces, and depending on which room they had decided on, the narrative adopted another development. Unlike in the *Kinoautomat*, the spectator of the Cinelabyrinth could therefore make individual decisions. In 1998, a new version of Cinelabyrinth was presented in Prague during the exhibition *100 Years of Czech Film*. Visitors to the exhibition had the possibility of experiencing the history of Czech film as a nonlinear narrative.

In the mid-1990s, Czech television staged an experiment with the interactive film presented at the Expo '67. Two different versions of the film were played on two different television stations: spectators could switch back and forth between the two stations, and thus between the two films.

In the 1960s, a group came into being in association with SCARS (Science Art Sense) that specialized in the development of multimedia presentations for various international occasions. The host countries were located on every continent in the world since it had become widely known that the former Czechoslovakia possessed a great deal of competence in the field of innovative and often complex multimedia performances. The technical head of the group was Jaroslav Frič, whom I have already mentioned in connection with the *Kinoautomat*. Besides numerous other systems, Frič developed the Spherorama and the vertical cinemascope for the British Columbia pavilion at Expo '70 in Osaka. The Spherorama was a slide projector that could produce a 360-degree dome projection using only one lens. Although Frič was responsible for innumerable inventions, there is very little documentation regarding his projects.

The backgrounds and the historical development of these unusual film formats possess a unique diversity and originality, yet it is nonetheless difficult to find adequate material about them, either in writing or in film. The phenomena described here certainly deserve more treatment at length, particularly the visual culture of moving images that served to produce so many great artists in Prague. Both the animated films (by Trnka, Švankmajer, Barte, and others) and the feature films (by directors including Formen, Chytilová, Juráček, Menzel, and Zeman) beautifully reflected the magical, surreal, absurd, and fantastical atmosphere of Prague, which can still be experienced everywhere in that city.

First published in Jeffrey Shaw and Peter Weibel, eds., *Future Cinema: The Cinematic Imaginary after Film* (Cambridge, MA: MIT Press, 2003), 96-101. Translated from the German by Sarah Clift.

Bibliography

Frič, Jaroslav Erik. *Scars - Science Art Sense 2* Prague: Art Centrum, 1968-1973.
Hrbas, Jiří. *Laterna magika: Sborník stati*. Prague: Filmový ústav, 1968.
Orbis Fictus - New Media in Contemporary Arts. Prague: Soros Center for Contemporary Arts, 1995.
Pešánek, Zdeněk. *Kinetismus*. Prague: Česká grafická unie, 1941.
Ripellino, Angele Maria. *Magic Prague*. Berkeley: University of California Press, 1993.
Scholem, Gershorn. *Encyclopaedia Judaica*, vol. 2. Frankfurt/M.: Suhrkamp, 1970.
Svoboda, Josef, and Milena Honzíková. *Tajemství divadelního prostoru*. Prague: Odeon, 1990.

Vilém Flusser, Edith Flusser, and Michael Bielicky in Robion, France, 1991.

GOLEM IS ALIVE
Michael Bielicky

There is a very old Jewish cemetery in Prague. Golem, the collective soul of the ghettos, renders every tombstone visible. The inscription suddenly comes to life. The square letters of the Hebrew alphabet merge with the pictograms. This letter formula is the information that brings golem to life. The information that controls a computer seems to be based on the same principle. First published in *4. Videonale in Bonn* (1990), 110. Translated from the German by Paul Kenig.

Broken Intentions, Blank Spaces of Memory: A Visit to the Jewish Museum, Berlin

Elena Lappin

Entering the Jewish Museum in Berlin is not very different from entering an airplane. The same sharp controls that inevitably remind us of America these days, the same screening of hand luggage and the usual alarm signal when passing through the lock, indicating something metallic that I have on me, maybe inside me. I do not know what it is. An employee pats me every time, and finally I can get on the plane – or enter the museum now. I look around, see the people next to me, and immediately notice the irony: they are Holocaust survivors, many of them having traveled from Israel, and are trying to show that they do not pose a threat to this Holocaust memorial, which was built on German soil. They willingly endure the procedure.

I am not even in the cafeteria and have already used the forbidden word *Holocaust* twice and possibly thought it four times. That is my mistake, because the press conference shortly before had stated that this museum is not primarily and not exclusively about the Holocaust. The director, Michael Blumenthal, even said that the museum was not intended for Jews. "It is a museum for the Germans. The Jews don't need it." The architect Daniel Libeskind

Media Golem: Between Prague and ZKM

Michael Bielicky

My older brother and I were standing on the curbstone on the main street in my Prague neighborhood. I was seven years old at the end of April 1961, two weeks after the historical moment when the first human flew into outer space. An open limousine suddenly appeared with cosmonaut Yuri Gagarin waving to the crowds. As a small-sized person in a dense crowd, not knowing in which direction to look, I missed seeing this hero of all humanity. Although I missed seeing him, I felt the vibrant energies of the cheering crowds for a long time afterward.

Four years later, cheering crowds standing along the curb greeted Pope Paul VI waving from an open limousine driving down Fifth Avenue. In the crowd was a Korean man who had recently arrived in New York. He was holding the first black-and-white portable video camera, shooting the scene. This young man was destined to become the father of video art. His name was Nam June Paik. I had the good fortune of being his student twenty years later only because of my escape to the West in 1969, after the Soviet tanks invaded the former Czechoslovakia.

In 1981, I drove a horse and open carriage down Fifth Avenue into Central Park. After studying medicine for several years upon graduating from high school in Germany, I realized that my future lay not in being a physician, as my father's and brother's had, but rather in the realm of visual media. I moved to New York and lived in the Westbeth art community on the Hudson River. To pay my rent, I gained a license as a horse-cab driver.

Perhaps I should start somewhere else. We are in the year 1942 at my parents' wartime wedding. They are wearing yellow stars on their chests, kissing their parents goodbye on the run, not knowing then that they would never see them again. As a small boy, I could not understand how my friends had grandparents and even great-grandparents. I had none. When I was twelve, I first learned about the Holocaust madness that had exterminated my parents' entire family because they were Jews. It was not surprising that my parents did not speak to me about this unspeakable horror until I was twelve, since we continued to live in the anti-Semitic environment of the former post-Stalinist Czechoslovakia, where it was best not to be identified as a Jew.

In my home, the integration of art and science flowed naturally, since my father was both a

Holocaust Memory Reframed: Museums and the Challenges of Representation

Jennifer Hansen-Glucklich

Michael Bielicky's video sculpture *Menorah* [1989/2001] demonstrates how the conventional imagery of menorah candles may be disfigured to create new meaning. Bielicky, a New Media artist, has worked in a wide variety of media, including photography, video installation, and New Media projects. His 1995 project *Exodus*, for example, tracked Moses's journey through the desert using GPS, and his 2004 work *Falling Stars* projected giant video images of constantly renewing, shifting constellations of media celebrities ("stars") on the Volksbühne (People's Theater) in Berlin. The child of Holocaust survivors, Bielicky was born in the former Czechoslovakia and fled with his family in 1968, at the age of fifteen, to Germany. A professor of media art and digital media at the ZKM | Center for Art and Media Karlsruhe, Bielicky creates

MENORAH
Frauke Syamken

A steel chandelier carries small monitors on the tips of its seven arms. On the screens, the slightly flickering flames of a wood fire burn silently, miniaturized, multiplied. The video image on the screens is fed in not via cables, but via antennas – the transmitter remains hidden. Thus, with all the clarity in plastic formulation, the sculpture nevertheless overcomes the field of classic sculpture. With this work, Michael Bielicky imperceptibly, subtly intervenes in the coordinates of space, sets traces, and visualizes immaterial information flows with the antennas.

The flames burn at the predetermined location of the menorah, the seven-armed chandelier, which is one of the most

```
package
columbus2;
import
java.awt.
Font;
import
java.util.
ArrayList;
import
java.util.
Random;
import
com.sun.
opengl.
util.j2d.
TextRen-
derer;
import
common.
Vec3f;
public
final
class
Drawer {
```

musician and a scientist. He had survived the war years with my mother, having acquired false identification papers that permitted him to work as a musician, often playing piano at parties where the Nazis were celebrating. After the war, he studied medicine and became a medical scientist. He would come home after a long day at work and play piano while I sat beside him listening. My father was also a composer, who composed Czech tangos and rumbas that were released as recordings and played on the radio.

Ironically, my Jewish identity was awakened after arriving in West Germany. I changed overnight from a young communist pioneer to a Western hippie. I grew long hair, wore a goat-skin jacket embroidered with colorful flowers, started to socialize within the Jewish community of Düsseldorf, and joined a Zionist group. The actual reason for joining this group had little to do with leaving for Israel. It gave me the opportunity to be accepted into a marijuana-smoking hippie circle of friends that helped transform the trauma of emigration into a positive experience, insulating me from the brown-shirt mentality of the older German generation. It was even more difficult for my parents to relate to a generation with a Nazi past that included their parents' murderers. I remember sitting with my parents in our new home in Germany watching the moon landing on our Czech black-and-white TV. This moment awakened in me the power of real-time media experience.

Earlier fascinating media experiences in my Prague childhood, however, had an impact on my work as a media artist – frequenting the cinema, developing photographs in my neighbor's makeshift darkroom, immersion in a 360-degree panoramic film occasion, seeing early time-base imagery in a technical museum, and creating an instant camera anticipating the Polaroid. There were two movie theaters near where we lived, and my friend and I would go there nearly every Sunday for the morning matinee. We saw Karel Zeman's fantastical films, which are often shown today in university film schools and New Media departments as early examples of compositing visualization. In contemporary terminology, it is called a *virtual set*, in which technology allows the combination of actual actors with virtual reality, creating a virtual setting and even individual characters. Zeman was a pioneer with this technology, and later I became interested in it as well. I remember another early experience with film when my father took me to the panoramic cinema at the Holešovice amusement park. Inside a round building was a circular screen on which a 360-degree panoramic film from a Russian projection system was projected. Spectators did not sit as in a normal cinema but stood in the middle watching the changing view from an airplane. I remember that the plane began to bank, making people lose their balance and fall to the ground. This was a powerful experience. In the same fairgrounds in 1891, the artist Luděk Marold created a panorama, an image in which reality and fiction were blurred, where three-dimensional objects emerged from a 360-degree panoramic painting. This interaction between reality and fiction later became one of the main features of my work. My friend and I made a make-believe “camera” from a cardboard box in which we placed pictures we had drawn in advance. We would go to the park and ask people walking by if we could photograph them. If someone agreed, we would click the “shutter release” and pull from the “camera” one of the pictures to give to the person we had “photographed.” My childhood invention was the “precursor” to the Polaroid camera. A few years later, the son of my parents' friends

```
FileLoader loader;

TextRenderer renderer;

ArrayList<TextSource> sources, sourcesOnBeach,

int index = -1;

WaterSurface surface;

float beach, horizon, xScaling, yScaling, halfWidth;

float rowDistance = 50f; // 50

static int rowAmount = 20;

float leftOfBeach, rightOfBeach, farOfBeach, leftOfHorizon, rightOfHorizon, farOfHorizon;

int[] sortingOfBeach, sortingOfHorizon, sortingOfBeachInverted, sortingOfHorizonInverted;

int firstSortingOfBeach = 0;

int firstSortingOfHorizon = 0;

float zInWaterSurfaceOfHorizon = 0f;

float m, c;

public Drawer(float right,
```

spoke of the “history of two thousand years of the Jews in Germany, which is not just a history of the Holocaust.” Both seemed extremely satisfied with the museum and congratulated each other on the success of their project. Blumenthal praised Libeskind's building, and Libeskind generously admitted that the building had won through the museum.

I wish I had seen Libeskind's architecture empty. On this rainy Monday, the metal cladding of the zigzag building looks so dull that it fits well with the ugliness of the high-rise buildings all around. After the

data visualization projects, including projections on buildings that interrogate concepts of news, media, and public spaces.[1] Bielicky's work stages an encounter between the spiritual and the technological. Sculptures like *Sefiroth Tree* [1990] and *Menorah* carry religious names and invoke traditional as well as Kabbalistic Jewish customs. At the same time, they bear small video screens and thus bring traditional ideas and images into dialogic

important icons of the Jewish rite and has become an emblem of Judaism throughout history. Here, the past and the present combine in an archaic religious symbol, the origin of which lies in the earliest biblical times. The spiritual and biographical, cultural identity and communicative processes flow together in a symbolic inventory. In the shape of the chandelier, Jewish culture and biblical traditions continue to be at work for thousands of years and at the same time absorb historical events and the experience of death and persecution, as can also be read in the flames as a reference.

In Bielicky's oeuvre, ***Menorah*** [1989] is certainly the most sculptural, physical work, but the wireless transmission technology of the video on

```
float top, float near, float far) {

beach = near;

horizon = far;

halfWidth = right;

xScaling = right / near;

yScaling = top / near;

farOfBeach = -getHorizonCushion();

farOfHorizon = -2 * getHorizonCushion();

m = (getSky(horizon) * 0.5f - (getSky(beach) * -1f - 100f)) / (horizon - beach);

c = -getSky(beach) - 100f - m * beach;

// initialize sorting arrays

sortingOfBeach = new;

sortingOfHorizon = new

for (int i = 0; i < rowAmount; i++) {

sortingOfBeach[i] = i;

sortingOfHorizon[i] = i; }

shuffle(sortingOfBeach);

shuffle(sortingOfHo-
```

press conference, which took place elsewhere, I have to ask my way to the museum. An elderly woman, whom I ask about the Jewish Museum – just a few meters away from Libeskind's eye-catching building – gives me a suspicious look and says harshly that she has no idea. Does she correspond with the type of visitor Blumenthal wants to bring to his museum?

Inside, I try to relate to the lines and angles first. I know from interviews and articles that Libeskind deconstructed the Star of David, and now I want to see how his experiment works. At first I'm a little confused, but soon I realize that you can only move in one direction, two at most. Everything is labeled and explained. There is the axis of continuity, the axis of exile, the memory void, the Holocaust tower. Everything is very clean and tidy and clear. But when I start reading the little signs, I start to get angry. "The architect Daniel Libeskind," it says, "prompts us to think about the Holocaust and about the people who managed to flee, about continuity and the people who live on." Libeskind's trademark is the Voids, vertical spaces, which are actually meaningful even without explanation. But still here you are taught: "With the Voids, Daniel Libeskind symbolizes the loss that the annihilation of European Jews has left in German and European history."

I enter the Voids – with my feelings, not with those that Libeskind wants to awaken in me. A young woman opens the heavy door to the Holocaust tower for me. It is high, cold, windowless – daylight comes in only through small openings. It

from New York came for a visit with an actual Polaroid. I was not at all surprised.

When I was fifteen years old, I saw what appeared to be an action movie in the making while hiking with my friend in the countryside not far from Prague. At the horizon, hundreds of tanks where rolling over the hills in the far distance. When we realized that what we were seeing on that summer morning in 1968 was not a movie, but the beginning of the invasion of the Russian army into Czechoslovakia, we ran down the road, tearing down all the direction signs to make it difficult for the invading soldiers to find their way. This image will forever remain etched in my mind along with the horrible feeling of being helpless and powerless.

I was fortunate to have been born in Prague, a city permeated by the myth of the golem, a prerobotic being created by mystical algorithms four centuries ago, invoked by Rabbi Judah Loew, the spiritual father of Norbert Weiner's cybernetic theory. Prague is the city in which the Czech word *robot* was conceived, the golem was born, and Kafka told the tale of the metamorphosis of a young man into a giant cockroach. It is also the city in which the first interactive cinema, *Kinoautomat*, and the phenomenon of *laterna magika*, the fluid transition between the stage and projected film, were invented. Publishing the first illustrated book for children in 1658, the visionary Czech educator Comenius pioneered in developing a system of media pedagogy of great significance in New Media studies.

I was fortunate once again to have immigrated to Düsseldorf, where I studied in a high school not far from Düsseldorf's illustrious Art Academy. The academy radiated out to the community at large, so I felt part of what was going on. I could not help but notice the reverberations being sent out by the life pulsating there. Near the academy were several cafés and bars where students and professors congregated. I spent a lot of time in one such local hangout named Creamcheese. This environment had a strong impact on me without my being entirely aware of everything that was going on around me. In our neighborhood, I often saw Joseph Beuys. He was indeed larger than life, and not just because of his height and hat, but because he drove a Bentley. The strength of his personality and work was not clear to me until two years

tension with new forms of technology and perception. As a child of seven or eight, Bielicky was deeply affected by the magical experience of developing photographs. In a 2009 interview, Bielicky related the story of how Rabbi Judah Loew used a magic lantern to transform his poor home in the Jewish ghetto of Prague into a castle in honor of Emperor Rudolf II's visit. The story of this "medieval virtual reality," as Bielicky describes it, reveals the visual mood and culture in which he was steeped as a child.[2]

In Bielicky's video sculpture *Menorah*, traditional menorah candles and extinguished memorial candles have been replaced by video screens with images of flickering flames. The installation is profoundly ironic. In the Hanukkah story, burning flames symbolize miraculous permanence: despite the lack of sufficient oil, the candles burned for eight days and nights. Here, the flames of the candles have been replaced by a more "permanent" and modern medium – the play of transmitted signals that express themselves as light and figure. These flames are clearly

the seven monitors already points to later projects in which he gives immaterial information flows a specific artistic – more performative, more ephemeral, and more mobile – form. His most radical work is the virtual teleperformance *Exodus*, which was performed during the Ars Electronica in 1995 in the Negev desert. Bielicky, guided by a satellite-controlled information system (GPS) and in permanent presence on the internet, moved on the biblical path through the Negev desert, which the people of Israel traveled after leaving Egypt. Exemplarily ancient, nomadic traditions of Jewish heritage merge with the latest technology in the motif of the journey, spanning history and future at the same time and giving shape to spiritual potential in a medial before I entered the academy. I became aware of the significance of the art scene in Düsseldorf when I saw a video installation for the first time in my life in the academy. Today, it is considered a seminal piece. It was created by Shigeko Kubota, Nam June Paik's wife, and was based on Marcel Duchamp's *Nude Descending a Staircase* [1912]. Although I appreciated the artistic energies in Düsseldorf, I decided to study medicine, which I enjoyed for three years and thought was going to be my profession. When I realized that the life of a physician was not what I really wanted for myself, I left medical school and left Düsseldorf for New York. I was always grateful for the ongoing support for my quest offered by my brother, Peter, himself a physician and collector of Czech avant-garde art.

When I first came to New York City in 1978, the cosmopolitan atmosphere of the city was liberating for me, even though my existence there was very tenuous. It was important to me that no one asked who I was or where I came from. It did not matter. Being in New York gave me a burst of energy that dissipated when I relocated at the edge of a Californian redwood forest, in the beautiful mountains around Santa Cruz. In this perfect paradise where I did not have anything particular to do, I felt no motivation to do anything at all. I soon realized I needed the vibrant energy and existential challenge of a big city and returned to New York to begin intensive work on photography. A turning point came when I definitively decided to pursue photography as a profession. This came from meeting New York photographer Fredrich Cantor, whose work I admired. He did not know it, but for me at that time, he was a real guru. I tried to imitate his work. My New York photographs, created under Cantor's influence, helped me eventually get accepted into the Düsseldorf Art Academy.

I returned to Germany to work for *Monochrom* magazine, which offered me the freedom to create a wide variety of photographs, which it published. The magazine was very progressive for its time, sometimes even provocative, in both content and design. I mostly did portraits of friends, people I was acquainted with, strong personalities for the most part. The photos were pseudo-staged in often-bizarre situations that were created without a lot of prior preparation. The magazine soon folded. I suppose it was too experimental for its time. During this period, however, I never really considered myself a professional photographer, even though it paid my rent.

I first applied to the Düsseldorf Art Academy in 1983. Although I was not accepted, something positive did come out of it, as Beuys organized a special exhibition of those who were rejected. He was already so famous that he could invite the press. This exhibition of the rejected threw into doubt the very social status of the "artist" and "art." The following year, I was accepted into Bernd Becher's photography atelier at a time when photography was starting to become accepted on an equal footing with the classical fine arts. My schoolmates who continued with photography, Andreas Gursky, Thomas Struth, and Thomas Ruff, later became successful artists. For me, the work in Becher's atelier was boring. The conceptualism he encouraged did absolutely nothing for me, although I appreciated it in Becher's work itself. I found the work his students were producing banal and foreign.

I met Nam June Paik by accident at the opening of an exhibition. I told him I would like to study under him, and he did not ask for any further details about me. He just said, "You are my student." When someone came up to him,

is completely clear to me: I am supposed to feel dread, fear, loneliness here. In fact, I almost feel comfortable in this room, which offers peace and quiet after the excited crowd outside. On to the blank space of remembrance: another cathedral-like vertical space, the floor of which is covered by an installation by the Israeli artist Menashe Kadishman. It is called *Fallen Leaves* and consists of a pile of rusty metal discs with milled holes for the eyes, nose, and mouth. You can walk over the faces or stop on them. Thus we may – no – thus we should remember the dead. This

and self-consciously artificial. As mere images of flames, they are mediated through screens and possess no natural light or warmth. No longer dependent on a sacred miracle for their power, these flames are made possible through technology and controlled by human will rather than divine intervention. Intriguingly, the source of the flame images remains hidden from view: the transmitter is concealed, and the installation thus maintains a hint

form in a vivid way. Like Nam June Paik and Vilém Flusser, Bielicky gains creative strength from modern communication technologies. Culture-spanning mobile forms of existence and experiences are central themes of his work. The communication between the hidden transmitter and the antennas of the seven monitors refers metaphorically beyond the elementary technical act of data transmission to a spiritual dimension. Associations arise. The sculpture remains in the room, and the thoughts set off on a journey.

First published in Heinrich Klotz, ed., ***Kunst der Gegenwart*** (Munich: Prestel, 1997), 55. Translated from the German by Paul Kenig.

--------------- PR OCESS ---------------

Java Threads: (=> current thread) 0x00007

```
rizon);
sortingOfBeachInverted = new

invertSorting(sortingOfBeach, sortingOfBeachInverted);

invertSorting(sortingOfHorizon, sortingOfHorizonInverted);

sortingOfBeach = sortingOfHorizon;

sortingOfBeachInverted = sortingOfHorizonInverted;

loader = new FileLoader();

renderer = new TextRenderer(new Font("Sans Serif", Font.BOLD, 100),

true, true); // 72

String[] lines = null;

if (loader.success) {

lines = ileParser.loadines("current-news.tsv");

} else {

lines = ("backup-news.tsv");}

if (lines.length == 0) {

System.exit(0);}

sources = new ArrayList<TextSource>();
```

```
String
code =
null;

int index
= 0;

String[]
headlines
= new
owAmount];

for (int
i = 0; i
< lines.
length;
i++) {

String[]
line =
lines[i].
lit("\t");

if
(!line[0].
als(code))
{

if (code
!= null) {

sources.
add(new
Text
Source
(renderer,
headlines,
code));

}

code =
line[0];

index =
0;}

head-
lines[in-
dex] =
line[1];

index++;}

source-
sOnBeach =
new Array-
List<Text-
Source>();

sources
OnHori-
zon = new
Array-
List<Text-
Source>();

addSources
ToHori-
zon();

pushHori-
zon();

surface
= new
WaterSur-
face();}

private
float
getSky(-
float z) {

return z *
yScaling;}
```

installation is so superfluous that I try to imagine the Void without the metal disks. What remains? An empty space that symbolizes nothing.

My disappointment with the architecture and artistic equipment of the museum would be complete had I not discovered the large steel menorah, a work by the young Czech artist Michael Bielicky with the simple title *Menorah* (1989). It is in one of the corridors and is so impressive that I have to sit on a bench to look at it for a while. A small television screen is attached to each arm of the menorah, on which the black-and-white video of a flame can be seen nonstop. Without any explanation, this menorah has an extraordinary effect. It triggers an emotional but unsentimental feeling that there is a connection between the dead and the living, between past and present. Unlike Libeskind's architecture, this installation is not about the artist, but about other people. It is often overlooked that Libeskind's first museum design was called *name model* because the names of murdered Jews should be recorded on the walls of the house. Only the empty walls remain of this concept – today it has only the name of Libeskind. The same applies to the Voids. There, too, you are asked to think and feel like the architect. I can hardly imagine a more egomaniacal monument. It almost forces you to distance yourself from the architect's intentions. And that should be exactly the opposite of what Libeskind wanted.

Back to Bielicky's menorah. I'm lucky, the artist is present and

he introduced me as his new student. I was really lucky because it was not so easy to get into his atelier. He did not take everyone. When I began to study with Paik, a new period began for me. I felt like I had found my métier working with video. Outwardly, he was very humble. He was even skeptical about his own work. But looking back now, I realize that maybe this was a tactic of his. What impressed me about Paik, though, was his lack of pretension, and his interest in just everyday things. I think that is why students liked him so much. He never played the star, and you could speak to him about anything. Most people do not know this, but there would be situations when if he liked a student's work, he would simply buy it. He did not do this because he was collecting these objects but so that he could use them in his own installations. He considered it a form of partnership. He was not misusing his students' work. For me, of course, what was most important about Paik was his openness to his students. That was the greatest lesson for me, the one I identified with the most. I try to maintain this sort of openness with my own students. I consider them more as partners whom I can learn from despite their age or limited experience.

At the academy, Beuys had created a space he called Freie lnternationale Universität (FIU). It was a gesture on his part to represent a clear alternative to academic seclusion, an open space within a closed space. Beuys, of course, always had his devotees around him. My friend, the Bolivian painter Ricardo Peredo, and I began to associate with Beuys and his group. He was such a charismatic personality that he attracted us to him. On the other hand, we felt uncomfortable with his students, who acted like members of a difficult-to-define sect. When Beuys spoke, it was like they were listening to a sermon. Beuys's lectures themselves were incredibly inspirational, and they forced us to think about the role of the artist and his work in a social context. He propagated a completely different type of artistic work. He thought the artist should create *social sculptures*, that is, the artist's work should be focused on mending the world. I still mull over this idea today and always return to it and try to discuss it with my students too.

My video installations evolved into video sculptures at the end of my studies in Düsseldorf. The difference between the two is not exactly clear. The term *video sculpture* did not exist

of mystery. The miracle of Hanukkah – the burning oil that defied natural laws – has been demystified and subjected through *Menorah* to a modern, technological explanation. *Menorah*, therefore, ironizes the use of the menorah and its candles as a commemorative cue to suggest miraculous permanence.

While the menorah and candle flames are clearly coded as sacred, television screens and video are simply part of mundane daily life and speak to the realm of the profane. The use of contemporary media to render images of flames and the juxtaposition between the sacred and the profane in this installation undermine and disfigure the sacred symbol. What opens up through this disfiguration is a glimpse of the fluidity of the sacred. *Menorah* reveals that the sacred cannot be imprisoned in static forms and that objects are not intrinsically sacred; rather, the sacred is refigured through this exhibit as a shifting evocation, invested in forms through ritual, placement, and contexts of remembrance. Moreover, for those cognizant of the connection between Zionism, Hanukkah, and the

fcef0ef d800 JavaThread "SIGHUP handler" daemon [_thread_ blocked, id=121731, stack (0x0000 70000ea 69000,0x00 007000 0eb69000)] 0x 0000 7fcef04d 1000 J avaThread "Java2D Queue Flusher" daemon [_thread_ blocked, id=107539, stack (0x0000 70000ff2 b000,0 x0000 70001002 b000)] 0x0000 7fcef16 38800 Java Thread "Java2D Disposer" daemon [_thread_ blocked, id=78351, stack(0x 0000 70001 054f000 ,0x0000 7000 1064f 000)] 0x00 007fc ef090 7000 JavaT hread "EMF Reference Cleaner" daemon [_thread_ blocked, id=21507, stack (0x00007 0000fe2 8000,0 x0000 70000ff 28000)] 0x000 07fcef0 029800 JavaThread "Service Thread" daemon [_thread_ blocked, id=20483, stack (0x00 0070000 fc2200 0,0x0000 70000f d22000)] 0x0 0007fce until it was used for the first time in 1986 (*Videoskulptur* in German) by the curator Wulf Herzogenrath for an exhibition at the Kölnischer Kunstverein. I guess one distinction is that video installations use monitors as the central element. In a video sculpture, the object itself is so central that if the monitors are switched off, it can still be a meaningful artwork. I created *Menorah/Inventory* [1989] at the end of my studies, without having any idea what sort of response it would eventually have. It had small TV monitors at the ends of each of seven branches of a large steel candelabrum. On the monitors' screens danced video images of flickering flames. These virtual flames emanated from a hidden video transmitter sending spiritual messages to antennas topping each of the seven monitors.

Menorah/Inventory directly referenced my Jewish identity in a German context. The first place in Germany that provided me some comfortable surroundings was the Düsseldorf Jewish community. Yet, it took me a long while before I was ready to acknowledge my Jewishness openly and publicly. The first time I publicly displayed *Menorah/Inventory* at the academy, I placed a ring around it made of defunct fire extinguishers. They were not so easy to find because at the time, everyone in Germany had the Baader-Meinhof gang and other terrorist groups still fresh in their minds, and their bombs were made of old fire extinguishers. Nevertheless, I wanted to show the installation like this. I wanted to say that these old extinguishers were like old Nazis, who no longer had the strength to snuff the flame of the menorah. This was the only time I used this literal interpretation when exhibiting *Menorah*. Actually, it was David Galloway, the noted curator and art critic, writing for the *International Herald Tribune*, who convinced me that the object was powerful enough on its own. The work was in great demand. I won several awards for it, and it went from exhibition to exhibition. Actually, there exist two copies of *Menorah*. One was bought from me by ZKM | Center for Art and Media in Karlsruhe as the very first work for the collection of its Museum of Media Arts (and so it was given identification number 001). The second was commissioned in 2001 by the Jewish Museum in Berlin at the architect Daniel Libeskind's request.

Shortly after the fall of the communist system in eastern Europe in 1990, I was invited to return to Prague to establish the first department of New Media arts in the region. When I spoke to my mentor, Nam June Paik, about the offer of a professorship in New Media at the Academy of Fine Arts in Prague, he told me, "Go for it! Good luck!" and spontaneously gave me 5,000 Deutsche Mark to get the new department started. With this money and some additional sponsorship, I purchased two video cameras and three video editing systems. This very basic video equipment was the basis for creating a lively and creative department in a cubistic villa next to the main Art Academy building. In the first years, I worked with my students on some early communications art projects, such as *IPI* (*International Painting Interactive*), in collaboration with students in many other countries who collectively created a virtual painting using a graphics tablet and modem. We were also involved in a pioneering interactive television project (*Piazza Virtuale*), which was presented at the 1992 documenta IX in Kassel, Germany. The seminal philosopher of media Vilém Flusser inspired my students with his highly original lectures. After his tragic death, we organized a series of Vilém Flusser symposia in collaboration with Prague's Goethe-Institut.

During this period in Prague, I developed projects using locative media, such as

explains to me how his seemingly simple object works. In the bench on which I am sitting, a transmitter sends out impulses to the screens. When visitors pass by, they disrupt the signal: Judaism, in this way, is alive; the flame may go out for a moment, but it will continue to flicker quickly. Originally, according to Bielicky, his menorah was supposed to fill the empty space of commemoration. Then Libeskind decided to install Kadishman. Of course, Bielicky was disappointed, mostly because he rejected Kadishman's work for artistic reasons. He even wrote to the museum project

Holocaust in the immediate post-World War II period in the new state of Israel, the ironic treatment of the sacred Hanukkah myth in the context of Holocaust remembrance is also significant on another level. It is not only the miraculous myth of Hanukkah that is ironized. Indeed, the entire ideological fabric connecting the heroic Maccabee revolt to the destruction of European Jewry and the establishment of Israel – that is, the fulfilment of the Zionist dream – as a solu-

```
private float getStarboard(float z) {
return z * xScaling + TextHeadline.widestSymbol;}

private float getPortside(float z) {
return -z * xScaling - TextHeadline.widestSymbol;}

public void draw(float t, float xTranslation, float zTranslation) {

renderer.begin3DRendering();

drawSources(t, xTranslation, zTranslation, sourcesOnHorizon,

sortingOfHorizon, sortingOfHorizonInverted, farOfHorizon,

firstSortingOfHorizon);

drawSources(t, xTranslation, zTranslation, sourcesOnBeach,

sortingOfBeach, sortingOfBeachInverted, farOfBeach,

firstSortingOfBeach);

renderer.end3DRendering();}
```

f001a0 00 JavaThread "C1 Compiler-Thread3" daemon [_thread_blocked, id=19971, stack (0x000070000fb1f000,0x00007000 0fc1f000)] 0x00007fcef1034000 JavaThread "C2 CompilerThread2" daemon [_thread_blocked, id=19459, stack (0x000070000fa1c000 ,0x000070000fb1c000)] 0x00007fcef2038800 JavaThread "C2 CompilerThread1" daemon [_thread_blocked, id=18947, stack (0x000070000f919000 ,0x000070000fa19000)] 0x00007fcef081b000 JavaThread "C2 CompilerThread0" daemon [_thread_blocked, id=18435, stack (0x000070000f81600 ,0x0 00 070000f91600 0)] 0x00007fcef201b000 JavaThread "Signal Dispatcher" daemon [_thread_blocked, id=17927, stack (0x000070000f713000, 0x0 000 70000f813000)] 0x00007fcef080e800

```
private void drawSources(float t, float xTranslation, float zTranslation,

ArrayList<TextSource> sources, int[] sorting,

int[] sortingInverted, float zPosition, int firstSorting) {

for (int i = 0; i < sources.size(); i++) {

// every source

TextSource source = sources.get(i);

float x = source.x + xTranslation;

float z = zPosition + zTranslation;

float y = getY(z);

float xInWaterSurface = source.xInWaterSurface;

float zInWaterSurface = source.zInWaterSurface;

int[] currentSorting = sortingOfHorizon;

if (i % 2 == firstSorting) {

currentSorting = sortingOfHorizonInverted;}

for (int j = 0; j < rowAmount; j++) {
```

manager but received no response. His letter is revealing in two ways. He documents the development of the exhibition and formulates his view of art that addresses the Holocaust. "I think it is very problematic to want to express something as indescribable as the Holocaust in a concrete, pictorial form. After talking to my mother and her sister, who had been in Auschwitz for two years, I can't think of a work of art that could represent the mass murder of the Jews." And: "It contradicts the Jewish perception, to create a concrete depiction of suffering."

The exhibition designers who filled the Libeskind building with evidence of the history of two thousand years of the Jews in Germany also had to make a choice. They opted for a minimalist presentation of personal items. Therefore, while looking into the showcases, I feel like a voyeur sniffing other people's private lives: diaries, postcards, toys, jewelry, suitcases. Survivors have presumably donated these things to the museum - proudly and hoping to give younger generations access to the past. And yet I had the feeling that I am not entitled to look at all these intimate things at such close range.

The small number of exhibits is astonishing. The museum appears empty. An old lady who was sitting next to me on the bench in front of the menorah agreed. "There's nothing left of us. What do they want to show here?" And then she told about herself. She spoke of her own Holocaust and how she had survived it. She opened her handbag and showed me two items the museum people

a global positioning system (GPS), that presented at Ars Electronica in Linz, Austria. My *Intelligent Mailman* [1994] at Ars Electronica was the first GPS artwork ever. I integrated GPS and internet technologies in a performance artwork that electronically transmitted my wandering through the Negev desert for four days, retracing the steps of Moses in the Exodus from Egypt. I also created virtual environments at the Babelsberg High-Tech Center in Berlin and at the ZKM | Center for Art and Media in Karlsruhe.

Living at the intersections of Czech and German cultures was and continues to be an amazing trigger for creative thought and action. Switching time-space while reflecting on one's encounter with changing environments is a great teacher for a creative person. I felt that the newly found freedom in eastern Europe produced a level of energy and creative potential at the time that was much stronger than what was happening in western Europe. I traveled extensively throughout the former communist world between 1990 and 2000 as adviser to the Soros Center for Contemporary Arts, creating educational departments and centers for New Media art from Bucharest, Odessa, and Moscow to Alma-Ata in Kazakhstan. I began the new millennium lecturing on New Media arts in Thailand and, along with Francis Wittenberger, founded the New Media Arts Festival in Bangkok. My experience in Asia led me to realize how much more dynamic this part of the world was in comparison to the staider culture of western Europe.

The challenges of educating future generations in the field of digital arts are the rapidly changing conditions that make today's media theory stale tomorrow. We know that ideas we taught a decade ago are irrelevant today. Perhaps, the most significant change is the democratization of video and computer technologies that makes everyone a potential digital artist. The aim to create Soros media centers in eastern Europe modeled after the ZKM | Center for Art and Media Karlsruhe and MIT's Center for Advanced Visual Studies and Media Lab required vast amounts of funding for sophisticated equipment and facilities. The concentration of digital art production in these centers has given way to powerful media tools that are both cheap and compact enough for anyone to create serious digital artworks in their own home. Presti-

tion to the age-old problem of Jewish exile is put into question.

Beyond refiguring the sacred, Uri Tzaig's *String*, Moshe Safdie's *Memorial to the Deportees*, and Bielicky's *Menorah* accomplish something more: all three resist the monumentalizing of the past and Holocaust memory. They avoid the process whereby objects are removed from history and turned into fetishes of the past. As Didier Maleuvre argues in *Museum Memories*: "To decree that the museum piece is an object henceforth removed from historical becoming turns that object into a sacrament of history, a history so absolute as to be above historical being itself. The museum artefact is crowned with a historical aura of such sacredness that history itself, in its becoming, cannot touch it." In such a manner, Maleuvre argues, the museum confers on its artifacts the "sanctity of an eternal judgment" so that "objecthood is invested with the aura of fate." In other words, the museum raises its objects into a realm above and outside history. This temporal disjunction and rupture transforms artifacts into monuments, which

JavaThread "Finalizer" daemon [_thread_blocked, id=14339, stack(0x000070000f610000,0x000070000f710000)]
0x00007fcef0809800 JavaThread "Reference Handler" daemon [_thread_blocked, id=13827, stack(0x000070000f50d000,0x000070000f60d000)]
0x00007fcef1001000 JavaThread "main" [_thread_blocked, id=775, stack(0x00007fff5d536000,0x00007fff5dd36000)]

Other Threads:
=>0x00007fcef102e000 VMThread [stack: 0x000070000f40a000,0x000070000f50a000] [id=13315]

VM state:at safepoint (shutting down)

VM Mutex/Monitor currently owned by a thread: ([mutex/lock_event])
[0x00007fcef1804c80] Threads_lock - owner thread: 0x00007fcef102e000

Heap:
total

gious media art festivals like Ars Electronica in Linz and Transmediale in Berlin are having to reinvent themselves to continue their claims of being innovative, risky, and fresh.

The primary question is, what is the role of the artist in society in the twenty-first century? We need to completely rethink stereotypical images of the artist and the concept of the art school, which is becoming obsolete. Perhaps art schools can be replaced by mobile educational units that adapt to alternative cultural environments. We need to acknowledge the hundreds of millions of pictures produced worldwide daily. This enormous proliferation of images is radically changing our sensibilities. It is causing cultural pollution of our environment that may be as great a threat to our minds and souls as physical pollution is to our bodies. Does it make sense to educate our students to produce more and more images? Perhaps we need to encourage the practice of *cultural ecology* by creating an ecological movement against the image pollution of our environment like those protesting against chemical pollution. Students in a post-digital age are already creating new forms of dematerialized art – Net art, locative media, data and information visualization, telematics – that reach into public spaces globally and even beyond our planet.

My impression is that most educational institutions are producing artists who are often swallowed up by the media industry – television, advertising, and other large media corporations. Although I recognize that students coming out of art schools have to pay rent and other costs of living, they should not sell out to industry, but rather should have the self-confidence to promote their unique qualifications as creative partners when negotiating projects with commercial enterprises. From the beginning, they should build a symbiotic relationship between themselves as media artists and commercial enterprises.

Although few art educators like to talk about it, I see many art schools around the world succumbing to financial pressures, which often forces them to accept less talented young people just because they bring tuition money to the school. I am very much aware of the privilege I had in Prague where this was simply not an issue.

My sixteen years teaching at the Academy of Fine Arts in Prague convinced me that the key to educating future digital artists is less the quality of the school and the professor than the quality of the student who gets accepted. In Prague, I was fortunate to always be able to choose the best of the best. Consequently, those students were from the beginning more my partners than students. My students in Prague were invited and won awards in such New Media art festivals as Ars Electronica in Linz or Transmediale in Berlin, where they were considered not students but professional artists.

I guess I was lucky again to be appointed as a full-time professor and head of the Department of lnfoArt / Digital Media at the Karlsruhe University of Arts and Design (HfG), Germany. The fact that the school is situated in the same giant building as the ZKM is a great advantage for the students. They can see world-class media art shows, attend events with top international performers, and hear lectures by some of the most important artists and theoreticians in the world. After sixteen years in Prague, I am leaving the dreamy and poetic city for the more rational and functional Karlsruhe. This is my third emigration between the Czech Republic and Germany.

Although primarily conceptual in orientation, my department at the Art Acad-

would have liked – her yellow Star of David with sewing marks and the last letter her mother had written, in 1942, before she was deported to Auschwitz and murdered there. The lady always has the Star of David and the letter in her pocket. "My children don't know about it. I don't know myself why I'm telling you this. Now please give it back to me; it belongs to me."

The moment I held the Star of David in my hand was more moving, more important, more instructive than everything this museum has to offer. Do I have to explain that in more detail? Blumenthal believes that he

appear as the "damaged, inauthentic" images of what they once were. From their original contexts and supplanted anachronistically into the present, the objects' ceremonial character keeps intact the "historical caesura" at their core. The objects are no more than ruins committed to the "holding tank of commemoration," appearing to us through a veneer of loss. Monumentalized objects expose, finally, what Maleuvre calls the "alienated status of memory

```
// every headline
Text-Headline headline = source.headlines[currentSorting[j]];
if (z > beach) {
break;}
if (z >= horizon) {
float currentPortside = getPortside(z);
float currentStarboard = getStarboard(z);
for (int k = 0; k < headline.amount; k++) {
// every symbol
float xOfSymbol = x + headline.xPositions[k];
float xOfSymbolInWaterSurface = xInWaterSurface
+ headline.xPositions[k];
// TODO: starboard value should fit to the right edge of the screen
if (xOfSymbol > currentStarboard) {
break;}
if (xOfSymbol > currentPortside) {
Vec3f coordinates =
```

118784K, used 117727K [0x000000076ab00000, 0x000000077a300000, 0x00000007c0000000) eden space 117760K, 99% used [0x000000076ab00000,0x00000000771d5fe78,0x0000000771e00000) from space 1024K, 59% used [0x00000000077a200000,0x000000077a298010, 0x000000077a300000) to space 10752K, 0% used [0x0000000778e00000, 0x0000000778e00000,0x00007 79880000) ParOldGen total 72704K, used 8603K [0x00000006c0000000, 0x00000006c4700000, 0x000000076ab00000) object space 72704K, 11% used [0 x000000006c0000000 ,0x00000006c0866f70, 0x00000006c4700000) Metaspace used 27902K, capacity 28146K, committed 28416K, reserved 1075200K class space used 3217K, capacity 3292K,

emy in Prague was also a technological laboratory in which students were given a lot of freedom and, in turn, were expected to assume individual responsibility. Most students understood this challenge. Others misused it to their disadvantage. I believe that it is important to work with the students on highly innovative, challenging, and risky issues. My experience has taught me that project-centered study motivates students more and is generally a more efficient educational methodology than more formal methods.

The significance of being open to learning from teachers and colleagues through ongoing dialogue has also taught me. My long-term dialogue and friendship with key thinkers and artists, such as Nam June Paik, Vilém Flusser, Woody and Steina Vasulka, Mel Alexenberg, and Peter Weibel, have enriched me and facilitated my ability to see alternative perspectives on life and art. Students should be encouraged to develop the need to break out of institutionalized frameworks. The younger generation should learn to take risks rather than always follow their teachers. Often students exhibit a fresh vision that exceeds those of their professors. It is our duty to support their vision even when our egos sometimes may get hurt. They should ask if the so-called art system (art school, gallery, museum, art critic, curator, art magazine, art fair, etc.) is the right framework for a digital artist at the beginning of the twenty-first century, knowing very well how much this system is corrupted, where often financial interests dominate and manipulate the art market independent of the quality of the artworks.

For the past two years, my wife, Kamila Bielicka Richter, and I have been collaborating on a project that we call *Falling Life* [2005–07]. It operates completely outside of the art system. It is an ongoing project that was introduced for the first time in Berlin in August 2005. This urban screening project needs neither a curator nor a gallery. It does not need a fixed place or access to electric power. We are equipped with a car, a laptop, a compact powerful projector, and a small power generator. With this mobile equipment, we can create an instant presence in the urban landscape. We transform city architecture into dynamic and living organisms. Without any on-site preparation and without any permits, we operate a kind of guerilla theater-style

has created a living museum, but despite its enticing multimedia offering, there can be no question he did. The Jewish Museum, Berlin, is an extension of the fascination that modern Germany has with dead Jews. Perhaps this is why the official opening had to have the character of a festive ceremony. According to the federal president, the museum shows that Jewish German history is more than the Holocaust and the Third Reich. In fact, the museum shows the utter insecurity of Germans about what their history actually is. Instead of looking at their own history, German historians concentrate on Jews. The best research into recent German history comes from British and American historians, while there are countless chairs for Judaism at German universities. Despite all this scientific research, the Berlin museum is unable to explain Jewish history because it overlooks the fact that German Jews are only a small part of the Jewish people, whose origins are in Palestine, not in Europe. By presenting the German Jews as a talented, successful, but always exotic minority, the museum paints a picture of Germany as a society that remains closed to people of different skin color, religion, and culture. At best, these people were or are tolerated; at worst, they were driven out or destroyed.

After the tour, visitors to the Jewish Museum can decide whether modern Germany is an open, multicultural society by pressing a green button for Yes or a red button for No. Who may have thought up this game? After visiting a museum documenting Germany's terrible past, isn't the

in modern times"; that is, they reveal that our reliance on ceremonial forms to remember the past is a symptom of our estrangement from an authentic culture or environment of memory.[3] In contrast to the display of monumentalized ruins of the past in the United States Holocaust Memorial Museum, *String*, the *Memorial to the Deportees*, and *Menorah* do not appear as ruins or monuments in a conventional sense. They do not escape the realm of history to become sacraments – rather, they remain rooted in the here and now as they wait for their actively engaged viewers to unveil their meanings.

Excerpt from Jennifer Hansen-Glucklich, "Refiguring the Sacred: Strategies of Disfiguration in *String*, the *Memorial to the Deportees, and Menora*," in *Holocaust Memory Reframed: Museums and the Challenges of Representation* (New Brunswick, NJ: Rutgers University Press, 2014), 178–80.

```
surface

.getCoordinates(xOfSymbolInWaterSurface,

zInWaterSurface, t);

coordinates.x += xOfSymbol;

coordinates.z += z;

renderer.draw3D(headline.symbols[k], coordinates.x,

y + coordinates.y, coordinates.z, 1f);}}}

z += rowDistance;

zInWaterSurface += rowDistance;

y = getY(z);
}}}

private float getY(float z) {

return m * z + c;}

@SuppressWarnings("unchecked")

public void pushHorizon()
{

sourcesOnBeach = (ArrayList<TextSource>) sourcesOnHorizon.clone();

// for (int i = 0; i < rowAmount; i++) {

// sortingOfBeach[i] = sortingOfHorizon[i];

// sortin-
```

committed 3328K, reserved 1048676K
Card table byte map: [0x0000000104361000, 0x0000000104b62 000]
byte_map_base: 0x0000000100d61000

Marking Bits: (ParMarkBitMap*) 0x0000000103 8efd20
Begin Bits: [0x000000010 50b8000, 0x00000001090b8 000)
End Bits: [0x000000010 90b8000, 0x000000010d0b8 000)

Polling page: 0x0000000101fbd000

CodeCache: size= 245760Kb used= 9030Kb max_used= 9047Kb free= 236729Kb
bounds [0x000000010e3d4000, 0x0000000010ed04000, 0x000000011d3d4000]
total_blobs= 3647 nmethods= 2684 adapters= 874
compilation: enabled

Compilation events (10 events):
Event: 164.628 Thread 0x00007fcef1034000 3284 ! 4 org.eclipse.swt.

projection. Within less than ten minutes, we can illuminate giant buildings with our artwork, reaching huge audiences that would probably never walk into a gallery or museum. We use a minimalist language of constantly appearing and disappearing pictograms. The moving icons often represent the collective reality of our interconnected, globalized world. *Falling Life* has been projected during the Prague-Berlin Festival, at a subversive public interference in Ars Electronica in Linz, at ZKM in Karlsruhe, at the DOX Centre for Contemporary Art in Prague, at Interferencia Barcelona, at MAF Bangkok, and will be shown in Jerusalem and Sevilla.

Falling Life has mutated into www.fallingtimes.info [the website is no longer available], an everlasting and growing online real-time news translation machine representing permanently appearing and disappearing information about our times as we witness the fall of Western civilization. *Falling Times* refers to the heavy info pollution in which we live. It is estimated that 1.5 exabytes of unique new information will be generated worldwide this year. That is estimated to be more than in the previous five thousand years. Half of what students in technical colleges learn today in their first year of study will be outdated by their third year of study.

The info society has created a new kind of consumer – the info consumer. The most consumed information is the news. The news has been turning more and more into entertainment, creating infotainment. The news producers are the biggest info polluters of our time and thus are the biggest contributors to info ecological disaster. In our *Falling Times* [2006–09] participatory artwork, the visualization of news content is reduced to headlines and keywords that appear most often in Google News. These news bytes are translated into a dynamic pictogram language that aims to be universal and instantly understandable. Online users have the opportunity collectively to define the meaning associated with each icon we have created. In this way, the users decide which icon represents which news and which news is being searched for and displayed. This open platform permanently grows and transforms itself by learning from collective contributions. Information does not transport meaning anymore but rather creates a pattern decorating our daily life with the feeling that we are connected to reality. It is urgently necessary to teach our students to deal with being inundated with massive amounts of information.

We projected on the facade of the grotesquely gigantic building built by the brutal Romanian dictator Nicolae Ceaușescu in Bucharest. With the fall of communism and the execution of Ceaușescu, the building constructed by his dictatorial regime is being shared by the parliament of a democratic government and a museum of contemporary art. There was an exhibition in the museum of social realist paintings glorifying the dictator that, after his fall, looked absurd and preposterous. Boorish parliamentarians did not get the satire of these kitsch artworks and accused the curators of promoting communist propaganda. Perhaps it is a sign of Isaiah's prophetic vision to beat swords into plowshares that the buildings of evil regimes are being transformed into centers for creative arts. The Media Department of the Düsseldorf Art Academy, where I studied with Nam June Paik, was housed in former Gestapo headquarters, and I currently teach in an enormous building shared by my art school and the ZKM that was a Nazi munitions factory, where slave laborers manufactured torpedoes.

First published in Mel Alexenberg, ed., *Educating Artists for the Future: Learning at the Intersections of Art, Science, Technology and Culture* (Bristol: Intellect, 2008), 193–202.

1 Sven Spieker, "Interview with Michael Bielicky" (audio), November 16, 2009, https://artmargins.com/interview-with-michael-bielicky-sven-spieker.
2 Ibid.
3 Didier Maleuvre, *Museum Memories: History, Technology, Art* (Stanford, CA: Stanford University Press, 1999), 12, 61, 63, 58f. Maleuvre builds here on Pierre Nora's concept of *lieux de mémoire* – "places of memory" that become necessary because of a lacking contemporary culture or environment of memory. See Pierre Nora, "Between Memory and History: Les Lieux de Mémoire," *Representations*, no. 26 (Spring, 1989): 7–24.

positive obvious? The answer must be easy. You just press the green button and go out with a good feeling. Yet, a handwritten note hangs on the device: "Not yet functioning."

First published in *Frankfurter Allgemeine Zeitung*, no. 220 (September 21, 2001). Translated from the German by Paul Kenig.

```
gOfBeachInverted[i] = sortingOfHorizonInverted[i];
// }
firstSortingOfBeach = firstSortingOfHorizon;
leftOfBeach = leftOfHorizon;
rightOfBeach = rightOfHorizon;
addSourcesToHorizon();}
private void addSourcesToHorizon() {
sourcesOnHorizon.clear();
// shuffle and invert sorting
// shuffle(sortingOfHorizon);
// invertSorting(sortingOfHorizon, sortingOfHorizonInverted);
float halfOfCurrentSourceWidth = 0f;
float x = getPortside(horizon);
while (x - halfOfCurrentSourceWidth < getStarboard(horizon)) {
TextSource source = getNextSource();
halfOfCurrentSourceWidth =
```

widgets.Display::sleep (74 bytes) Event: 164.657 Thread 0x00007fcef1034000 nmethod 3284 0x000000010ebf1590 code [0x000000010ebf18a0, 0x0000 00010ebf2c88] Event: 176.896 Thread 0x00007fcef001a000 3285 1 sun.java2d.pipe.RenderBuffer::position (11 bytes) Event: 176.896 Thread 0x00007fcef001a000 nmethod 3285 0x000000010e97e990 code [0x000000010e97eae0, 0x000000010e97ebf0] Event: 202.288 Thread 0x00007fcef001a000 3286! 3 java.util.logging.Log Manager::ensureLogManagerInitialized (128 bytes) Event: 202.289 Thread 0x00007fcef001a000 nmethod 3286 0x000000010ebb6990 code [0x000000010ebb6b40, 0x000000010ebb71c8] Event: 202.289 Thread 0x00007fcef001a000 3288 3java.util.

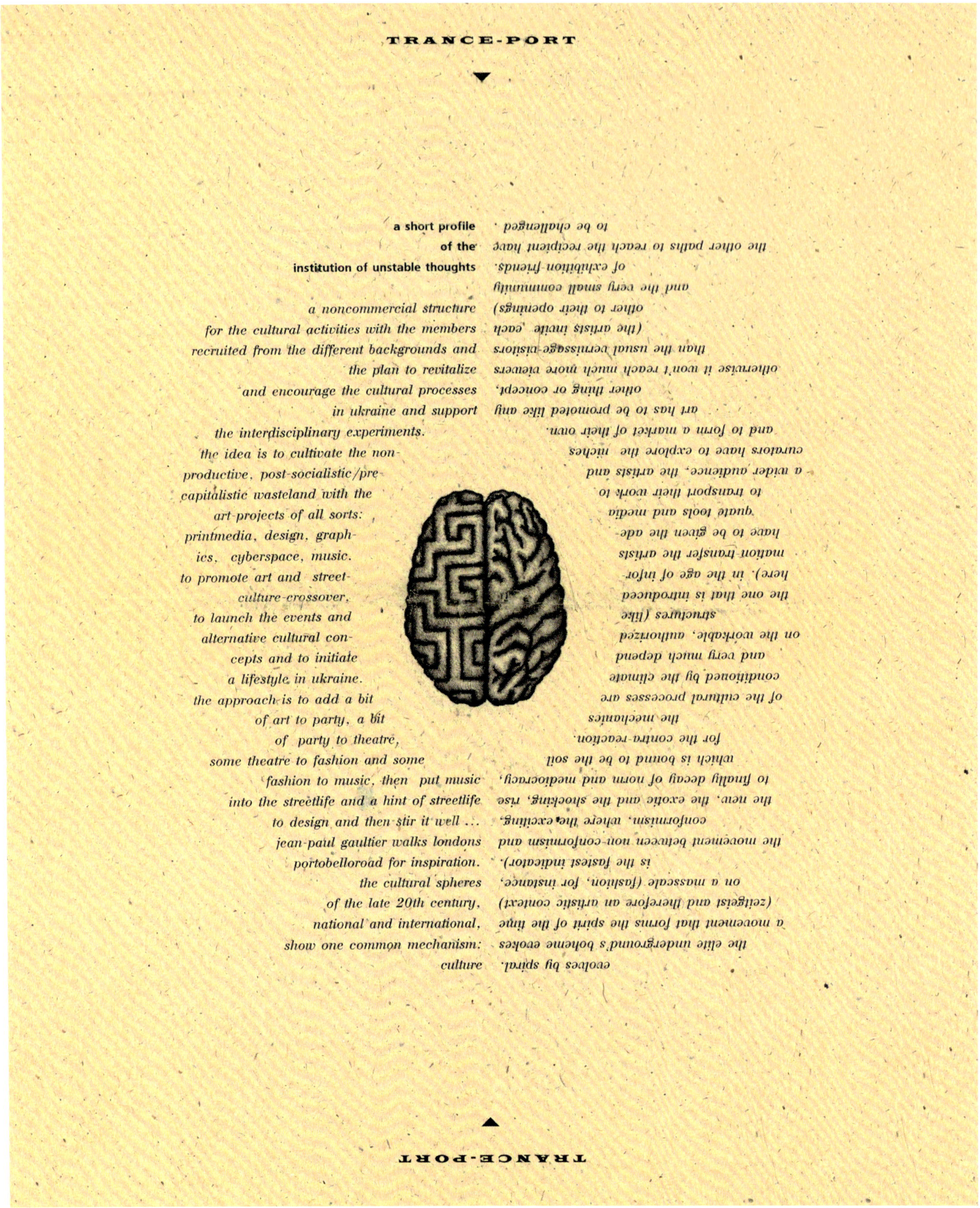

TRANCE-PORT

a short profile of the institution of unstable thoughts

a noncommercial structure for the cultural activities with the members recruited from the different backgrounds and the plan to revitalize and encourage the cultural processes in ukraine and support the interdisciplinary experiments. the idea is to cultivate the non-productive, post-socialistic/pre capitalistic wasteland with the art-projects of all sorts: printmedia, design, graphics, cyberspace, music, to promote art and street-culture-crossover, to launch the events and alternative cultural concepts and to initiate a lifestyle in ukraine. the approach is to add a bit of art to party, a bit of party to theatre, some theatre to fashion and some fashion to music, then put music into the streetlife and a hint of streetlife to design and then stir it well ... jean-paul gaultier walks londons portobelloroad for inspiration. the cultural spheres of the late 20th century, national and international, show one common mechanism: culture evolves by spiral. the elite underground's boheme evokes a movement that forms the spirit of the time (zeitgeist and therefore an artistic context) on a masscale (fashion, for instance, is the fastest indicator). the movement between non-conformism and conformism, where the exciting, the new, the exotic and the shocking, rise to finally decay of norm and mediocracy, which is bound to be the soil for the contra-reaction. the mechanics of the cultural processes are conditioned by the climate and very much depend on the workable, authorized structures (like the one that is introduced here). in the age of information transfer the artists have to be given the adequate tools and media to transport their work to a wider audience. the artists and curators have to explore the niches and to form a market of their own. art has to be promoted like any other thing or concept, otherwise it won't reach much more viewers than the usual vernissage-visitors (the artists invite each other to their openings) and the very small community of exhibition-friends. the other paths to reach the recipient have to be challenged .

TRANCE-PORT

Institution of Unstable Thoughts (Alexander Gnilitsky, Lesja Zajac), flyer for the Guerilla exhibition project *Trance-Port* in various exhibition venues in Odessa (August 24–25,1996). The Institution of Unstable Thoughts was founded in 1996 and was initiated by Michael Bielicky.

Perpetuum Mobile

Pepe Rojo in conversation with Michael Bielicky

Pepe Rojo: In several of your works, you fuse contemporary technology with mystical symbols, particularly Jewish. You have *Menorah*, *Golem Is Alive*, and *Next Year in Jerusalem*. Why? Is technology mystical? Is mysticism technological?

Michael Bielicky: Of course the technology is mystical and also the mysticism can be technological. The technology, especially the computer technology, can be mystical, because it has its own life; it creates sometimes unpredictable results, and so it can create real surprises. The new media are unstable media. And vice versa, the mysticism can have technological quality; for example, Kabbalah, the Jewish mystical system, is based on complex mathematical principles. The great Rabbi Loew of Prague, the creator of golem, was one of the first applied mathematicians.
But those arguments are not the reasons why I use the new technologies. I simply believe that the old philosophical systems can be made visible with the tools of contemporary technology. I would even go further and insist that computer and information technology are ideal tools to make some of the old ideas accessible and readable for men of today.

Rojo: Although most of your work is technologically challenging, you have relied on figures of the past, "appropriating" them in your work: Benjamin, Flusser, Delvaux, Švankmajer, even Paik's face going through his video alteration techniques; you even have some work titled in Latin. How do you supply the technological "newness" of your work with a historical heritage? How do you explain the nexus between new media and the traditional arts?

Bielicky: Again I have to repeat: the older some ideas are, the more modern technologies are needed to make those ideas accessible. I was always fascinated about the old Jewish philosophical systems, and the only way to deal with those ideas was to use electronic media. Later on, I got confirmation that I was on the right track through the writings of the great artist and educator Mel Alexenberg. He argues that the Jewish idea of artistic and creative acts is the opposite to the Greek or Hellenistic approach. He says that entering the postmodern age is nothing else than applying the Jewish (cabalistic) principles of nonlinearity and multiple truths. And in this sense, computer technology is an ideal creative tool in our age. The possibility of creating interactivity or hypertextual art is an analogy for cabalistic principles. Mel Alexenberg is currently in the process of writing a book, *The Future of Art in a Postdigital Age*, with the subtitle *From Hellenistic to Hebraic Consciousness* [the book was published in 2011].
To answer the last part of your question, I think there is not much of a nexus between the new media and traditional art. But there are lots of links between new media and old attempts of using the *laterna magika* and camera obscura, or other technological tools.

Rojo: How do you explain the relationship between art and new media? Can we talk about art in new media? You once told me you were kind of skeptical about the whole idea of art. Why? How does this view reflect on your work as an artist?

Among the Twitter Critters: The Artist Michael Bielicky Presents His Garden of Error and Decay

Niklas Maak

Berlin. For a moment one could think that they were doing a painting exhibition again, that they were illuminating a mural in the Czech embassy with spotlights – but then one could see from the outside that this was something completely different: not a painting but a film projection, a procession of drawn figures that drifted slowly over the wall as if in a slow river. Sometimes someone picked up a kind of joystick, like those in video games, aimed at the characters passing by, and then there was an entertaining bang; people were happy, and the characters on the wall swelled to twice their size.

What did it all mean? What was projected on the wall was an interactive work by Prague-born artist Michael Bielicky, who was a master student of Nam June Paik and has been a professor of media art in Karlsruhe for five years now. His work is called *Garden of Error and Decay* and, as it shone on the wall, pretty much corresponded to what Diego Rivera's political murals – the so-called Murales – were for the twenties: large-format hidden object pictures that want to highlight what determines our time. Something like this rarely takes place in oil paintings today, if only because the crucial image production has largely migrated to the media and the Internet. There you can also look at the "garden" (www.gardenoferroranddecay.net), and the first thing you notice about this website, which was enlarged during the Prague-Berlin Festival for an evening of interactive murals, is the gentle beauty of the illustrations: with its colors and the stylized light blue Mount Fuji in the background, the "garden" could also be an idyllic children's book. But like Henry Darger, you will soon see only pictograms of horror in this idyll: cars with smoking exhaust pipes and terrorists and oil cans and fires and nuclear explosions, pulsating, mutating icons for all the world's problems, which are constantly changing. Visually, it all looks very nice – as if a Japanese graphic artist had mixed Paul Chan's *Happiness after 35,000 Years of Civilization* with Bosch's *Garden of Earthly Delights* and a few war films; in terms of content, the project wants to establish a new narrative form: the *data-driven narrative*. Twitter feeds and stock-market data are fed into the work in so-called real time, changing the passing world panorama of animated pictograms with the help of sophisticated algorithms, while the joystick commands, which are given in the belief that the virtual world is influenced like a video game, remain completely without consequences.

As a political message, that might sound something like "the world is controlled by networked power systems and forces of nature; you are only fooled into believing that you have design options" – but this would be very Diego Rivera–like, simple and misanthropic. As an attempt to render a picture of the invisible global movements on the internet, it is all the more exciting: what one sees here is the beginning of an art that within the internet wants to make visible what determines there – without leaving pictures – how things look here and elsewhere.

First published in *Frankfurter Allgemeine Sonntagszeitung*, no. 5 (February 6, 2011). Translated from the German by Paul Kenig.

Bielicky: The new media as a creative tool has a very different character to the tools of traditional media. Dematerialization and ubiquity are highly symptomatic of the use of new technologies. The aesthetics of communication is not interested in the creation of physical objects; it is more interested in time space. I am not skeptical towards the creative process itself, but I am very skeptical of the frame in which art is viewed and practiced these days. I am talking about the so-called art system, like art school, art historian, art magazines, curators, galleries, and especially the art market. It seems that the art market dictates what is in and what is out, and what is art and what is not art. This is an absurd situation. It seems that at the moment, more interesting art happens outside of the art system. I have always tried to operate outside of this system so as not to be dependent on weird and fucked-up situations. And I must say, it is partly the fault of artists themselves: they do not have enough imagination to seek other frames; they are often blinded too much by fame and money, and so they play this stupid game.

Rojo: You also told me you were skeptical about the whole idea of teaching. How does this reflect on your work as head of the Prague School of New Media? In which way are you skeptical about the idea of teaching?

Bielicky: It seems that in the field of natural science, for example, it is normal to adapt the research conditions and also the education to the latest results we are aware of. But in art research and education, there is this strange conservatism. Often the educators are teaching things that were of interest about thirty years ago.
In the art school of today, students should be learning more about the aesthetics of disappearance, telepresence, genetic coding, subversive strategies, et cetera. Instead of this, they are learning about painting techniques or printing techniques, and so on. This is not very responsible. The students have the right to learn about topics of our times. The teaching should also be more project orientated, and in certain ways, teachers should be more like partners with the students than some kind of guru.

Rojo: One of your constant themes is cyclic representations. Your spiral is perhaps the main metaphor: *Circulus Viciosus*, *Perpetuum Mobile*, even *Room with a View*. Even still, the repetition never "lands" in the same place. Each cycle changes. How do you approach the idea of nonlinearity?

Bielicky: As I've already mentioned, the nonlinearity, the interactivity or ubiquity are new and very challenging conditions for the creative act. Those possibilities have to be explored, and we are still at the very beginning. Why should the artist be recognizable by her or his art? This is also a very old idea, which only serves the art market. The artist should be taking risks all the time, and she or he should be open to experiment, even if it meant failure.

Rojo: The nature of a work of art changes radically through the use of new media. How would you describe these changes?

Bielicky: I think I've already answered this question above. The fact that I am creating dematerialized artifacts which can be presented anywhere, anytime, is such a radical change as much in the production as in the reception that first we have to get used to these new conditions.

Rojo: In your writings, you use the word *interface* continually. You have created truly interactive pieces. What happens when you exchange the idea of spectator for the idea of user?

Bielicky: Well, why should the recipient always be just a passive receiver of art? It is almost a kind of handicap. When I involve the spectator in my project and she or he can actively communicate with the piece, this interaction opens many more possibilities for reading the artwork's message. I am also giving the spectator more options, and this is a very important moment. I think it is wonderful when the spectator can have his own choice of perceiving the artwork. The dynamic relationship between the art piece and the spectator opens up very interesting sociological, psychological, and, of course, artistic diversity.

Rojo: Most of your installations remind me of a game. What's the difference, in the age of electronics, between art and entertainment?

Bielicky: I wouldn't say that most of my projects are game-like. But it doesn't matter. This question is very important in the moment. It seems that some computer games are much more sophisticated and exciting in every sense than so-called high art products, and we must be allowed to ask whether we are facing a situation turned upside down or not. Because it could be that so-called high art is, in reality, less powerful than the art of popular culture, like, for example, interactive computer games.

Rojo: How do you understand the idea of place, of site? You've gone from manipulating images to manipulating places. What have you learned from your explorations on pieces like *Delvaux's Dream*, *Room with a View*, and *Exodus*? What is movement?

Bielicky: Well, in the case of *Delvaux's Dream* [a walk-in painting], my main aim was to create the possibility of overcoming the separation between the subject (the viewer) and the object (the painting). By using virtual set technology and a special tracking system, the viewer could become part of the perceived painting and even interact with the figures in the painting. This experience gives a new perspective from which to reflect on art history. *Room with a View* (a 360-degree interactive, real-time generated environment) allows the spectator to actively create her or his way through different realities, which do not only surround the viewer with images but also with sound. Maybe future cinemas could have this kind of shape. And finally, *Exodus* was a virtual teleperformance from the Negev desert, using internet, GPS (global positioning system), cellular phone, and three-dimensional graphics. Here, the real-time experiences of the artist and the viewer were very different; there were lots of challenges in this project, and we didn't know if it would work at all. All of those projects became a great school for me and the teams that collaborated on them.

Rojo: What is an *act* in the electronical age? How does virtuality affect our life? Are we really changing, or is this change only cosmetic?

Bielicky: The simple fact that we can be anytime, anywhere, definitely affects our perception and behavior. Entering virtual spaces evokes strong sensual experiences. I am not saying that we will be saved by technology. In

Video game on the Fat Corner in the Art Museum: Eyes in the Cheese

Ulrike Merten

"Turn your TV into a video sculpture. Tilt your device to the right side. With this gesture you honor Joseph Beuys." If this is all it takes. This recommendation comes from Michael Bielicky and Ricardo Peredo Wende, two Paik students. Beuys's fat was in the fire – to be precise, on October 9, 1986, the *Fettecke* [fat corner] of the art prophet ended up in the waste bin. The video work of the artists encircles the rise and fall of the wall object in Beuys's former studio with technical gadgets, wit, and dexterity.

The two TV sets in the *Creamcheese* room of the art museum are upside down. Yet, the portrait format alone does not create a new perspective. It was unpredictable cuts, fades, snippets of words, and trembling still images that irritated viewing habits. Nonetheless, whether the visual confusion is suitable enough to sweep our heads empty to ask ourselves, "What is art and where does it end?" remains to be seen.

The video "sculptors" let the experts – Kasper König, Klaus Staeck, Harald Naegeli, Johannes Stüttgen, Irmin Kamp [...] – have their say, sometimes cutting them off spontaneously, sometimes with only a goulash of sound, thus emphasizing the sentences on the *Fat Corner* that they left unaltered. Beuys puttied ordinary fat high up in the right corner of his studio and stated that when one looks at the corner of fat, one is able to penetrate into personal spiritual depths. Sprayer Naegeli sees the destruction of the artwork as a provocation for thought. Beuys's disciple Stüttgen is outraged by the ignorance and sees the crime as a sign that there is no freedom, only a free space at the academy: "an eye in the cheese."

While the video somersaults in the viewer's head for forty minutes, Beuys's *Spirit* descends the stairs of the academy: sad, speechless, with a film camera in his hand.

First published in *Neue Ruhr Zeitung*, no. 63 (March 16, 1987). Translated from the German by Paul Kenig.

Excursions from within Time

Wolfgang Werth

The archaic and the contemporary, the historical and the timeless, the motionless and the flowing, the spiritual and the material: in his work Michael Bielicky permits only apparent contrasting to clash, which occasionally interconstitutes itself. His view is aimed, over timely correspondences, at those with which continuity, tradition, and the specific newness about a crystalized point in the present can be made explorable. Bielicky assumes an expression of modesty through cultural cognate in an eloquent way, which, as a rule, is lacking in the approach to the new media, indicating doubt as to the immortality of things. This assumed attitude is not coquetted from the standpoint of a supposed evolutionary futuristic extreme point but is in the center of an imaginary nondirectional development, equivalents on the wrong terrain that can be subsumed under one formula – in this case: information – and that become clear in the installation *Spiral*. The walk-in sculpture is a symbol of the unrelenting flow of information that every person is subjected to and that he himself disassociates. The asymptotic rejuvenating spiral reminds us of the double-helix genetic code as the natural, or even the prayer, functions of Torah, as the cultural expression of the archetypical structure by means of which information is transferred and in the form of which our solar system moves through the universe. Bielicky takes the liberty of preserving the heterogeneous, the off-hand, the noncompound, the duration of his artistic performance and of connecting it to a third, new one. Isolated from the original familiar context, history is fictionalized and excursions into over-timeliness are possible. The affinity of the widest variety of forms that the inconceivable has the power to assume is of interest to the artist in his archaistic search for traces. The things themselves – from which man remains excluded, as they are only accessible to him in an imparted manner – will nevertheless in no way be instrumentalized. Bielicky's art is at one and the same time oxymoronic: ideas become visibly perceptible without even the Judaic image prohibition being infringed – a testimony of respect to the widest range of manifestations of knowledge that does away with graphical hierarchy. The contemporary does not have the final decision regarding his position in the incessant flow of time but does acknowledge his provisional position, which is inherent in this. He reclaims that he is a part of that future – which is understood to be permanently developing in the present – supplied from the past. The mere presence of the symbol, for example, in the installation *Menorah*, opens up a flood of associations that disregard – not directed by the object – the limitation of the historical moment and penetrate into regions that close themselves off to the possibility of depiction. The consequences of archetypical motives in Bielicky's sculptures – be it the recurrent number seven, the menorah, the circular and spiral structure, fire and water as metaphysical symbols of meaning – speaks for the synchronicity of the diachronies, for the simultaneousness of nonsimultaneousness, for dated parallels. Tribute is paid to the inherent antiquatedness of man, which replies to an increasingly dehumanized world of life with a recourse to the irrational, which occasionally can be found in the aesthetic. The complications of the conditions of the spiritual are proved by the fact that these symbols are reproduced, that is, they only become clear in simulation. The voluntarily effected collective farewell from the authentic in the world of consumer goods consequently becomes conspicuous. The sculptures, nevertheless, indicate the inability to give up the desire for the spiritual, which cannot be simulated nor reproduced. In contrast to the tangential omnipotent media, art respects the misunderstood, the nondepictable. The transmitter of visually perceptible information is always located in the "somewhere" in Bielicky's work, the closest to which comes a cryptic globe. Even here, the terms of reception can be reconstructed and rationally made accessible – and so we more or less know that in the installation *The Inner Observer*, an infrared camera is concealed in the black globe, which picks up the word *light* in all secrecy, broadcasting it by means of a coupled transmitter to the monitors that are switched on to receive – yet Bielicky aims deliberately at the dark opaque form inaugurated by the secretive black globe. A metaphoric approach to the relativity of human perceptive processes.

In his art, Michael Bielicky opposes the omnipotent mania of that hybrid rationality, which, in the wake of Enlightenment acts, is the relieving principle. Performed with the aid of artificial gestures and with technical media, Bielicky tracks down the deceivable dialectics of synchronism and difference, continuity and alternity, the calculated and the chance; and reminds us, with man-made means, of the reality that exists away from anthropocentric world pictures and evolutionary-cultural superiority.

First published in Karl Gerbel and Peter Weibel, eds., *Endo und Nano: Die Welt von innen* (Linz: Veritas-Verlag, 1992), 126–29. Translated from the German by Paul Kenig.

Ricardo Peredo, Michael Bielicky, *Menschen verstehen durch Missverstehen II/IV (Inka & Naty)*, 1988, single-channel video series II/IV. Video stills.

the future we will have great difficulties in distinguishing between reality and simulated reality. The philosopher Vilém Flusser said once: "We are no longer the objects of a given objective world, but projects of alternative worlds. From the submissive position of subjection we have arisen into projection. We grow up. We know that we dream. [...] With us, the adventure of becoming human has entered a new phase. This becomes most apparent in the indistinguishability between truth and apparition, or between science and art."[1]

Rojo: What would be, in your opinion, the most important aspects of our lives that would be changed by new technologies?

Bielicky: Oh, there are so many aspects, which will have an effect on future generations. There is the possibility of misusing those technologies to control humans in totalitarian ways. Modern societies could also become pretty stupid by getting brainwashed by all kinds of modern media, and so, in this sense, new media artists will have greater responsibility in the future. They will become a kind of control mechanism within society. Even hackers could play an important role on this issue. We have great technologies and lots of bandwidth, and what will be needed is relevant content. Of course, there are also many positive aspects to new technologies. The possibility of democratization for greater numbers of people on this Earth gives us some hope.

Rojo: Economic changes and globalization are also byproducts of technology. What do you think about their impact on eastern and central Europe since the fall of the Berlin Wall?

Bielicky: Well, first we have to differentiate – as eastern Europe is not a homogenous structure – between countries like Poland, Hungary, or the

Czech Republic that have almost become Western societies, while Romania, the Ukraine, and others are facing serious problems. You must know that in the early days, for example, in the year 1995, as far as I know, the use of the internet within Czech universities was partly higher than in some Western countries. Before the Second World War, the Czech Republic used to be a high-tech country. The plane industry and the automobile industry, for example, were highly advanced, and even during the communist era, some interesting technologies were developed in the Czech Republic. An instance of these was a passive radar system, which had the ability to track the so-called invisible American planes. Hungary has a very similar history. I would say that at the moment, the impact of new technologies on some of the above-mentioned east European countries is similar to those in western Europe.

Rojo: Many critics have been saying central and eastern Europe are the places to look for new trends in art. How do you feel about this? Have the political changes unleashed an artistic boom? What's new over there?

Bielicky: I know that some people will not like to hear what I have to say now. But it is very true. Those trends simply don't exist. Definitely not in the so-called fine arts. There is a strange cultural identity crisis in the former communist countries. Before the political changes, artists in eastern Europe could define themselves clearly against the communist governments. But since the communists have gone, it seems to be very difficult in a globalized world, which of course has reached large parts of eastern Europe, to find this identity.
Since so-called contemporary art in the West is also struggling, the struggle in eastern Europe has doubled. Most contemporary art in eastern Europe is a kind of second-class Western art. I would say that in the field of cinema, literature, or theater, the situation is better; in those disciplines you can find some interesting works.

Rojo: How do you work? How do you approach the creative process? How does collaborating with other people affect this process?

Bielicky: I work from one extreme to the other, which means there are periods when I am concentrated on a single project, and periods where I take a kind of multitask approach. Mostly, I work with teams of highly specialized experts, because actually I have no idea about programming or building hardware; I know what is possible to do with the technology, and that's enough. But since life and work are in my case the same issues, it is as with life: sometimes everything goes fine, and sometimes everything goes wrong. But I love it how it is, because I can never predict how things will turn out, if the project will succeed, if somebody will like it, if I will not go broke, and if I will not dream of doing something completely different. I believe that over the course of a lifetime, a human being should live in different cultures and do at least three different professions.

Rojo: What's the future like?

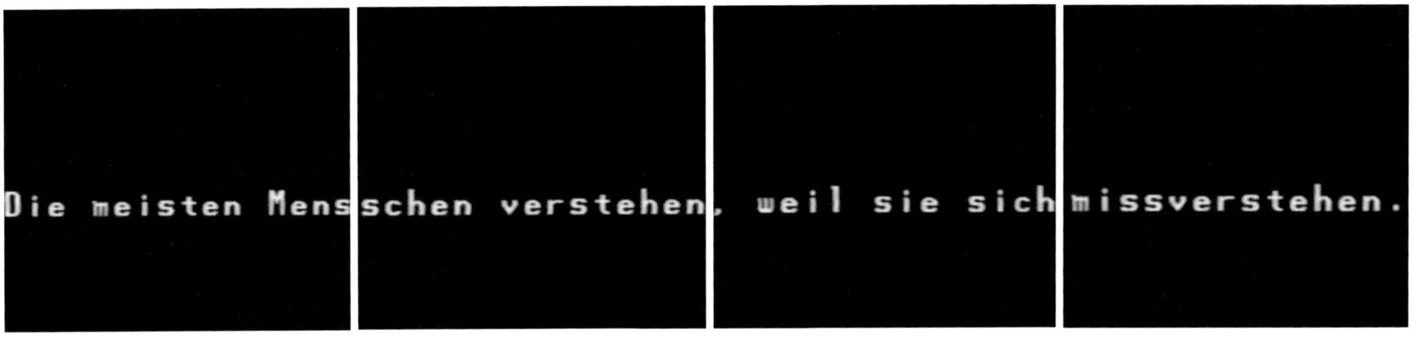

Ricardo Peredo, Michael Bielicky, *Menschen verstehen durch Missverstehen II/IV (Inka & Naty)*, 1988, single-channel video series II/IV. Video stills.

Bielicky: Ten Commandments

1. Most people understand each other because they misunderstand each other.
2. Ubiquity of information, interconnected interactive documents, reciprocal and asynchronous telecommunications within groups and between groups: the virtualizing and deterritorializing character of cyberspace makes it the vector of an open "Universe." (Pierre Lévy)
3. We have to reconsider the meanings of the fixed terms like *soul*, *spirit*, *identity*, *me*, and *self*. (Vilém Flusser)
4. Since we have no idea of the future, we have no idea of the present either.
5. We are not the subjects of an existing world anymore, but the projections of alternative worlds. (Vilém Flusser)
6. The term *interactive media* is pretty imprecise; it would be more accurate to use *instable media*".
7. In the future we will distinguish not between different kinds of information but different kinds of noise.
8. The universe is an information-seeking and information-giving system: it has a consciousness.
9. The conscience of the future will be the hackers.
10. The future is not what it used to be.

This interview was first published in the magazine *complot 34* (2002): 40–45. Translated from the Spanish by Pepe Rojo.

1 Vilém Flusser, "Digital Apparition," in *Electronic Culture: Technology and Visual Representation*, ed. Timothy Druckry (London: Aperture, 1996), 244f.

Unknown, Nam-June Paik, entrance exam,
Düsseldorf Art Academy, 1987.

Nam June Paik in Between

Michael Bielicky

Is Nam June Paik really a Korean? Is Nam June Paik really an artist? Is Nam June Paik a person at all? Or is he/she/it just a virtual being that has become synonymous with the myth of the times, becoming avant-gardist, magician, world citizen, player, and so on? It was around 1976 when I saw a video installation for the first time in my life at the Düsseldorf Kunsthalle. The installation was not by Paik, but by his wife Shigeko Kubota. It was the well-known work *Nude Descending a Staircase* (1976). I still remember very well that I stood in front of it fascinated for quite a long time, and even after seeing the rest of the exhibition, I quickly returned to Kubota's work.

This Düsseldorf time was very exciting in many ways. The Düsseldorf Art Academy and its surroundings were loaded with creative energy. The artist group ZERO, with Mack, Piene, and Uecker, has shown just as many new perspectives with their presentations as the young music group Kraftwerk irritated the audience with their electronic music in the legendary Creamcheese Club (designed by ZERO). At this time, Joseph Beuys caused ripples, and Paik was no longer a stranger on the scene. I met Paik in 1983, when he opened his permanent video installation at the Düsseldorf Art Academy. I spoke to him, and after we had talked for a while, I asked him whether I could switch from Bernd Becher's photo studio to Paik's studio. He immediately agreed, and when a friend of his came over, he introduced me as his student. So, for the following years, I witnessed Paik's highly improvised style not only as a professor, but above all as a constantly changing artistic agitator. After he found out from me that I was from Czechoslovakia, he said I absolutely needed to get to know Woody Vasulka, an important pioneer of video art and founder of The Kitchen in New York. I did so a few years later, lucky to work together with two of the embodiments of a new art direction for many years.

Paik's video class had some specifics. For example, there was the colorful mix of his students. It was no coincidence that students of all different nations were attracted to his studio, or atelier. There were students from Bolivia, Poland, China, Austria, Iran, France, India, Yugoslavia, Ireland, Israel, Czechoslovakia, Mexico, Korea, Spain, Finland, Japan, and so forth. There were also a few German students, who were called foreigners by the international students. This multicultural mix itself was full of productive dynamism.

In 1984, I was a fresh student of Paik's and witnessed the *Good Morning, Mr. Orwell* project. This networked intercontinental satellite transmission left me enormously impressed. Discovering the satellite network as a new cultural space for itself was a highly innovative experience, especially when we look at it from today's perspective of global internet networking. Paik's lectures, and not only in our Düsseldorf Art Academy, were more like a performance, where Paik often talked about everything but video art itself. So, I was often a witness of various presentations, where the audience held itself in great anticipation to learn something about the new art but in the end had heard rather strange stories of sociological character.

At the inauguration of the unique museum project Insel Hombroich near Düsseldorf, Paik let a remote-controlled violin with a radio controller swim back and forth in a garden on a small lake. Paik would almost have fallen into the water if someone had not held him at the last second. In our studio, when there was a meeting with Paik at all, problems were often discussed that had to do with the studio's future equipment. When the student work was

Woody Vasulka at the Studio for Electro-Instrumental Music (STEIM), Amsterdam, 1996.

presented, Paik repeatedly bought parts or whole works from some students and integrated them into his own videotapes. In this case, all sides of such a "business" were extremely satisfied. Paik's unique linguistic mix of German and English with a strong Asian accent and an indefinable use of grammar often resulted in a sort of Western haiku poetry form.

It was sometimes difficult to distinguish between intention and misunderstanding. Later, when I became his assistant, misunderstandings happened all the time. For example, when we were supposed to meet at the airport, the only problem being that I thought in Düsseldorf and he thought in Frankfurt. So, I always had to drive to Frankfurt Airport when we would, in addition to the problem of his studio, discuss his art projects; and not only that, but we would also design them on the go. Within twenty minutes he scribbled three video installation drafts on paper for his employee, so that his employee had foundations for new works by Paik. Paik was always the initiator of various exhibitions for his students. We had trips to Paris and Berlin together and made several trips to New York. Again and again, unexpected events occurred during these trips. My Bolivian friend Ricardo Peredo, for example, sprayed a whole can of shaving cream on Paik's head while Paik presented our work at a public event in Paris.

Paik came to the meetings with his students fairly irregularly. I don't mean to say that this was bad. For most of us, it felt right and useful. There were always new students who tried to become a student of Paik. So he told them he was a bad professor since he was never present anyway. That did not put the newcomers off; they insisted that the legendary video master watch their videotapes. He always asked how long the tapes were, and then the lights went out, and the videos were shown. The candidates waited nervously and full of anticipation for his comments. In most cases, after the light was turned on again, Paik was sleeping. Then he would wake up and say, "Not bad, but a little too long." But who knows? In an interview, Paik explained that good tapes are those during which he falls asleep.

Shigoko Kubota, *Duchampiana: Nude Descending a Staircase*, 1991, single-channel video installation.

Nam June Paik at École nationale supérieure des arts décoratifs (EnsAD), Paris, 1987.

Jennifer Miller and Cathy Weiss, Veletržní palác, Prague, 1996.

Jennifer Miller and Cathy Weiss, Prague Castle, 1996.

Cathy Weiss and Jennifer Miller, performance, Veletržní palác, Prague, 1996.

It was not Paik that decided who would be accepted as a new student in his class; he let his students decide, which was sometimes not a nice experience for new students. It wasn't always easy to be Paik's assistant: he called me from New York from time to time, often between 3 a.m. and 6 p.m. – early, as you can imagine. I didn't always understand everything correctly. This sometimes led to irritation.

The Paik class at the Düsseldorf Art Academy existed between phantasmagoria and reality as a collection of strange individuals – people fiddling with old machines in dark rooms, young artists who were on the trail of a new medium. Paik always avoided being a role model; rather, he provoked and allowed experimental things. He emancipated his students by refusing them. He was more likely to be present in his absence.

The fall of communism was a big catalyst, especially in eastern Europe. I had been lucky enough to be appointed to the Prague Academy of Fine Arts (AVU), and established the first studio for new media in the country. Paik spontaneously gave me 5,000 DM and just wished me good luck. That was during the opening of another exhibition of former Paik students at the Anthology Film Archive in New York. I can still remember that I invited a friend from New York to the exhibition opening, the excellent performance artist Jennifer Miller. Her extremely irritating appearance has quite frightened some of the exhibition visitors.

The nineties prefigured in some ways the trends of the twenty-first century: MTV, the Gulf War, the internet, globalization, high-tech revolution, genetic engineering revolution, and so on. Paik was sensitive enough to think about some of these phenomena very early on.

First published in Yonsei University, Institute of Media Art (IMA), *Proceedings of MAC2002 Symposium* (Seoul: Yonsei University, 2002), 65–67. Translated from the German by Paul Kenig.

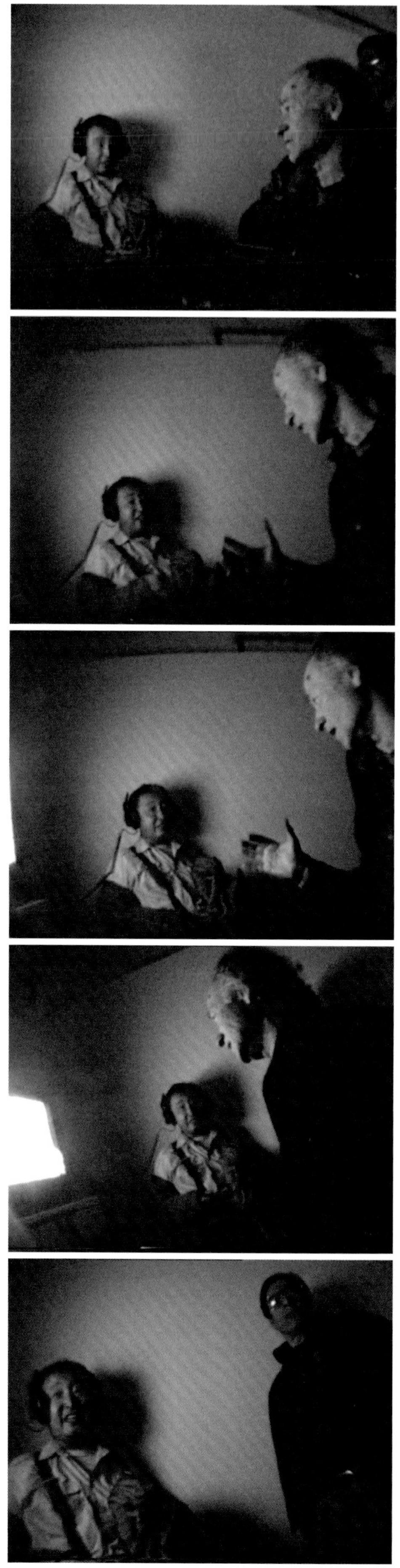

Nam June Paik and Jonas Mekas at Anthology Film Archives, New York. 1990. Screenshots.

Woody Vasulka, Michael Bielicky, and Nam June Paik, Hotel Metropol, Düsseldorf, 1987.

Video Works
1985–1990

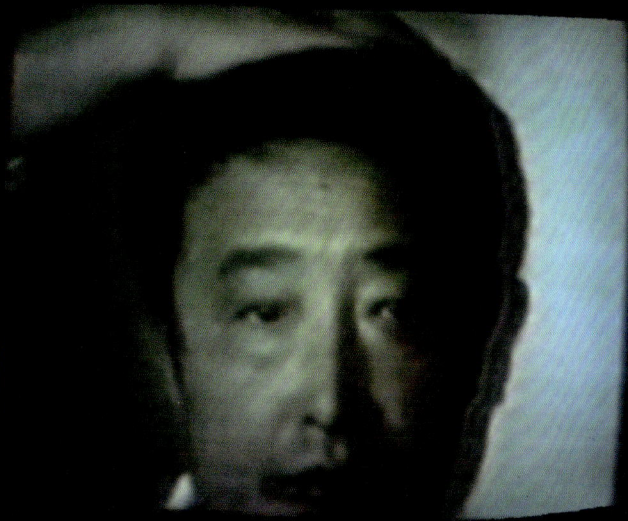

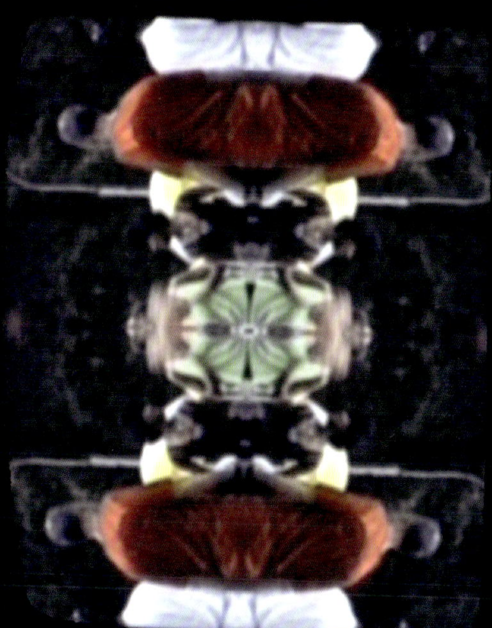
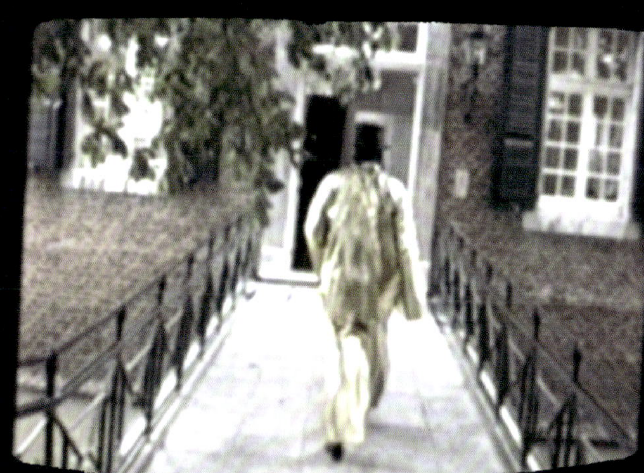
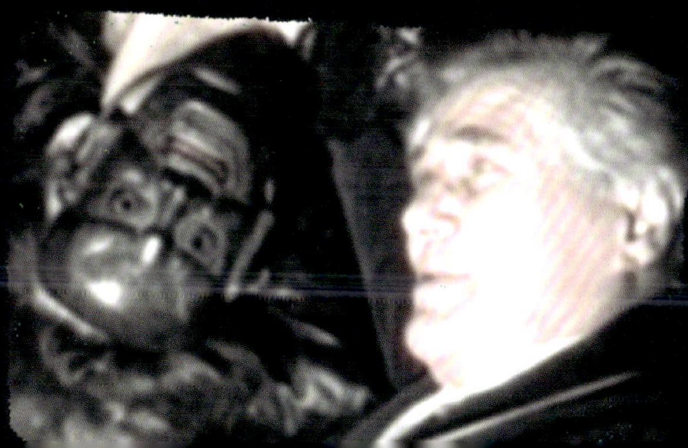

1 See Micky Kwella and Jörg Himstedt, eds., *VideoFilmFest '88 des 18. internationalen forums des jungen films*, exhib. cat. (Berlin: MedienOperative, 1988), 19.
2 See Michael Bielicky, *Four Seasons* (Amsterdam: LIMA, 1984), http://www.li-ma.nl/site/catalogue/art/michael-bielicky/four-seasons/1862; Kwella and Himstedt, *VideoFilmFest*, 19; Michael Bielicky, *Perpetuum Mobile* (Amsterdam: LIMA, 1986-87), http://www.li-ma.nl/site/catalogue/art/michael-bielicky/perpetuum-mobile/10; Petra Unnützer, ed., *3. Videonale: 11-16.9.1988*, exhib. cat. (Bonn: Videonale, 1988), 53; Michael Bielicky, *Next Year in Jerusalem* (Amsterdam: LIMA, 1988), http://www.li-ma.nl/site/catalogue/art/michael-bielicky/next-year-in-jerusalem-hommage-a-rabbi-lw/14; Dario Ghanai, ed., *5. Videonale: 15-20.9.1992* (Bonn: Videonale, 1992), 110; and Michael Bielicky, *Golem Is Alive* (Amsterdam: LIMA, 1989), http://www.li-ma.nl/site/catalogue/art/michael-bielicky/golem-is-alive/13.
3 See Klaus Bußmann and Florian Matzner, eds., *Nam June Paik: Eine Data Base* (Stuttgart: Edition Cantz, 1993), 148.
4 See Mel Alexenberg's essay "From the Golem of Prague to Waze from Israel," in this volume.
5 See Ulrich Gregor and Peter B. Schumann, eds., *17. Internationales Forum des jungen Films* (Berlin: Felgentreff and Goebel, 1987), 58; and Christoph Blase and Peter Weibel, eds., *Record again! 40Jahre-Videokunst.de Teil 2* (Ostfildern: Hatje Cantz, 2010), 86-89, 411-12.

Video Works 1985–1990

One of Michael Bielicky's first video works, *Perpetuum Mobile*, was produced in 1986 in Düsseldorf.[1] He drew on the major technical building blocks when reinventing his artistic practice, starting with the first digital video editing techniques, such as stop motion via U-Matic, time-base correction, and drop-out compensator (DOC); then turning to wireless transmissions and infrared cameras in the 1980s; and in the 1990s to GPS, the internet, and real-time data. He always tried to provoke and document aesthetic errors in the specter of the machine, both in parallel and in reflected contradiction to the media industry's ongoing technical refinement processes.

In the 1980s, Bielicky unintentionally developed techniques with the first digital video editing machines that could alter, distort, and rearrange video material, similar to his mentor Nam June Paik's debut exhibition in 1963, in which Paik used magnets to distort his exhibits based on television sets. Works, such as *Four Seasons* (1984), *Circulus Viciosus* (1985), and *Paik Hat* (1986) disturb linear narrative traditions through techniques such as literally cutting the celluloid and stop motion alone, whereas *Perpetuum Mobile* (1986), *Next Year in Jerusalem (Homage to Rabbi Loew)* (1988), and *Golem Is Alive* (1989) introduce digital editing techniques to create videos that appear haunted by the specters of early eastern European media culture, deeply rooted in Jewish formations, or patterns of thought.[2] Bielicky's video works lack a distinctive opening sequence or even starting point, as well as a definite end or closing sequence. They characteristically feature a certain duration, albeit of random length, and if this owes to environmental circumstance, then perhaps it is to Paik's remark on students' work being "not bad, but maybe a little bit too long" every time he stood up during his famous evaluation sessions held in his atelier at Düsseldorf Art Academy.[3] Parallel to this possible subconscious influence of group dynamics, Bielicky's work rides on the crest wave of technical boundaries in video editing; his video works follow Jewish patterns of thought meticulously, most strikingly their circularity, or, to use Mel Alexenberg's formulation, their "spiral consciousness." "Jewish consciousness is shaped by spiral forms: [...] Jews are called [...] 'People of the Scroll.' [...] The medium is such an integral part of the message that if the biblical words written in a scroll form are unavailable, the Torah is not read in the synagogue, even if the exact same words are available in printed book form. The Torah printed on separate pages, imprisoned between two rectangular covers, destroys the message of the endless flow of divine wisdom."[4]

Not only do the titles *Four Seasons*, *Perpetuum Mobile*, *Circulus Viciosus, Next Year in Jerusalem*, *This Year in Jerusalem*, and *Golem Is Alive* scream circular, recurring, peripatetic, infinite, birth, death, and resurrection – the contents shown in Bielicky's video works circle around general human patterns of behavior: the behavioral repetitions of everyday life are set in both fast and slow motion on screen and can thus be considered comical and absurd, often bordering on the insane. For Bielicky, technology always harbors the danger of accelerating toxic human impulses, and his works frequently comprise metaphors on the imperatives of exercising discretion toward our technical realities before they overpower us.

In collaboration with Ricardo Peredo in 1987, Bielicky examines a janitor's destruction of Joseph Beuys's *Fettecke* [Fat Corner]. The resulting documentary video sculpture is a "who's who" of Beuys's students and disciples, as well as a gush of partly absurd, partly fascinating explanations on how and why this case of a janitor's complete ignorance of art has implications for the future of art in general.[5]

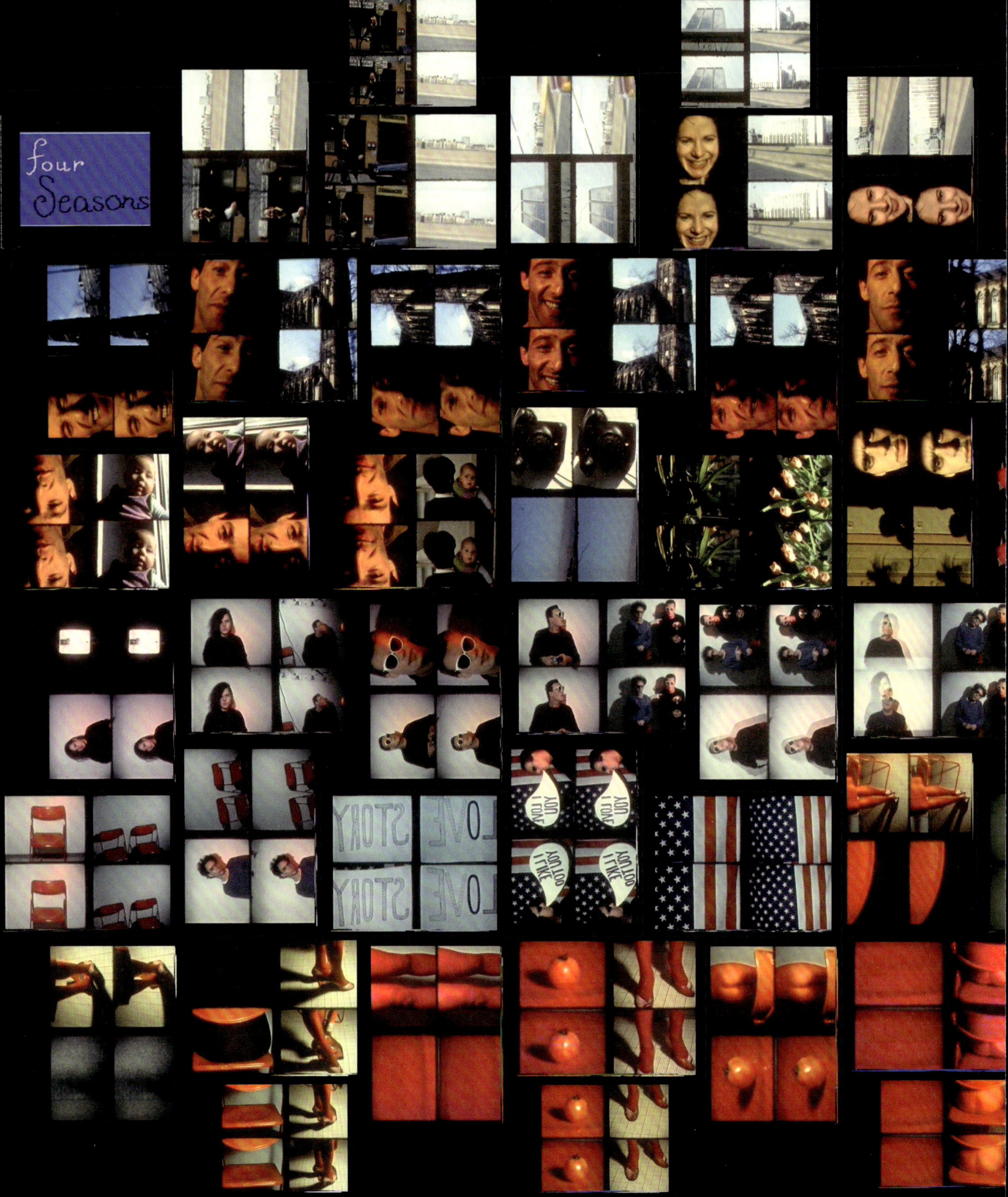
four
Seasons

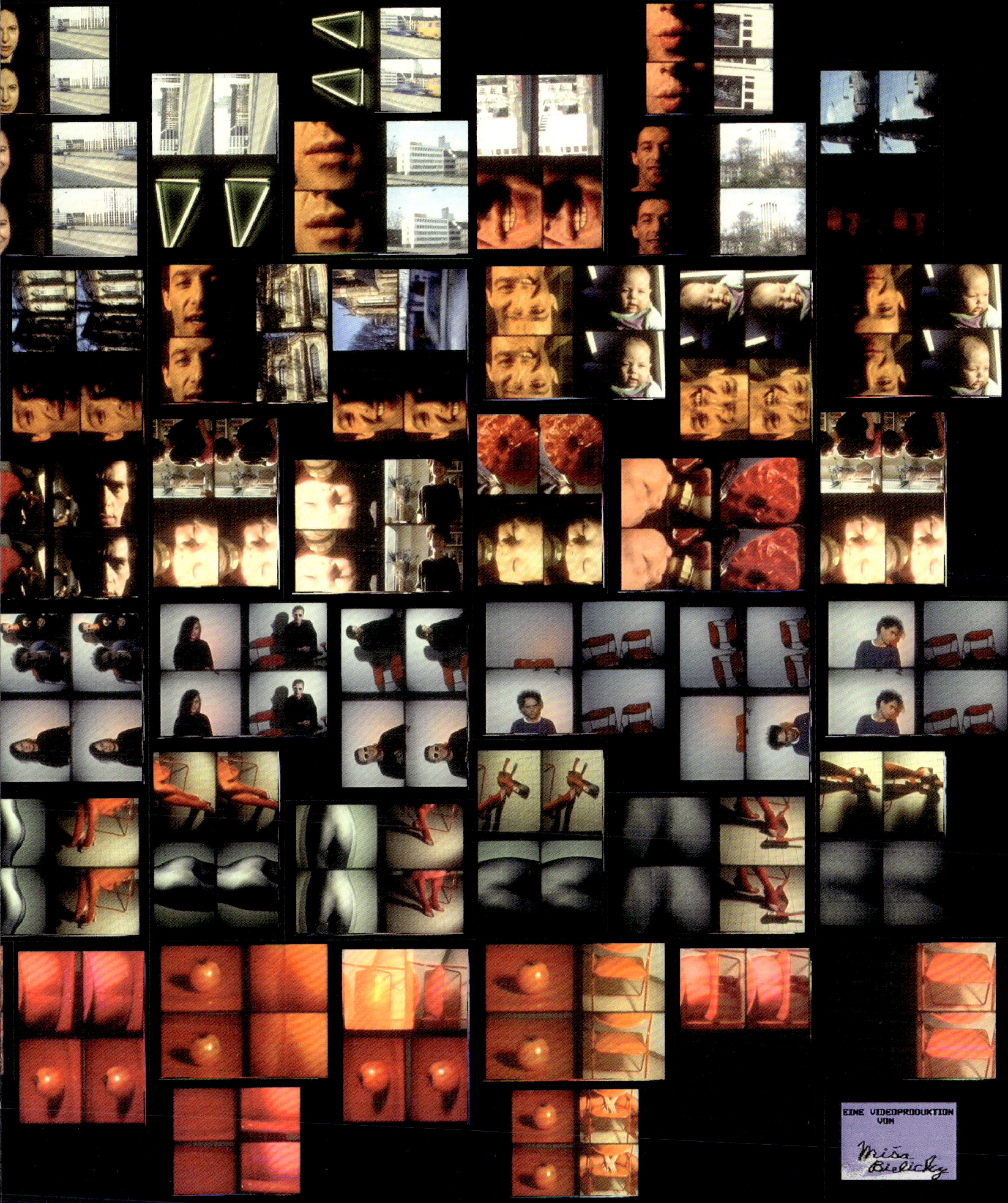

Four Seasons, 1984, single-channel video. Screenshots.

CIRCULUS
VICIOSUS

BIELI
CURRENT COLOR
MISH
CKY

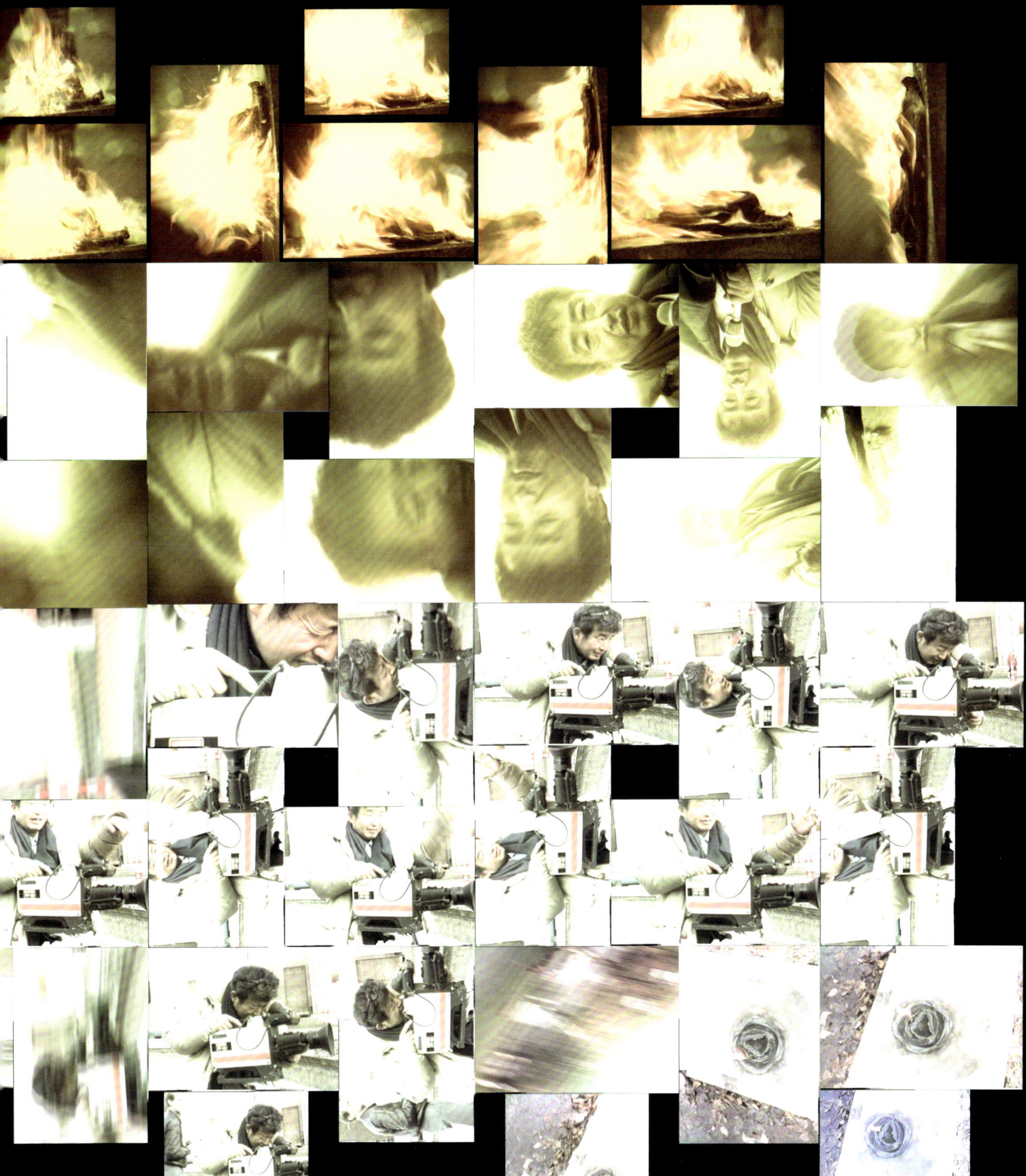

Paik Hat, 1986, single-channel video. Screenshots.

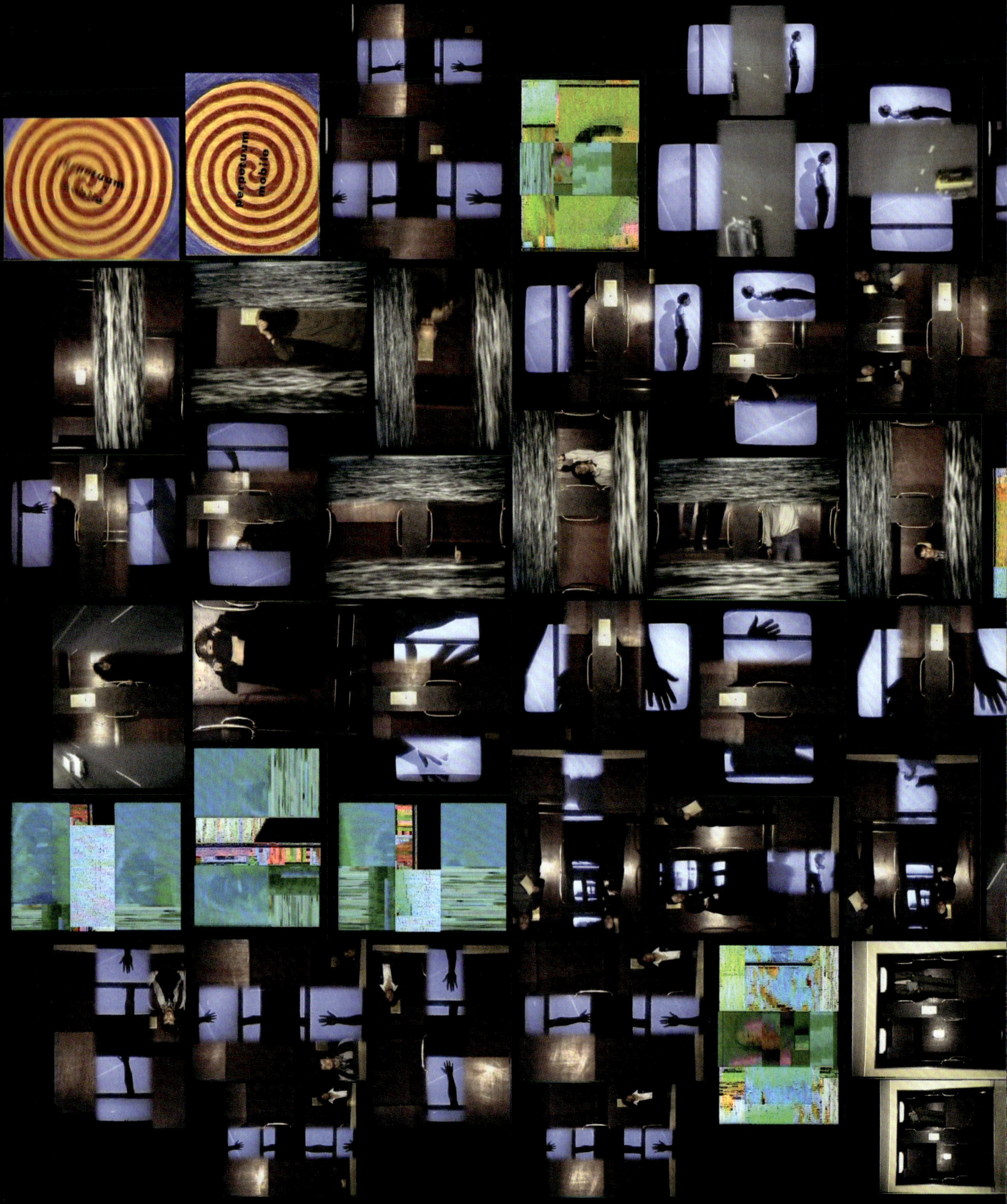
perpetuum
mobile

PERPETUUM MOBILE

Perpetuum Mobile is the depiction of the elementary manifestation of nature and human existence. Without the permanent movement and change, life would be in a static state, for example death. What remains unchanged is the ornament of the flowing space.

P A I K

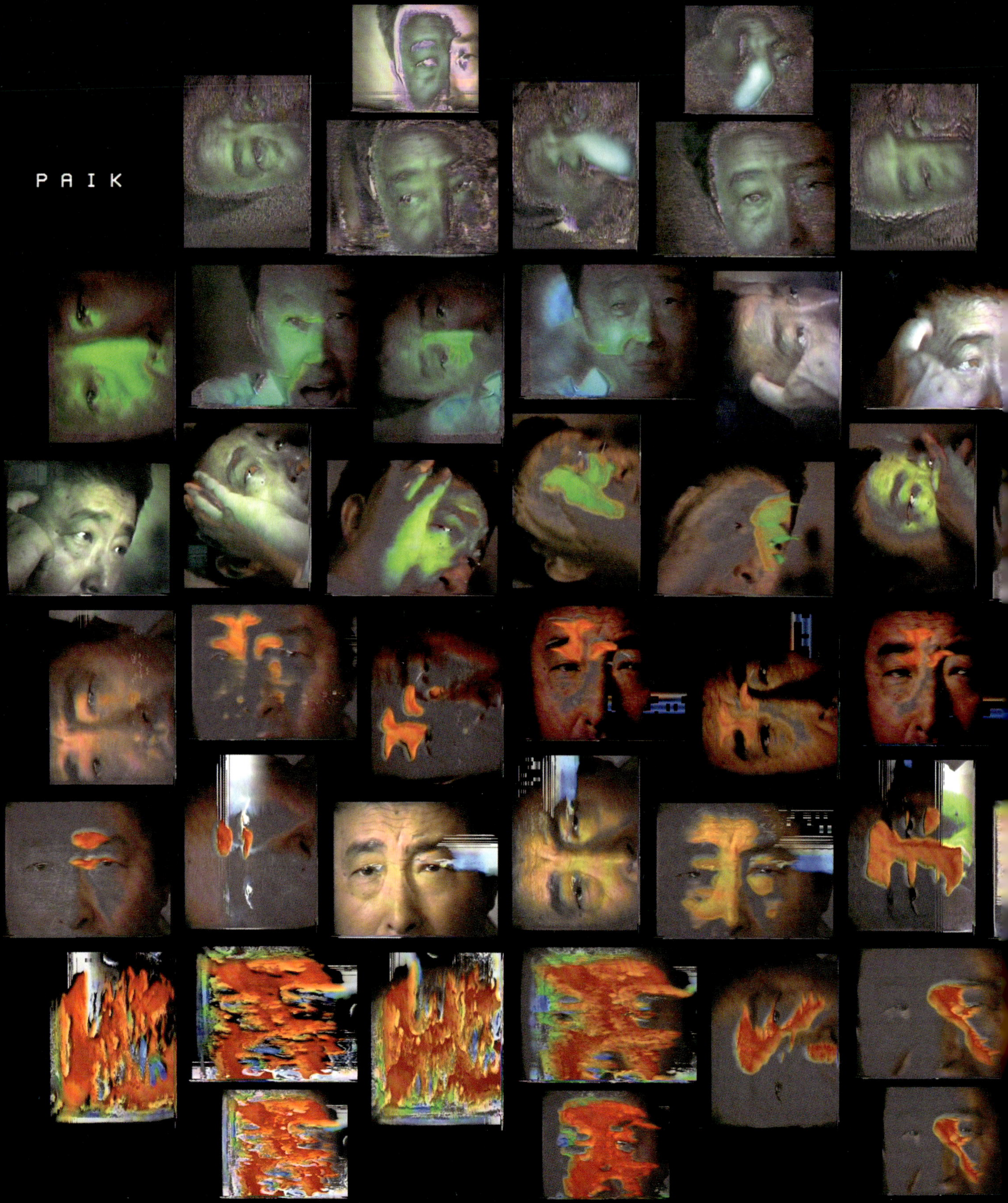

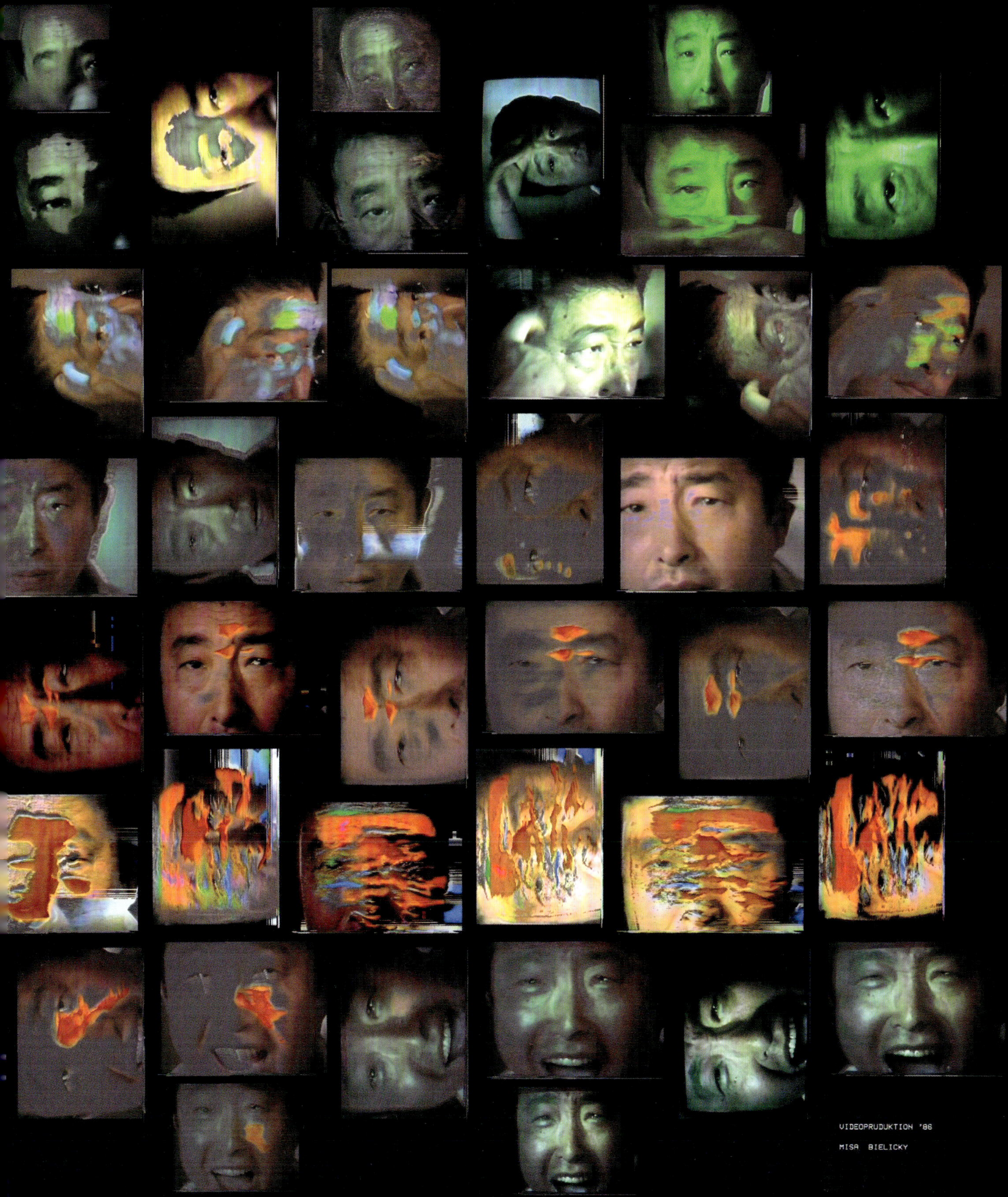

Paik – I'm an Experimentalist, 1987, single-channel video. Screenshots.

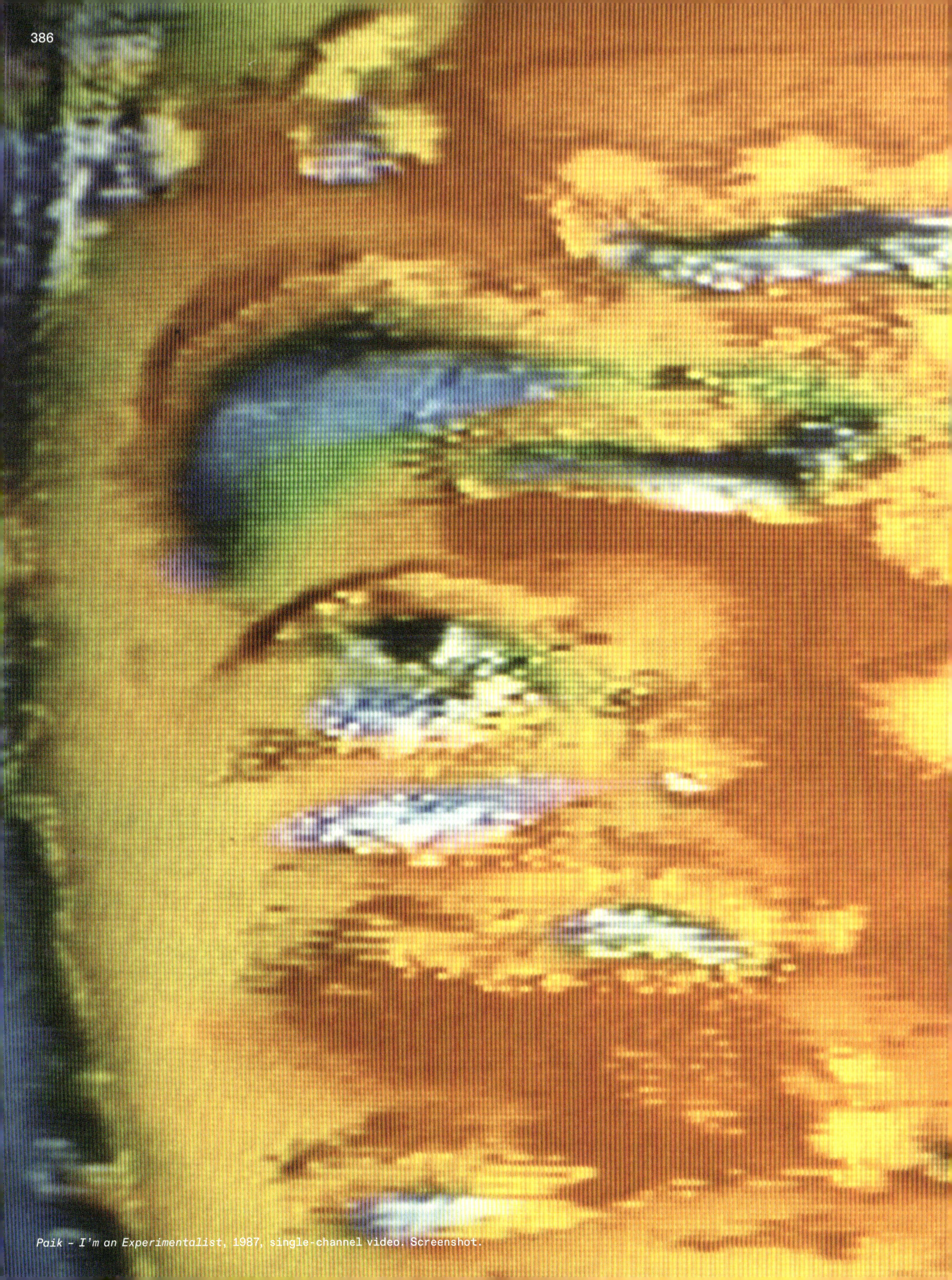

Paik – I'm an Experimentalist, 1987, single-channel video. Screenshot.

Michael Bielicky. Düsseldorf
Paik – I'm an Experimentalist

Let us now praise video art! Here's one for the "old master" in the late, great Paik-Abe color synthesizer style. Yes, we have no banalities.

Mischa Bielicky has studied video as student of Nam June Paik at the Kunstakademie Düsseldorf (Düsseldorf Art Academy).

First published in Keiko Sei, Alfred Birnbaum, eds., *Infermental 8: In the Afterglow of TV Land* (Tokyo, 1988), 16.

NEXT YEAR IN
JERUSALEM

Next Year in Jerusalem (Homage to Rabbi Loew), 1988, single-channel video. Screenshots.

Year in Jerusalem (Homage to Rabbi Loew), 1988, single-channel video. Screenshot.

GOLEM IS ALIVE

Golem Is Alive, 1989, single-channel video. Screenshots.

JLB-Perfect Day of Joseph Beuys, 1989, single-channel video. Screenshots.

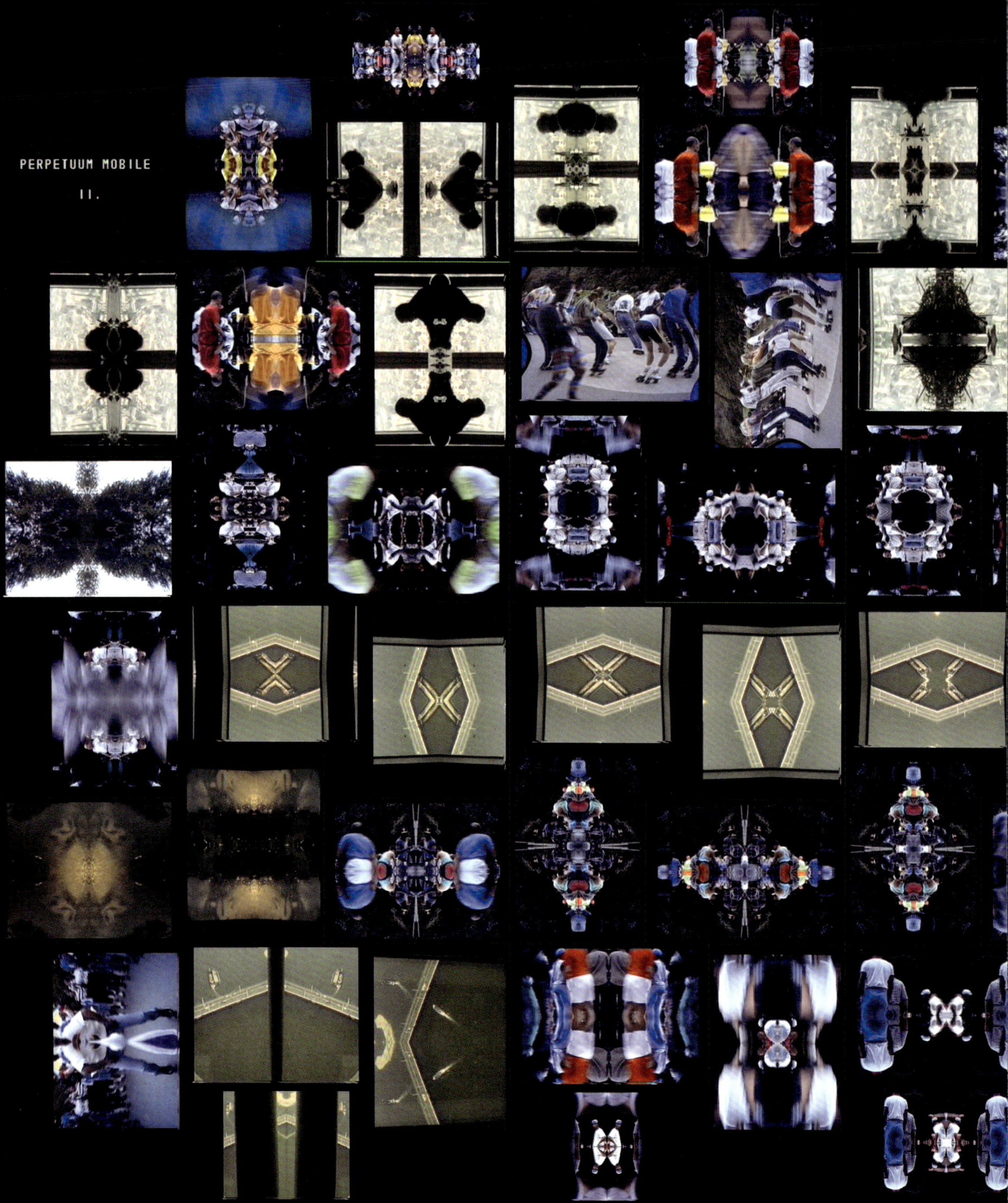
PERPETUUM MOBILE
II.

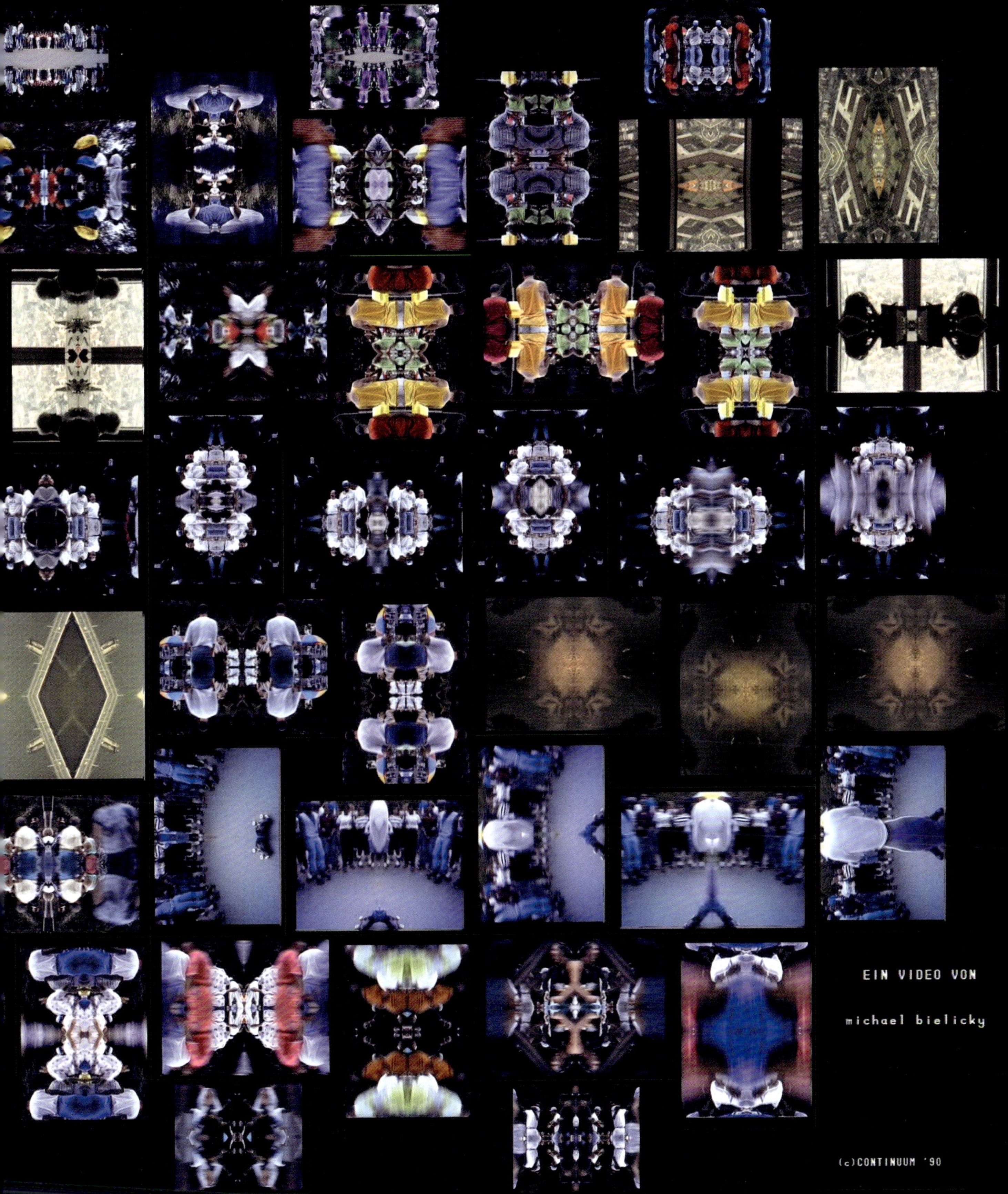

Perpetuum Mobile II, 1990, single-channel video. Screenshots.

he Visit, 1985, single-channel video. Screenshots.

DER
BESUCH

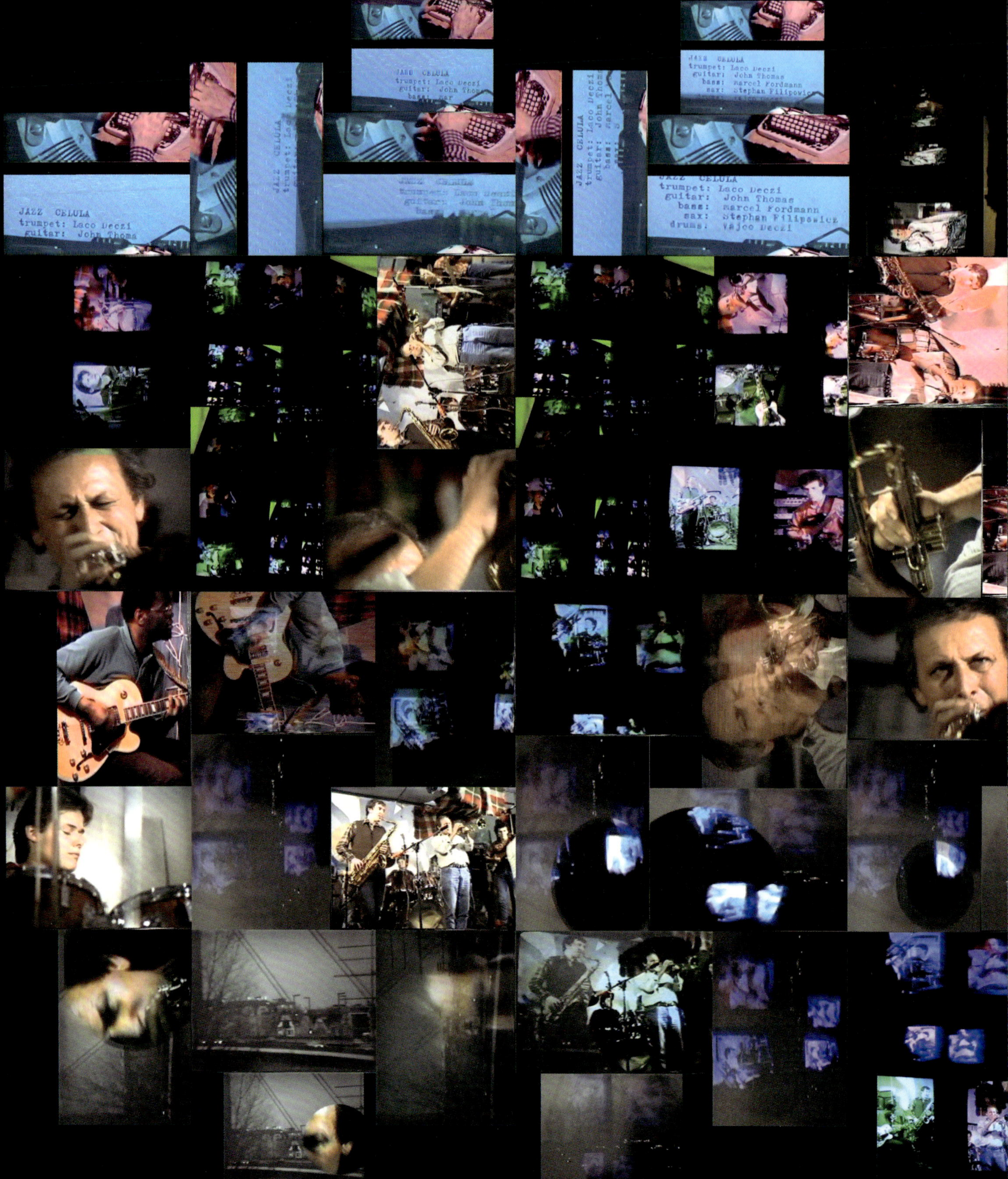
JAZZ CELULA
trumpet: Laco Deczi
guitar: John Thomas
bass: marcel Fordmann
sax: Stephan Filipowicz
drums: Vajco Deczi

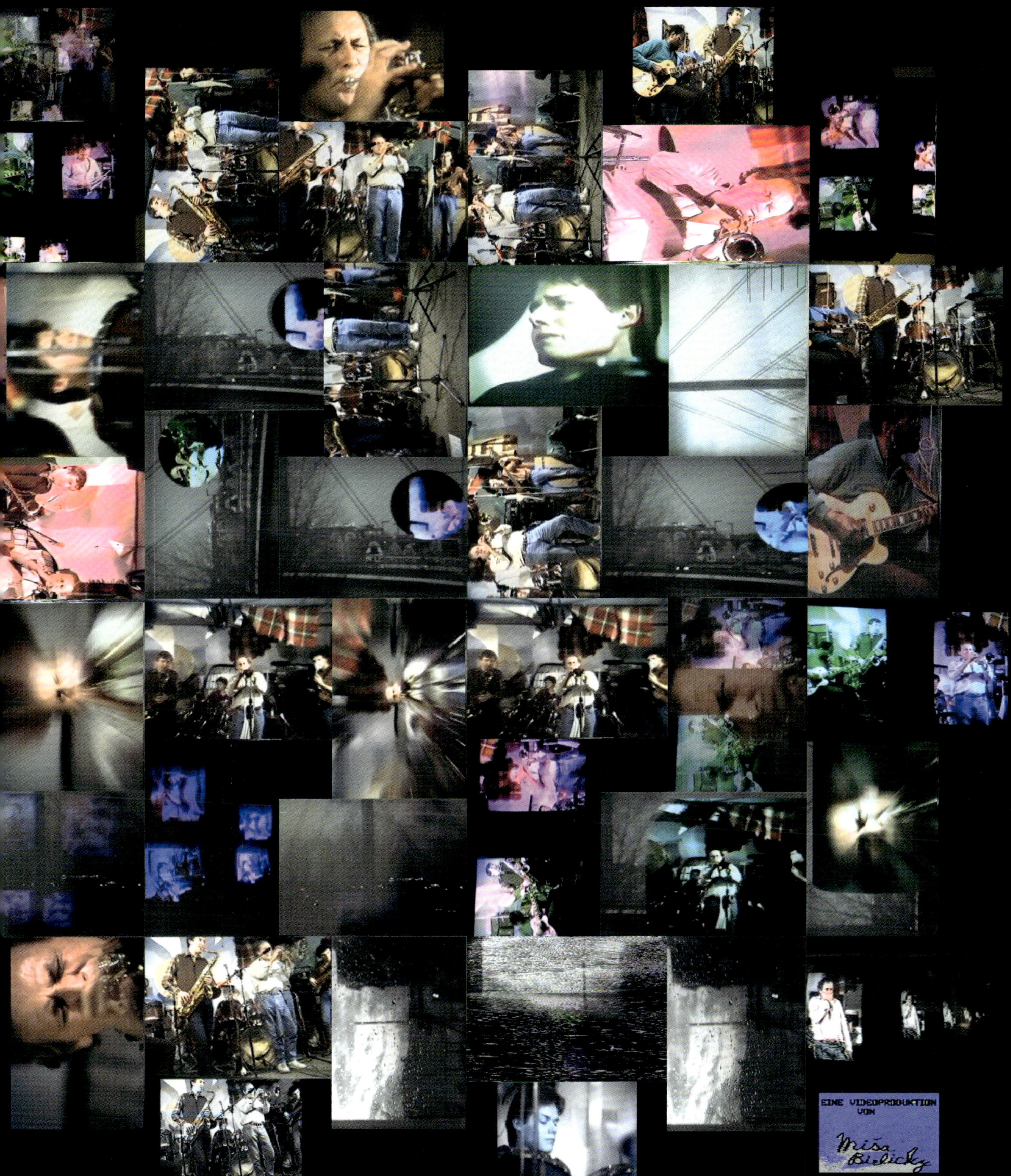

Jazz Celula, 1989, single-channel video. Screenshots.

Fat Corner, with Ricardo Peredo, 1987, single-channel video. Screenshots.

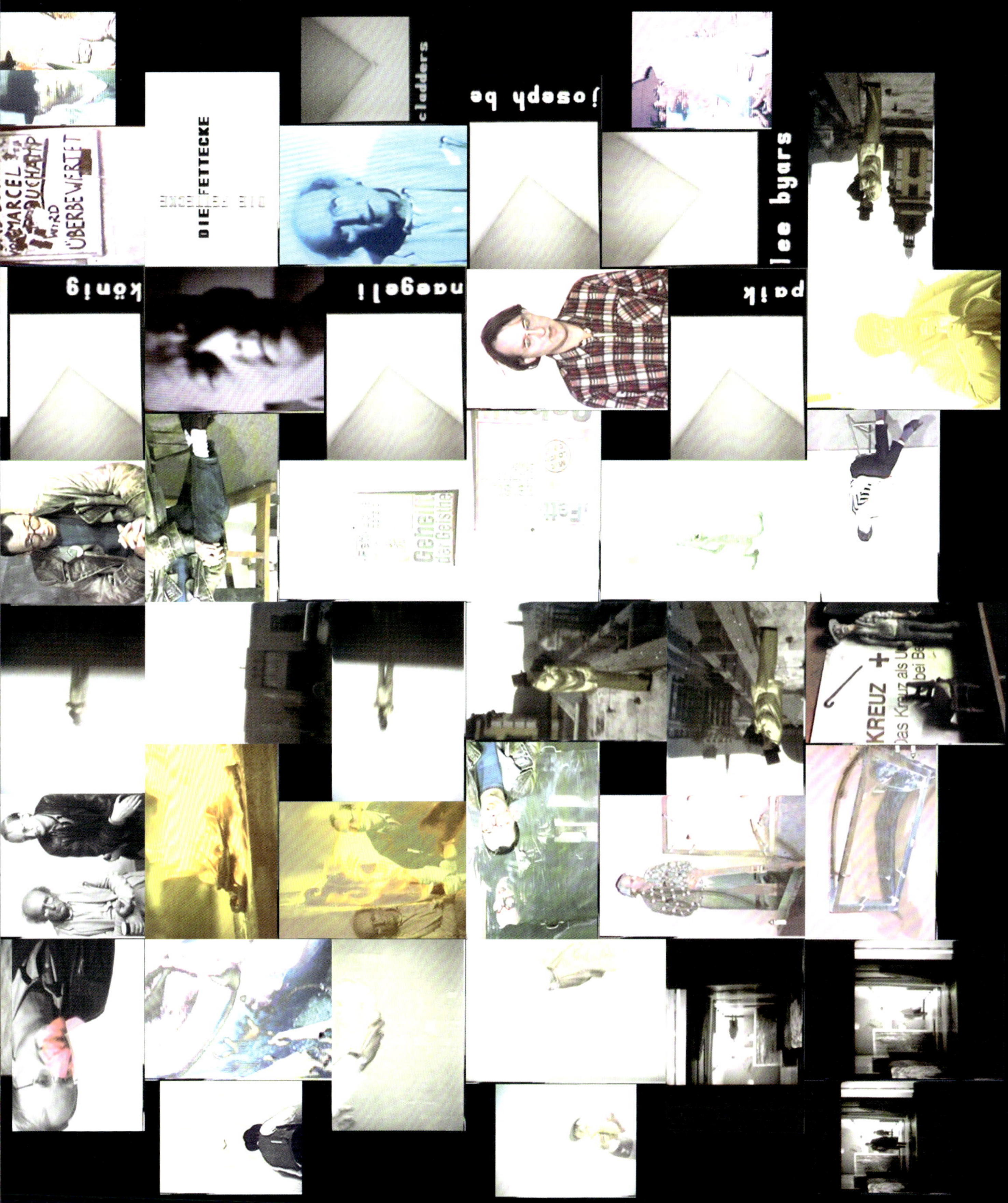

cladders
joseph be
lee byars
könig
naegeli
paik
DIE FETTECKE
MARCEL DUCHAMP WIRD ÜBERBEWERTET
KREUZ
Das Kreuz als U

Wolf Vostell, *MultiMediale 2*, ZKM | Karlsruhe, 1991.

Wulf Herzogenrath and Shigeko Kubota, Museum Kunstpalast, Düsseldorf, 2010.

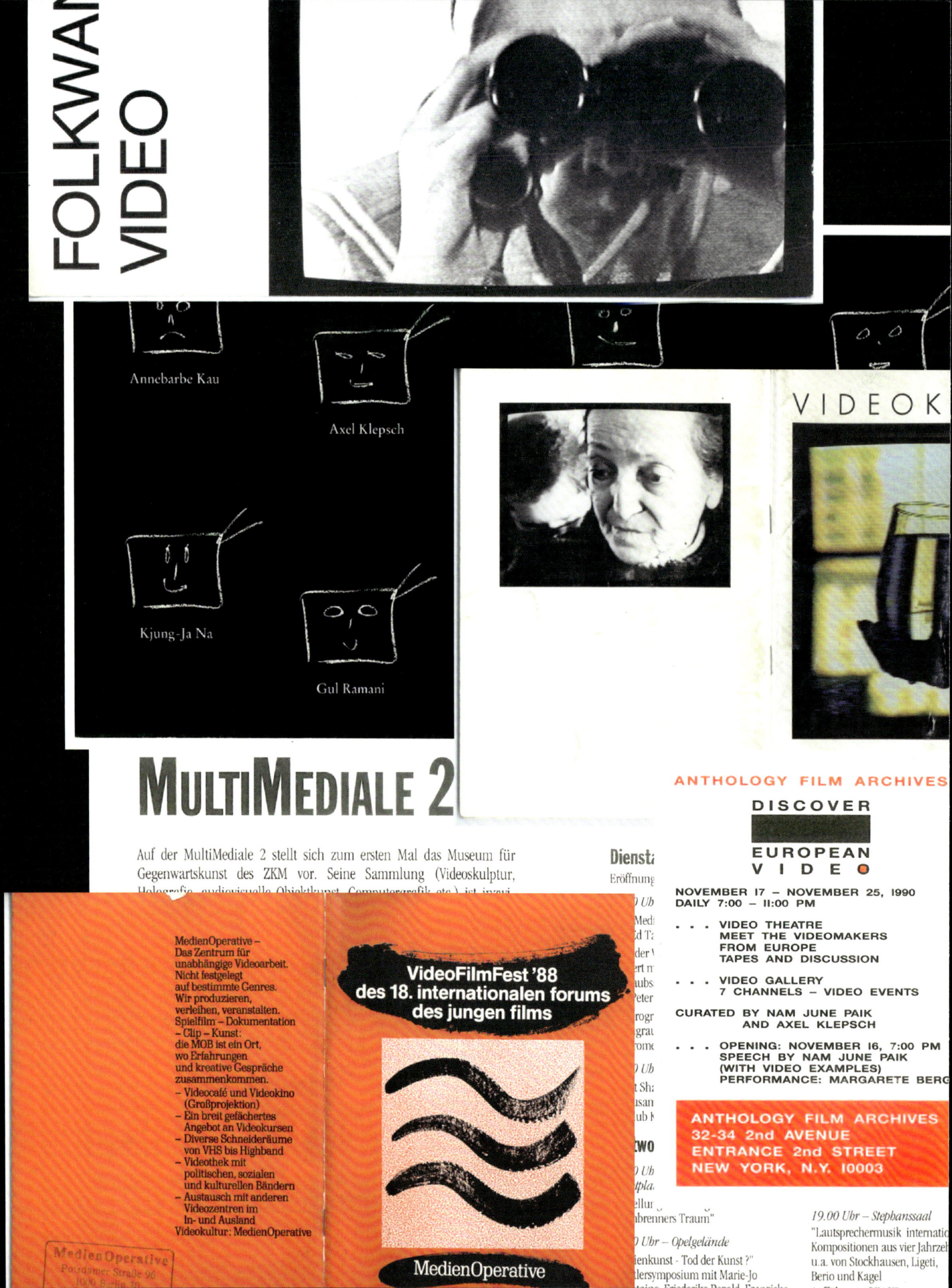

FOLKWAN
VIDEO
Annebarbe Kau
Axel Klepsch
Kjung-Ja Na
Gul Ramani
VIDEOK
MULTIMEDIALE 2
Auf der MultiMediale 2 stellt sich zum ersten Mal das Museum für Gegenwartskunst des ZKM vor. Seine Sammlung (Videoskulptur,
ANTHOLOGY FILM ARCHIVES
DISCOVER
EUROPEAN
VIDEO
NOVEMBER 17 – NOVEMBER 25, 1990
DAILY 7:00 – 11:00 PM
. . . VIDEO THEATRE
MEET THE VIDEOMAKERS
FROM EUROPE
TAPES AND DISCUSSION
. . . VIDEO GALLERY
7 CHANNELS – VIDEO EVENTS
CURATED BY NAM JUNE PAIK
AND AXEL KLEPSCH
. . . OPENING: NOVEMBER 16, 7:00 PM
SPEECH BY NAM JUNE PAIK
(WITH VIDEO EXAMPLES)
PERFORMANCE: MARGARETE BERG
ANTHOLOGY FILM ARCHIVES
32-34 2nd AVENUE
ENTRANCE 2nd STREET
NEW YORK, N.Y. 10003
MedienOperative –
Das Zentrum für
unabhängige Videoarbeit.
Nicht festgelegt
auf bestimmte Genres.
Wir produzieren,
verleihen, veranstalten.
Spielfilm – Dokumentation
– Clip – Kunst:
die MOB ist ein Ort,
wo Erfahrungen
und kreative Gespräche
zusammenkommen.
– Videocafé und Videokino
(Großprojektion)
– Ein breit gefächertes
Angebot an Videokursen
– Diverse Schneideräume
von VHS bis Highband
– Videothek mit
politischen, sozialen
und kulturellen Bändern
– Austausch mit anderen
Videozentren im
In- und Ausland
Videokultur: MedienOperative
VideoFilmFest '88
des 18. internationalen forums
des jungen films
MedienOperative
19.00 Uhr – Stephanssaal
"Lautsprechermusik internati
Kompositionen aus vier Jahrze
u.a. von Stockhausen, Ligeti,
Berio und Kagel

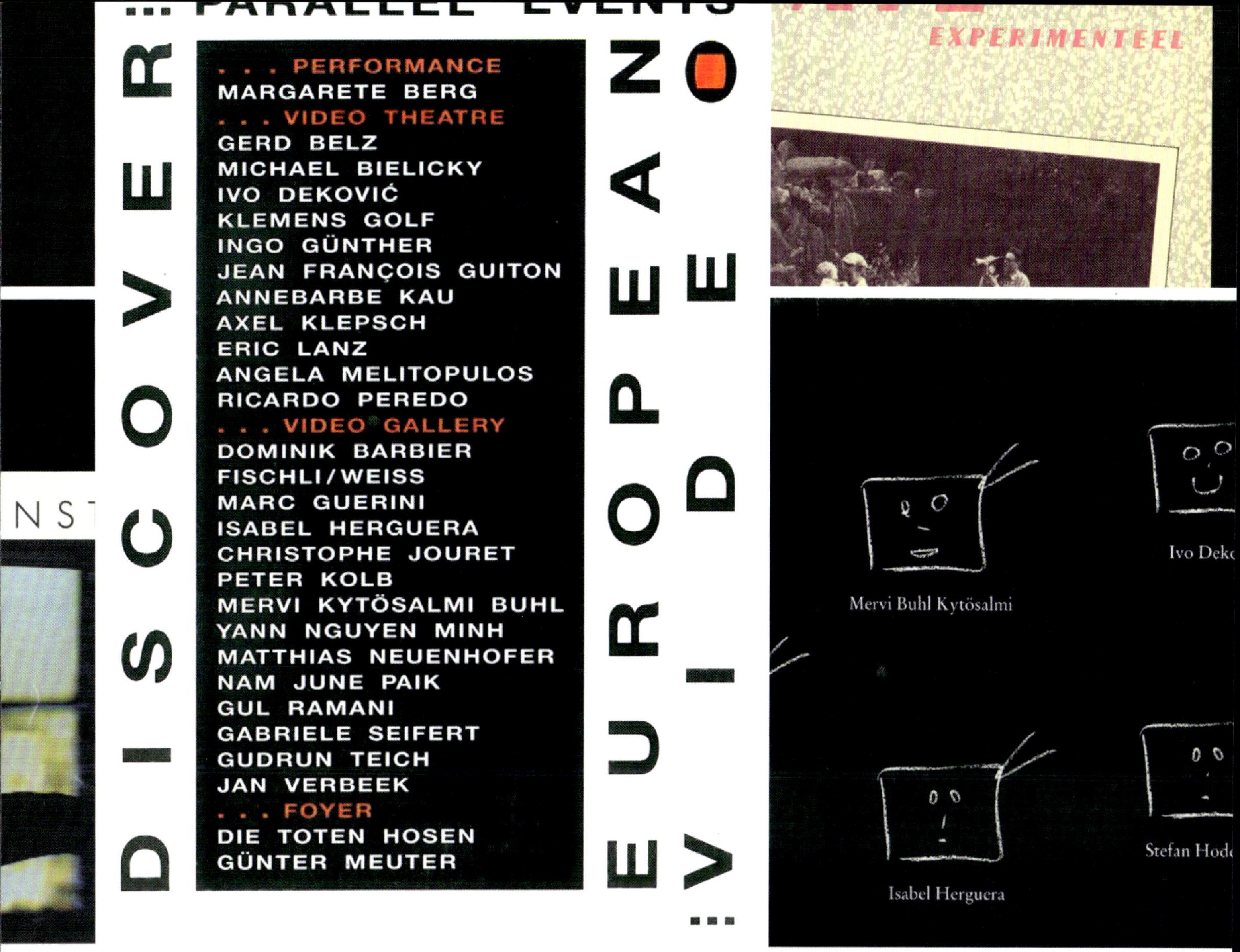

Collage of flyers and brochures Michael Bielicky collected over the years.

Nam June Paik at his studio, Düsseldorf Art Academy, 1987.

Nam June Paik and students of Düsseldorf Art Academy at Paik's Studio, New York City, 1990.

Nam June Paik

Nam June Paik in conversation with Michael Bielicky, Ivo Deković, Gul Romani, and Ricardo Peredo

Nam June Paik has achieved his greatest publicity in the realm of music, Fluxus, and video. His work is not limited to that of a pure visualist – in addition to art history, he originally studied music history and composition theory, and worked with Stockhausen among others. In the early 1960s he shocked the world with music performances, including one with the cellist Charlotte Moorman. As in a collage, he homogeneously combines the sensitive qualities of a musician and an artist with the intelligence and rationality of a scientist, the irreconcilably shocking quality of an anarchist with the smile of a wise man and the knowledge of technical fundamentals of technology. He was the first to use TV sets as a carrier for abstract shapes and was one of the first to build a video synthesizer to produce all imaginable electronic shapes and colors. His concern is communication, and he does not designate a style in any particular art genre.

Although he speaks English and German excellently and has read philosophical treatises in original languages early on, in interviews in the 1970s, he used to combine both languages, both ways of thinking and even verbal peculiarities. These peculiarities are difficult to reproduce, especially if he has a more casual conversation with four different students of four different nationalities.

Nam June Paik: What do my shoes cost?

Ivo Deković: What do your shoes cost?

Paik: Eight hundred Deutschmark [DM] a pair.

Deković: How much?!

Paik: Well, eight hundred DM!

Deković: How long can you use them?

Paik: For a very long time, but I have thirty pairs of shoes; an awful lot, isn't it?

Michael Bielicky: But those are only for months with thirty days?

Paik: No, no – I have thirty different pairs of shoes that don't fit, and I already own them a couple of years, but that doesn't matter.

Ricardo Peredo: Can you ride a motorcycle?

Paik: No, no – I have very bad coordination. I also have a bad, um, stomach, so it could get cold.

Bielicky: Do you think Kafka would have been interested in video if he had known about it?

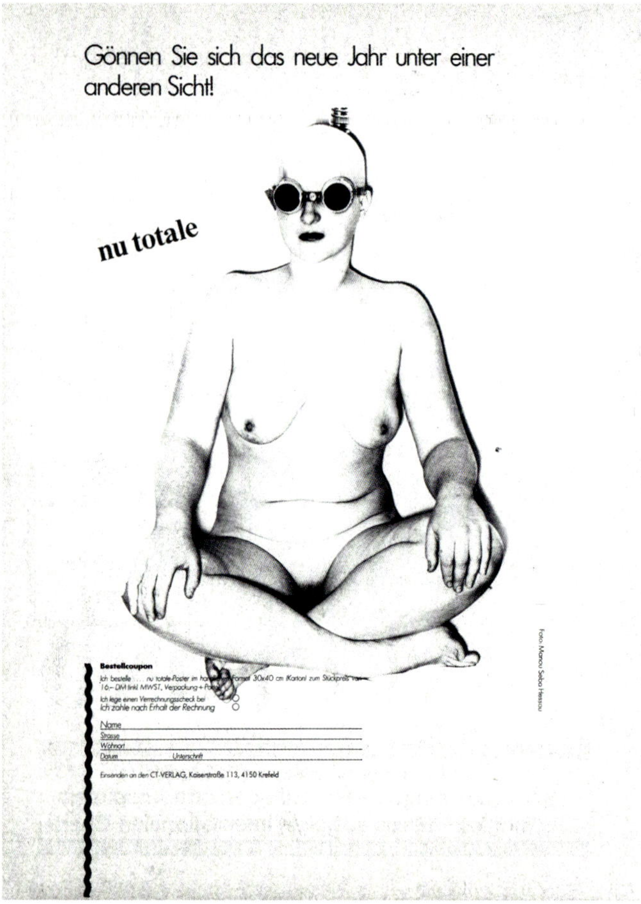

Unknown artist, *nu totale*, photograph in: *Zukunft issue* of *Monochrom Extra*, 1985.

Fredrich Cantor, *Atomic Brain*, 1982. Portrait of Michael Bielicky in: *Zukunft issue* of *Monochrom Extra*, 1985.

Paik: I don't think Kafka [...] maybe Joyce – yes, James Joyce would have been, but Kafka probably not.

Bielicky: What medium would you have worked with if you had lived in the Middle Ages?

Paik: Probably I would not have become an artist.

Bielicky: And if you were born again in the year 3000?

Paik: In the year 3000 – if I did art a second time, it would be boring. I would do something else.

Deković: Business?

Paik: No, no business – I could have done business with my father. Still, I think art is better than business.

Deković: What would you want to do other than art?

Paik: I wanted to make music history, science – music [...] I would like to have something to do with music or art.

Deković: In any case, always –

Paik: – But I didn't know that I could be successful or that I could live – that is very difficult – to remain anonymous, of course! But I don't expect that one can earn money with it in Germany, so [...] as a means of security, if I were a professor of music history in Korea, that would satisfy me. But I never wanted more.

Peredo: And if you had become a woman, would you have liked to have done that too?

Paik: [laughs] I thought you would ask that. But I've never had any problems with that. I would probably have done the same things. A good question that nobody has asked me before.

Deković: What do you think of children?

Paik: I can only barely feed myself; I have enough obligations – my life is getting expensive.

Deković: And your art requires so much commitment that you don't have time for children?

Paik: No, no, actually, I've always liked children – but I didn't want to take responsibility. There are enough children who are just conceived, then sent to university, et cetera. I myself had a great deal of freedom as a child, and when a child is as free as I was, then I have would have to earn a lot of money for a child like me. This is a little too much.

Paik: [keeps browsing through *Monochrom* no. 5 and in the end keeps coming back to the photo *Nu totale*] That is shocking – that is really shocking. You see that a lot in the US.

Bielicky: [points to his portrait of Cantor] What do you think of the photo?

Paik: Bizarre, eh – that might be a punk, mightn't it? But it's good, I think [...] like a little ego trip, eh?

Bielicky: A New York photographer did that while I was there.

Paik: But that's shocking, yes. Others always want to have more shocking [...] How old is this newspaper?

Bielicky: I'm not sure. This picture was taken by an African.

Deković: Your last installation with eighty-eight monitors, was it your biggest so far?

Paik: The biggest one? No! The next one at the Centre Pompidou will be even bigger.

Deković: Mine is not so much a memorial [...] or something –

Paik: [laughs] – permanent, yes, – very permanent.

Deković: Have you planned a new one?

Paik: I have a date in Paris in early December.

Deković: What do you like to eat most?

Paik: Korean soup!

Deković: Is that something special does it have a name?

Paik: Yukgaejang – something like Hungarian goulash.

Peredo: Do you still have family in Korea [...] how many women?

Paik: Oh, maybe you mean my mistress from kindergarten. [...] She became famous, a writer. [...] I see her. She is as old as me.

Gul Romani: Has Korea changed now?

Paik: Yes, yes – through my project, [...] but there is nothing else to do there.

Bielicky: Do you like doing interviews?

Paik: I do a lot, sometimes.

Bielicky: And the questions are always the same?

Paik: But today?

Peredo: How is it when you are in New York, do you feel like a New Yorker there?

Paik: Oh, I don't know. The New Yorkers are too snobbish for me. I am not a snob!

Peredo: And when you are in Germany?

Paik: Am I a German? No, I feel the same almost everywhere, no matter where I am! An old lady once asked me if I lived here, and she said, yes, she too, or something similar.

Deković: Do you think that you have something like a nomad in you? Have you always wanted to see new countries?

Paik: No, no, that was more of a compulsion, but [...] I probably also have nomadic traits because Koreans have always been nomads in some way, similar to Hungarians or Finns, et cetera. But if I, for example, come to Kenya, Nairobi, et cetera, then I can still see and experience something. But I probably have something like an escapist tendency – or, how do you say, escapade in German?

Bielicky: Refugee tendency!

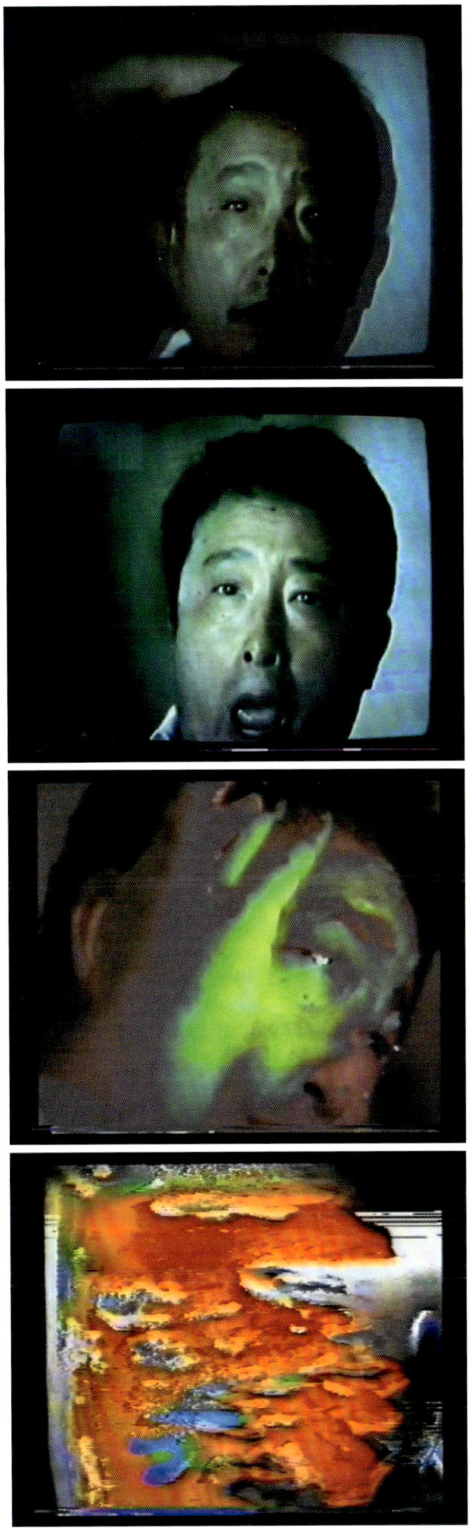

Paik – I'm an Experimentalist, 1987, single-channel video. Video stills.

Paik: Escapade is not a refugee. Escapist tendency.

Bielicky: We are all foreigners!

Paik: Yes, yes – but escapist is something else. A mental phenomenon. What is it called when you don't just see reality and think something else and then deviate from reality again? (Adventure?) With the Marxists, for example, all the curios, abstracts, artists were called escapists – if one wasn't a social realist.

Peredo: Are you a realist?

Paik: No, I'm an experimentalist!

Deković: Do you love sports?

Paik: No, do I look like that? I saw sumo wrestlers in Japan, and I saw baseball in New York – some spend a lot of time with it. I thought I had to keep my head free for other things because it often seemed too time consuming to me to always win.

Deković: And why are you in Wiesbaden of all places and not in Düsseldorf or Cologne?

Paik: Wiesbaden is a spa; that's good because of my sugar levels. That's why I have the professorship there; otherwise I would have given it up long ago.

Deković: How is your relationship with the people in the pension where you live?

Paik: It's difficult. They all go to bed at 10 p.m. – just older people, and I always wake them up. Like the old Wehrmacht major who injured his foot. He's already eighty, and I always wake him up.

Deković: And how long do you want to stay in Wiesbaden?

Paik: Maybe another four years.

Deković: Are you a rich man?

Paik: Maybe.

Deković: What is money for you? What is a materialistic man?

Paik: Money is just there to pay for my shoes, to pay for my teeth. [...] My life is very expensive.

Peredo: Do you have any idea at what age you would like to die?

Paik: When the balance between joy and pain is no longer right! If there's a little more pain, [...] I don't want to live long and then be able to determine my own death. I'm half man, half insect, dependent on

Nam June Paik, *Wrap around the World*, 1988, global broadcast with performances by David Bowie, Ryuichi Sacamoto, Merce Cunningham, the Viennese Art Orchestra and others. Video stills.

insulin. I could use some other mechanism and take potassium cyanide instead.

Bielicky: Will there be more video artists or more painters in a hundred years?

Paik: Oh yes, definitely a lot more people who work with video. How few people paint in oil, and every child today already has a computer.

Deković: So, you see the development as completely natural and normal?

Paik: I don't necessarily want to judge whether this is good or bad. Not even who should earn more money with it or not. But when I see the many different processes involved in oil painting, then I would like to make it easier for myself by just pressing a button.

Deković: Which zodiac sign are you?

Paik: I was born on July 20th.

Bielicky: Leo?

Paik: Leo, probably – eh, Leo – Cancer.

Deković: In Chinese?

Paik: Monkey, [...] yeah, I'm quite a monkey!

Deković: Do you believe that?

Paik: Probably [...] there are certain scientific reasons. Yes, yes, I think so [...] There are a lot of people for whom this is always a little bit true. For example, my wife is an ox. She is much slower – I'm too fast, yes! This year is the year of the ox; in the Chinese horoscope, it comes back every twelve years, and I know some ox. These people are even slower! And there is a certain scientific background insofar as there are a number of medial places in the galaxy from which one can assume certain traits in the year of one's birth, which are influenced by a kind of electromagnetism. That is very possible. I think I can say – no, I am sure that there are scientific reasons. In America at a party, and here too, women often ask what year you were born.

Deković: It's very popular in America.

Paik: Yes, you are always asked about your year of birth, but then you should also compare the Chinese and Western horoscopes, because that's where palmistry comes from. There is probably a similarity here – and probably also with the Indian one. Is there an Indian palmistry?

Romani: Yeah, yeah, [...] that's when someone keeps checking on my mother before coming into my house.

Paik: And is it more related to European or Chinese, or brand new? There was no palmistry before the English?

Romani: Um, yes, there was.

Paik: You have to have that in your head! If you compare the ancient palmistry book and the horoscope, you get a pretty good idea of the humanistic history before the time of Noah's Ark. [...] Last week there was a cover story in *Time* magazine about the importance of dinosaurs – next week it will probably be published in *Der Spiegel* and then in *Stern* [German magazines], et cetera. In *The New York Times*, Professors Müller and Alvarez put forward an interesting theory that explains why the dinosaurs became extinct; that is to say that every 26 million years a defect in our organism is supposed to die off.
The mean thing now is that *Time* printed all the scientists who were involved in the findings and in the theory by name – all but the Italian scientists who made the first significant discoveries about it. That is very mean – and nationalistic!

Deković: That's politics! How many people roughly are there in New York making video?

Paik: Yes, there are very many, around one thousand film students at the university alone. But they also pay over 10,000 dollars. [...] You should be very happy here because you hardly have to pay any money. There, you have to pay over one hundred thousand dollars, and you can't even use a cutting device, and one thousand people are of course difficult to teach. In America it is simply the case that the more people attend the university, the more they earn from it; university is a business there! The competition in America is very tough. Usually when I've been in Europe for six months, I'm almost gone. You also have to be there a lot because you never know when *The New York Times* will call, at least once a year, and if you don't go there regularly, you lose time and are forgotten.

Bielicky: Have you ever thought of making a real feature film?

Paik: I don't think so. If someone comes, it has to be a North Korean. I've been thinking of – if you offer me a few million dollars and then tell me what to do [...] but most likely not.

Deković: What about your plans? Do you want to do a satellite project again?

Paik: Yeah, sure, in '86 and then '88 something is planned from Korea. The last satellite project was on the America-Europe axis; this time the theme is East-West worldwide. The whole thing is analogous to the Olympic Games and has its beginning and ending in Korea. In between there are cities and countries like Poland, Japan, Israel, Cologne [Germany], Pakistan, France, England, Madrid [Spain], Italy, India, Morocco, Beijing [China], Tokyo [Japan], and the last stop is Seoul [South Korea] – something will also appear as music. We don't know yet, but it must be new and interesting and politically relevant!

This interview was first published in *Monochrom* (1980). Translated from the German by Paul Kenig.

Michael Bielicky and Nam June Paik, Düsseldorf, 1986.

Lost, 2017, immersive data-driven installation. Installation view, Centro de Arte Contemporáneo Wifredo Lam, Havana, 2017.

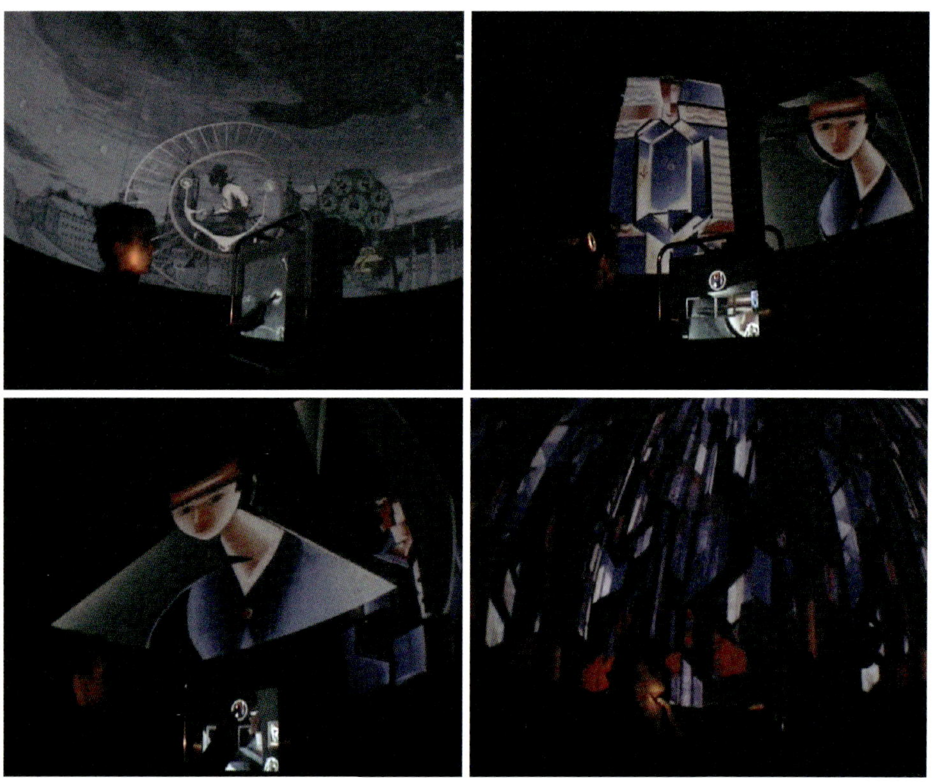

Room with a View, 2000, immersive interactive installation with 360 degree dome projection. Installation views, ŠKODA Pavilion, Autostadt, Wolfsburg, 2000.

From the Golem of Prague to Waze from Israel

Mel Alexenberg

Michael Bielicky invited me to give the inaugural lecture at the launching of the Institute for Postdigital Narrative that he founded at Karlsruhe University of Arts and Design (HfG). My talk explored the definition of "postdigital" as the humanization of digital technologies through narrative art forms, the thesis of my 2011 book *The Future of Art in a Postdigital Age: From Hellenistic to Hebraic Consciousness*.[1]

Bielicky's artworks exemplify story-telling formats that illustrate the confluence between action-centered Hebraic consciousness shaped by biblical narrative and postdigital thought expressed in dynamic narrative art fashioned by digital culture. The storyline flow of Bielicky's artworks demonstrates the lively, spirited, playful, and ever-changing energy that characterizes Jewish thought and experience. He wrote: "Mankind has always operated on narrative to explain and understand its own existence. Our times, in particular, call for the exploration, expression, and especially, creation of new story-telling formats."[2]

In *The Art of Biblical Narrative* (1981), University of California Professor Robert Alter explains that the Bible "has a great deal to teach anyone interested in narrative because its seemingly simple, wonderfully complex art offers such splendid illustrations of the primary possibilities of narrative."[3] The Bible, the most read book on earth, tells the story of the creation of the universe, the creation of all human beings, and the creation of a family enslaved in a foreign land that grew into the nation Israel living in freedom in its own land.

As a background to all of Michael's artworks, both those with and without Jewish symbolism, I will begin this essay with a postdigital reading of three key biblical passages. I start with "In the Beginning" by presenting my translation of the first two verses of the Bible in the vocabulary of digital culture. I then translate, in terms of psychology and sense modalities, the first verse that starts the story of the Jewish people though the life of the patriarch Abraham. The third passage examines concepts of deconstruction and reconstruction in the episode of Moses breaking stone tablets engraved with Ten Commandments that is met with praise rather than punishment for smashing an object that is "Made by God".

It is most appropriate when discussing Bielicky's artworks for me to translate biblical passages from the original Hebrew language of the Bible into the language of digital culture. These translations are based upon ideas in my 2018 book *Through a Bible Lens: Biblical Insights for Smartphone Photography and Social Media*.[4] In reviewing my book, Michael Bielicky wrote that it is inspiring on many levels because it gives us an amazing perspective on our own existence, especially in the age of the interconnected iPhone culture.

In the Beginning God Created Media Systems

"In the network of networks, God created media systems for creating heaven and earth. When the earth was absolutely empty and dark, God created light and separated between light and darkness (1 and 0)." (Genesis 1:2)

The Hebrew word for "in the beginning" is *b'reshit*, akin to the word *b'reshet*, meaning "network." The media system of heaven, the spiritual realm, is made up of the 22 Hebrew letters that form the words of the Torah, (the first five books of the Bible). The media system of earth in the digital realm returns us to the primeval binary creation of darkness and light, 0 and 1, on and off. "God separated between the light and darkness." (Genesis 1:4) Bits and bytes are basic elements of digital media systems. Every internet website, blog, video, song, and text that you access in The Cloud – the network of all networks – is written with the binary system of the first day of Creation.

The other media system of earth, the material realm, is written with electrons and protons that form atoms and molecules. Atoms and molecules are basic elements of material systems. Supersized molecules like DNA contain the binary code of all life forms written with two pairs of two letters: A-T, T-A; and C-G, G-C, on the rungs of double helix ladders.

Most English translations of the first verse follow the *King James Bible*: "In the beginning God created the heaven and the earth." (Genesis 1:1)

However, when I read it in Hebrew, the language in which it was originally written, and the language in which I teach and speak everyday living in Israel, it has the additional word *et* twice. "In the beginning God created et the heaven and et the earth."

The Hebrew word *et* in the language of the Bible signifies the first creations before heaven and before earth. In translations, *et* drops out since it has no equivalent in English. It is a grammatical form indicating a direct object linking verb to noun. It links "created" to "heaven" and to "earth." It is spelled *aleph-tav*, the first and last letters of the Hebrew alphabet. Spanning the full set of 22 Hebrew letters from *aleph* to *tav*, *et* represents a prototypic media system used to create a spiritual system called "heaven." The ancient Hebrew language is a prototype of media systems used to create spiritual systems like the Bible itself. The biblical narrative explores the spiritual dimensions of living in a material world. It teaches how to bring heaven down to earth, how to experience spirituality in everyday life.

Biblical Formula for Envisioning New Realities

God gave Abraham a kinesthetic formula to see from new perspectives. "Walk yourself away from your land, from your birthplace, and from your father's house, to the land that I will show you." (Genesis 12:1) Applied to today, this formula can be read as: "Move both physically and psychologically away from those things that are most familiar to you and you will come to see from a fresh viewpoint."

The Bible identifies Abraham as a Hebrew, which means "one who crosses over to envision new realities." It is told that in the world of idolatry where he lived, Abraham was charged to mind his father's idol shop. He took a stick and smashed all the clay idols, leaving the largest one whole. He placed the stick in the hand of the large idol. When his father returned to his shop and saw the shocking scene, he demanded an explanation from his son. Abraham told him that the largest idol had smashed all the others.

Seventy Faces of Torah

"The tablets were the work of God, and the writing was the writing of God, engraved on the tablets. As Moses approached the camp and saw the calf and the dancing, he burned with anger and threw the tablets out of his hands, smashing them at the base of the mountain. Then God told Moses, 'Chisel out two stone tablets like the first ones and write on them the same words that were on the tablets that you smashed.'" (Exodus 32:16, 32:19, 34:1)

The biblical object of supreme worth is the Ten Commandments engraved on stone tablets with Divine laser light. What did Moses do with this object that is "Made by God"? He smashed it to bits. Did God reprimand or punish him for what would appear to be an immensely sacrilegious act? No. God tells Moses that he should carve out a second set of stone tablets and write on the tablets the words that were on the first tablets he had smashed.

In the Talmud, we hear a group of rabbis ask why God reminded Moses that he had broken the tablets that were "Made by God". He knew that he had smashed them. The words "that you smashed" seem superfluous. One of the rabbis, Reish Lakish, plays with the Hebrew word "which" – *asher* – that can also be read as *ashrei*, "praiseworthy." God praises Moses for the wisdom he had in breaking what was divinely engraved in stone to prevent our idolizing a frozen formulation. The Torah must be written by a human hand. We must create an intimate bond with it, rather than holding it in distant awe.

One legend tells that the Hebrew letters from the smashed tablets spread out over the desert as an invitation for each generation to collect them and rewrite the Torah for itself in the spirit of the times. The Divine original is replaced by human copies and copies of copies over generations to our day.

Although the original that was "Made by God" needed to be smashed to bits to prevent it from being kept at a distance and idolized, only high-touch Torah scrolls flawlessly copied by hand retain ritual power. Printed or digital copies are valued for Torah study, but not for public reading in the synagogue. Judaism teaches that the essence of biblical study is to conceptually smash the text to bits and put it back together in seventy alternative ways. This postmodern-like deconstruction leads to reconstruction with multiple insights and fresh perspectives gleaned from the Torah.

Michael Bielicky's Art is an Expression of Hebraic Consciousness

My postdigital analysis of the three above passages in the biblical narrative gives us clues to Michael Bielicky's expression of Hebraic consciousness in all his artwork, not just in his artworks using Jewish symbolism. He translates ideas and experiences in life into the language of digital culture that radically defies tradition as if the first passage in the Bible reads: "In the network of networks, God created media systems for creating heaven and earth." Like the patriarch Abraham, Bielicky walks away from all that is most familiar in the art world to see alternative opportunities. The Bible identifies Abraham as a Hebrew, who crosses over to envision new realities. Bielicky is clearly a descendent of Abraham. And like Moses, he has the daring and audacity to break down the very definition of art and reassemble it for a postdigital age.

Bielicky created urban artworks in collaboration with his wife Kamila B. Richter that they called *Falling Life* (2005–06). They operate completely outside of the art system. Equipped with a car, a laptop, a compact powerful projector, and a small power generator, they are able to create an instant presence in the urban landscape. They transform city architecture into dynamic and living organisms. Without any on-site preparation and without any permits, they create guerrilla-theater projections. Within less than ten minutes, they can illuminate giant buildings with their computer-animated urban screening project, reaching vast audiences that would probably never walk into a gallery or museum.

Hebraic consciousness, which colors Bielicky's outside-the-box art, is summarized by the Norwegian Christian theologian Thorleif Boman (1894–1978) in his seminal work *Hebrew Thought Compared to Greek* (original 1954, English translation 1960). He analyzes and compares passive, immobile Hellenistic thought that dominated Western art until Modernism

Falling Times, 2006–09, data-driven installation. Installation views, Barcelona, 2007.

with action-centered, ever-changing Hebraic thought. He describes Hebraic thought as "dynamic, vigorous, passionate, and sometimes quite explosive" compared to Hellenistic thought that is "static, peaceful, moderate, and harmonious in kind."[5]

Bielicky wrote: "What interests me the most is the phenomenon of permanent changes in life – the appearance and disappearance of things. In my work I try to get closer to the inner meaning of life. My images are in permanent movement. There is no simple image."[6]

An Artist's Narrative

It seems appropriate for me to discuss Bielicky's creative and innovative artworks as the story of our shared interests and close friendship. It began in the summer of 2002 when my wife Miriam and I were enjoying a vacation in Prague while making plans for my exhibition, *Cyberangels: Aesthetic Peace Plan for the Middle East* that took place in the Robert Guttmann Gallery at the Jewish Museum of Prague in 2004.

We went to see an exhibition of Otto Piene's innovative artwork at the Prague City Gallery. I had worked closely with him for five years during the 1980s at the MIT Center for Advanced Visual Studies where he was the Center's director and I was a research fellow. The Prague Gallery director told me that I must meet with Professor Bielicky, the head of new media arts at the Prague Academy of Fine Arts, before I returned home to Israel. He gave me his phone number.

When Miriam and I returned to our hotel, I phoned Michael. He answered in a tired voice explaining that he had just that moment returned home from lecturing on new media arts in Thailand. When I introduced myself, he asked if I was the Mel Alexenberg who collaborated with Otto Piene on the exhibition *LightsOROT* (1988). When I said yes, he excitedly asked where I was. When I told him that I was in Prague, he said he'd get a taxi and come immediately to my hotel.

Michael explained that he had created a video-sculpture *Menorah* (1989), culminating his studies at the Düsseldorf Art Academy. He admired Professor Otto Piene, who had been invited to Düsseldorf from MIT to be juror of the projects submitted for the Master of Fine Art degree. Years earlier, as a high school student in Düsseldorf, Michael spent a lot of time in a local hangout where students and professors of the illustrious Art Academy congregated. Its interior was created by members of the ZERO group, Otto Piene, Günter Mack, Heinz Ücker, and was later installed in Düsseldorf's museum kunst palast (today Kunstpalast). This environment had a strong impact on him.

He told Miriam and me that as Otto Piene approached his *Menorah*, he offered to explain what a menorah meant in Jewish life. Although not Jewish, Otto quickly responded that he knew very well what a menorah was, having collaborated with Mel Alexenberg in creating the exhibition *LightsOROT: Spiritual Dimensions of the Electronic Age* at Yeshiva University Museum in New York. Otto gave him the catalogue of the 1988 exhibition.[7] He explained how that catalogue had a monumental influence on his thought and art. That evening, we began a vibrant dialogue and deep friendship that is continually developing.

Menorah as a Branching Tree-form

In his chapter "Media Golem: Between Prague and ZKM," which he wrote for my 2008 book *Educating Artists for the Future: Learning at the Intersections of Art, Science, Technology and Culture*, Michael describes his *Menorah* and its significance in his life as artist and Jew: "I created *Menorah* at the end of my studies without having any idea what sort of response it eventually would have. It had small TV monitors at the ends of each of seven branches of a large steel candelabrum. On the monitors' screens, video images of flickering flames danced. These virtual flames emanated from a hidden video transmitter sending spiritual messages to antennas topping each of the seven monitors.

Menorah directly referenced my Jewish identity in a German context. The first place in Germany that provided me some comfortable surroundings was the Düsseldorf Jewish community. However, it took me a long while before I was ready to openly and publicly acknowledge my Jewishness. The first time I publicly displayed *Menorah* at the Academy, I placed a ring around it made of defunct fire extinguishers. They weren't so easy to find because at the time everyone in Germany had the Baader-Meinhof Gang and other terrorist groups still fresh in their minds and their bombs were made out of old fire extinguishers. Nevertheless, I wanted to show the installation like this. I wanted to say that these old extinguishers were like old Nazis who no longer had the strength to snuff the flame of the menorah. This was the only time I used this literal interpretation when exhibiting *Menorah*. Actually, it was David Galloway, the noted curator and art critic writing for the *International Herald Tribune*, who convinced me that the object was powerful enough on its own.

The work was in great demand. I won a number of awards for it and it went from exhibition to exhibition. Actually, there exist two copies of *Menorah*. One was bought from me by ZKM in Karlsruhe as the very first work for the collection of its Museum of Media Arts (so it was given identification number 001). The second was commissioned in 2001 by the Jewish Museum in Berlin at the architect Daniel Libeskind's request."[8]

Elena Lappin, in her critique of Libeskind's museum design, "Vacancies of Remembrance: A Visit to the Jewish Museum Berlin," writes of her encounter with Bielicky's *Menorah*: "My disappointment about the museum's architecture and exhibits is complete, when I spot a large menorah made of steel, a work by a young Czech artist Michael Bielicky with the simple title 'Menorah,

2001.' She is to be found in one of the corridors and is so impressive that I have to sit down on a bench and look at it for a while. On every arm of the menorah a small TV screen in attached, on which a black and white video flame can be seen. An extraordinary impact emanates from this Menorah, emanates with no explanation at all. She provokes the existence of an emotional, yet unsentimental sensation of connection between the dead and the living, between past and present."[9]

Jennifer Hansen-Glucklich, in her 2014 book, *Holocaust Memory Reframed: Museums and the Challenges of Representation* that Bielicky's *Menorah* reveals that the sacred cannot be imprisoned in static forms and that objects are not intrinsically sacred. She adds that the sacred is refigured as a shifting evocation, and is invested in forms through ritual, placement, and contexts of remembrance.[10]

The most prominent object in the *Mishkan* – the portable Tabernacle built in the Sinai Desert – was the menorah, a candelabrum with the form of a tree with seven branches: different parallel pathways emerging from a common root. At the top of each branch is a vessel of olive oil that is kindled to illuminate the *Mishkan*. Like the Torah, the menorah is called a Tree of Life. "Its ways are ways of pleasantness and all its paths are peace" (Proverbs 3:17). "Ways" and "paths" are plural. No one way and no single path, but rather alternative ways and multiple paths.

Spiral Video Installation The Name

Michael describes his 1990 video installation *The Name*: "Information always moves through time and space in the same form of a spiral. The genetic code is stored in the double-helix spiral in the same way as the information in the two rolls of the Torah, the sacred book of Judaism. The sounds of human language move through space in the same way as our solar system moves through the universe. We store information on a computer disc in a spiral form. The light – a word – a name – a code – information is invisible and comes from the darkness, from 'somewhere,' made visible through the various media. The universe is an information-seeking and -giving system (consciousness). The installation consists of a metal spiral on which seven small b & w monitors (information carriers) are mounted. One can walk through the spiral like through a tunnel. At the end of that 'tunnel' there is a black sphere – the 'somewhere.' A small TV transmitter transmits 'the information' (in the form of a flame) to the carrier – the spiral and the receivers (TVs)."[11]

The Medium is an Integral Part of the Message

Jewish consciousness is shaped by spiral forms: from the Torah scroll, to *tzitzit* fringes, to the ram's horn *shofar*, to spiral *hallah* bread. Jews are called *Am HaSePheR* (Hebrew: "People of the Scroll"). The medium is such an integral part of the message that if the biblical words written in a scroll form are unavailable, the Torah is not read in the synagogue, even if the exact same words are available in printed book form. The Torah printed on separate pages, imprisoned between two rectangular covers, destroys the message of the endless flow of divine wisdom. Indeed, the Hebrew word *malben* means both "rectangle" and "brickyard" where the Israelites were enslaved in Egypt.

The message of the endless flow of a Torah scroll is apparent when the annual cycle of reading the Torah scroll comes to an end and is rewound. The reading of the end is immediately followed with reading the beginning. The last letter of the last word *IsraeL* is *L*. It is linked to the first letter of the first word *B'reshit* (Hebrew: "in the beginning"), that is, *B* to spell the word *LeB*

Menorah/Inventory, 1989, video sculpture. Installation view, Düsseldorf Art Academy, 1989.

Menorah/Inventory, 1989, video sculpture. Screenshots

The Name, 1990, video sculpture. Installation view,
Galerie René Coelho, Amsterdam, 1991.

("heart"). The heart of the Torah is when the end connects to the beginning in an endless flow. The SPR root of *SePheR* as "scroll" has found its way into the English words SPiRal, SPiRitual and inSPiRation.

In the Sabbath morning liturgy, we recite: "The righteous will flourish like a palm tree, and grow like a cedar tree in Lebanon" (Psalm 92:12). Judaism aims to nurture the growth of righteous individuals as expressed by the two alternative growth patterns of trees. Michael expresses both of them in each of his earliest artworks. The spiral growth of the palm tree is seen in his spiral video installation. In Kabbalah – the down-to-earth mystical tradition of Judaism – the *sephirot* are the ten stages by which spirituality spirals down into everyday life. The branching growth of the cedar tree is seen is his *Menorah* that demonstrates multiple paths.

Media Golem and Emergence of Jewish Consciousness

Michael Bielicky describes the emergence of his Jewish consciousness in his chapter, "Media Golem: Between Prague and ZKM" in my book *Educating Artists for the Future*. He reveals the influence on one of his artworks, extending from those with Jewish symbolism to those with undercurrents of dynamic thought patterns of Judaism hidden beneath the surface of all his artworks. It also explains the origins of his creative work at the interface of art, science, and technology.

He begins his story in 1942 at his parents' wartime wedding in Prague. They were wearing yellow stars on their chests, kissing their parents goodbye, never to see them again. As a young boy, he did not understand why his friends had grandparents and even great-grandparents, and he had none. When he was twelve, he first learned about the Holocaust madness that had exterminated his parents' entire family because they were Jews. It was not surprising that his parents did not speak to him about the unspeakable horror until he was twelve, since they continued to live in the anti-Semitic environment of post-Stalinist Czechoslovakia where it was best not to be identified as a Jew.

In his home, the integration of art and science flowed naturally since his father was both a musician and scientist. He had survived the war years with his wife having acquired false identification papers that permitted him to work as a musician, often playing piano at parties where Nazis were celebrating. After the war, he studied medicine and became a medical scientist. Michael described how his father would come home after a long day of work and play piano while he sat listening beside him. His father was also a composer who composed Czech tangos and rumbas that were released as recordings and played on the radio.

When he was fifteen, he saw what appeared to him like an action movie in the making while hiking with his friends in the countryside not far from Prague. On the horizon, hundreds of tanks were rolling over the hills in the far distance. Then they realized that what they were seeing on that summer morning in 1968 was not a movie, but the beginning of the Russian invasion of Czechoslovakia. He and his friends ran down the road tearing down the direction signs to make it difficult for the invading soldiers to find their way. Michael stressed how that image was forever etched in his mind along with the horrible feeling of being helpless and powerless.

His parents packed him and his brother into their car and drove to West Germany. Ironically, it was in Germany that his Jewish identity was awakened. Michael described how he changed overnight from a young Com-

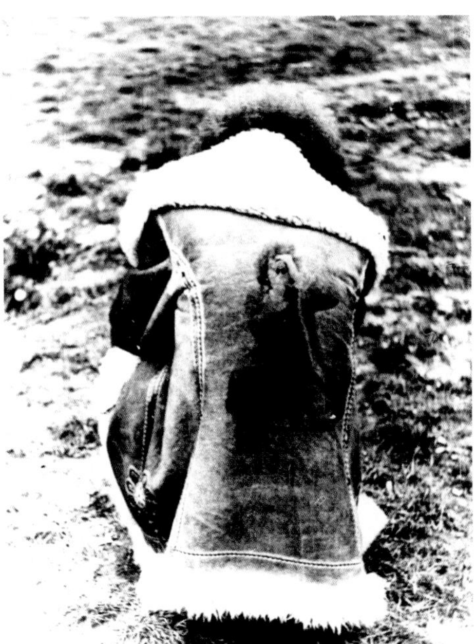

Untitled, 1970s, sandwich printing analog black-and-white photograph.

munist Pioneer to a Western hippie. He grew long hair, wore a goat-fur jacket embroidered with colorful flowers, started to socialize within the Jewish community of Düsseldorf, and joined a Zionist group. Acceptance in a hippie circle of Jewish friends helped transform the trauma of emigration into a positive experience, isolating him from the brown-shirt mentality of the older generation of Germans. It was more difficult for his parents to relate to a generation with a Nazi past that included the murderers of his parents and their entire family.

Golem Is Alive

Bielicky's video *Golem Is Alive* (1989) is a jarring ride through the Prague Jewish cemetery where the Hebrew letters are etched into gravestones, or bulging out of them in relief. They are peeking out from behind mounds of snow. His 1989 video artwork sensed the 22 ancient Hebrew letters anticipating our age of digital media while commemorating centuries of vibrant Jewish life in his birthplace, Prague. He writes: "In Prague there is a very old Jewish cemetery [...] Golem, the common soul of the ghetto makes each aktinolit (gravestone) visible. The inscription suddenly becomes alive. The quadratic letters of the Hebrew alphabet fuse together with the symbol-images [...] The information in the form of a letter formula makes Golem alive; the information, which needs to make a computer work, seems to work on the same principle."[12]

The word *golem occurs in the Bible in* Psalm 139:16, which uses the word *galmi* ("my golem"), translated as "unformed substance" or "raw material," connoting the unfinished human being before God's eyes. The golem narrative involves Judah Loew ben Bezalel, the late sixteenth century rabbi of Prague – *known as the* Maharal – who reportedly created a golem, a giant human figure formed out of clay from the banks of river near his synagogue. He brought the golem to life by inscribing on his clay forehead three Hebrew letters, *alef-mem-tav*, spelling the word *emet* (a Divine name meaning "truth"). The golem was programed to defend Prague's Jews from anti-Semitic attacks and genocidal pogroms. It is told that as the golem grew larger and stronger its program went haywire and he went on a rampage. To stop him, Rabbi Loew erased the letter *alef* from his forehead so only the *mem* and *tav* remained to spell *met* (Hebrew: "death"). The golem collapsed into a lump of muddy clay.

Golem Is Alive, 1989, single-channel video. Screenshots.

Next Year in Jerusalem

Next Year in Jerusalem (1988) is a video sequel to *Golem Is Alive* that honors the man who Bielicky calls "the harbinger of visual media and cybernetics."[13] In it, he shows images and sounds of running water to symbolize the process of movement flowing over the huge stone blocks of the Western Wall retaining the Temple mount in Jerusalem, against which we gain a sporadic glimpse of a Jew swaying in prayer before the ancient stones.

Michael Bielicky tells the story of how Rabbi Loew used a magic lantern to transform his poor home in Prague's Jewish ghetto into a castle in honor of Emperor Rudolf II's (1552–1612) visit. This story of medieval virtual reality colored Bielicky's experience of growing up in Prague. Rabbi Loew's thoughts flowed between his world of Kabbalah – the down-to-earth mysticism of Judaism – and new concepts being generated by the leading scientific minds of the 1700s, with whom he personally exchanged ideas.

Next Year in Jerusalem (Homage to Rabbi Loew), 1988, single-channel video. Screenshots.

From The Golem of Prague to The Golem of Rehovot

The super-computer created in 1965 at the Weizmann Institute of Science in Rehovot, Israel, was named "The Golem of Rehovot" at the suggestion of Professor Gershom Scholem (1897–1982) of the Hebrew University of Jerusalem – one of the twentieth century's foremost authorities of Kabbalah. He explained why it should be named after the Golem of Prague at the dedication ceremony for the new computer. In his remarks, Scholem provided what he felt was an obvious comparison between the classic tale of the golem and the giant new computer.

Scholem gave several reasons for the name to be bestowed on the Israeli super-computer. He explained that at their foundation, the golem – "Rabbi Loew's robot" – and the digital golem had the same basic function. The Golem of Prague was brought to life by the combination of letters from the 22 letter Hebrew alphabet. The golem computer, however, knows only two symbols, the 0 and 1 that make up the binary system. Everything can be translated into just these two terms so that the Weizmann Institute golem can process it. "I daresay the old Kabbalists would have been glad to learn of this simplification of their own system. This is progress," said Scholem.[14] Decades before the emergence of smartphones, Scholem compared the growth potential of the two creations. The golem, after flying into a fit of rage, grew in size wherein the golem computer was expected to only shrink as improvements are made in the future.

This Year in Jerusalem: A Telematic Installation

Bielicky's telematic installation *This Year in Jerusalem* was the exhibition at The Robert Guttmann Gallery at the Jewish Museum of Prague from November 2005 through January 2006.

The installation is entitled *This Year in Jerusalem* as a reference to *L'Shana Haba'ah b'Yerushalayim* (Next Year in Jerusalem), the traditional saying that Jews in the Diaspora have uttered for centuries as a hope that the unification of their people in their own land will soon arrive. For nearly two thousand years this dream had remained unfulfilled.

As Michael Bielicky's installation demonstrates, advanced telecommunications technology and the internet allow us to travel without ever physically leaving home. Just as we are able to penetrate the picture surface and enter its third dimension, we may also transfer ourselves to a virtual landscape of our imaginings. Bielicky's telematic installation electronically captured the bodies of visitors to the gallery and transported them in real time to the plaza facing the Western Wall in Jerusalem.

The Western Wall (Hebrew: *ha-Kotel ha-Ma'aravi*) is the retaining wall of the Second Temple located on the western foot of the Temple Mount, the holiest site in Judaism, which legend considers the center of the world. On this site stood the Temple built by King Solomon more than three thousand years ago and the Second Temple destroyed by the Romans two thousand years ago.

Immediately after the founding of the State of Israel in 1948 the Arab League expelled Jews from Jerusalem's Old City and denied them access to the Western Wall. This situation continued until the Six-Day War in 1967 when the Israeli army took control of the Old City and the Western Wall once again became a center of Jewish religious life. People come 24 hours a day to pray, bringing their most intimate wishes and heartfelt aspirations. It would be difficult to find anywhere else in the world with an atmosphere comparable to that of the Western Wall.

This Year in Jerusalem, 2006, telematic installation. Installation views, Jewish Museum Prague, Robert Guttmann Gallery, 2005/06.

The gallery in Prague was equipped with a special device to track movement (a motion capture tracking system). This system worked on the basis of four lamps that emit infrared rays whose reflections off the bodies of visitors to the gallery were recorded by special cameras. This data was transferred to the system's center, which then generated an image according to set parameters. The image is a double, or avatar, of each visitor, a three-dimensional model composed of voxels (3D pixels). When someone moved in the designated area his/her figure and movement were captured and immediately transmitted into the image projected on the screen in front of him/her. Visitors to Bielicky's interactive exhibition saw themselves in mingling with worshipers at the Western Wall.

This image of the Western Wall was transmitted by a web camera on a balcony overlooking the Wall and streamed in real time via a high-speed internet connection into the Robert Guttmann Gallery for the entire length of the installation, thereby offering visitors to the gallery in Prague a unique opportunity to find themselves in Jerusalem without having to overcome any geographical distance between the two cities, or cross any boundaries whatsoever. The web camera located in the gallery enabled visitors to view this revolution in travel in real time and in a virtual space.

Exodus: A Virtual Teleperformance in the Israeli Desert

Bielicky's 1995 virtual teleperformance *Exodus* was enacted in the Israeli Negev Desert. It is a place I know well. My wife Miriam and I lived in the Negev town of Yeroham for seven years. Our fourth child, Moshe was born there and our older son continues to live there after forty years with his wife, six children, daughter-in-law, and grandson. Moshe is the Hebrew name for Moses. Moses led the Israelites through the desert for forty years from

Exodus, 1995, telematic performance. Photographs of the vehicle GPS-antenna, and the expedition vehicle.

Exodus, 1995, telematic performance. Screenshots of the online travel log.

slavery in Egypt to freedom in their own land. Moses's trek through the desert was Bielicky's inspiration for *Exodus*.

Bielicky's four-day journey through the desert was tracked at Ars Electronica in Linz, Austria. His equipment included a portable global positioning system (GPS) device, which in turn was connected to a modem and a cellular phone. The GPS data received from several navigation satellites was transmitted via radiotelephone to the nearest server where digital desert landscapes were stored. These could be viewed worldwide through the internet with his movement perceived in real time. At the same time, the GPS data was transmitted via the internet to Linz where it was made visible in specially developed 3D graphics on a projection screen. Three times a day, he was in contact with the audience in Linz for a period of about ten minutes through a live voice telephone connection.

Bielicky explains that when Moses brought his people out of enslavement, no one knew what a radical effect this event would have on the evolution of human history. Humanity gained a new consciousness both through the experience of gaining freedom and receiving the Ten Commandments. He used this important event in human history as a metaphor for the emerging new human being at the end of the twentieth century. His virtual teleperformance artwork explored the emigration of humans into virtual nets and the associated liberation of time and space that changes consciousness.

He writes: "Information technology doesn't produce material objects anymore, only immaterial ones. The network artists may be in Siberia, New York, Tokyo, Berlin, or elsewhere and they all are part of an organism which is constantly developing its own unique dynamics and which has its own effects on their creative efforts. [...] The museum of the future will be able to be everywhere: at home, at the North Pole, in the desert, in a dance club, in prison, or at one's deathbed."[15] He anticipated by two decades that the entrance to the museum of the future would be through smartphones in the palms of millions of hands.

Three creative young Israelis developed a real-time interactive system using a GPS that simultaneously navigates thousands of vehicles with their drivers interacting with one another. In 2013, they sold their company, Waze to Google for over a billion dollars to make Google Maps come alive. More than 100 million people worldwide use Waze with directions in 27 different languages. Waze's headquarters is in Ra'anana, the small city where I live that is a half-hour's drive north of Tel Aviv when following Waze's directions for the most time-saving route.

I am ending my essay on Michael Bielicky's groundbreaking artworks with translations of biblical passages from the original Hebrew of the Bible into the language of digital culture. I began this essay by translating: "In the beginning God created the heaven and the earth" as *"In the network of networks, God created media systems for creating heaven and earth."* Here, I offer postdigital translations of two sentences in the Bible that make sense in terms of Waze. Both sentences use the term "straight circles" that can only be translated metaphorically, since a literal translation makes no sense. My translations below follow the most common translations in both the Jewish and Christian traditions.

The Artscroll English Tanach[16] translation of Proverbs 4:11 is: "I instruct you in the way of wisdom: I lead you in the course of fairness." The *King James Bible* translates it as: "I have taught thee in the way of wisdom; I have led thee in straight paths." My digital age translation is: "The wise way is to use Waze; Follow my directions – at the roundabout continue straight."

The ArtscrollEnglish Tanach translation of Proverbs 4:26 is: “Weight the course of your feet, and all your ways will be established.” The *King James Bible* translates it as: “Ponder the path of thy feet; stay on the safe path.” When I hear directions while driving on Israel’s roads, the same passage makes sense to me when I hear the Waze voice tell me: “At the roundabout continue straight and you will arrive at your destination.”

1 See Mel Alexenberg, *The Future of Art in a Postdigital Age: From Hellenistic to Hebraic Consciousness* (Bristol: Intellect, 2011).
2 See Michael Bielicky, “Manifesto for the Institute of Postdigital Narrative” (IPN), November 21, 2010, http://infoart.hfg-karlsruhe.de/manifesto/.
3 Robert Alter, *The Art of Biblical Narrative* (New York: Basic Books, 1981), 6.
4 See Mel Alexenberg, *Through a Bible Lens: Biblical Insights for Smartphonne Photography and Social Media* (Nashville: Elm Hill, 2018).
5 Thorleif Boman, *Hebrew Thought Compared with the Greek* (New York: Norton, 1960), 27.
6 Michael Bielicky, “Michael Bielicky,” in *Images Du Futur’91,* eds. Ginette Major and Hervé Fischer, exhib. cat. (Montréal: La Cité des Arts et des Nouvelles Technologies de Montréal, 1991), 18.
7 See Melvin Alexenberg, Otto Piene (eds.), *LightsOROT: Essays and Catalog of an Exhibition at the Yeshiva Museum in New York City* (New York: CAVS; Cambridge, MA: MIT, 1988).
8 Michael Bielicky, “Media Golem: Between Prague and ZKM,” in *Educating Artists for the Future: Learning at the Intersections of Art, Science, Technology and Culture*, ed. Mel Alexenberg (Bristol: Intellect, 2008), 193-202, here 197ff.
9 Elena Lappin, “Zerbrochene Intentionen – Leerstellen der Erinnerung: Ein Besuch im Jüdischen Museum Berlin,” *Frankfurter Allgemeine Zeitung*, 220 (September 21, 2001): 62. Translated from the German.
10 See Jennifer Hansen-Glucklich, *Holocaust Memory Reframed: Museums and the Challenges of Representation* (New Brunswick: Rutgers University Press, 2014).
11 Michael Bielicky, *Der Name*, https://transmediale.de/content/der-name.
12 Michael Bielicky, *Golem Is Alive*, video, 1998, see http://bielicky.net/projects/go-lem-alive-1988.
13 Michael Bielicky, *Next Year in Jerusa-lem*, single-channel (Umatic), 5:44 minutes, (Videosculptures Exhibition: Cite Internationale des Arts, Paris), 1988, http://bielicky.net/projects/next-year-jerusalem-homage-rabi-low-1988.
14 Gershom Scholem, “The Golem of Prague and the Golem of Rehovot,” in *The Messianic Idea in Judaism and other Essays on Jewish Spirtuality* (New York: Schocken, 1995), 339.
15 Michael Bielicky, “Exodus,” in *Mythos Information – Welcome to the Wired World*, eds. Karl Gerbel and Peter Weibel, exhib. cat. Ars Electronica 1995 (Vienna: Springer, 1995).
16 See the *Artscroll English Tanach* (New York: Artscroll Mesorah Publications Ltd., 1996).

Nira Pereg, Mel Alexenberg, and Kamila B. Richter, Karlsruhe, 2008.

Video Sculptures
1980–1991

1 Karl Gerbel and Peter Weibel, eds., *Ars Electronica'92: Die Welt von innen. Endo & Nano* (Linz: Veritas-Verlag, 1992), 126-29; and Jennifer Hansen-Glucklich, *Holocaust Memory Reframed: Museums and the Challenges of Representation* (New Brunswick, NJ: Rutgers University Press, 2014), 178-80.
2 For why Jews are "The People of the Scroll" and Jewish religion is primarily based on the media format of an "endless flow of divine wisdom," see Mel Alexenberg's essay "From the Golem of Prague to Waze from Israel," in this volume.
3 Michael Bielicky, *The Name*, in *Images du future '91: 31 mai - 22 septembre*, ed. Ginette Major (Montreal: Cité des Arts et des Nouvelles Technologies de Montréal, 1991), 18.
4 Verein der Freunde und Förderer des Kunstraum Neuss, *Discover European Video*, ed. Axel Klepsch (New York: Anthology Film Archives, 1990), 11, 46; and Wendelin Renn, ed., *Schirm-Herrschaft - Video Kunst: 27. Juni bis 25. Juli 1993* (Villingen-Schwenningen: Städtische Galerie, Lovis-Kabinett, 1993), 16.
5 Wulf Herzogenrath, ed., *Video-Skulptur retrospektiv und aktuell: 1963-1989* (Cologne: DuMont, 1989).

Video Sculptures 1980–1991

Unlike many of his contemporaries, Michael Bielicky's art concept does not progress from video art to tube television grid art, but instead it leaps from video to video sculptures. Still, Bielicky used tube television grids as a means of video display in parallel and from the very start of his career, without imposing new titles on them. Already in his first student year, he arranged small televisions on the scaffolding in Paik's atelier at Düsseldorf's Kunstakademie. Bielicky displayed a variety of his video works this way, years before he was honored by Paik to display the very same works on *Fish Flies on Sky* at the Museum Kunstpalast. In 1989, the same year *Golem Is Alive* was released and only five years after his first video release, Bielicky expanded the two-dimensional screen into an exhibition space. With his *Menorah* (1989) he extended the screen frames with the intention of dissolving them into a symbolically powerful sculpture – one of the main symbols of Jewish religion.[1] One year later, in 1990, he did away with the concrete religious symbolism and housed his videos in the most universal yet abstract Jewish symbol – the spiral.[2]

"One can walk through the spiral-like tunnel. At the end of that tunnel is a black sphere (the somewhere). A small TV transmitter transmits the information (in the form of a flame) to the carrier, the spiral, and the receivers (TVs). Information always moves through time and space in the same form. It always has the form of the spiral. The sounds of human language move through space in the same way as our solar system moves through the universe. We store information on a computer disc in a spiral form, as we do on a videotape."[3]

The Name (1990) is technically akin to *Menorah* but is an attempt to foreground Bielicky's great sensitivity for the deep time of spirituality, while even further eclipsing technical time.[4] He tries to unmask technology as just one meta-narrative among many: technology might appear to be the more contemporary meta-narrative, but it has only recently replaced religion and continues to amplify certain human behavioral patterns just as its ideological predecessor did. Technology is neither more neutral nor more universal than religion; in fact, it aligns with the most linear and simple algorithms known to man: along the meta-narrative of networks. Yet it aligns most obviously with the quantum computing meta-narrative; digital principles are questioned not only in a metaphysical or sociological way, but increasingly by the most prominent technological traits: advancement and efficiency. Nowadays, the predominant meta-narrative is shifting slowly once more in favor of the cyclical and spiral. This notion is only cemented by the fact that in 1989, Bielicky first exhibited *Menorah* with defunct fire extinguishers to show every visitor that he is well aware that his work – the fearless remix of religion and technology – might be hotwired for heated ideological discussions.

Later works even include Duchampian video sculpture experiments: *Output now* (1988) and *Easel* (1988), which Bielicky displayed at the Cité Internationale des Arts Paris, are reactions to the narrow *l'art pour l'art* concept of art in Paris and more widely in France – a time Bielicky often refers to as the most unproductive of his career. Yet he shows his first retrospective exhibition in the Salon 2e *Étage*, the Cité's largest Salon, facing the Seine. In 1988, he exhibited printed video work screenshots and his Duchampian video sculptures among other works and promoted them with his own flier design, calling the exhibition *Videosculptures*, which was a visionary title in view of how it preceded the publication of Wulf Herzogenrath's seminal book by one year.[5]

The transient culmination of this collection of works, aside from *Perpetuum Mobile* (2019), is *Perpetuum Mobile* (destroyed) at the Montreal *Images Du Futur* exhibition in 1991. Bielicky sent sketches, drafts, and video material abroad, and he commissioned a huge installation consisting of thirteen small televisions surrounded by a circular neon tube that displayed his video works. Although this installation recalled the tube television grids of that time, it also resembled a clock and more of a sculpture than a grid. Symptomatic of the grid-laden television exhibition landscape of that time, the 1991 version of *Perpetuum Mobile* does not appear in the exhibition catalogue at all (despite its dimensions and prominent positioning), whereas *The Name* is discussed with much emphasis and at great length. Bielicky's only genuine display grid, perhaps his most Paikian work ever, is *Perpetuum Mobile*, shown at his first major retrospective at the ZKM | Karlsruhe in 2019. It comprised a construction site fence module with sixteen tablets attached with Velcro, displaying digitalized versions of video works that dated back to 1986 and showing the USB cables powering the installation – ultimately foregoing the moment of mysterious discovery when the observer asks themselves where the signal might be coming from. There is indeed a time before and a time after the internet: the source is dead.

Untitled, 1980,
video sculpture with scaffolding.
Installation view,
Düsseldorf Art Academy, 1987.

Easel, 1988, video sculpture. Installation view,
Cité Internationale des Arts, Paris, 1988.

ONWA
VOLUME
TUNING

WC

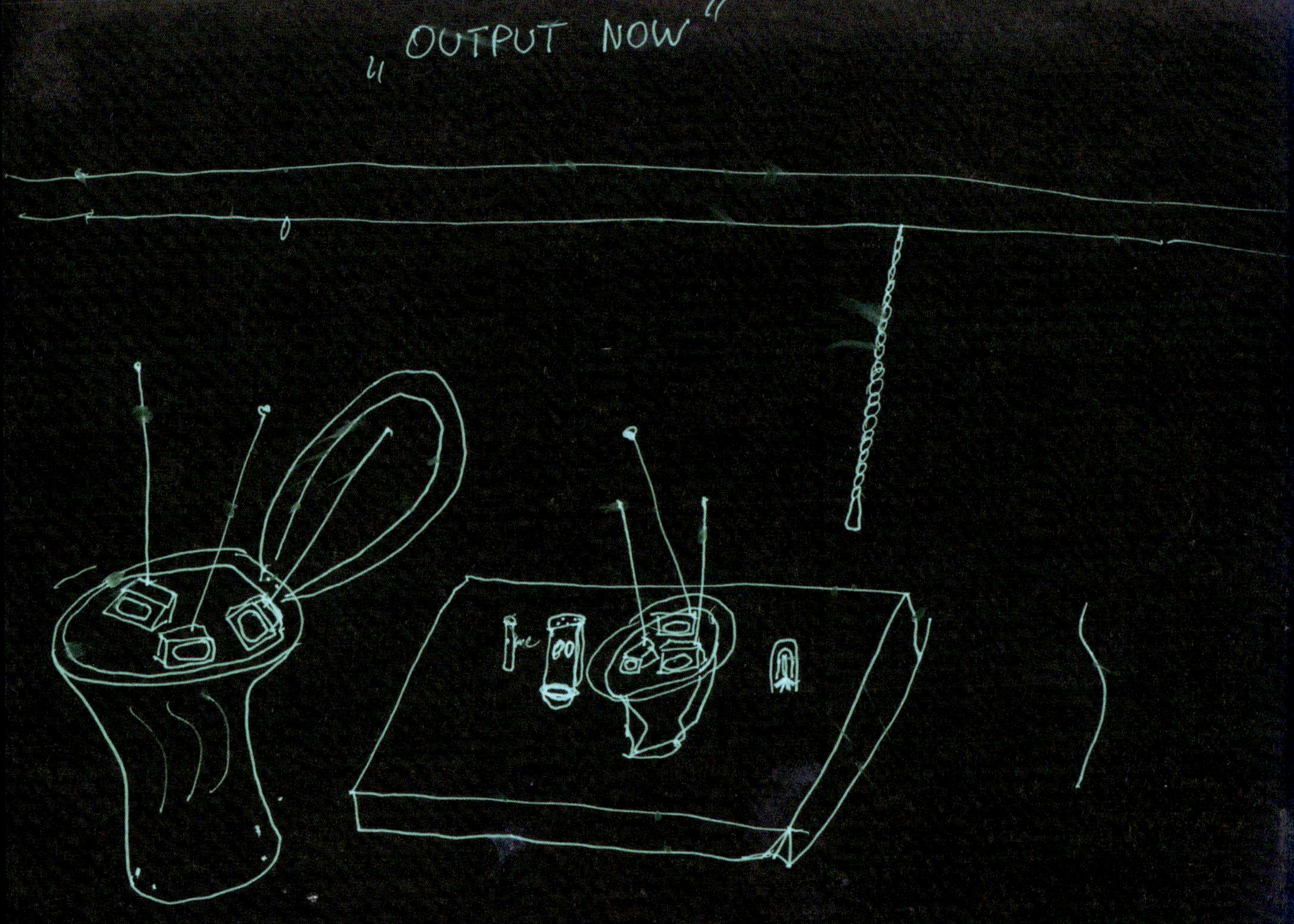
„OUTPUT NOW“

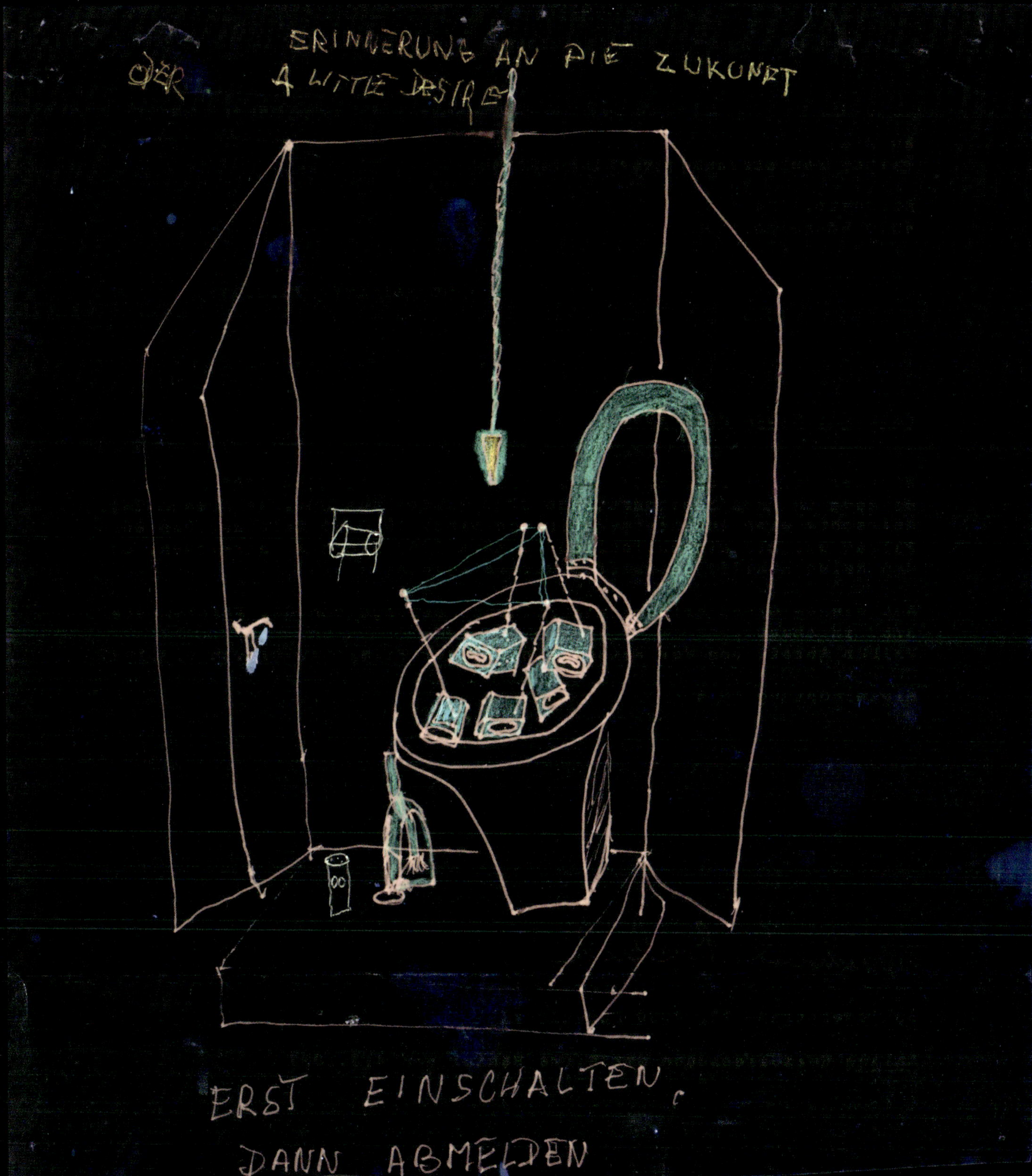

Output Now, 1988, video sculpture, Cité Internationale des Arts, Paris, 1988. Sketches.

JLB Perfect Guest 2, 1989, multi-monitor video sculpture. Installation view, Düsseldorf Art Academy, 1989.

What interests me the most is the phenomenon of permanent changes in life – the appearance and disappearance of things. I am not interested in telling stories about art. In my work I try to get closer to the inner meaning of life. My images are in permanent movement. There is no simple image.

Michael Bielicky in Vilém Flusser, Nam June Paik, Discover European Video: Anthology Film Archives, ed. by Axel Klepsch (New York: Anthology Film Archives, 1990), 11.

Menorah/Inventory, 1989, video sculpture.
Sketches, 1988.

Menorah/Inventory, 1989, video sculpture.
Sketches, 1988.

The Name

Information always moves through time and space in the same form. It always has the form of a spiral. Genetic code, for example, is stored in the double-helix spiral in the same way as the information in the two rolls of the Torah, the sacred book of Judaism.

The sound of human language moves through space in the same way as our solar system moves through the universe. We store information on a computer disc in a spiral form, as we do on a videotape.

The light – a word – a name – a code – information is invisible and comes from the darkness: from "somewhere." They first become visible through various media. The universe is an information-seeking and information-giving system (consciousness). The installation consists of a metal spiral of three turns, on which are mounted seven little black-and-white TV monitors (information carriers).

One can walk through the spiral as through a tunnel. At the end of that "tunnel" is a black sphere (the "somewhere"). A small TV transmitter transmits "the information" (in the form of a flame) to the carrier – the spiral, and the receivers (TVs).

First published in Ginette Major, ed., *Images du future '91* (Montreal: Cité des arts et des Nouvelles technologies de Montréal, 1991), 18.

The Name, 1990, video sculpture. Installation view, Galerie René Coelho, Amsterdam, 1991.

The Inner Observer, 1992, video sculpture. Installation view,
Ars Electronica, Linz, 1992.

LICHT

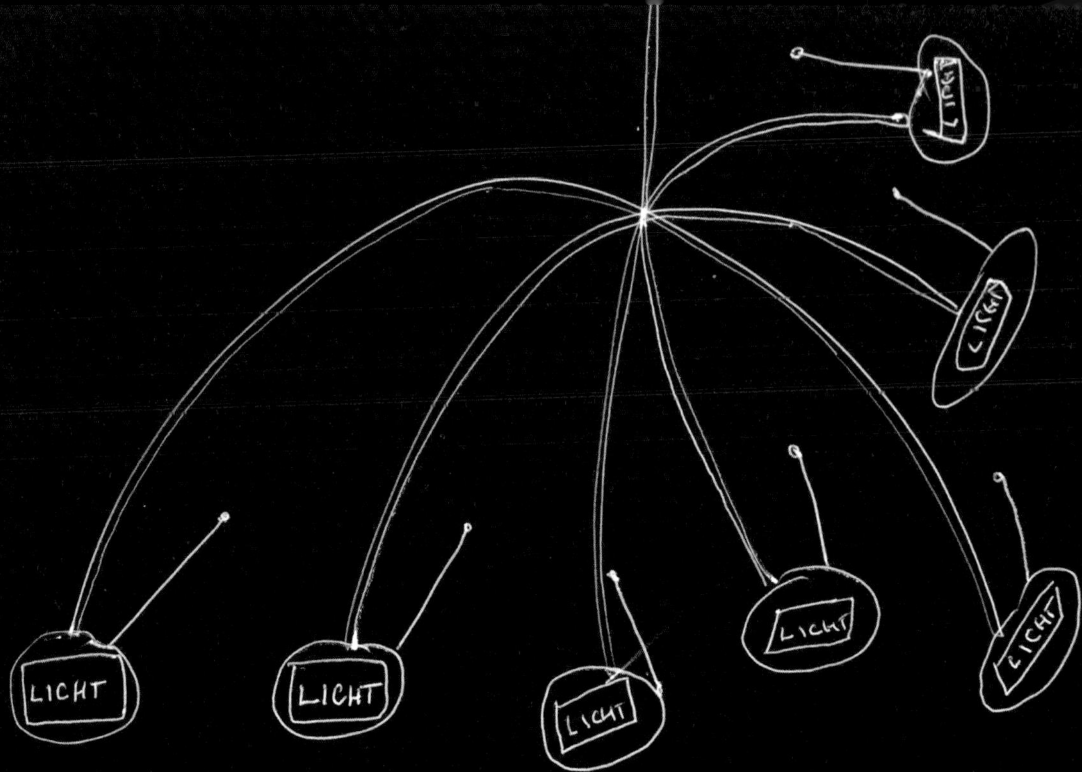

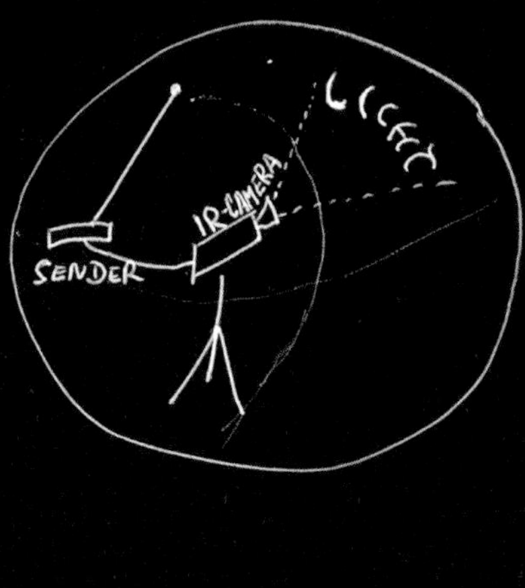

The Inner Observer, 1992, video sculpture.
Sketches, 1991.

The Inner Observer, 1992, video sculpture.
Sketches, 1991.

Wire model of the video sculpture *Perpetuum Mobile* for the *Images du futur* exhibition in Montreal. Photographed at the Theodor-Heuss-Bridge, Düsseldorf, 1991.

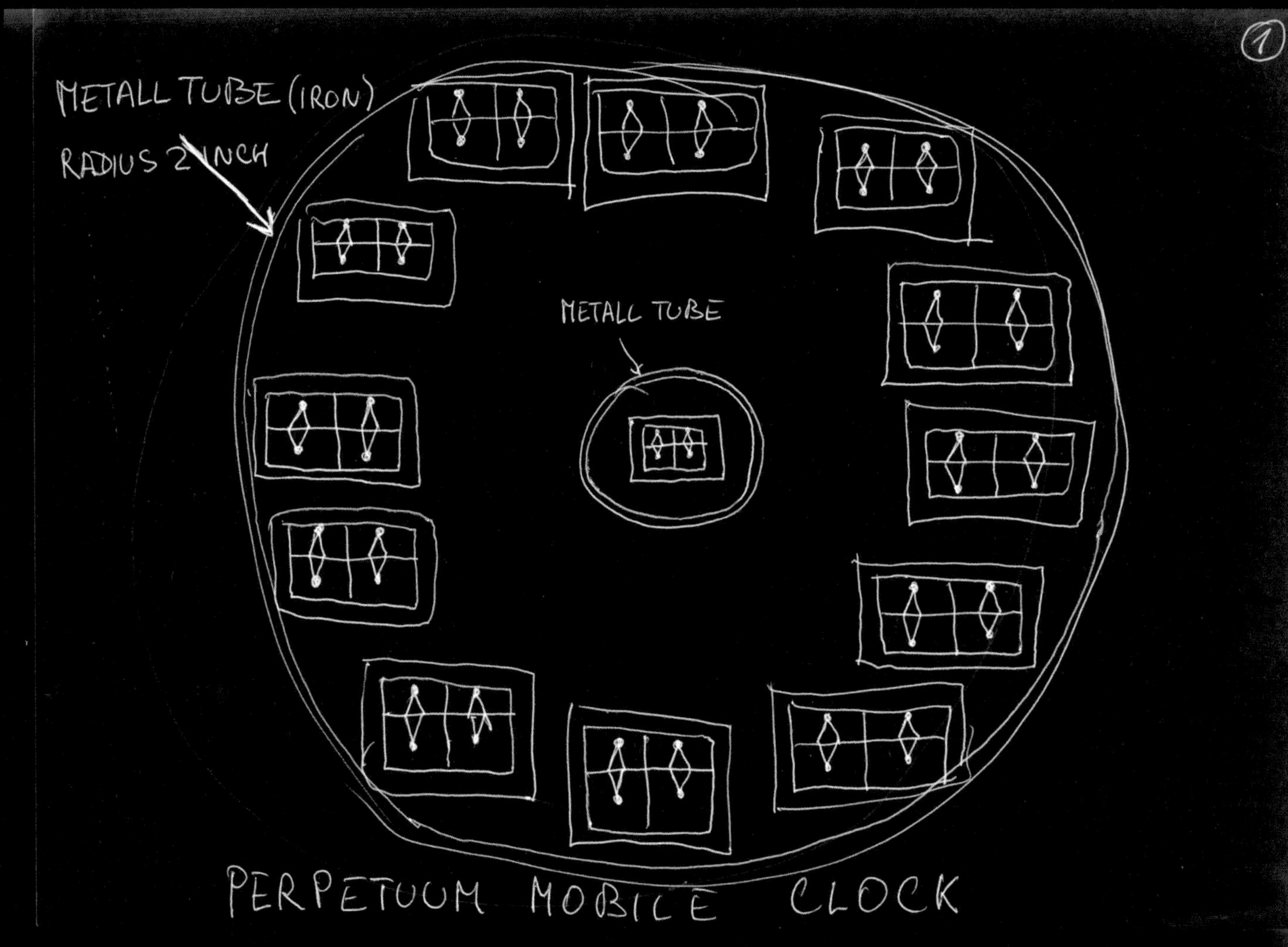

Perpetuum Mobile. Sketches, 1991.

Perpetuum Mobile. Sketches, 1991.

Perpetuum Mobile. Sketches, 1991.

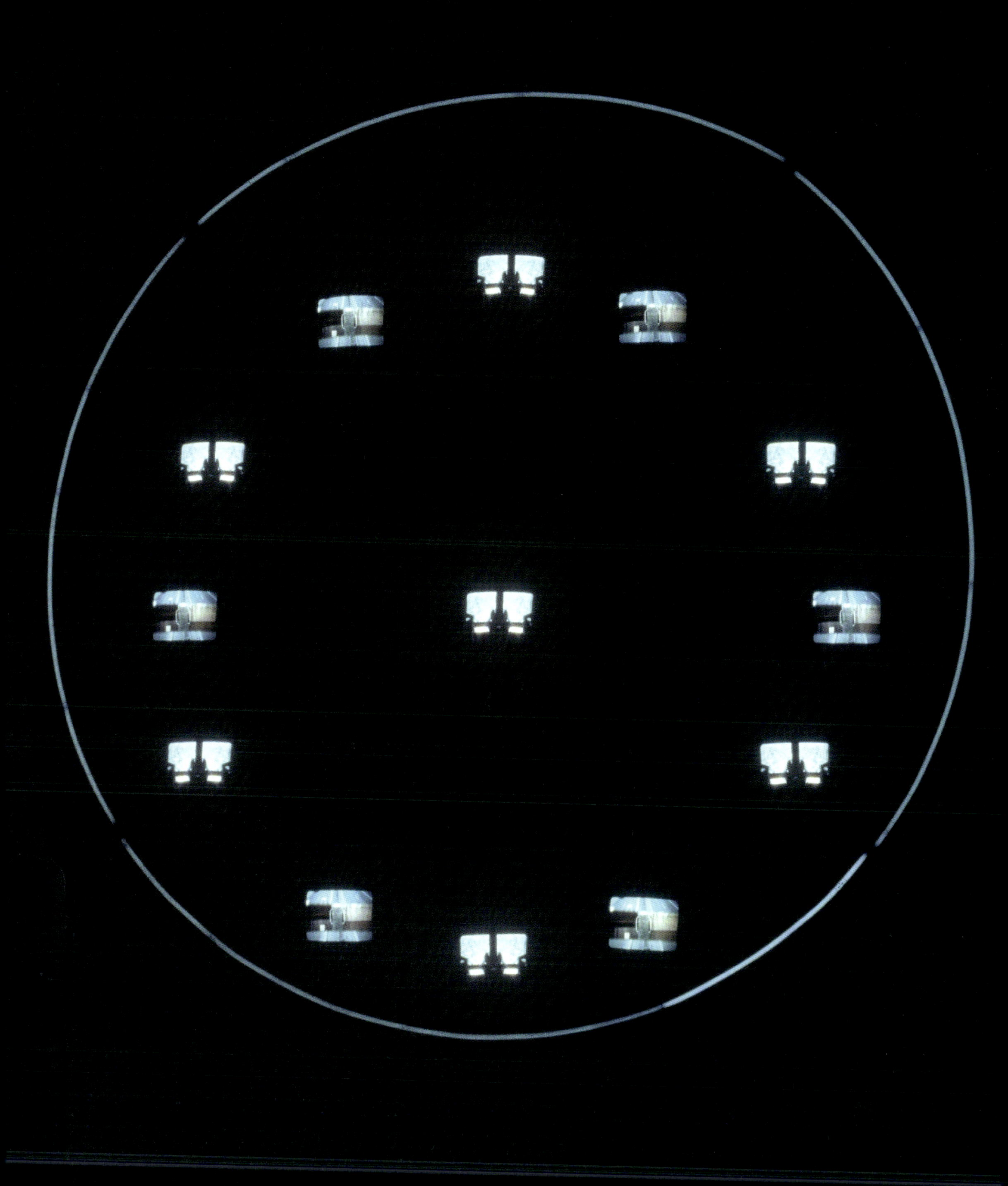

Perpetuum Mobile, 1991, video sculpture. Installation view, Cité des Arts et des Nouvelles Technologies de Montreal, Montreal, 1991.

The Sixth Sense

Michael Bielicky

When humans began to gather around the fire to allow themselves to be illuminated by its magical warmth and image, the fireplace became an archetypal place of communication for the following hundreds of thousands of years.

The telephone has radically changed the communication space; the perception of time has been redefined. The networking that is made possible by the telephone line enables a simultaneous flow of information. This "always everywhere" presence developed into a kind of new sense. In addition to the sense of sight, hearing, smell, sense of taste and touch, people develop an "everywhere sense." The omnipresence that we experience through this new sense apparently has a diametrical impact on our perception and reception: on the one hand, we expand by networking our knowledge and information potential; this is how we expand our brain capacity. On the other hand, there is a possibility that the amount and variety of information leads to general disinformation. This is no miracle, because before humans had this new sense, their perception was "only" three dimensional. By developing the sense for this new dimension, we are witnessing our own evolution.

This evolution today irritates various social structures around the world. They are too paralyzed to be able to respond adequately to such challenges. And so Mother Nature will, as always, use her selective principle to enable those who are willing to adapt to the new conditions.

The generations in our time are at a stage comparable to the stage at which fishlike creatures found themselves when they began to get to know the medium of air and land in addition to the water medium.

The military recognized the benefits of being everywhere very early on. The field phones from the 1950s can be networked. In this interactive installation you can experience a conference call. On the telephones, the phrase "Warning, the enemy is listening" is incised in the Czech language.

Michael Bielicky

David Galloway

In retrospect, German art of the 1980s resembles a rollercoaster ride of trends and *-isms*. None, however, seemed so full of promise as video sculpture, which took definitive form in the last Kassel documenta of 1987. The focus on video, and on "extended video" in the form of sculpture or installations, owes much to Nam June Paik, who teaches at the Düsseldorf Art Academy. One of his most gifted protégés is Czech-born Michael Bielicky, whose work has found substantial recognition in the last two years. Bielicky's family sought political asylum in Germany when he was only a child. He still maintains a studio in Düsseldorf and spends long periods in Prague and New York; it was in New York that his artistic ambitions first took shape. A self-taught photographer, he produced in 1981 a striking portrait series of New York street people that was published in Germany. Bielicky was thirty years old when he began his studies with Paik in 1984. A year later in Düsseldorf, he showed his first video sculpture: a toilet brimming over with portable television sets. On each was running a different program; hanging on a wall nearby were sheets torn from a TV guide. A video documentation of the destruction of Joseph Beuys's *Fettecke* (allegedly by a cleaning crew) at the Düsseldorf academy brought Bielicky his first significant recognition: it was featured at media festivals and museums throughout the world. Several subsequent works, including some exploring his Jewish heritage, were acquired by German television. But the artist was increasingly intrigued by the fusion of video and sculpture. He discovered the virtues of inexpensive mini-TVs. "The screen shouldn't overwhelm the sculptural presence," he argues, "and the work doesn't cease to exist when the set is turned off."

Water and fire, both suggestive of "the permanent flux of existence," became the artist's recurrent motifs. His first major work, produced in 1989, was a six-foot menorah entitled *Menorah*. Each of its seven arms bears a mini-TV whose antenna points toward the heavens. Flickering on each screen is a flame – a symbol of meditation, enlightenment, and Holocaust. *Menorah* was one of the first works acquired for the new ZKM | Center for Art and Media Karlsruhe. Seven "flaming" monitors also complete *Spiral*, to premiere this month at MonteVideo [today Netherlands Media Art Institute], in Amsterdam. Bielicky sees the spiral, through which visitors can walk, as a symbol for the flow of information through time and space, but he also refers to the genetic code stored in the double helix and sees a parallel to the life-giving information contained in the twin rolls of the Torah. Bielicky also teaches at the Prague Art Academy, which has turned over its entire staff since 1989. Returning to the city he fled as a child was initially disorienting, but he was soon inspired by its intellectual vigor. That's no surprise, considering the intersections of time, history, religion, and media that distinguish his work.

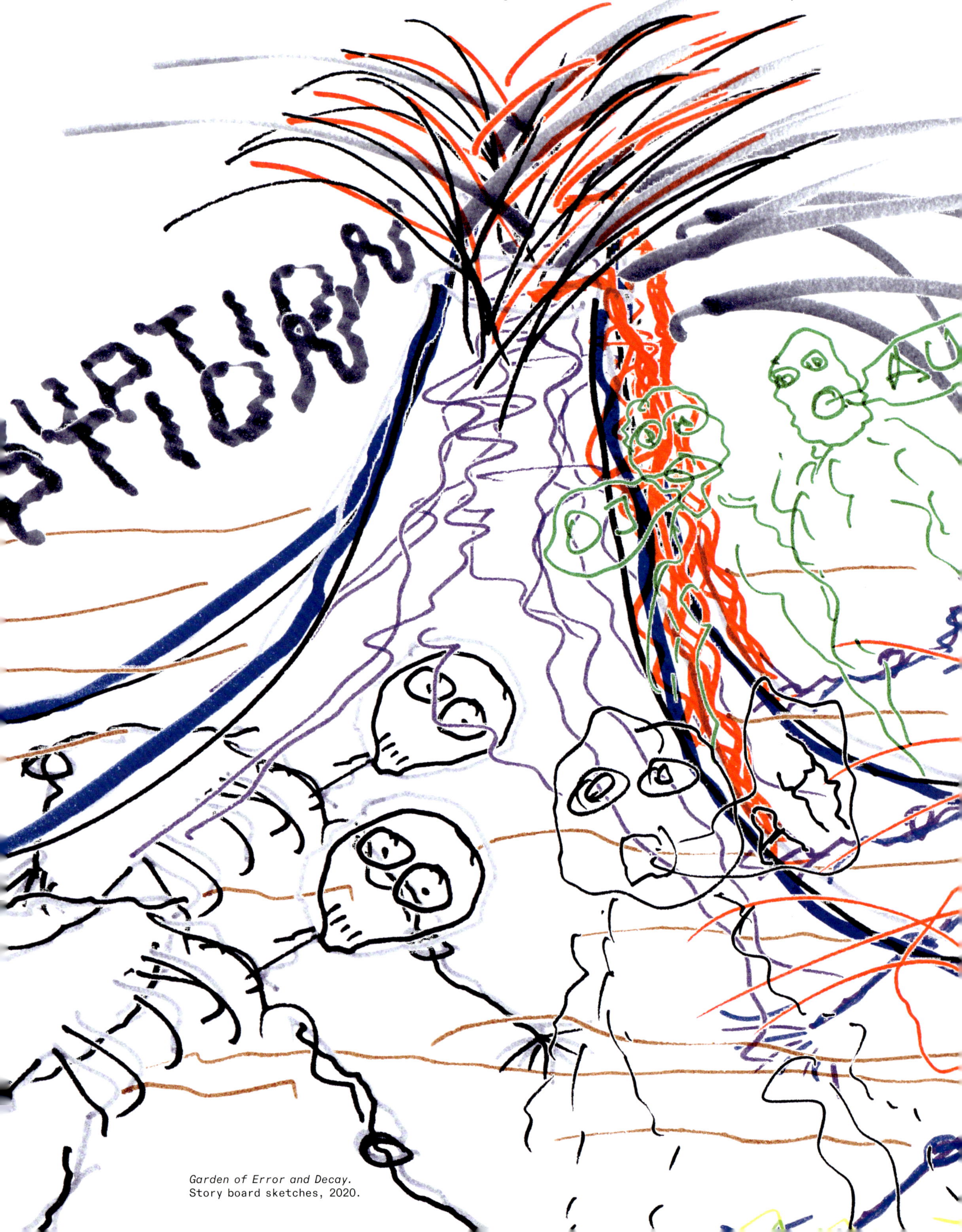

Garden of Error and Decay.
Story board sketches, 2020.

Golem, Leviathan, Behemoth: On a Few Irregularities at the End of the Sixth Day of Creation

Peter Sloterdijk

A common misunderstanding is that the definitive creation narrative in the *Tanakh* (what Christians traditionally call the Old Testament) is found right at the beginning of the Book of Genesis, where the often quoted six-day work and subsequent rest day is told in exalted monotonous verse.

This misunderstanding is related to the invalidated assumption that the Genesis depiction provided a complete survey of the basic divisions of beings, as well as the general categories of plant and animal species – with the exception of the single-celled and microbial organisms, whose existence, as closer examination reveals, is not covered by a corresponding execution order.

Furthermore, we note that the Creator, however he may be named, was consistent, creating only genuses and species by means of "let there be" orders, ergo in the logocratic mode; whereas, in the figures of Adam and Eve, he brought forth individuals – and did so through an act of artisanal handling: Adam was initially created, thanks to ceramic art, as an anthropomorphous clay statue, hollow inside, since a solid form would have precluded its later inspiration with life breath.

In the Book of Job, which belongs to the wisdom books of the *Tanakh*, the veil enshrouding several mysterious moments of the six-day work is lifted slightly – and instantly monstrosities appear that no sympathetic Creation believer would have anticipated.

One might describe the scene as follows: Suffering Job, having – it seems –lamented too loudly and apparently asked the Creator a few too many questions concerning the sense of the whole affair, receives an hour of tutoring from the supreme side, to learn humility toward the Creation – but above all to relinquish his error of thinking he had understood something about the miracles of Creation.

For this purpose, God summonses a monster, which at this point nobody knew was among his creatures. The Lord presents it in the following way:

> 40:15 Behold now, Behemoth, which I made as well as you; He eats grass like an ox.
>
> 40:16 Behold now, his strength in his loins; And his power in the muscles of his belly.
>
> 40:17 He bends his tail like a cedar; The sinews of his thighs are knit together.
>
> 40:18 His bones are tubes of bronze; His limbs are like bars of iron.
>
> 40:19 He is the first of the ways of God; Let his maker bring near his sword.
>
> 40:20 Surely the mountains bring him food, And all the beasts of the field play there.
>
> 40:21 Under the lotus plants he lies down, the covert of the reeds and the marsh.
>
> 40:22 The lotus plants cover him with shade; The willows of the brook surround him.
>
> 40:23 If a river rages, he is not alarmed; He is confident, though the Jordan rushes to his mouth.
>
> 40:24 Can anyone capture him when he is on watch, With barbs can anyone pierce *his* nose?[1]

It comes as no surprise that Job is silenced by so much irony. He will have known that a god jealously guards his sovereignty; that a god to whom a sufferer complains can be scornful as well, he learns here. Even more confounding is the statement put in the mouth of God that this monster was the zenith of the works of God. Then a second monster is presented:

41:1 Can you draw out Leviathan with a fishhook? Or press down his tongue with a cord?
41:2 Can you put a rope in his nose, Or pierce his jaw with a hook?
41:3 Will he make many supplications to you, Or will he speak to you soft words?
41:4 Will he make a covenant with you? Will you take him for a servant forever?
41:5 Will you play with him as with a bird, Or will you bind him for your maidens?
41:6 Will the traders bargain over him? Will they divide him among the merchants?
41:7 Can you fill his skin with harpoons, Or his head with fishing spears?
41:8 Lay your hand on him; Remember the battle; you will not do it again!
41:9 Behold, your expectation is false; Will you be laid low even at the sight of him?
41:10 No one is so fierce that he dares to arouse him; Who then is he that can stand before Me?
41:11 Who has given to Me that I should repay *him*? *Whatever* is under the whole heaven is Mine.
41:12 I will not keep silence concerning his limbs, Or his mighty strength, or his orderly frame.
41:13 Who can strip off his outer armor? Who can come within his double mail?
41:14 Who can open the doors of his face? Around his teeth there is terror.
41:15 *His* strong scales are *his* pride, Shut up *as with* a tight seal.
41:16 One is so near to another; That no air can come between them.
41:17 They are joined one to another; They clasp each other and cannot be separated.
41:18 His sneezes flash forth light, And his eyes are like the eyelids of the morning.
41:19 Out of his mouth go burning torches; Sparks of fire leap forth.
41:20 Out of his nostrils smoke goes forth; As *from* a boiling pot and *burning* rushes.
41:21 His breath kindles coals, And a flame goes forth from his mouth.
41:22 In his neck lodges strength, And dismay leaps before him.
41:23 The folds of his flesh are joined together, Firm on him and immovable.
41:24 His heart is as hard as a stone, Even as hard as a lower millstone.
41:25 When he raises himself up, the mighty fear; Because of the crashing they are bewildered.
41:26 The sword that reaches him cannot avail, Nor the spear, the dart or the javelin.
41:27 He regards iron as straw, Bronze as rotten wood.
41:28 The arrow cannot make him flee; Slingstones are turned into stubble for him.

41:29 Clubs are regarded as stubble; He laughs at the rattling of the javelin.
41:30 His underparts are *like* sharp potsherds; He spreads out *like* a threshing sledge on the mire.
41:31 He makes the depths boil like a pot; He makes the sea like a jar of ointment.
41:32 Behind him he makes a wake to shine; One would think the deep to be gray-haired.
41:33 Nothing on earth is like him, One made without fear.
41:34 He looks on everything that is high; He is king over all the sons of pride.[2]

This full quotation of the two passages, in their entire length, is necessary in order to reveal an aspect nearly concealed elsewhere – an aspect one might call the second face of Creation. The author of Job is seeking to elevate the eminence of the Creator by presenting two monsters, with which God plays, for His own entertainment. This is the sole motive that would justify the appearance of beings that do not belong to orthomorphic Creation. There is of course a remarkable flaw in the author's reasoning: by presenting Behemoth and Leviathan as animate creatures of God, he is using an incorrect term to refer to these sterile singularities ("Behold now, Behemoth, which I made as well as you"); in truth, they embody authentic monsters, which by definition can exist only as singular examples. Meanwhile, it is evident that authentic creatures have always and without exception been invested with a potential for creativity – at least with that amount that is required for the "pro-creation" of their species. This "as well as you" could refer to the sheer fact of being created – then it would be skipping over the difference between

Garden of Error and Decay. Story board sketches, 2020.

Garden of Error and Decay. Story board sketches, 2007.

Garden of Error and Decay: Anger of God Pictogram, 2020. Software screenshot.

human being and monster; or it would refer to an analogous monstrosity of monster and human being – a thought one had better, for now, not ascribe to the author. At the end of the world, the monsters tear each other apart, God kills them in their entirety with his sword and distributes their flesh among the pious. He thus eliminates the traces of the clandestine excess creation.

It would seem to make more sense to understand the monsters Behemoth and Leviathan to be surplus beings, unmentionable in the regular Genesis, for good reason. They symbolize the two giant masses of marine and land matter, in which enormous supplies of uncompleted creation are plausibly likely to exist, far beyond the orthodox eumorphic fauna in the water and on the Earth. What they called "matter" comprised vast numbers of terabytes of unformed information; Greek: *teras,* the monster. Both miscreations have a typical chimeric structure, since they form hybrids, combining the genetic elements of other well-formed beings. Chimeras are normally genetically mixed singularities and, as such, are incapable of breeding similar offspring. It is no coincidence that Thomas Hobbes, in the seventeenth century, derived the emblem of the British empire from the Leviathan – even the greatest empires are, like the monster from the deep, the toys of God.

Being hyper-hybrids, both Behemoth and Leviathan refer to the sleeping potential of the matter that was already present while the spirit of God was already hovering over the dark waters. They are suited for far more than bringing to his senses a human being from the land of Uz, lamenting his misery. They herald the restless activity in the epigenetic sphere, where God – outside of the official Creation – had already esoterically set foot. It teems with creatures of the second order, whose endocreative potential is as yet undetermined. With this in mind, at any rate, anyone unprepared to acknowledge the fermentations in the darkroom of epigenesis should remain silent about the publicly announced Genesis. The two *teras*-form creatures show: when God rested on the seventh day, his Creation was – despite being deemed *valde bonum*-grade – unfinished. In the surpluses of the semi-finished and the unformed wait monsters – under the pretext of art, of engineering, of communication, and of medicine, they are drawn forth from latency.

Of course, these considerations of monstrosity have an anthropological aspect too. According to Genesis, Adam is unmistakably a creation derived from a ceramic procedure. We can only imagine him initially as an anthropomorphous clay sculpture. If clay is brought into play here as an exemplary form of vaguely defined characteristics or even featureless matter (Nicholas of Cusa calls this matter without characteristics *confusum chaos*), it simultaneously stands for the accommodation of "matter" to "form" – which is why it presents a model example of the event called "information." Clay precedes silicon.

At the end of the sixth day of Creation (the Jewish Friday evening, or the Christian Saturday evening), the clay man is created with the application of pottery methods, whose form is human because he is required to match the Creator's "image". In the later Jewish retelling of the story of Adam, the as yet soulless clay man is called a golem. His deficit, the absence of spiritual and vital breath, is ameliorated through an act of inspiration.

Nothing would seem more likely, in a civilization with a strong creation conception of the notion of imitation, that sooner or later the creation of life would be manifest the abundant in spirit. Once this happens, it revives the feeling that, at the end of the sixth day of Creation, a lot of work was left unfinished. This was addressed on the eighth day with the introduction of fire; on the ninth day, domesticated animals and metallurgical objects were added; as well as written characters, the fine arts, minted currency, telephones and long-range artillery.

Meanwhile, by all indication, the third day of the second week of Creation has dawned. Awaking from their clayey sleep, the golems declare their willingness to take on more daily tasks than the Rabbi Loew of Prague would have ever dreamed of. The computers are beginning to say "I" and "you," they are learning to behave like petit bourgeois citizens whose actions are driven by reason; they will shortly be paying taxes and voting for the "party of lesser evils"; they will attend ethics courses and love their fellow robots as they do themselves.

Soon we will be reading in the cultural news about a robot that has cut off one ear; about him being admitted to a clinic for defective nontrivial systems; about him lying in a coma, hallucinating sunflowers that he recently painted – in a style never see before by human eyes. They will be saying, he wanted to emigrate; he was looking for wooden clogs for walking in on moon dust.

Translated from the German by Lonnie Legg.

1 Job 40:15-24 (New American Standard Bible).
2 Job 41:1-34 (New American Standard Bible).

Pavlina Pudil and Petr Pudil, Karlsruhe, 2021

Peter Fischli and David Weiss, *The Way Things Go*, 1987, 16 mm, color, sound, 29:45 min. Video stills.

The Guilt of Experience

Michael Bielicky

When I found out about the topic of this year's symposium, I first remembered an old Prague Christmas story. Many years ago, on Christmas Eve, a man was admitted to a Prague hospital with the following injuries: a huge laceration on the head, a fishbone stuck in the throat, and a badly burned butt. The doctors did not know which of the injuries they should treat first and were puzzled how one could get such different injuries at the same time. The injured person's wife then made the following statement about the incident: during the traditional carp dinner to celebrate the birth of Christ, a fish bone got stuck in the man's throat. Then he went to the toilet, his thoughts revolving around the fact he had to go to the hospital. He smoked nervously while sitting on the toilet, not realizing that his wife had thrown drops of petrol into the toilet after cleaning earlier. The poor man threw his burning cigarette into the toilet, whereupon a flash of flame burned his back. Then he jumped up reflexively and smashed his head into the window, which was open toward the light shaft of the house. Half-dazed, he fell back, and the flame injured him even more.

You may be wondering what this story has to do with our topic. And you would be right if you found that it does not much. In any case, there is just as little a relationship between them as there is between the concept of experience and the concept of innocence itself. In this Christmas story we find a principle that questions the relationship between experience and the concept of guilt/innocence projected by humans. I would like to replace the terms *guilt* and *innocence* with a single term, namely the concept of original guilt. This term should first be considered value free. It should rather be understood as a constant accompanying circumstance of every experience. Just like the Christmas story, the film *The Way Things Go*, by Fischli and Weiss, also reveals superordinate mechanisms that similarly show no relationship between the concepts of experience and innocence. I am talking about the chain of events mechanism.

Allow me to express my doubts here as to whether it makes any sense to discuss the topic at hand. The English philosopher John Locke, representative of empiricism, believes that all knowledge is dependent on experience and that knowledge is under its control. In this context, I would like to mention two circumstances that have shaped my experience of reality over the past few weeks while I have been thinking about the topic of the symposium, and that in turn have made a strong reflective impression on my thoughts. Again and again, while I was sitting at my portable computer in a variety of environments to continue writing my contribution, I also dedicated a long time to a game that is on said computer. It is a Chinese game that is several thousands of years old and in some ways resembles chess. The principle of this game is to develop a strategy with which you can clear stones with the same symbols in pairs in such a way that not a single stone remains in the end. This fascinating game with enormous strategic options is a wonderful metaphor for acting in life and for the uncertain outcome of what we do. We make permanent decisions to get to goals, and depending on how we choose to do it, we make ourselves "guilty" insofar as we possibly miss the desired goal. And just as with this game, it does not help to bring any experience from the old to the next game, because you always find a new constellation of circumstances: so it is mostly difficult to apply old experiences to new experiences in life. Nevertheless, people always tend to apply old experience patterns to new experiences, assuming that they will master the new situation better and can reach the goal safely and without "guilt." This abstract game, through which I have repeatedly rehearsed the thinking process itself, step by step on one side and at the same time with a necessary foresight to achieve the hoped-for result, taught me that we have only very limited control of consciousness, and thus responsibility (guilt/innocence) for our actions, even when awake. This rational exercise in experience and active, deliberate action contrasted with a very opposite experience on a meta level I experienced as well, namely an emotional experience. I have had an extremely intense love affair in the past few weeks, which brought my partner and I into such an absolute state that all other experiences have begun to lose importance. This pure state of being, which is clearly outside time and space, has repeatedly given me the thought (when I reached my full consciousness from time to time) that this extreme experience can in no way touch the question of innocence or even guilt and that it must rather be the wish of the people themselves who want to establish a connection. Of course, you could create a relationship between guilt and innocence, for example, then, when you consider that in such an extreme state, which is certainly not going to last forever, you are ready to ignore all other realities for at least a certain time – for example, professional or social obligations. You can feel guilty for a moment, but mostly the feeling is much stronger than leaving the guilt too much space. In this context, I would like to deny the thesis that pure innocence is the main phenomenon in the absolute state of love. I am sure that this state is accompanied by a highly destructive element, and that you accept this consciously and even with some joy.

The transcendent element of the love experience is subject to other laws, to which the concept of guilt or innocence cannot be applied, even if the poets have repeatedly tried to express such a relationship. The deep fear that strikes every habit-dependent being every time he deviates from his habitual behavior is a primitive drive, which is very powerful even in premature living beings, but it also plays an indispensable role in the complex motivational structure of human cultural life. It is essential to the fearful feeling of having sinned, in short, of feeling guilty, and thus contributes significantly to the compliance of civilians with the law.

I remember the story of a husband suddenly returning from a business trip, who rang the bell and waited for a long time at his own house door. When his wife finally opened the door and tried to talk him into washing his hands in the kitchen and not in the bathroom as usual, he stormed into the bathroom and was faced with a stranger. Then the strange gentleman politely said, "Do not be angry, but I have a tender affair with the lady from the upper floor, and her husband has come unexpectedly, so the only thing I could do was to climb out of the window into your bathroom. Surely you will help me out of this embarrassment and let me out through the door?" The surprised husband smiled cheerfully and let the unknown gentleman pass. Around midnight, the husband was still wide awake next to his deeply sleeping wife when he suddenly ferociously slapped her in the face. Startled she said to him, "Are you crazy? Why are you hitting me?" He replied, "Something just occurred to me. We don't have a second floor above us."

So, wherever guilt arises, lies may appear, but you should be careful not to consider all lies with the same rating, as can be seen from the following conversation between two train travelers:

"Where are you going?" asks one.
"I am going to Warsaw, to buy wood," the other replies.

Flussers Fluss, 1991–94, single-channel video. Video stills of Vilém Flusser and Michael Bielicky playing chess, Robion, France. 1991.

Four Seasons, 1984, single-channel video. Video stills.

Then the first says, “Why the lie? I know if you say you are going to Warsaw to buy wood, then you are actually going to Lernberg, to sell grain. But I happen to know that you are actually going to Warsaw to buy wood. So why are you lying?”

Should we adopt what we perceive as true? Would the untruth be avoided as soon as nobody contradicts, neither the neighbor, our conscience, or the senses? Or if they argue, again: Who should be trusted? Me, or the collective majority of opinions? Or can it be reason that recognizes the truth from all deception? Truth and lies of the gods, demagogues, society, and imagination populate the whole world theater, like all the smaller stages of individual consciousness, amid the colorful backdrop of revelation and incantation, humbug and incompatibility of our whole history. The repeated attempt to view humanism as a guarantor of human knowledge has long since overtaken itself. The belief in the cultivation of the human spirit and to finally reach human paradise has lost its meaning at the latest, since we know that at the infamous Wannsee Conference on the final solution for the Jews, at least six participants sat at the decision table who were honored with a doctorate of philosophy.

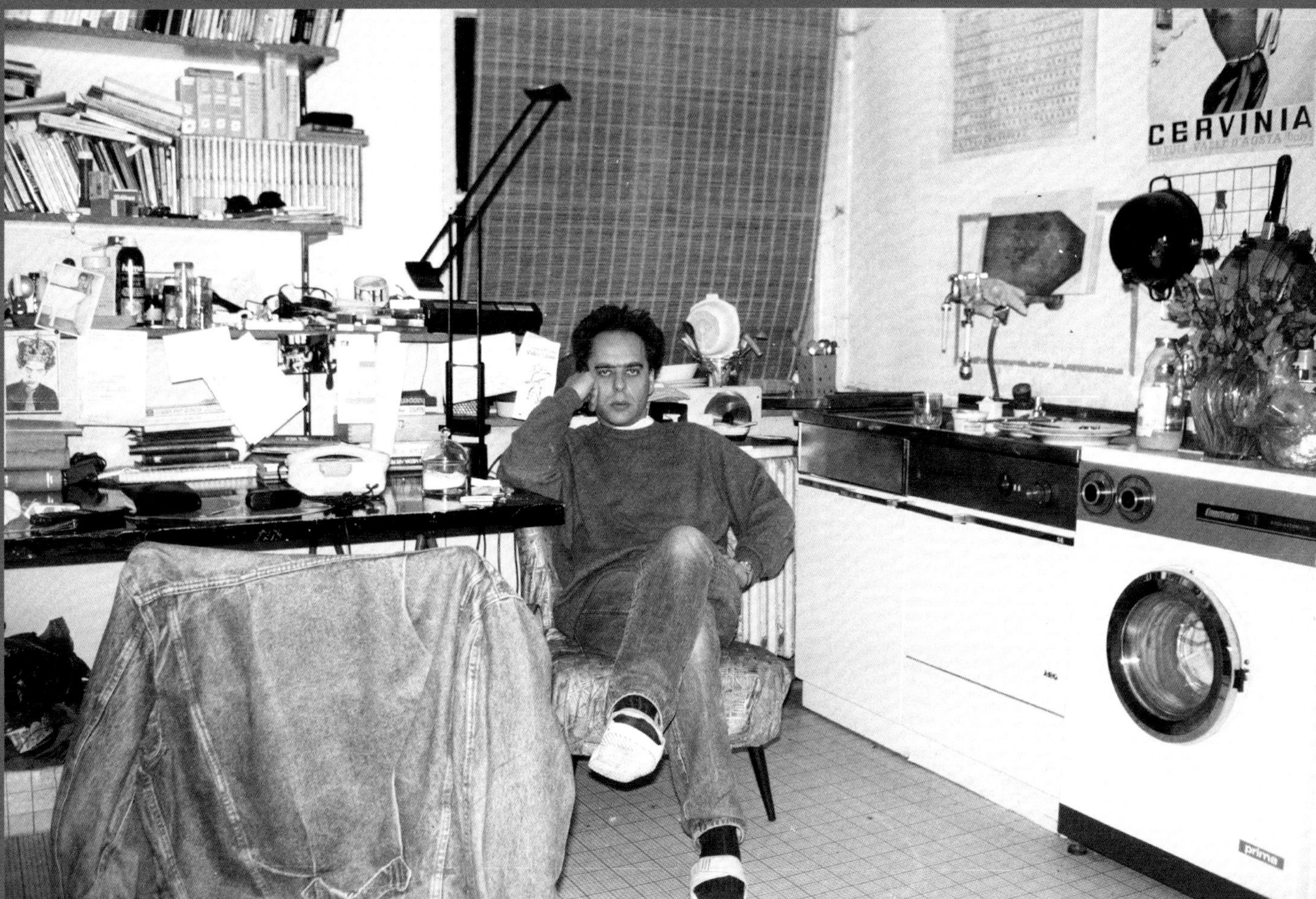

Michael Bielicky, Düsseldorf, 1988.

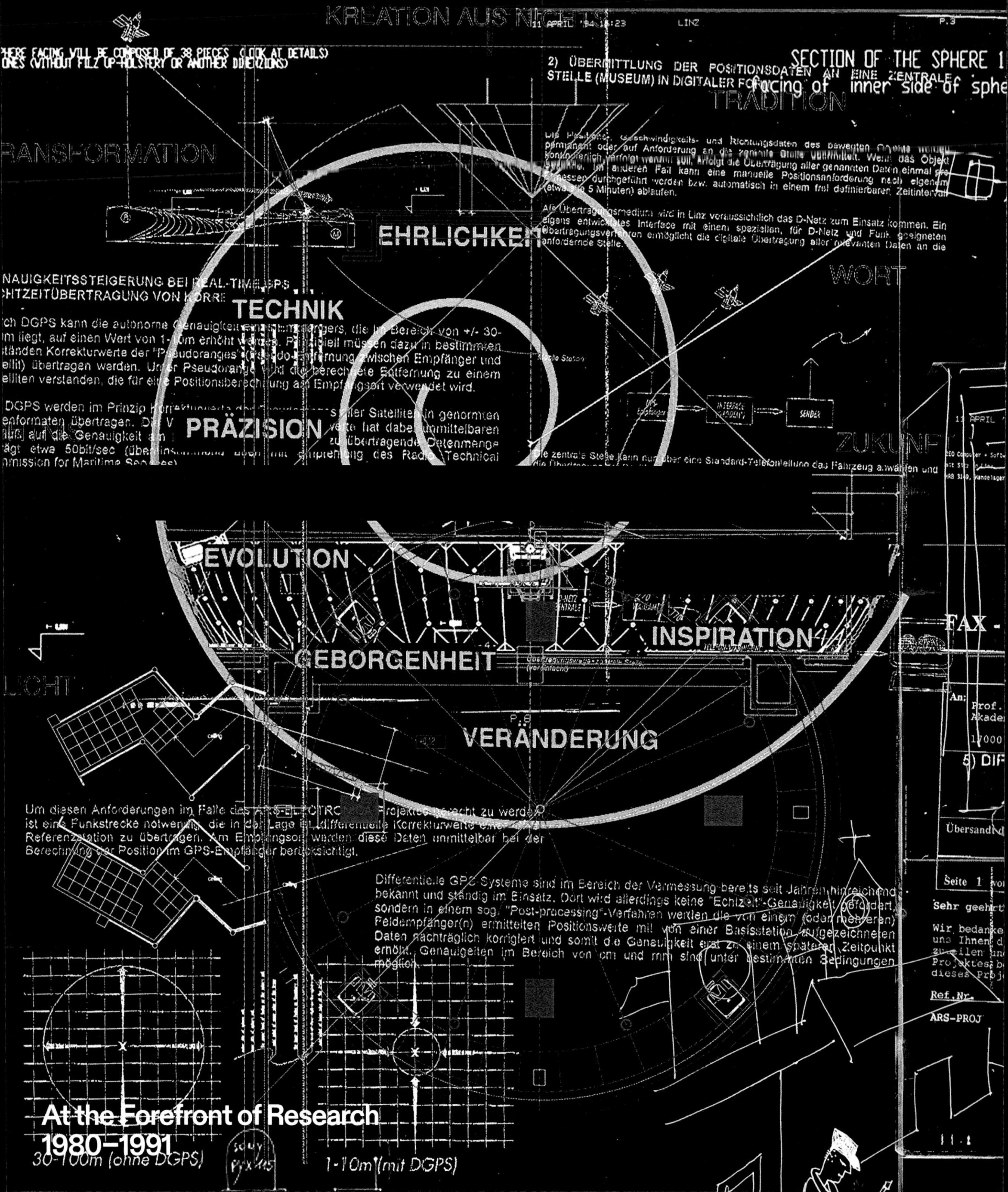

At the Forefront of Research 1980–1991

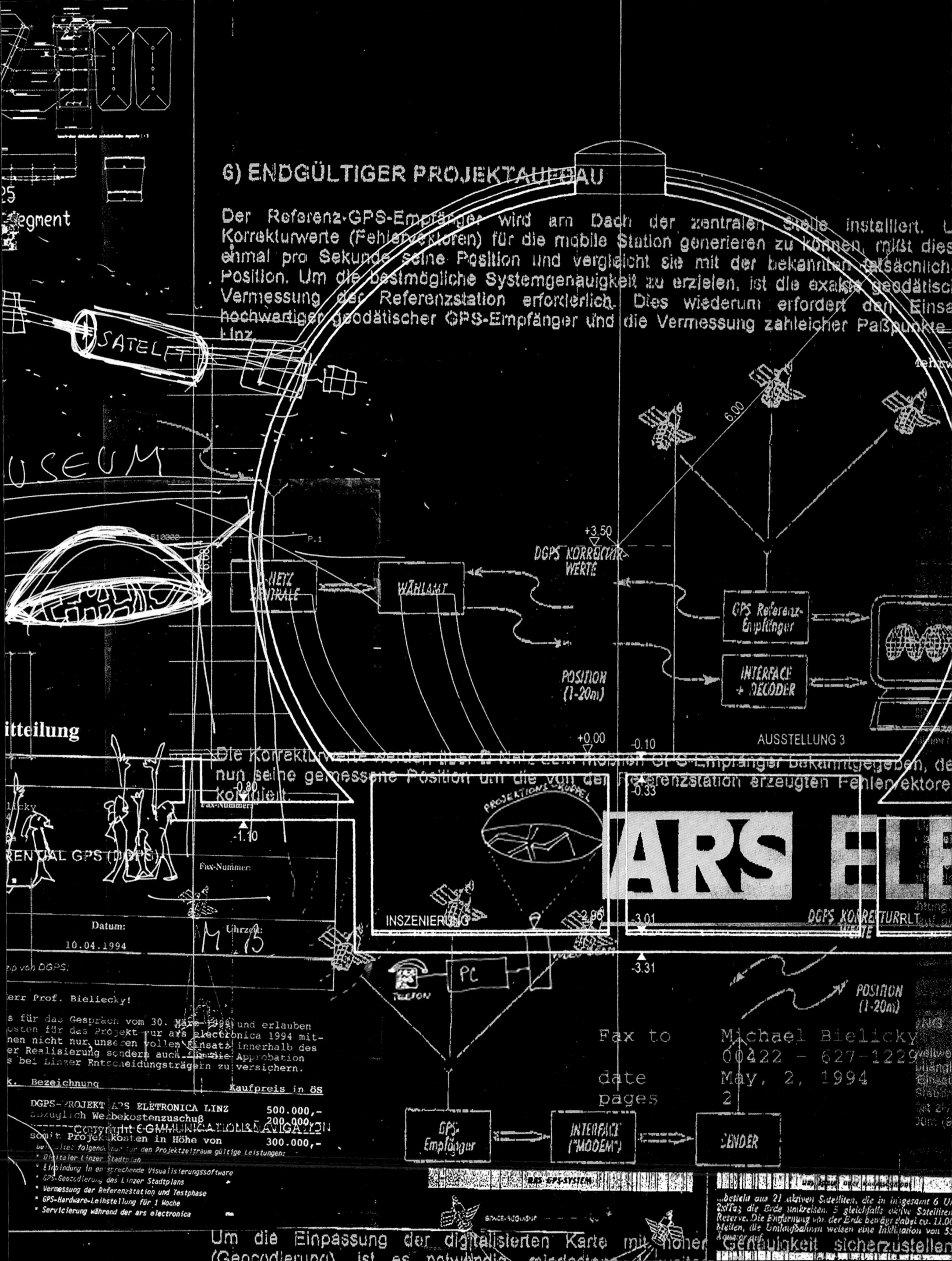

6) ENDGÜLTIGER PROJEKTAUFBAU
Der Referenz-GPS-Empfänger wird am Dach der zentralen Stelle installiert.
Korrekturwerte (Fehlervektoren) für die mobile Station generieren zu können, mißt dies
einmal pro Sekunde seine Position und vergleicht sie mit der bekannten tatsächlich
Position. Um die bestmögliche Systemgenauigkeit zu erzielen, ist die exakte geodätisc
Vermessung der Referenzstation erforderlich. Dies wiederum erfordert den Einsa
hochwertiger geodätischer GPS-Empfänger und die Vermessung zahlreicher Paßpunkte
Linz.
SATELIT
egment
USEUM
6.00
+3.50
DGPS KORREKTUR-WERTE
WÄHLAMT
GPS Referenz-Empfänger
INTERFACE + DECODER
POSITION (1-20m)
+0.00
-0.10
AUSSTELLUNG 3
Die Korrekturwerte werden über D-Netz dem mobilen GPS-Empfänger bekanntgegeben, de
nun seine gemessene Position um die von der Referenzstation erzeugten Fehlervektore
korrigiert.
itteilung
-0.80
-0.33
-1.10
RENTIAL GPS (DGPS)
Fax-Nummer:
PROJEKTIONS-KUPPEL
ARS ELE
INSZENIERUNG
2.96
-3.01
DGPS KORREKTUR-WERTE
Datum:
10.04.1994
Uhrzeit:
-3.31
PC
TELEFON
POSITION (1-20m)
Fax to Michael Bielicky
00422 - 627-1229
date May, 2, 1994
pages 2
Herr Prof. Bieliecky!
s für das Gespräch vom 30. März 1994 und erlauben
osten für das Projekt zur ars electronica 1994 mit-
nen nicht nur unseren vollen Einsatz innerhalb des
er Realisierung sondern auch für die Approbation
s bei Linzer Entscheidungsträgern zu versichern.
k. Bezeichnung
Kaufpreis in öS
DGPS-PROJEKT ARS ELETRONICA LINZ 500.000,-
abzüglich Werbekostenzuschuß 200.000,-
somit Projektkosten in Höhe von 300.000,-
Copyright C-COMMUNICATION&NAVIGATION
Digitaler Linzer Stadtplan
Einbindung in entsprechende Visualisierungssoftware
GPS-Geocodierung des Linzer Stadtplans
Vermessung der Referenzstation und Testphase
GPS-Hardware-Leihstellung für 1 Woche
Servicierung während der ars electronica
GPS-Empfänger
INTERFACE ("MODEM")
SENDER
Um die Einpassung der digitalisierten Karte mit hoher
Genauigkeit sicherzustellen

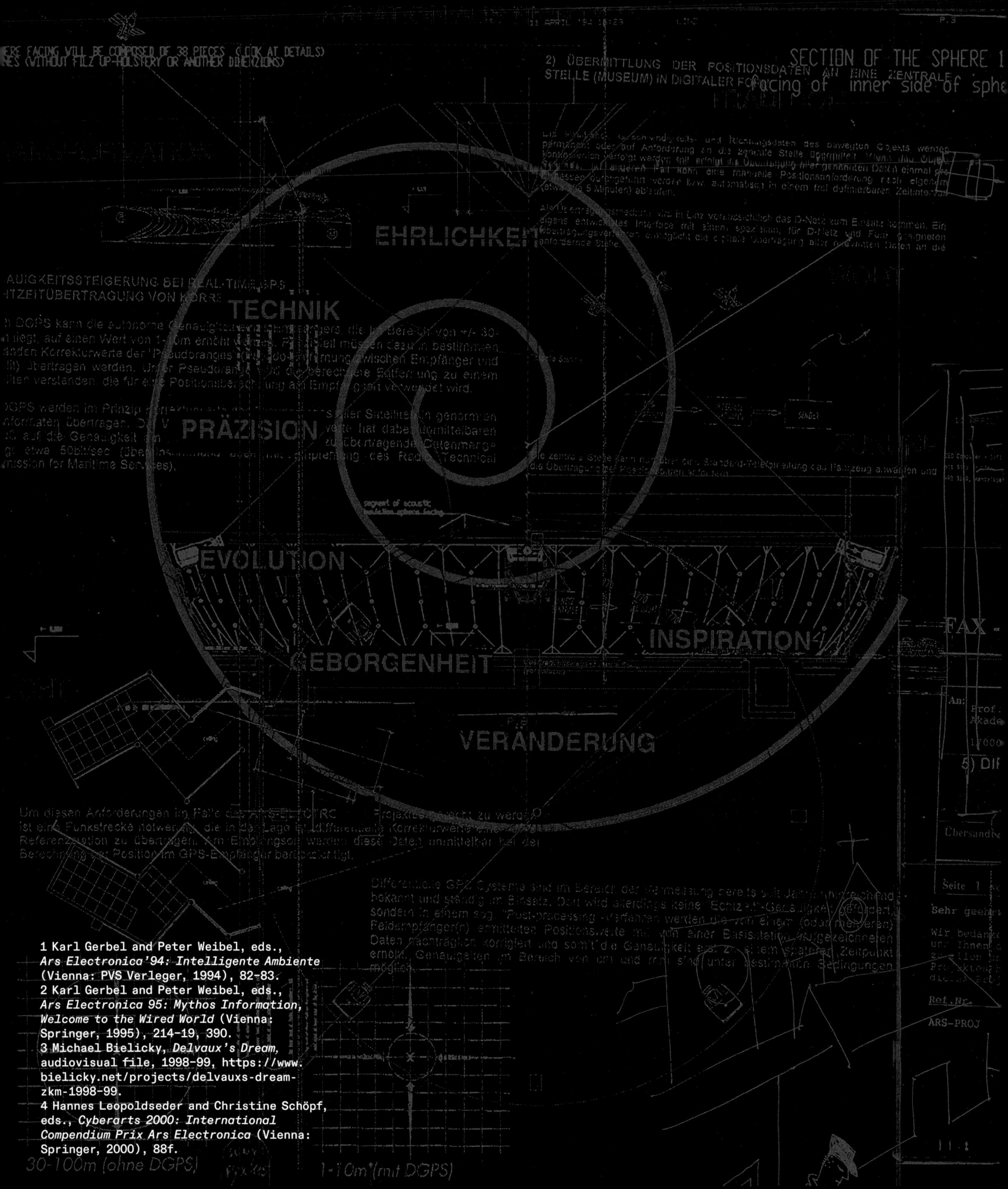

1 Karl Gerbel and Peter Weibel, eds., *Ars Electronica'94: Intelligente Ambiente* (Vienna: PVS Verleger, 1994), 82–83.
2 Karl Gerbel and Peter Weibel, eds., *Ars Electronica 95: Mythos Information, Welcome to the Wired World* (Vienna: Springer, 1995), 214–19, 390.
3 Michael Bielicky, *Delvaux's Dream*, audiovisual file, 1998–99, https://www.bielicky.net/projects/delvauxs-dream-zkm-1998-99.
4 Hannes Leopoldseder and Christine Schöpf, eds., *Cyberarts 2000: International Compendium Prix Ars Electronica* (Vienna: Springer, 2000), 88f.

At the Forefront of Research 1994–2001

Michael Bielicky began to experiment with GPS in an art context in 1994: his work *Intelligent Mailman* (1994) is the first of its kind worldwide and marks the onset of numerous foundational research projects on interactive media art. The mailman, viewed as a medial archetype, is the intellectual starting point of this work. The *Intelligent Mailman* is an anachronism and is the first artistic work in art history based on GPS technology: viewed one way, Bielicky's mailman is still transferring information from place to place, and he even does so by hand, but viewed another, he is simultaneously transmitting his location and movements over an imaginable distance as well as to several locations "live" or, in more contemporary terms, in real time. All this suddenly becomes possible with the help of a GPS that one mailman can carry in his hand and in a messenger sack.

With this anachronistic double function, *Intelligent Mailman* symbolizes a strange intermediate stage of being on the path to a complete information and surveillance age, while still experiencing the physical reminder that a considerable amount of technology is required to keep one within that stage. Today's smartphones do not lay on our shoulders anymore and certainly do not bump against our thighs when we walk. Today we simply feel a light sensation in our pocket, which only leaps into conscious awareness when we feel the slight panic of it being potentially lost somewhere. The intermediate prosthetic stage of technology addressed in *Intelligent Mailman* is completely lost in today's world.[1]

In another technologically pioneering project, Bielicky sets out to inscribe the biblical Exodus route into the prototype of what we all have come to know as the internet. Calling it a teleperformance in 1995, Bielicky et al. – equipped with a Jeep packed with what was then high-end technology – set out to track the Exodus route in the Negev desert, collecting GPS data and storing it on one of the first websites as they traveled.[2] That project, at the very junction of religion and narrative technology, marks a turning point in Bielicky's work. Technology is not mystified by specters anymore; the equilibrium between technology and religion that his work once reached with *The Name* (1990) tips the balance of favor toward technology. Bielicky literally traces the biblical history of Jewish culture with scientific means, and scientific means only.

From 1999 to 2001, he led the Virtual Set Project, a seminal research program at the ZKM | Center for Art and Media Karlsruhe. One of the first of the *produced@zkm-series* is the virtual reality blue-screen environment *Delvaux's Dream* (1998–99).[3] *Delvaux's Dream* is about the universal human dream of wandering through paintings and ultimately through photographs and moving images. This work displays the world of Belgian artist Paul Delvaux and was reconstructed with the help of chroma key technology and a complex tracking interpreter system. The visitors wander around the painting and interact with the staffage. Returning to the teleperformance concept, the mixed-reality stream is projected on a screen facing the main entrance atrium of ZKM | Karlsruhe for other visitors to see.

Room with a View (2000), for Volkswagen on the site of Autostadt Wolfsburg, again in collaboration with the ZKM and a *produced@zkm* project, was realized in a dome twelve meters in diameter and nine meters high, built from the ground up for this purpose. Visitors could interactively explore seven thematic environments. The surroundings revolved around the present and historical culture of the Czech Republic. They opened up new perspectives on development, influences, and their impulses in areas such as literature, art, and architecture. When the visitor approached the navigator in the center of the dome – a twelve-inch touchscreen monitor mounted on a revolving column – the image sections on the projection surface would change depending on the orientation and input.[4]

Intelligent Mailman, 1994, telematic performance.
Ars Electronica, Linz, 1994. Sketch.

SATELIT
SATELIT

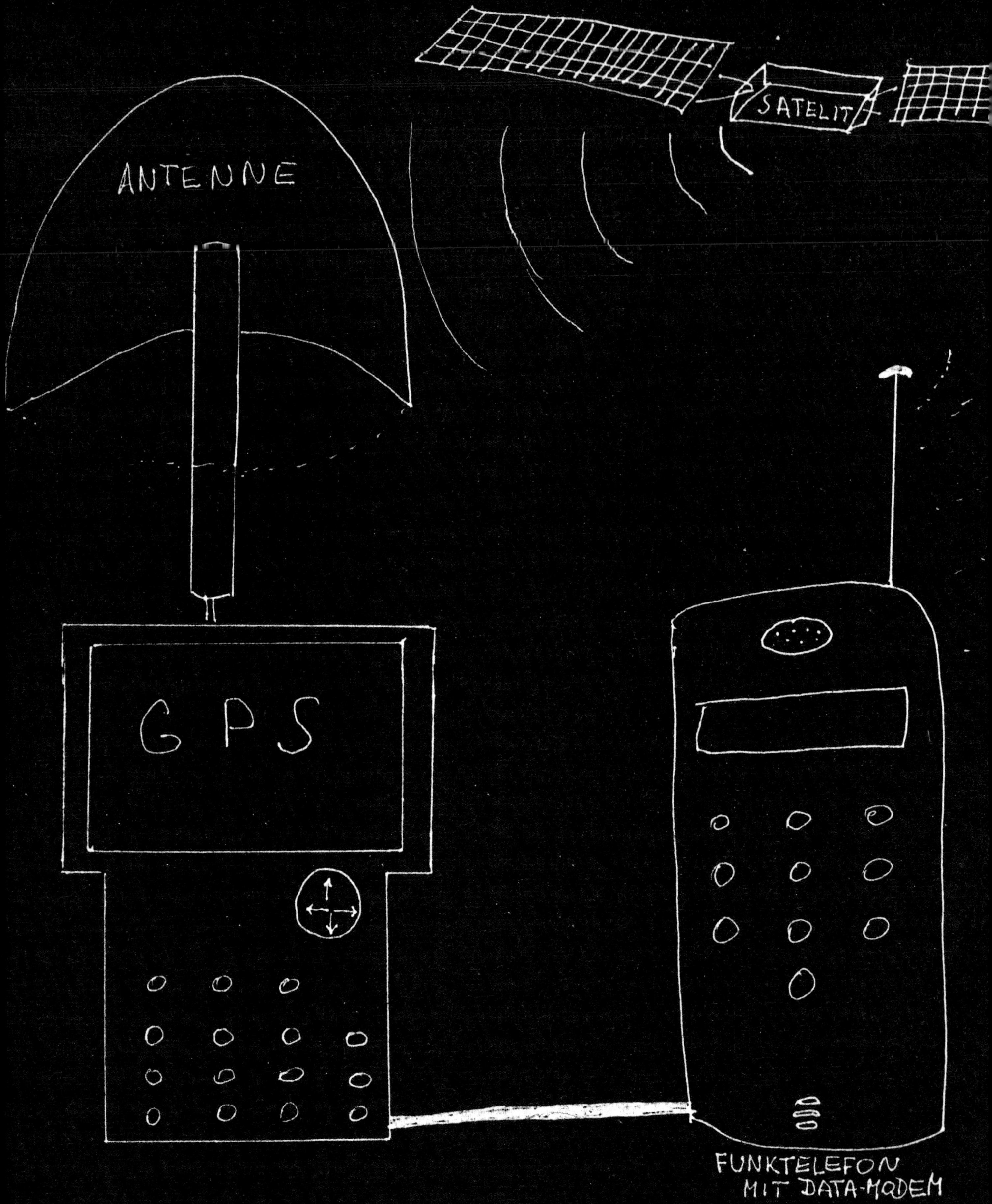
SATELIT
ANTENNE
GPS
FUNKTELEFON
MIT DATA-MODEM

Intelligent Mailman, 1994, telematic performance. Ars Electronica, Linz, 1994. Sketch.

Intelligent Mailman, 1994, telematic performance.
Ars Electronica 1994, Linz, 1994.

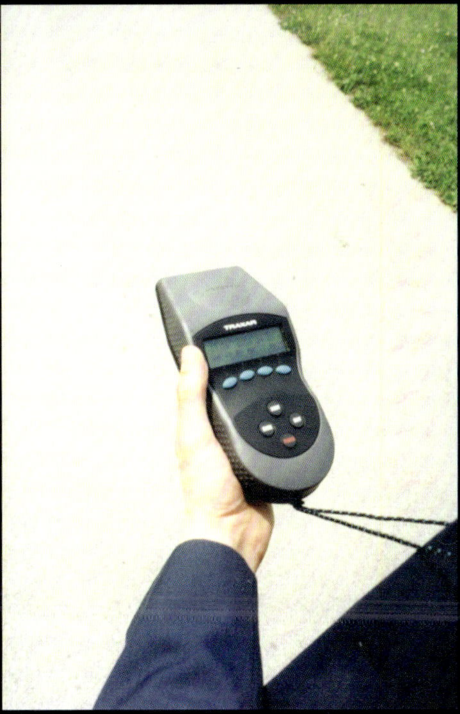

Research – Intelligent Mailman (1994)

The Motorola Traxar portable GPS device is connected to a Nokia GSM cellular phone with the U.S. Robotics World-port plug-in modem. At that time, the rental fees for the telephone and fees for a 45-hour private data transmission frequency were DM 2000 (Deutschmark), or 1000 euro in total. The wearer's movement data is transmitted as GPS data to a modem and an Intel i486 computer in the exhibition room, where it is interpreted by custom-made software and blended over a digital city map. The resulting image is projected onto a screen.

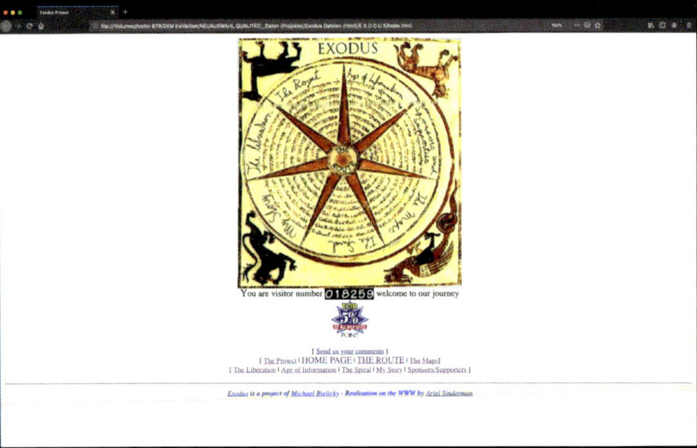
EXODUS
You are visitor number 018259 welcome to our journey
[Send us your comments]
[The Project | HOME PAGE | THE ROUTE | The Maps]
[The Liberation | Age of Information | The Spiral | My Story | Sponsors/Supporters]
Exodus is a project of Michael Bielicky - Realisation on the WWW by Ariel Sinderman

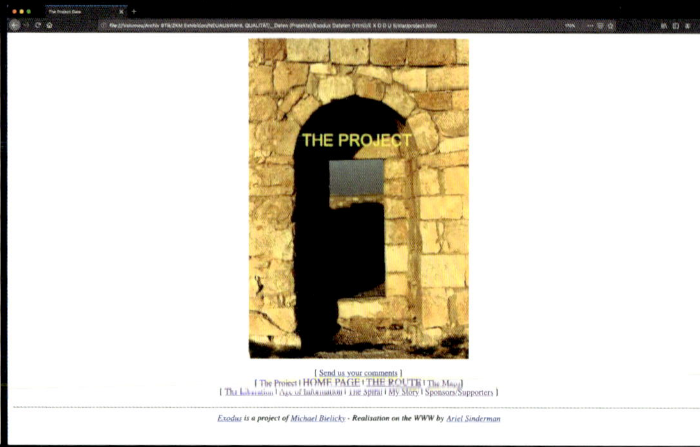
THE PROJECT
[Send us your comments]
[The Project | HOME PAGE | THE ROUTE | The Maps]
[The Liberation | Age of Information | The Spiral | My Story | Sponsors/Supporters]
Exodus is a project of Michael Bielicky - Realisation on the WWW by Ariel Sinderman

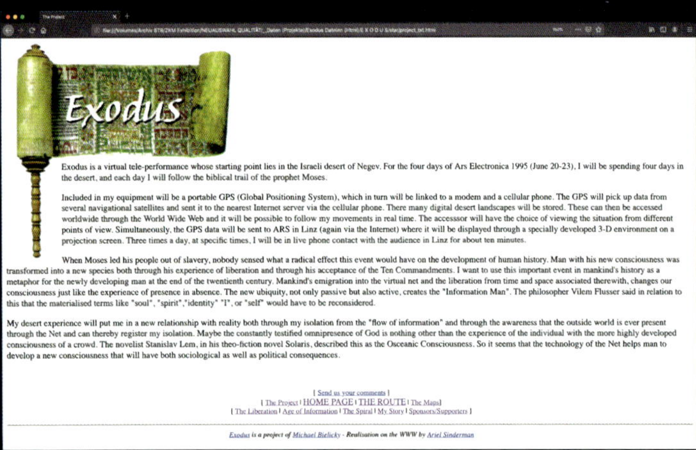
Exodus
Exodus is a virtual tele-performance whose starting point lies in the Israeli desert of Negev. For the four days of Ars Electronica 1995 (June 20-23), I will be spending four days in the desert, and each day I will follow the biblical trail of the prophet Moses.
Included in my equipment will be a portable GPS (Global Positioning System), which in turn will be linked to a modem and a cellular phone. The GPS will pick up data from several navigational satellites and sent it to the nearest Internet server via the cellular phone. There many digital desert landscapes will be stored. These can then be accessed worldwide through the World Wide Web and it will be possible to follow my movements in real time. The accessor will have the choice of viewing the situation from different points of view. Simultaneously, the GPS data will be sent to ARS in Linz (again via the Internet) where it will be displayed through a specially developed 3-D environment on a projection screen. Three times a day, at specific times, I will be in live phone contact with the audience in Linz for about ten minutes.
When Moses led his people out of slavery, nobody sensed what a radical effect this event would have on the development of human history. Man with his new consciousness was transformed into a new species both through his experience of liberation and through his acceptance of the Ten Commandments. I want to use this important event in mankind's history as a metaphor for the newly developing man at the end of the twentieth century. Mankind's emigration into the virtual net and the liberation from time and space associated therewith, changes our consciousness just like the experience of presence in absence. The new ubiquity, not only passive but also active, creates the "Information Man". The philosopher Vilem Flusser said in relation to this that the materialised terms like "soul", "spirit", "identity" "I", or "self" would have to be reconsidered.
My desert experience will put me in a new relationship with reality both through my isolation from the "flow of information" and through the awareness that the outside world is ever present through the Net and can thereby register my isolation. Maybe the constantly testified omnipresence of God is nothing other than the experience of the individual with the more highly developed consciousness of a crowd. The novelist Stanislav Lem, in his theo-fiction novel Solaris, described this as the Oceanic Consciousness. So it seems that the technology of the Net helps man to develop a new consciousness that will have both sociological as well as political consequences.
[Send us your comments]
[The Project | HOME PAGE | THE ROUTE | The Maps]
[The Liberation | Age of Information | The Spiral | My Story | Sponsors/Supporters]
Exodus is a project of Michael Bielicky - Realisation on the WWW by Ariel Sinderman

THE ROUTE
During the four day performance, you will have an opportunity to experience, in a double sense, different types of landscapes.
The first two days you will get an impression of a desert which looks like a 3-D map from close up. During the third and fourth day, the landscape will change not only in reality, but in the digital form as well. "On the road" you will get a chance to see different views and perspectives (both present and past).
From the images that you collect, you may either create your own large scale animations, or you can simply download the versions which have been prepared for you. After four days you will have a collection of images of the trip, as well as four movies from the journey.
Get full size picture (60Kb)
PRESENT
PAST
[Send us your comments]
[The Project | HOME PAGE | THE ROUTE | The Maps]
[The Liberation | Age of Information | The Spiral | My Story | Sponsors/Supporters]
Exodus is a project of Michael Bielicky - Realisation on the WWW by Ariel Sinderman

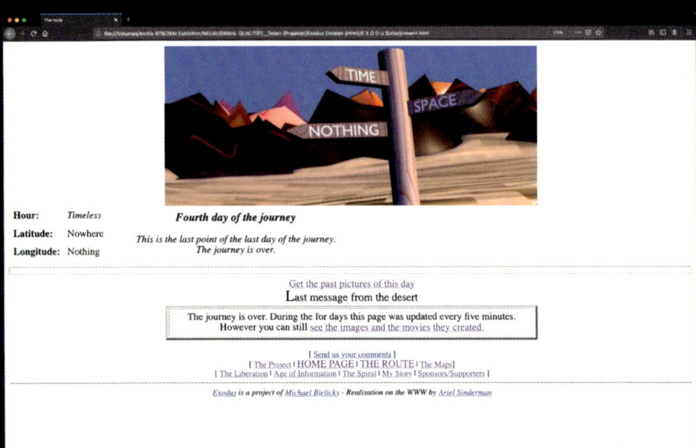
TIME
SPACE
NOTHING
Hour: Timeless
Latitude: Nowhere
Longitude: Nothing
Fourth day of the journey
This is the last point of the last day of the journey.
The journey is over.
Get the past pictures of this day
Last message from the desert
The journey is over. During the for days this page was updated every five minutes.
However you can still see the images and the movies they created.
[Send us your comments]
[The Project | HOME PAGE | THE ROUTE | The Maps]
[The Liberation | Age of Information | The Spiral | My Story | Sponsors/Supporters]
Exodus is a project of Michael Bielicky - Realisation on the WWW by Ariel Sinderman

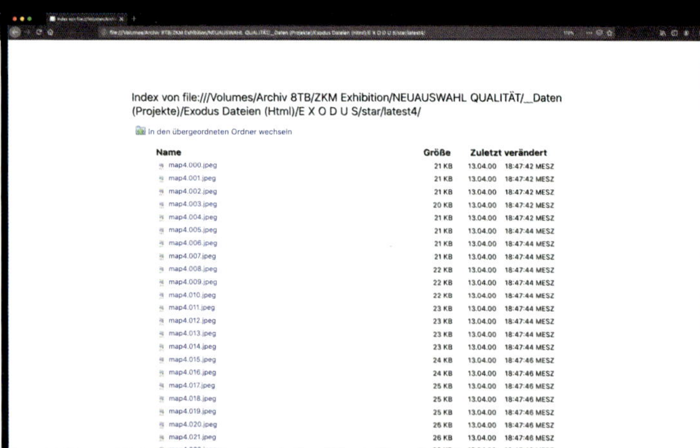
Index von file:///Volumes/Archiv 8TB/ZKM Exhibition/NEUAUSWAHL QUALITÄT/_Daten (Projekte)/Exodus Dateien (Html)/E X O D U S/star/latest4/
In den übergeordneten Ordner wechseln
Name Größe Zuletzt verändert
map4.000.jpeg 21 KB 13.04.00 18:47:42 MESZ
map4.001.jpeg 21 KB 13.04.00 18:47:42 MESZ
map4.002.jpeg 21 KB 13.04.00 18:47:42 MESZ
map4.003.jpeg 20 KB 13.04.00 18:47:42 MESZ
map4.004.jpeg 21 KB 13.04.00 18:47:42 MESZ
map4.005.jpeg 21 KB 13.04.00 18:47:44 MESZ
map4.006.jpeg 21 KB 13.04.00 18:47:44 MESZ
map4.007.jpeg 21 KB 13.04.00 18:47:44 MESZ
map4.008.jpeg 22 KB 13.04.00 18:47:44 MESZ
map4.009.jpeg 22 KB 13.04.00 18:47:44 MESZ
map4.010.jpeg 22 KB 13.04.00 18:47:44 MESZ
map4.011.jpeg 23 KB 13.04.00 18:47:44 MESZ
map4.012.jpeg 23 KB 13.04.00 18:47:44 MESZ
map4.013.jpeg 23 KB 13.04.00 18:47:44 MESZ
map4.014.jpeg 23 KB 13.04.00 18:47:44 MESZ
map4.015.jpeg 24 KB 13.04.00 18:47:46 MESZ
map4.016.jpeg 24 KB 13.04.00 18:47:46 MESZ
map4.017.jpeg 25 KB 13.04.00 18:47:46 MESZ
map4.018.jpeg 25 KB 13.04.00 18:47:46 MESZ
map4.019.jpeg 25 KB 13.04.00 18:47:46 MESZ
map4.020.jpeg 26 KB 13.04.00 18:47:46 MESZ
map4.021.jpeg 26 KB 13.04.00 18:47:46 MESZ

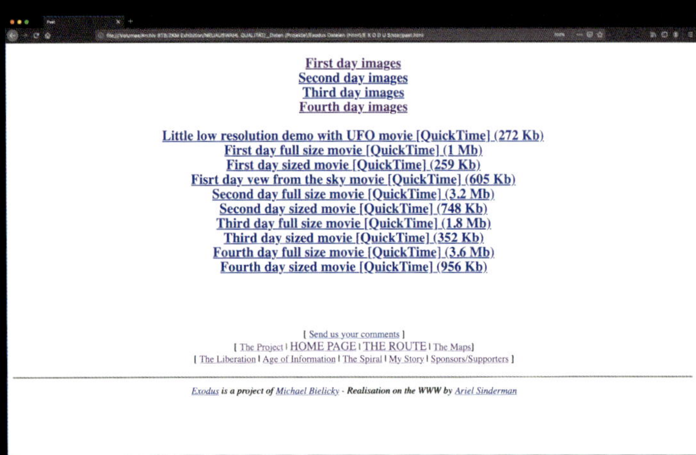
First day images
Second day images
Third day images
Fourth day images
Little low resolution demo with UFO movie [QuickTime] (272 Kb)
First day full size movie [QuickTime] (1 Mb)
First day sized movie [QuickTime] (259 Kb)
Fisrt day vew from the sky movie [QuickTime] (605 Kb)
Second day full size movie [QuickTime] (3.2 Mb)
Second day sized movie [QuickTime] (748 Kb)
Third day full size movie [QuickTime] (1.8 Mb)
Third day sized movie [QuickTime] (352 Kb)
Fourth day full size movie [QuickTime] (3.6 Mb)
Fourth day sized movie [QuickTime] (956 Kb)
[Send us your comments]
[The Project | HOME PAGE | THE ROUTE | The Maps]
[The Liberation | Age of Information | The Spiral | My Story | Sponsors/Supporters]
Exodus is a project of Michael Bielicky - Realisation on the WWW by Ariel Sinderman

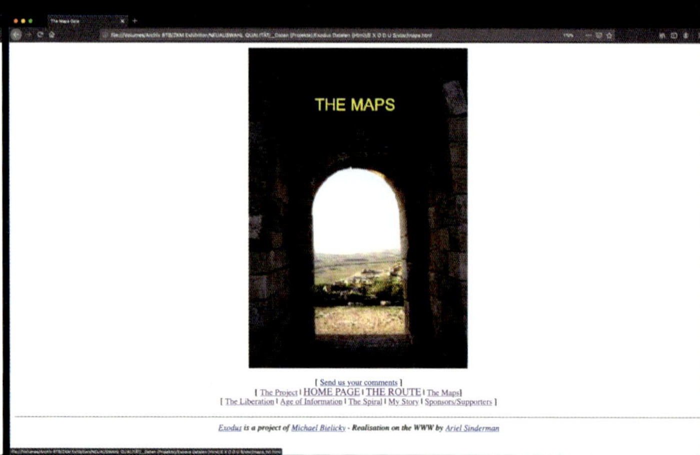
THE MAPS
[Send us your comments]
[The Project | HOME PAGE | THE ROUTE | The Maps]
[The Liberation | Age of Information | The Spiral | My Story | Sponsors/Supporters]
Exodus is a project of Michael Bielicky - Realisation on the WWW by Ariel Sinderman

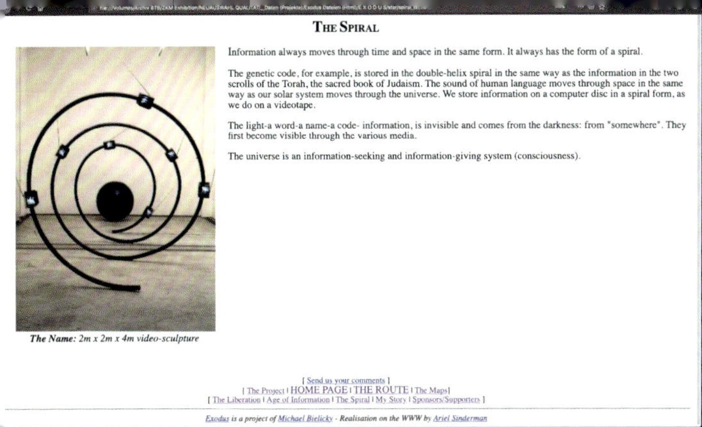

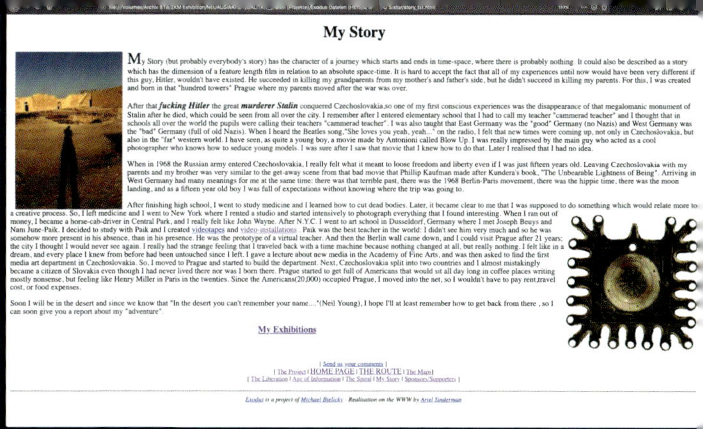

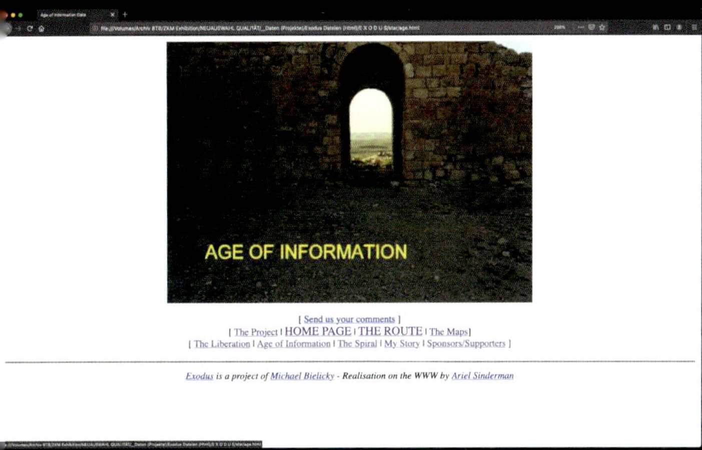

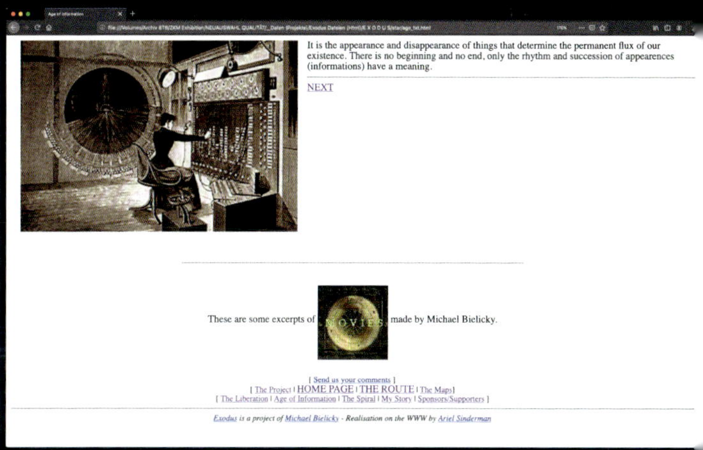

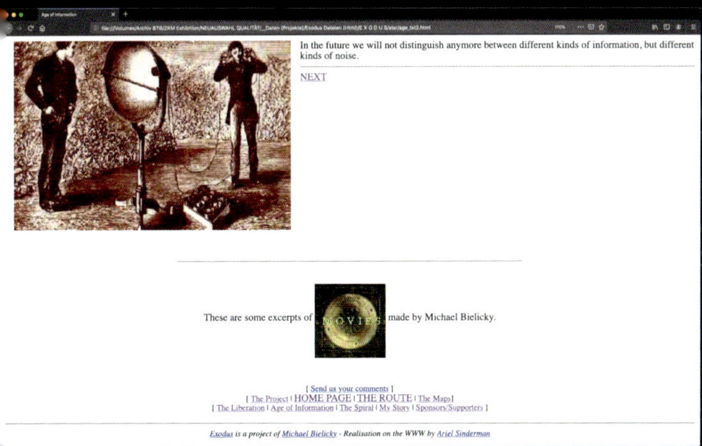

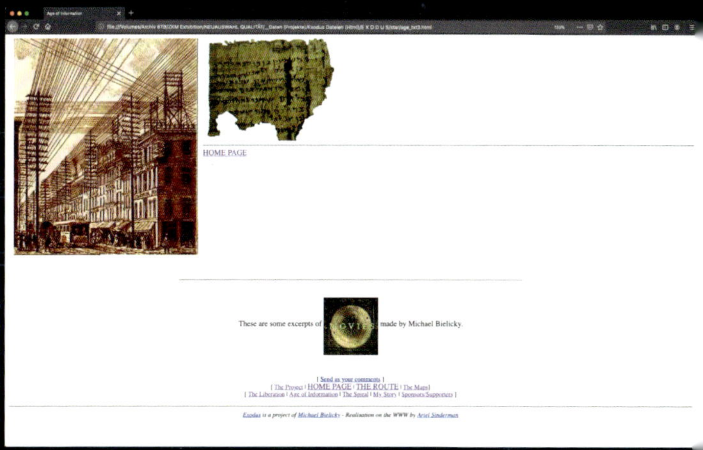

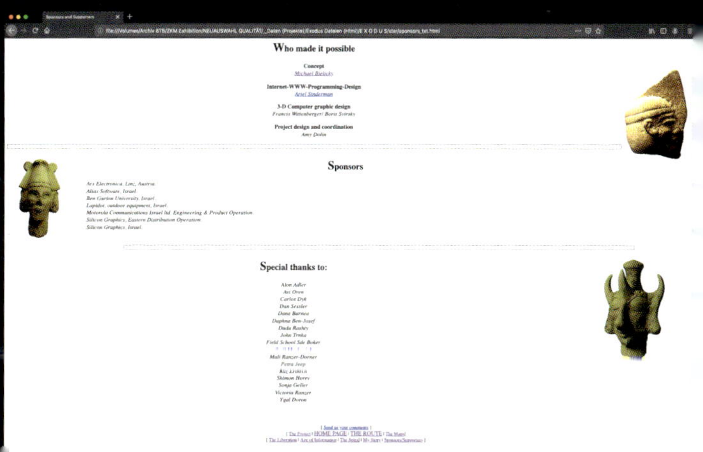

Exodus, 1995 ,telematic performance.
Screenshots of the online travel log

Research – Exodus (1995)

The GPS transponder, which is per-

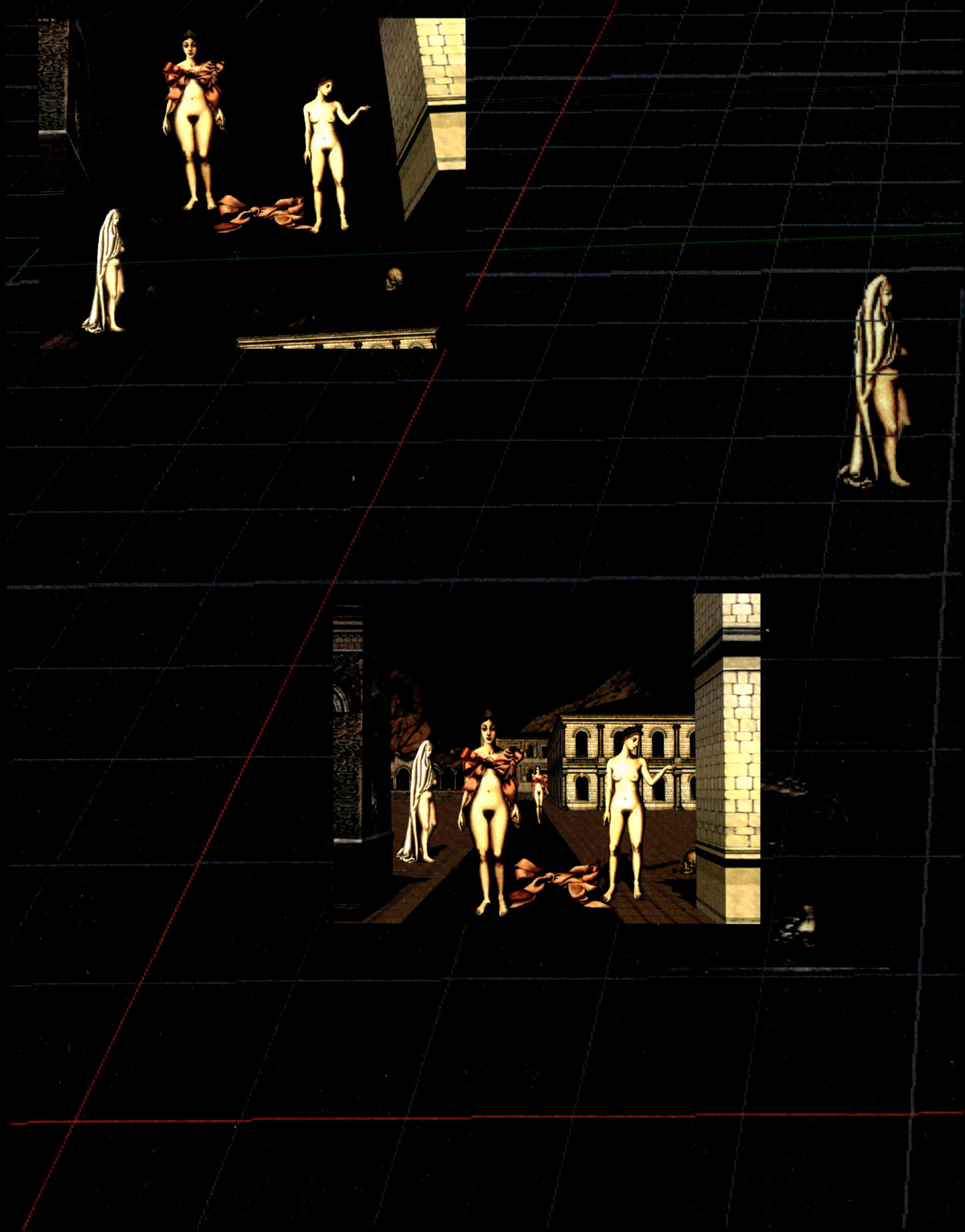

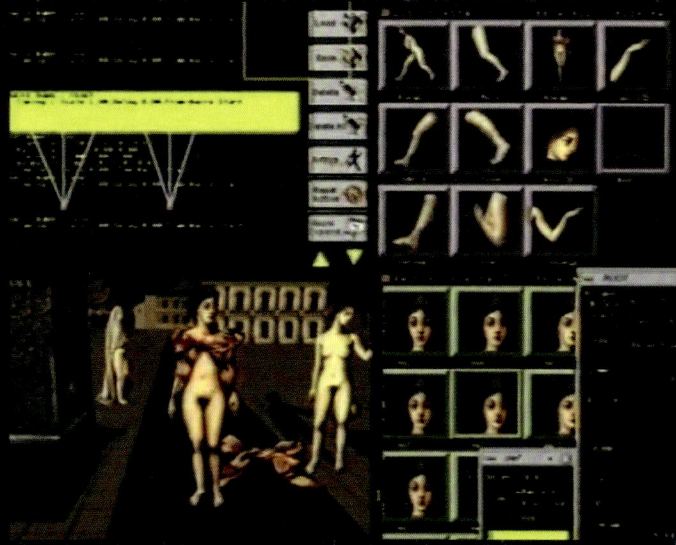

Research – Delvaux's Dream (1998–99)

The visitors in the blue screen environment are filmed by a camera and interpreted by André Bernhardt's tracking system. The resulting data are converted to function as a three-dimensional model of the Delvaux painting by Petr Savorsky using software from Gideon May. His software compiles this constant flow of information from tracking and image data in real time and projects the mixed-reality image of the model space onto a projection surface on the opposite wall, where visitors can see themselves in the painting. The image signal can also be seen in the atrium of the ZKM as an overall image construction without the possibility of grasping either the hypertechnical structure behind it or the real-time performative character of it.

Delvaux's Dream, 1998–99, interactive mixed reality environment. Installation view, ZKM | Karlsruhe, 1998–99.

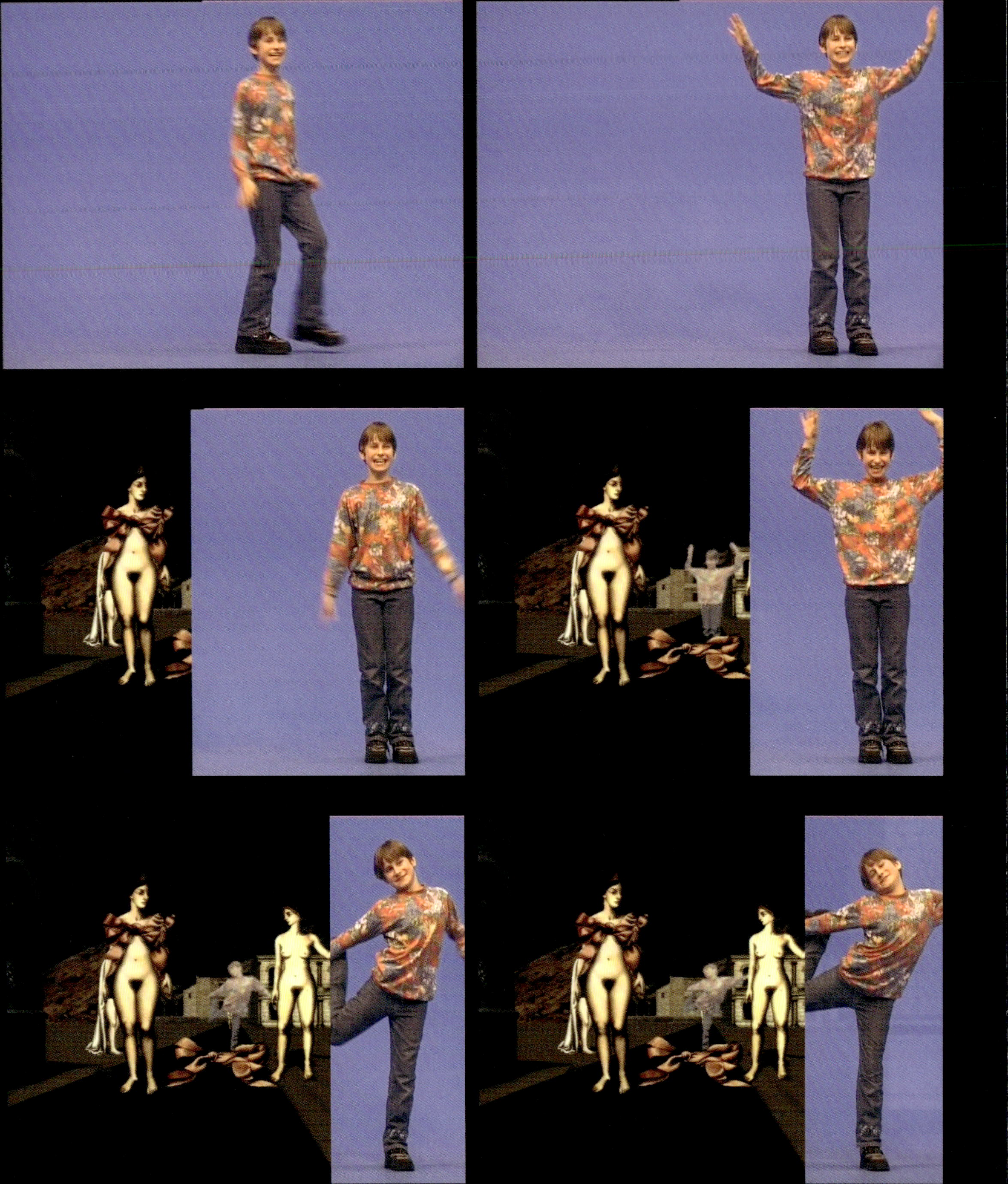

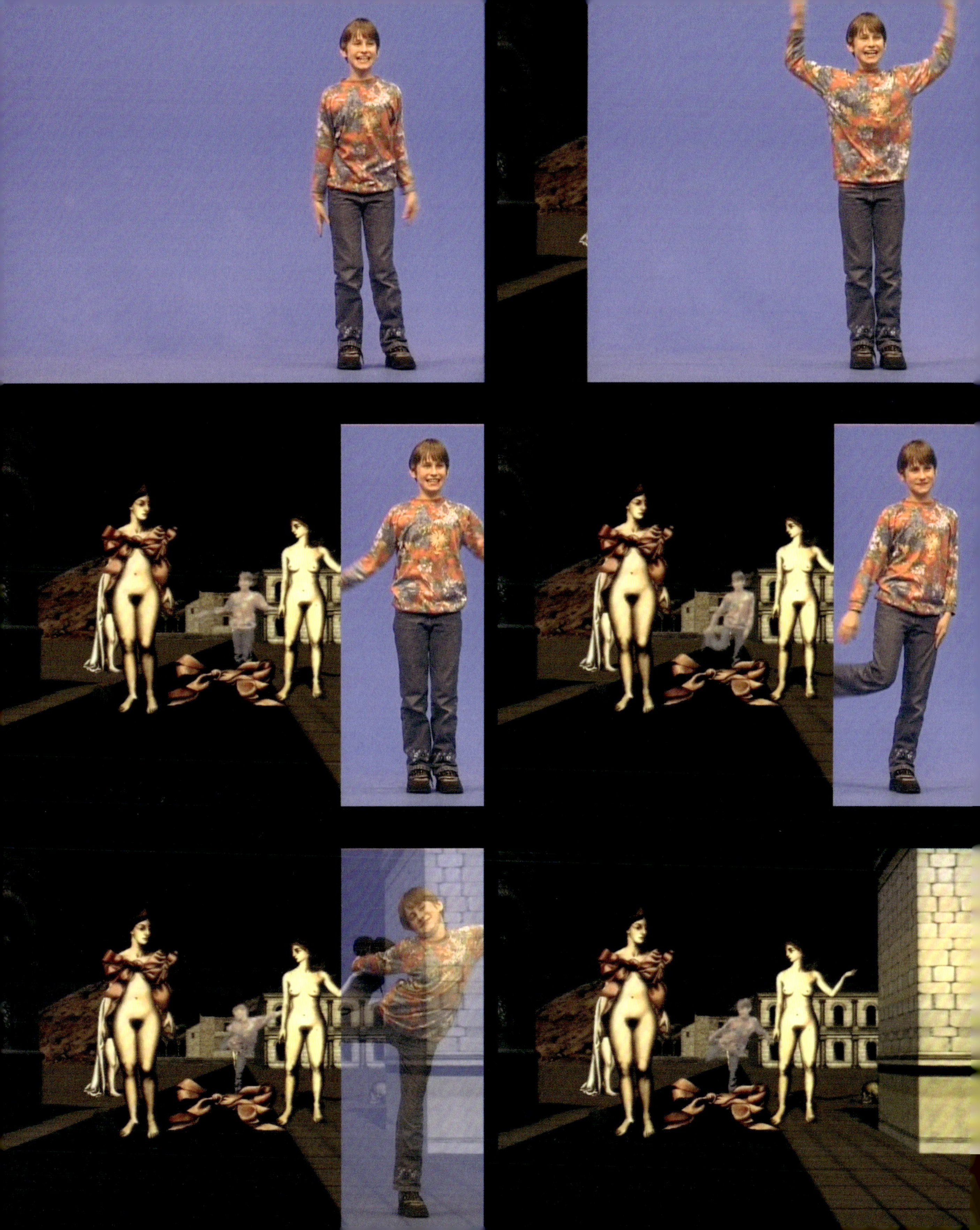

Research – Room with a View (2000)

A 360-degree dome projection with four VPL-S2000 LCD projectors, eight-channel surround audio, sixteen speakers and four subwoofers, a total of 2 million pixel resolution power, as well as a continuously rotating touchscreen – that is *Room with a View*. The graphics, which were rendered by four SGI Infinite Reality computing units, are based on a networked audio, graphics, and video setup. An additional SGI unit also interprets and renders the touchscreen graphics.

The user interaction concept is designed for intuitive user friendliness and use by all ages and (computer) experience levels: it offers immediately visible image and sound feedback on actuations of the touchscreen with simultaneous (re)activation of autonomous, emergent behavior processes: user interaction changes algorithm parameters and content events at the same time.

The content concept offers seven worlds: the golem symbol enables the user to select a world or multiple worlds. When activated, the dynamic symbols change the projected worlds. The dynamic symbols are influenced by the respectively active (selected) worlds and additionally by the orientation of the touchscreen. The projection just generated by all the interactions mentioned above is also recorded and displayed on the touchscreen and in turn influences its appearance. This concept, which at that time had hardly any technical implementation and was rather a theorem than a concept, has rarely been implemented so comprehensively or so systematically integrated to this day: this concept is augmented reality.

Bernd Lintermann's software *MTK* and the software *Xfrog* algorithmically define the graphic animations. *Xfrog* is still used today by Disney, Pixar, Sony Imageworks, Electronic Arts, Konami, and Microsoft. The audio design can also be heard directly and interactively in response to actuations of the touchscreen, but it is also algorithmically linked to content events.

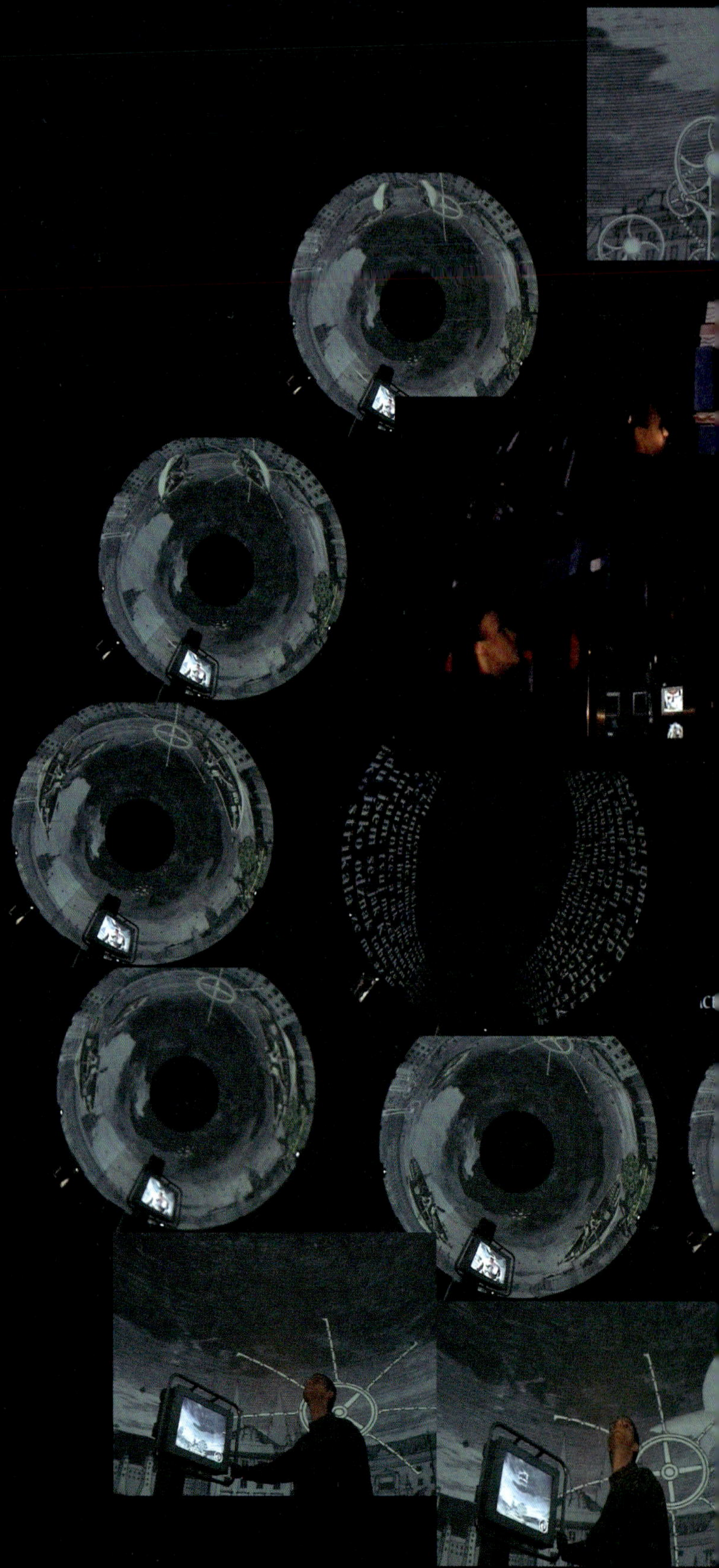

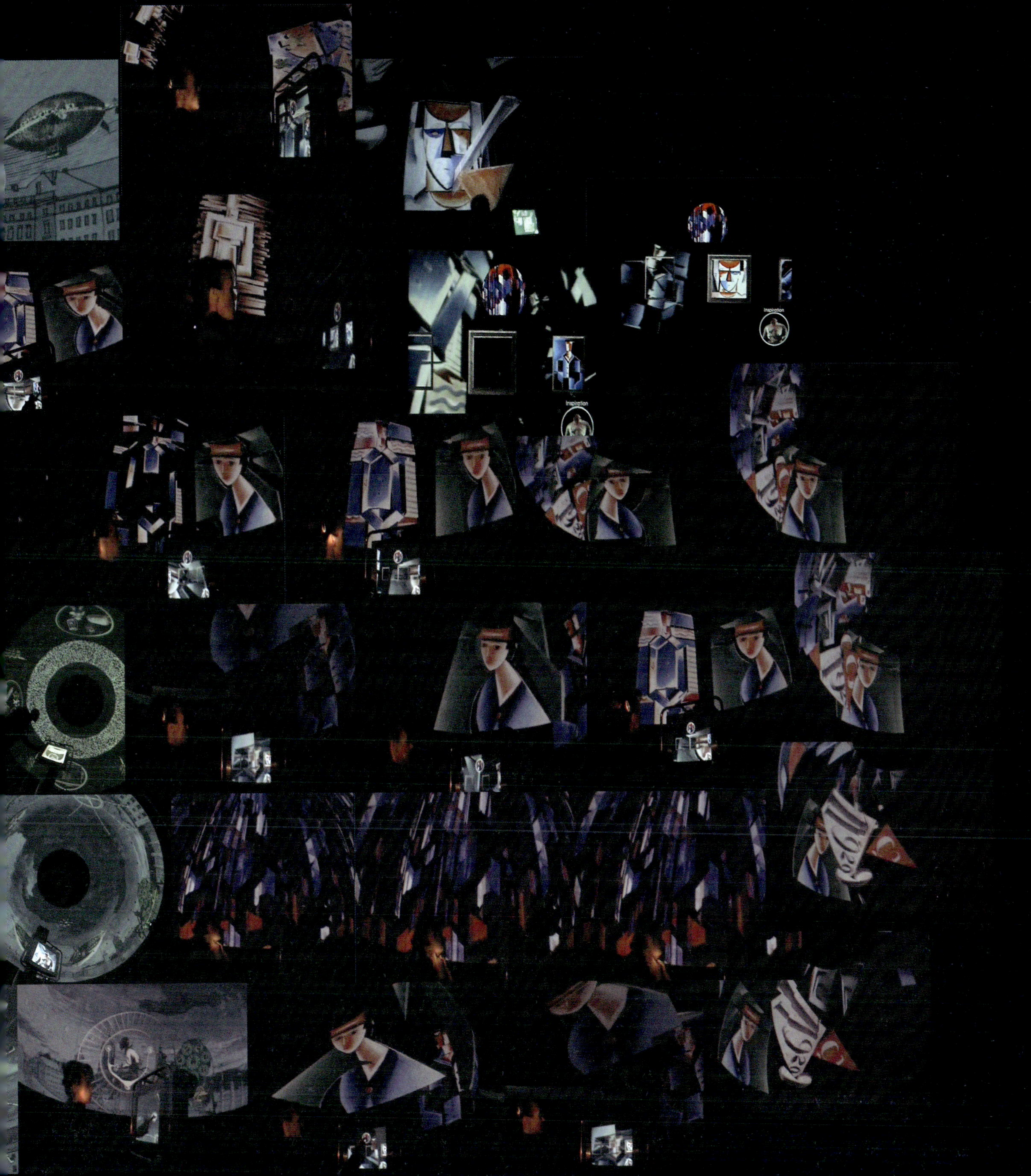

Room with a View, 2000, immersive interactive installtion with 360 degree dome projection. Installation views, ŠKODA Pavilion, Autostadt, Wolfsburg, 2000.

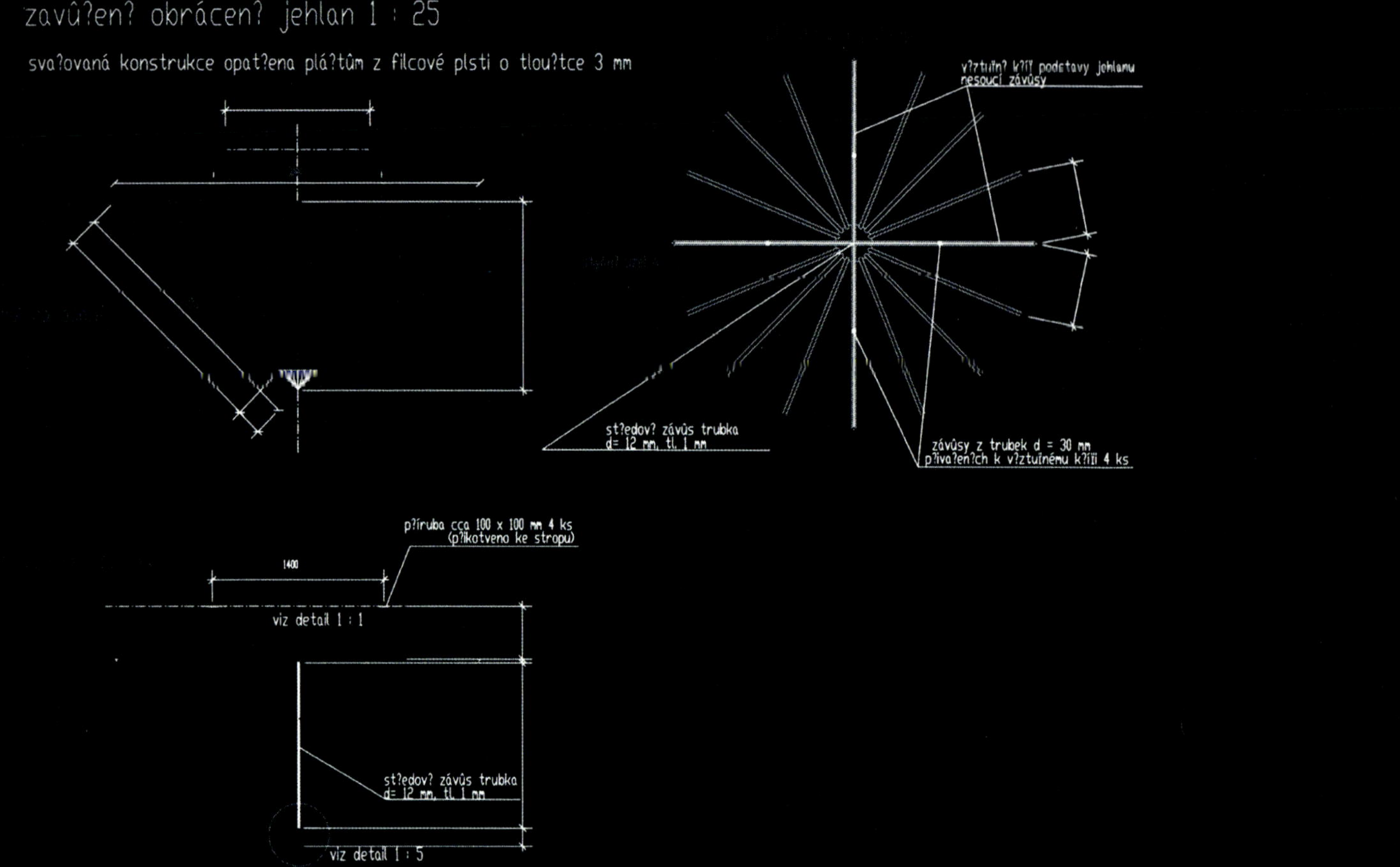

***Room with A View*, 2000, dome contruction site, Autostadt Wolfsburg, Wolfsburg, 2000.**

Room with A View, 2000, test for the 360 degree dome projection in the EVE-Exentded Virtual Environment, ZKM | Karlsruhe, 1999.

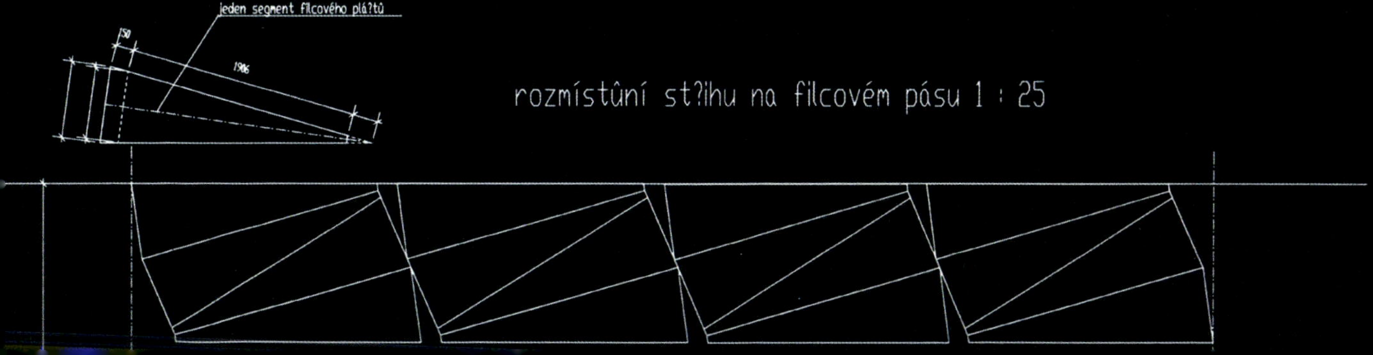

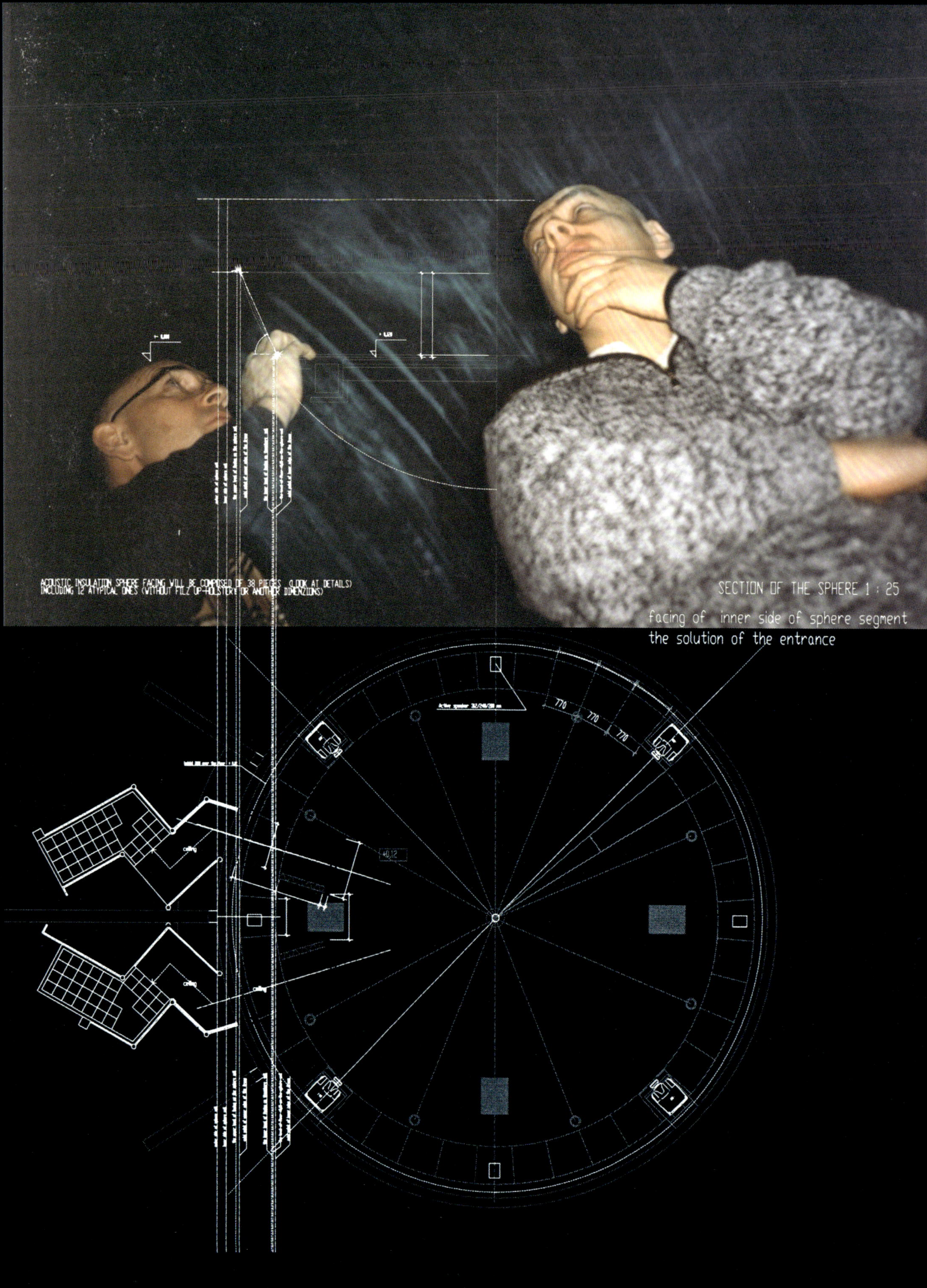
ACOUSTIC INSULATION SPHERE FACING WILL BE COMPOSED OF 38 PIECES (LOOK AT DETAILS)
INCLUDING 12 ATYPICAL ONES (WITHOUT FILZ UP-HOLSTERY OR ANOTHER DIMENZIONS)
SECTION OF THE SPHERE 1 : 25
facing of inner side of sphere segment
the solution of the entrance
770
770
770
+0,12

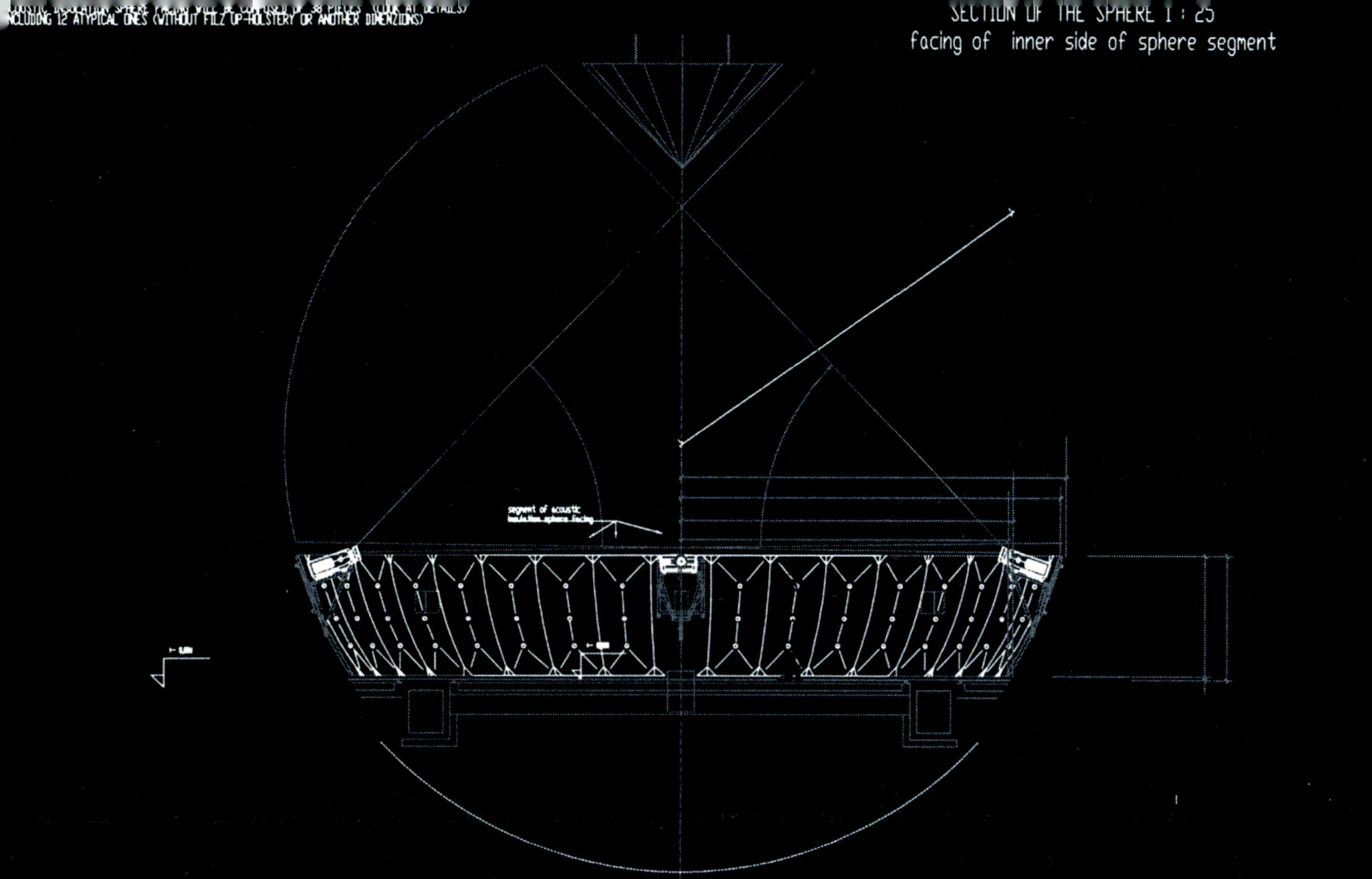

Jeffrey Shaw and Michael Bielicky testing the 360 degree dome projection
in the EVE-Exentded Virtual Environment, ZKM | Karlsruhe, 1999.

Room with a View, 2000, immersive interactive installation with 360 degree dome projection. Installation view, ŠKODA Pavilion, Autostadt, Wolfsburg, 2000.

EnBW

Flashouse, 2018, data-driven installation on facade (permanent). EnBW City, Fasanenhof, Stuttgart.

Flashouse, 2018, data-driven installation on facade (permanent). EnBW City, Fasanenhof, Stuttgart.

EnBW

Flashhouse, 2018, data-driven installation on facade (permanent). EnBW City, Fasanenhof, Stuttgart.

Flashhouse, 2018, data-driven installation on facade (permanent).
EnBW City, Fasanenhof, Stuttgart.

Seventynine, 2022, interactive, AI-driven installation. Kunsthalle Prague.

Michael Bielicky (Prague, 1954) & Kamila B. Richter (Olomouc, 1976)

Paul Kenig

Without vowels, the Hebrew words for *letter*, *number*, and *speaking* are identical. In their original writings, the old cabbalists regarded the Holy Scriptures as the code of God in which they assigned letters to numerical values: for them the universe is essentially built on the prime elements or numbers, because God's words reflected in human language are concentrations of His energy. For the cabbalists it was the numerical code that possessed the infinite power to create new realities: an *imitatio Dei*. The idea of the homunculus was later derived from these numerical world-creating principles.

The mythical homunculus worked on similar principles as the modern computer of today: only a combination of words or numbers – a code – could make it alive. The artificial being could only do the bidding of its master and could perform all kinds of chores for her or him, just like today's computers. This mythical servant was nothing but a replica of Adam, the first human. God created Adam from clay and invested him with His divine life force and thus intelligence. Before the divine spark was breathed into him, Adam was nothing but a homunculus. Thus, the creation of the artificial being was based not only on the numerical code and the letter code, but also on the resonances of the vocalised letter combinations or the names of God: sound is an important code, too, when creating new realities. Since a tiny bit of God's creative power was passed on to the first human, it is no wonder that in our small way we try to do what God did in the beginning. But there were some things that for a long time we were unable to give our products: speech, reason, and intuition. Just as the homunculus' spontaneous intelligence lagged behind the human – so, too, did AI's spontaneous intelligence for decades. All theological trappings notwithstanding, the creation of the homunculus is an affirmation of the creative and productive power of humankind. It repeats, on a small scale, the work of creation. Although it would seem that what began on the mythological or spiritual plane became a technical servant of humankind's needs, our AI evolves ever so rapidly into the mythological and spiritual again, without us noticing it too consciously. Today's homunculus or AI is able to create new homunculi through *imitatio Hominis* and these can then create further AI ad infinitum through *imitatio Robotum*, akin to the *imitation Dei* of the old cabbalists. In fact, according to Gershom Scholem, the old cabbalists would have been glad to learn that the Hebrew alphabet, a 22 element system, was simplified by the binary system with its two basic elements: the 0 and 1.

The interactive project *SEVENTYNINE* is an artificial being whose *head* manifests itself in a specially engineered spherical screen. The visitors can use their language to induce "the being" to react in a singing mode. The name of the artificial being is encoded in the number SEVENTYNINE. This liturgical artificial intelligence enables an immersive spiritual experience as one might expect of the 21st century.

In the 1990s, Kamila B. Richter's *o-System* (1997) and *M-System* (1998) were pioneering web art projects, her *Emporium Spirit* (2010) is a groundbreaking data visualisation project, which was the predecessor to later data-driven work by the artist duo, such as the *Garden of Error and Decay* (2010–2019) and the *Columbus 2.0* (2008–2019) series. Today Richter's oil paintings are generated from uncontrollable software glitches and she, as an individual artist, might be considered the organic algorithm that visualises these glitches in larger-than-life formats. Michael Bielicky coined the term "data-driven" and instituted an entire media art department and innumerable own and student projects on this sensitive media categorisation at the Karlsruhe University of Arts and Design. And, in the 1980s, his art was dealing in part with Jewish religion tropes. However, within the oeuvre of Kamila B. Richter and Michael Bielicky *SEVENTYNINE* is an autonomous being: although it is software based, *SEVENTYNINE* is not *driven* by data, it *is* data, it *drives* data, and as such cognition. Kamila B. Richter and Michael Bielicky have brought conscious data into being, which will challenge museum visitors in audible, visible, and cognitive ways.

The unqiue software by Kimin Han is able to re-interpret or remodulate spoken words in the form of contemplative chants. At the same time, an AI implemented by Nikolaus Völzow makes *human-like* communication with a liturgical artificial intelligence possible. His voice-based AI enables visitors to create a new, spiritual, comical, absurd, and sometimes bizarre sort of interaction. The many different algorithmic *senses* are orchestrated by a software *backbone* by Alex Wenger.

The head is installed on the body, a custom-designed bottle dryer. Any resemblance to the famous Marcel Duchamp ready-made is coincidental. The 80 cm diameter sphere display was developed in China.

Since 2020, the being is coming to life through programming code as well as its visitors' communication sparks. We hope it will come to life peacefully and won't destroy the world.

friday.
master
holy
cubistic

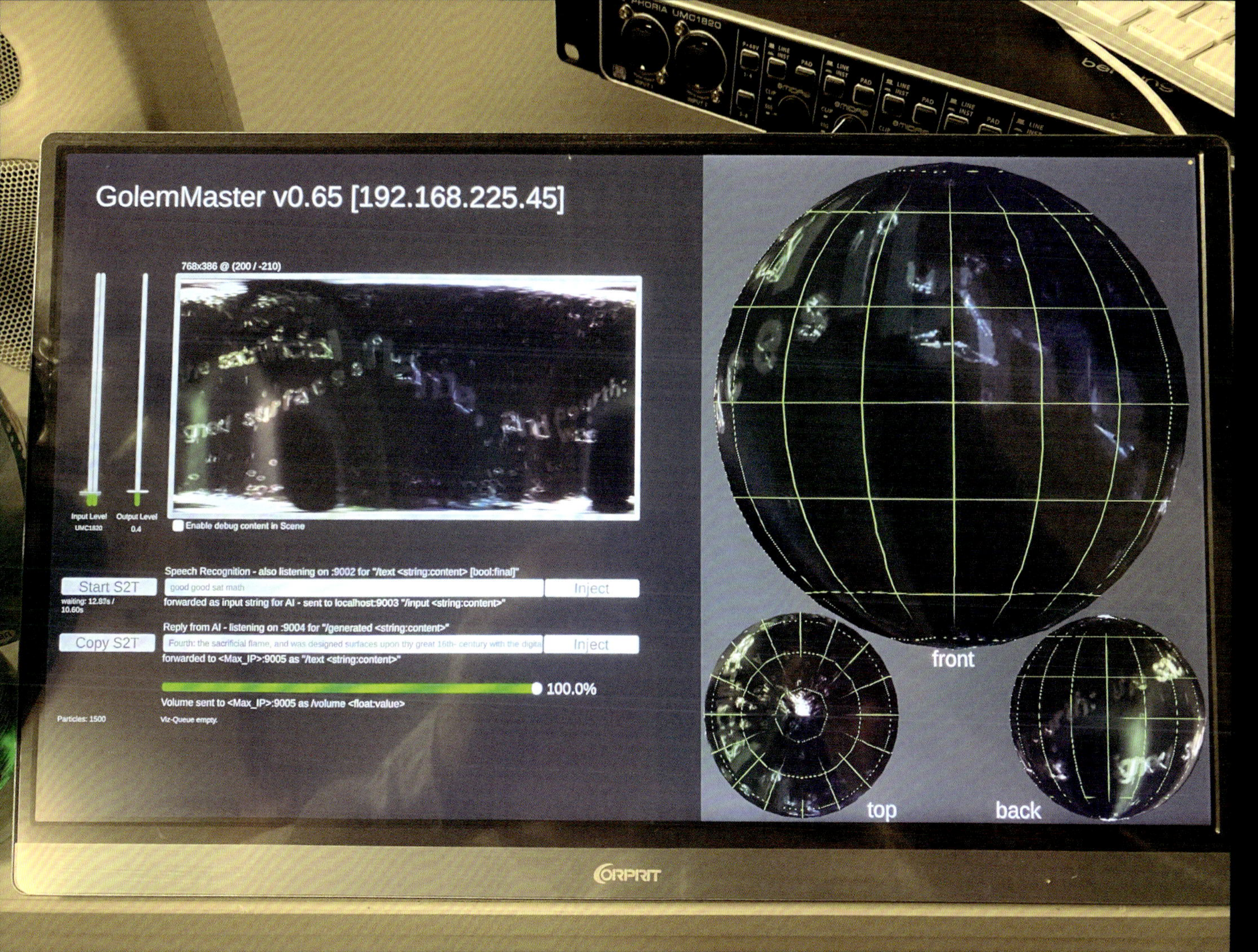
GolemMaster v0.65 [192.168.225.45]
768x386 @ (200 / -210)
Input Level
UMC1820
Output Level
0.4
Enable debug content in Scene
Speech Recognition - also listening on :9002 for "/text <string:content> [bool:final]"
Start S2T
good good sat math
Inject
forwarded as input string for AI - sent to localhost:9003 "/input <string:content>"
Reply from AI - listening on :9004 for "/generated <string:content>"
Copy S2T
Fourth: the sacrificial flame, and was designed surfaces upon thy great 16th- century with the digita
Inject
forwarded to <Max_IP>:9005 as "/text <string:content>"
100.0%
Volume sent to <Max_IP>:9005 as /volume <float:value>
Particles: 1500
Viz-Queue empty.
front
top
back

Vortext, 2020, public space installation.
Schlachthof, Karlsruhe.

wir? Was wir

Kamila B. Richter, *Errorless Error (Mother + Child II)*, 2019-2020 and *To Err is Divine VI*, 2018-2019, oil and amber paintings, 2020, within *Vasulka's Wave*, immersive projection, 2021. Installation view *Infosphere: Kamila B. Richter, Michael Bielicky, Peter Weibel, Nam June Paik*, Galerie Zdeněk Sklenář, Prague.

Narcissistic Machine, 2021, data-driven interactive installation, Ansbach. 2021.

Peter Weibel, Michael Bielicky, and Peter Sloterdijk, Baden Baden, 2022.

Jean Baudrillard, ZKM | Karlsruhe, 2004.

Lothar Späth, unknown person, ZKM | Karlsruhe, 2008.

Henry Zemel and Stephan Doesinger, Karlsruhe University of Arts and Design (HfG), 2008.

Tony Conrad and Steina Vasulka, Karlsruhe, 2007.

Jennifer Miller and Cathy Weiss, Prague, 1996.

List of Works

ANALOG PHOTOGRAPHS

Untitled, 1975-84, Germany
Analog photographs.

Untitled, 1983, Germany
Analog photographs, sandwich technique.

Digital Andy, 1987, Germany
Video prints altered by the first digital video editing techniques time base correction and drop-out compensator (DOC).

Untitled, 1980-81, New York
Analog photographs.

Untitled, 1985, Germany
Analog photographs for *Monochrom Zukunft* issue of *Monochrom Extra*, 1985.

VIDEOS

Four Seasons, 1984, Düsseldorf, Germany
Single-channel video, creative misuse of the standard 8 mm format; double spools were not cut after development.

Circulus Viciosus, 1985, Düsseldorf, Germany
Single-channel video, creative misuse of the standard 8 mm format; double spools were not cut after development.

The Visit, 1985, Düsseldorf, Germany
Single-channel video, 14 min., an experimental love story.

In Autumn, 1986, Düsseldorf, Germany
Single-channel video, creative misuse of the standard 8 mm format; double spools were not cut after development.

Paik Hat, 1986, Düsseldorf, Germany
Single-channel video.

Perpetuum Mobile, 1986, Düsseldorf, Germany
Single-channel video, creative misuse of the standard 8 mm format; double spools were not cut after development.

Fat Corner, with Ricardo Peredo, 1987, Düsseldorf, Germany
Single-channel video, 40 min., creative misuse of time-base correction and drop-out compensation.

Paik - I'm an Experimentalist, 1987, Düsseldorf, Germany
Single-channel video, creative misuse of time-base correction and drop-out compensation.

Menschen verstehen durch Missverstehen II/IV (Untitled), Ricardo Peredo and Michael Bielicky, 1988
Menschen verstehen durch Missverstehen II/IV (Inka & Naty), Ricardo Peredo and Michael Bielicky, 1988
Menschen verstehen durch Missverstehen III/IV (Harald Oskar Naegeli), Ricardo Peredo and Michael Bielicky, 1988
Menschen verstehen durch Missverstehen IV/IV (Untitled), Ricardo Peredo and Michael Bielicky, 1988
Single-channel video series I-IV.

Next Year in Jerusalem (Homage to Rabbi Loew), 1988, Düsseldorf, Germany
Single-channel video, creative misuse of time-base correction and drop-out compensation.

Golem Is Alive, 1989, Düsseldorf, Germany
Single-channel video, creative misuse of time-base correction and drop-out compensation.

JLB Perfect Guest, 1989, Düsseldorf, Germany
Single-channel video.

Jazz Celula, 1989, Düsseldorf, Germany
Single-channel video, 16 min., experimental music video, creative misuse of time-base correction and drop-out compensation.

Perpetuum Mobile II, 1990, Düsseldorf, Germany
Single-channel video, creative misuse of time-base correction and drop-out compensation.

Circulus Viciosus X (Gulf War coverage), 1991, Düsseldorf, Germany
Single-channel video.

Flussers Fluss, 1991-94, Robion, France
Single-channel video.

Crossings: The Last Path of Walter Benjamin, 2002, Strasbourg, France
Single-channel video.

Reise/Führer, 2004, Wolfsschanze, Gierłoż, Poland
Single-channel video.

VIDEO SCULPTURES

Untitled, 1987, Düsseldorf, Germany
Video sculpture, analog antenna TV sets, video recorder, platform in Nam June Paik's atelier at the Düsseldorf Art Academy.

Output now, 1988, Düsseldorf, Germany
Video sculpture, toilet bowl, analog antenna TV sets, analog sender and receiver, nail, wood plank, TV magazines, chained cistern handle, pedestal.

Easel, 1988, Paris, France
Video sculpture, analog antenna TV sets, analog sender and receiver, easel.

JLB Perfect Guest 2, 1989, Düsseldorf, Germany
Multi-monitor video sculpture, analog antenna TV sets, video recorder.

Menorah/Inventory, 1989, Düsseldorf, Germany
Video sculpture, steel frame, analog antenna TV sets, analog sender and receiver, defunct fire extinguishers, 275 × 200 × 100 cm.

Menorah, 2001, Berlin, Germany
Video sculpture, steel frame, analog antenna TV sets, analog sender and receiver, 275 × 200 × 100 cm.

The Name, 1990, Düsseldorf, Germany
Video sculpture, steel frame, analog antenna TV sets, analog sender and receiver, 500 × 200 × 200 cm.

Sefiroth Tree, 1990, not exhibited
Video sculpture, steel frame, analog antenna TV sets, analog sender and receiver.

The Inner Observer, 1992, Ars Electronica, Linz, Austria
Video sculpture, steel frame, steel spheres with analog antenna TV sets, fluorescent paint, camera, analog sender and receiver.

The Inner Observer, 2001, Museum Ostdeutsche Galerie, Regensburg, Germany
Video sculpture, analog antenna TV sets, fluorescent paint, camera, analog sender and receiver.

Perpetuum Mobile, 2019, ZKM | Karlsruhe, Germany
Video sculpture, digital multi-channel video, tablet computers, USB wiring, construction sitefence.

RESEARCH

Intelligent Mailman, 1994, Ars Electronica, Linz, Austria
GPS-driven telematic performance, Traxar portable GPS device, Nokia GSM cellular phone, U.S. Robotics Worldport plug-in modem, Intel i486 computer, projector, digital map.
Consulting engineer: Werner Oberegger.

Exodus, 1995, Ars Electronica, Linz, Austria
Telematic performance, military-grade GPS transponder, off-road vehicle, military-grade satellite phone, military-grade portable computer.
Internet programmers: Ariel Sindermann, John Trnka; internet design: Ariel Sindermann, Amy Dolin; project coordinator: Amy Dolin.

Delvaux's Dream, 1998-99, ZKM | Karlsruhe, Germany
Interactive mixed reality environment, produced at ZKM, blue-screen environment, camera, tracking system, three-dimensional model of the painting, interpreter software, screen, projector.
3D-modeling: Petr Savorsky; tracking system: André Bernhardt; interpreter software: Gideon May.

Room with a View, 2000, ŠKODA Pavilion, Autostadt, Wolfsburg, Germany
Immersive interactive installation with 360 degree dome projection, *PanoramaScreen*, VPL-S2000 LCD projectors, networked audio, graphics and video setup consisting of eight-channel surround audio, sixteen speakers, and SGI Infinite Reality computing units, touchscreen, MTK software, Xfrog software.
Programming: Bernd Lintermann; sound: Torsten Belschner.

Ex Nihilo, 2019, ZKM | Karlsruhe, Germany
Data-driven digital wooden screen, custom-made software, Arduino hardware, LEDs, wood.
Programming: Alex Wenger.

INSTALLATIONS

The Sixth Sense, 1993-94, Prague Academy of Fine Arts, Czech Republic
Installation, field telephones.

Exhibition (On the Web), 2000, Espace EDF Electra, Paris, France
Digital installation, software, webcam, meat grinder, monitor, table.
Programming: Xicht (pseudonymously).

Perpetuum Mobile, 2003, Autostadt, Wolfsburg, Germany
Single-channel video installation, public digital screen.

Falling Stars, 2004, public facade, Volksbühne, Berlin, Germany
Data-driven installation, flash video, projector.
Programming: Kamila B. Richter; pictograms: Kamila B. Richter.

ICONUU, 2005, Karlsruhe, Germany
Graphic communication app.
Programming: brainz studios, Prague, Czech Republic; Axel Heide.

Falling Life, 2005, public facade, Linz, Austria
Falling Life, 2006, public facade, Berlin, Germany
Falling Life, 2007, public facade, Barcelona, Spain
Data-driven installation, flash video, projector.
Programming: Kamila B. Richter; pictograms: Kamila B. Richter.

Falling Times, 2006, public facade, Berlin, Germany
Falling Times, 2007, public facade, Barcelona, Spain
Falling Times, 2007, public facade, ZKM | Karlsruhe, Germany
Falling Times, 2008, public facade, São Paulo, Brazil
Falling Times, 2009, New York, USA
Data-driven installation, flash video, projector.
Programming: Kamila B. Richter; pictograms: Kamila B. Richter.

This Year in Jerusalem, 2006, Prague, Czech Republic
Real-time telematic installation, custom-made software, Kinect motion-sensing input device, projector, Western Wall Cam video stream.
Programming: Xicht (pseudonymously).

Columbus 2.0, 2007, public facade, Wuhan, China
Columbus 2.0, 2008, public facade, Bienal Internacional de Arte Contemporáneo de Sevilla (BIACS), Spain
Columbus 2.0, 2008, ZKM | Karlsruhe, Germany
Columbus 2.0, 2011 Thessaloniki, Greece
Data-driven installation, custom-made Java software, steering wheel, computer mouse, projector, wall.
Programming: Dirk Reinbold, Andreas Siefert, Andres Jungwickel.

Columbus 2.0, 2019, ZKM | Karlsruhe, Germany
Data-driven installation, custom-made web application, projector, wall.
Programming: Christian Lölkes; pictograms: Kamila B. Richter.

Riding the Mind, 2009, public facade, ZKM | Karlsruhe, Germany
Data-driven installation, custom-made application, projector, wall.
Programming: Kamila B. Richter, Axel Heide; pictograms: Kamila B. Richter.

Garden of Error and Decay, 2010, Wuhan, China
Garden of Error and Decay, 2011, Berlin, Germany
Garden of Error and Decay, 2011, Moscow, Russia
Garden of Error and Decay, 2011, Venice, Italy
Garden of Error and Decay, 2011, Florence, Italy
Garden of Error and Decay, 2011, Vancouver, Canada
Garden of Error and Decay, 2011, Karlsruhe, Germany
Garden of Error and Decay, 2012, Vienna, Austria
Garden of Error and Decay, 2012, Havana, Cuba
Garden of Error and Decay, 2012, Prague, Czech Republic
Garden of Error and Decay, 2013, Düsseldorf, Germany
Garden of Error and Decay, 2017, Havana, Cuba
Garden of Error and Decay, 2018, Freiburg, Germany
Garden of Error and Decay, 2019, Karlsruhe, Germany
Data-driven installation, custom-made Flash software, joystick, New York Stock Exchange data stream, Twitter data stream, projector.
Programming: Kamila B. Richter, Axel Heide; pictograms: Kamila B. Richter.

Garden of Error and Decay, 2013, Seoul, South Korea
Immersive data-driven, LED inlets on the Art Center Nabi facade (screen-band), custom-made Flash software, New York Stock Exchange data stream, Twitter data stream, projector.
Programming: Kamila B. Richter, Axel Heide; pictograms: Kamila B. Richter.

Why Don't We Wagner, 2013, Vienna, Austria
Why Don't We, 2013, Berlin, Germany
Why Don't We, 2013, Bad Rothenfelde, Germany
Why Don't We, 2014, Düsseldorf, Germany
Why Don't We Surveil, 2015, ZKM | Karlsruhe, Germany
Why Don't We, 2017, Bad Rothenfelde, Germany
Data-driven installation, custom-made Flash software, Twitter data stream, projector.
Programming: Kamila B. Richter, Axel Heide; pictograms: Kamila B. Richter.

Data Steel, 2015, Ostrava, Czech Republic
Data Labyrinth, 2016, Karlsruhe, Germany
The Names, 2018, ZKM | Karlsruhe, Germany
Vasulka's Wave, 2018, Brno, Czech Republic
Data-driven immersive, custom-made Java software, projector.
Programming: Wilhelm Brodt, Pantos (pseudonymously).

Lost Objects, 2015, Prague, Czech Republic
Data-driven immersive postminimalist opera, digital single-channel video, orchestra, scaenae frons, projectors, mosquito net stripes.
Programming: Kamila B. Richter, Axel Heide; pictograms: Kamila B. Richter.

Data Dybbuk, 2015, ZKM | Karlsruhe, Germany
Data-driven installation, custom-made web application, projector, wall.
Programming: Wilhelm Brodt, Pantos (pseudonymously).

IMAGIT (ICONUU project), 2017, Karlsruhe, Germany
Graphic communication app.
Programming: brainz studios, Prague, Czech Republic.

Lost, 2017, ZKM | Karlsruhe, Germany
Lost, 2017, Centro de Arte Contemporáneo Wifredo Lam, Havana, Cuba
Immersive data-driven installation, digital single-channel video, projectors, mosquito net stripes.

Narcissistic Machine, 2017, ZKM | Karlsruhe, Germany
Data-driven interactive, LCD-Spot Showtec Spectral M300 Q4 MKII, webcam, custom-made software, bare bone computer, mosquito net stripes.
Programming: Lukas Feller, Lukas Böhm.

Narcissistic Machine, 2018, Galerie Zdeněk Sklenář, Schönkirchovský palác, Prague, Czech Republic
Data-driven interactive installation, LCD-Spot Showtec Spectral M300 Q4 MKII, easel, LCD-screen, webcam, custom-made software, barebone computer.
Programming: Lukas Feller, Lukas Böhm.

Flashouse, 2018, EnBW City, Fasanenhof, Stuttgart, Germany
Data-driven installation on facade (permanent).
Design and circuit layouts: Alex Wenger; construction team: Benjamin Breitkopf, Paul Kenig; project coordinator: Paul Kenig.

Exhibition (On the Net), 2019, ZKM | Karlsruhe, Germany
Web-based digital installation, custom-made software, webcam, meat grinder, monitor, table.
Programming: Daniel Heiss.

Kostka, 2019, Prague, Czech Republic
Immersive data-driven installation, custom-made web application, projector, chimney.
Programming: Wilhelm Brodt, Pantos (pseudonymously).

Rawmaterial, 2019, ZKM | Karlsruhe, Germany
100 channel video.
Composition and editing: Paul Kenig.

Subjektprojektionen (Subject projections), 2019, ZKM | Karlsruhe, Germany.
50-channel video.
Composition and editing: Paul Kenig.

This Year in Jerusalem, 2019, ZKM | Karlsruhe, Germany
Real-time telematic installation, Kinect, motion-sensing input device, projector, Western Wall Cam video stream.
Programming: Xingbo Wang, Yiran Huang.

Vortext, 2020, ZKM | Karlsruhe, Germany
Public space installation, custom-made software, projectors, computers, cables.
Programming: Alex Wenger.

Perpetuum Mobile 3×3, 2021, Galerie Zdeněk Sklenář, Schönkirchovský palác, Prague, Czech Republic.
Video sculpture, Sony CRT TVs, media players, cables.

Seventynine, 2022, Kunsthalle Praha, Prague, Czech Republic
Interactive installation, custom-made steel bottle dryer, custom-made spatial audio software by Kimin Han, custom-made visual software by Nikolaus Völzow, custom-made AI by Alex Wenger, spherical LCD display, computers, microphone, cables, speakers.
Programming: Alex Wenger, Kimin Han, Nikolaus Völzow.
Purchasing/logistics/artistic consultant: Paul Kenig.

Michael Bielicky

Born in 1954 in Prague, Czech Republic
Lives and works in Düsseldorf and Karlsruhe, Germany

1969 transmigration to the Federal Republic of Germany
1975–78 works as a photographer in the USA
1984–87 studies at the Düsseldorf Art Academy – first as student of Bernd Becher, then as student of Nam June Paik
1984 first video works
1987 master student (Meisterschüler) of Nam June Paik; works as his assistant until 1991
1991 founding professor of the New Media Department at the Prague Academy of Fine Arts (AVU), Czech Republic
Since the mid-1990s interactive installations and performances
Since 2005 cooperation with the media artist Kamila B. Richter
2006 media art professor for digital media art at the Karlsruhe University of Arts and Design (HfG), Germany
2020 art director of lichtsicht 7, Projection Triennial, Bad Rothenfelde, Germany

AWARDS, PERMANENT COLLECTIONS, AND GRANTS

2001 acceptance of *Menora* into the permanent collection of the Jewish Museum, Berlin, Germany
2000 honorable mention at the Prix Ars Electronica for *Room with a View*, Cyber Arts, Linz, Austria
2000 acceptance of *Der Name/The Name* into the permanent collection, National Gallery in Prague, Czech Republic
1999–2000 guest artist at the Institute for Visual Media at the ZKM | Center for Art and Media Karlsruhe, Germany
1998 acceptance of *Menora* into the permanent collection, ZKM | Center for Art and Media Karlsruhe, Germany
1988 scholarship of the Cité Internationale des Arts de Paris, France
1988 honorable mention at the 3rd Marler Video-Art-Prize, Marl, Germany

SOLO EXHIBITIONS BY THE ARTIST DUO BIELICKY AND RICHTER

2017 *Lost*, Centro de Arte Contemporáneo Wifredo Lam, Havana, Cuba
2016 *Lost*, Apollonia Échanges Artistiques Européens, Strasbourg, France
2013 *Garden of Error and Decay*, Anna Klinkhammer Gallery, Düsseldorf, Germany
2011 *Garden of Error and Decay*, Embassy of the Czech Republic, Berlin, Germany
2009 *Falling Times*, Czech Centre, New York, USA
2006 *Falling Life*, Autostadt, Wolfsburg, Germany

SOLO EXHIBITIONS

2020 *Perpetuum Mobile*, ZKM | Center for Art and Media Karlsruhe, Germany
2018 *Flashhouse*, EnBW City, Stuttgart, Germany
2015 *Lost Objects*, National Theatre, Prague, Czech Republic
2013 *Garden of Error and Decay*, Art Center Nabi, Seoul, Korea
2006 *This Year in Jerusalem*, Robert Guttmann Gallery, Prague, Czech Republic
2004 *Falling Stars*, facade of the Volksbühne, Berlin, Germany
2004 *Reise/Führer* (Travel/leader), Galerie im Palais am Festungsgraben, Berlin, Germany
2003 *Perpetuum Mobile*, Autostadt, Wolfsburg, Germany
2000 *Room with a View*, Autostadt, Wolfsburg, Germany (in association with ZKM | Center for Art and Media Karlsruhe, Germany)
2000 *Exhibition (On the Web)*, Espace EDF Electra, Paris, France
1999 *Delvaux's Dream*, ZKM | Center for Art and Media Karlsruhe, Germany
1997 Czech Cultural Center, Berlin, Germany
1993 Czech Cultural Center, Bucharest, Romania
1993 Roter Salon, Volksbühne, Berlin, Germany
1991 *Time Based Arts*, MonteVideo Gallery, Amsterdam, Netherlands
1988 *Videosculptures*, Cité Internationale des Arts, Paris, France

GROUP EXHIBITIONS

2022 *Kinetismus – 100 Years of Art and Electricity*, Kunsthalle Prague, Prague, Czech Republic.
2021 *Infosphere: Kamila B. Richter, Michael Bielicky, Peter Weibel, Nam June Paik*, Galerie Zdeněk Sklenář, Schönkirchovský palác, Prague, Czech Republic.
2020 *Seasons of Media Arts*, City Center of Karlsruhe, Germany (curated by ZKM | Center for Art and Media Karlsruhe, Germany)
2019 *Laterna Magika: The Memory of an Experiment*, Meetfactory/Kostka Gallery, Prague, Czech Republic
2018 *Vasulka's Wave*, Vašulka Kitchen Brno, Brno, Czech Republic
2018 *1685 Days and Nights*, Galerie Zdeněk Sklenář, Schönkirchovský palác, Prague, Czech Republic
2018 *Dia-Logos: Ramon Llull and the Ars Combinatoria*, ZKM | Center for Art and Media Karlsruhe, Germany
2018 *Your North Is My South*, Museum für Neue Kunst, Freiburg, Germany
2017 *Lichtsicht VI*, Bad Rothenfelde, Germany
2017 *Open Codes: The World as a Field of Data*, ZKM | Center for Art and Media Karlsruhe, Germany
2015 *Data Steel*, presented by Galerie Zdeněk Sklenář at Bolt Tower, Dolní Vítkovice during the Colours of Ostrava Festival 2015, Ostrava, Czech Republic
2015 *Globale: Global Control and Censorship*, ZKM | Center for Art and Media Karlsruhe, Germany
2015 *Globale: Without Firm Ground – Vilém Flusser and the Arts*, ZKM | Center for Art and Media Karlsruhe, Germany
2015 *Morphing*, the Nordic House, Reykjavik, Iceland
2014 *700IS Reindeerland Screening*, Slaughterhouse, Egilsstadir, Iceland
2014 *Über das Morgen hinaus* (Beyond Tomorrow), Quadrennial, IMAI, Düsseldorf, Germany
2013 Lichtsicht 4, 4th Projection Biennial, Bad Rothenfelde, Germany
2013 *Wagner Extase*, Telegrafenamt, Vienna, Austria
2013 *Why Don't We*, Czech Centre, Berlin, Germany
2012 *Cartographies of Hope: Change Narratives*, DOX – Centre for Contemporary Art, Prague, Czech Republic
2012 La Bienal de La Habana – 11th Havana Biennial, Havana, Cuba
2012 *Plakartive*, Bielefeld, Germany
2012 *Zeit(lose) Zeichen* (Time[less] Signs), Künstlerhaus, Vienna, Austria
2011 4th Moscow Biennale of Contemporary Art, Moscow, Russia
2011 *Declining Democracy*, Palazzo Strozzi, Florence, Italy
2011 *Global Contemporary: Art Worlds after 1989*, ZKM | Center for Art and Media Karlsruhe, Germany
2011 *Tracing Home*, SIGGRAPH, Vancouver, Canada
2011 *Windows upon Oceans*, State Museum of Contemporary Art, Thessaloniki, Greece
2010 *IV. Semana de Teatro Alemán en La Habana*, Havana, Cuba
2010 *DIDF CINMAI – International Interactive Design Forum and International Contemporary New Media Art*, Wuhan, China
2010 *Esse, Nosse, Posse: Common Wealth for Common People*, National Museum of Contemporary Art, Athens, Greece
2010 *Gangnam Media Pole*, Seoul, South Korea
2010 *Record > Again! – 40yearsvideoart.de – Part 2*, Edith-Ruß-Haus für Medienkunst, Oldenburg, Germany
2009 *20 Jahre ZKM*, ZKM | Center for Art and Media Karlsruhe, Germany
2009 *Collider: Interactivity and New Media*, Myers School of Art at the University of Akron, Ohio, USA
2009 *Contemporary Art from Germany and China (Zeitgenössische Kunst aus Deutschland und China – Gemeinsam in Bewegung)*, Wuhan Museum of Art, China
2009 *Incheon International Digital Art Festival*, Incheon, Korea
2009 *KAMUNA*, Karlsruhe, Germany
2009 *Light Up the Night at the Complex*, Santa Fe, New Mexico, USA
2009 *Notation: Calculation and Form in the Arts*, ZKM | Center for Art and Media Karlsruhe, Germany
2009 *Record > Again! – 40yearsvideoart.de – Part 2*, Kunsthaus, Dresden, Germany
2009 *Record > Again! – 40yearsvideoart.de – Part 2*, Ludwig Forum, Aachen, Germany
2009 *Record > Again! – 40yearsvideoart.de – Part 2*, ZKM | Center for Art and Media Karlsruhe, Germany
2009 *Uncharted: User Frames in Media Arts*, Santralistanbul Museum, Istanbul, Turkey
2009 *Windows upon Oceans*, Strasbourg, France
2009 *YOU_ser 2.0: Celebration of the Consumer*, ZKM | Center for Art and Media Karlsruhe, Germany
2008 VII. Festival tschechischer Kunst und Kultur (7th Festival of Czech Art and Culture), Berlin, Germany
2008 Bienal Internacional de Arte Contemporáneo de Sevilla (BIACS), Spain
2008 *Mostra SESC de Arte*, São Paulo, Brazil
2008 *Urban Screens*, Melbourne, Australia
2008 *Welcome to Capitalism!*, DOX – Centre for Contemporary Art, Prague, Czech Republic
2007 *Columbus 2.0*, public facade, Wuhan, China
2007 VI. Festival tschechischer Kunst und Kultur (6th Festival of Czech Art and Culture), Berlin, Karlsruhe, Germany
2007 *Interferencia*, Barcelona, Spain
2007 *Sibiu: European Cultural Capital 2007*, Sibiu, Romania
2007 *YOU_ser: Century of the Consumer*, ZKM | Center for Art and Media Karlsruhe, Germany
2006 V. Festival tschechischer Kunst und Kultur (5th Festival of Czech Art and Culture), Berlin, Germany
2006 *Falling Life*, the National Museum of Contemporary Art, Bucharest, Romania
2006 *Landscapes of Desire*, Projections in the Quarry, Fertörakosz, Hungary
2006 New Media Arts Festival, Bangkok, Thailand

2005 IV. Festival tschechischer Kunst und Kultur (4th Festival of Czech Art and Culture), Berlin, Germany
2005 *Die Lange Nacht* (The Long Night), Autostadt Wolfsburg, Germany
2005 *Light Art from Artificial Light*, ZKM | Center for Art and Media Karlsruhe, Germany
2005 *Projections in the Streets of Linz*, unofficial contribution to the Ars Electronica Festival, Linz, Austria
2005 *This Year in Jerusalem*, Robert Guttmann Gallery at the Jewish Museum in Prague, Czech Republic
2004 *Baustelle Europa* (Europe - A Construction Site), MAK - Museum für Angewandte Kunst, Vienna, Austria
2004 *Brooklyn Euphoria*, Brooklyn Museum, New York, USA
2004 *E.U. Positive*, Akademie der Künste, Berlin, Germany
2004 European Media Art Festival, Osnabrück, Germany
2004 *Masterpieces of Media Art*, ZKM | Center for Art and Media Karlsruhe, Germany
2004 *Totally Hidden Books*, America House, Berlin, Germany
2003 *Ejhle svetlo* (This Light), Moravská galerie, Brno, Czech Republic
2003 *Paesaggio di desiderio* (*Landscapes of Desire*) Galleria Lattuada Studio, Milano, Italy
2002 *Lanterna Magika: New Technologies in Czech Art of the 20th Century*, Espace EDF Electra, Paris, France
2002 *Paik*, Museum Kulturforum, Düsseldorf, Gemany
2002 *The Paths of Europe*, Apollonia / Centre Européen d'Aide aux Créations Artistiques, Strasbourg, France
2002 *POLITIK-UM / New Engagement*, Prague Castle, Prague, Czech Republic
2001 *Installation Licht*, Museum Ostdeutsche Galerie, Regensburg, Germany
2000 *Crossings: Presence in Absence*, Walter Benjamin International Conference, University of Barcelona, Spain
2000 *Paths of Europe*, Macedonian Museum of Contemporary Art, Thessaloniki, Greece
2000 *Konec sveta? / The End of the World?*, National Gallery in Prague, Czech Republic
2000 *Next Sex*, Ars Electronica Festival, Linz, Austria, and ISEA, Paris, France
1998 *Internet Performance Prague - New York City* (with Frank London), New Media Department at the Prague Academy of Fine Arts, Czech Republic and the Kitchen, New York, USA
1997 *Kunst der Gegenwart*, ZKM | Center for Art and Media Karlsruhe, Germany
1997 *Terminal Bar Project in X-space*, Ars Electronica Festival, Linz, Austria
1996 *Bridge the Gap*, Rialto, Amsterdam, Netherlands
1996 *Butterfly Effect*, Mücsarnok / Kunsthalle, Budapest, Hungary
1996 *Internet Performance*, Terminal Bar, Prague, Czech Republic and the Kitchen, New York, USA
1996 *Jitro kouzelniku / Dawn of the Magicians*, National Gallery in Prague, Czech Republic
1996 *Mixed Pixels*, Kunstmuseum Düsseldorf, Germany
1995 Galerie Wunschik, Düsseldorf, Germany
1995 Goethe-Institut, Naples, Italy
1995 *LAB5: International Exhibition of Film, Photography, Video, and Computer Art*, Centre for Contemporary Art, Castle Ujazdowski, Warsaw, Poland
1995 *Mythos Information*, Ars Electronica Festival, Linz, Austria
1995 *OSTranenie: International Video Forum*, Bauhaus, Dessau, Germany
1994 European Media Art Festival, Osnabrück, Germany
1994 *Intelligente Ambiente*, Ars Electronica Festival, Linz, Austria
1994 *Joseph Beuys*, Centre Georges Pompidou, Paris, France
1994 *Príroda v pohybu. Video '94 / Nature in Motion, Video '94*, Mánes Gallery, Prague, Czech Republic
1993 *Na ja, gut, aber trotzdem* (Well, yes, but still), Saint-Gervais, Geneve, Switzerland
1993 *OSTranenie: Shattered Myths - New Realities*, 1st International Video Festival at the Bauhaus, Dessau, Germany
1993 *Schirm-Herrschaft*, Museum Heidenheim, Germany
1993 *Village Gaze*, Anthology Film Archives, New York, USA
1992 *Committed Visions*, MoMA, New York, USA
1992 *Endo und Nano - Die Welt von Innen* (Endo and Nano - The World from Within), Ars Electronica Festival, Linz, Austria
1992 *International Painting Interactive*, SIGGRAPH, Chicago, Illinois, USA
1992 International Videofest, Berlin, Germany
1992 *Moving Image - Electronic Art*, Foundation Juan Miró, Barcelona, Spain
1992 Videonale 5, Bonn, Germany
1991 *Artware Special*, Dortmund, Germany
1991 *Images of the Future*, Cité des Arts Nouvelles Téchnologies, Montreal, Canada
1991 *Multimediale*, ZKM | Center for Art and Media Karlsruhe, Germany
1991 *My Way Only*, House of the Artist, Moscow, Russia
1991 *Transitions*, Korean National Museum, Seoul, South Korea
1990 *Artware*, Hannover, Germany
1990 *Discover European Video*, Anthology Film Archives, New York, USA
1990 *East Meets West*, Museum Folkwang, Essen, Germany
1990 *Kunstminen*, Kunstmuseum Düsseldorf, Germany
1990 Videonale 4, Bonn, Germany
1989 International JVC Video Festival, Sydney, Australia
1989 *Man and Technology*, Nixdorf Building, Düsseldorf, Germany
1989 *Viper*, Luzern, Switzerland
1988 3rd Marl Video Art Prize, Marl, Germany
1988 10th International JVC Video Festival, Tokyo, Japan
1988 38th International Film Festival, Berlin, Germany
1988 European Media Art Festival, Osnabrück, Germany
1988 Infermental 7, Tokyo, Japan
1988 Videonale 3, Bonn, Germany
1987 33rd West German Short Film Festival, Oberhausen, Germany
1987 37th International Berlin Film Festival, Berlin, Germany
1987 documenta 8, Ottoneum, Kassel, Germany
1987 Kunstmuseum, Bern, Switzerland
1987 Kunstmuseum, Düsseldorf, Germany
1987 São Paulo Biennial, Brazil
1986 *Ave Experimental*, Arnheim, Netherlands
1986 DAAD Gallery, Berlin, Germany
1986 *Folkwang Video I*, Museum Folkwang, Essen, Germany
1986 Kunstmuseum Düsseldorf, Germany
1985 Atelier de Rencontre, École Nationale Supérieure des Arts Décoratifs de Paris (ENSAD), Paris, France
1985 *Continuum*, Art d'Ameublement Gallery, Bielefeld, Germany

Kamila B. Richter

Born in 1976 in Olomouc, Czech Republic
Lives and works in Düsseldorf and Karlsruhe, Germany

1997 first self-programmed web projects
2001 Master of Fine Arts at the Prague Academy of Fine Arts, Czech Republic
2000–2002 studies at the Technikon Natal, Durban, South Africa
Since 2005 cooperation with Michael Bielicky
2010 PhD at the Prague Academy of Fine Arts, Czech Republic

SOLO EXHIBITIONS BY THE ARTIST DUO BIELICKY AND RICHTER

2017 *Lost*, Centro de Arte Contemporáneo Wifredo Lam, Havana, Cuba
2016 *Lost*, Apollonia Échanges Artistiques Européens, Strasbourg, France
2013 *Garden of Error and Decay*, Anna Klinkhammer Gallery, Düsseldorf, Germany
2011 *Garden of Error and Decay*, Embassy of the Czech Republic, Berlin, Germany
2009 *Falling Times*, Czech Centre New York, USA
2006 *Falling Life*, Autostadt, Wolfsburg, Germany

SOLO EXHIBITIONS

2019 *Divine Error: Data Paintings by Kamila B. Richter*, Galerie Zdeněk Sklenář, Schönkirchovský palác, Prague, Czech Republic

GROUP EXHIBITIONS

2020 *Seasons of Media Arts*, City Center of Karlsruhe, Germany (curated by ZKM | Center for Art and Media Karlsruhe, Germany)
2019 *Laterna Magika: The Memory of an Experiment*, Meetfactory/Kostka Gallery, Prague, Czech Republic
2018 *Vasulka's Wave*, Vašulka Kitchen Brno, Brno, Czech Republic
2018 *1685 Days and Nights*, Galerie Zdeněk Sklenář, Schönkirchovský palác, Prague, Czech Republic
2018 *Dia-Logos: Ramon Llull and the Ars Combinatoria*, ZKM | Center for Art and Media Karlsruhe, Germany
2018 *Your North Is My South*, Museum für Neue Kunst, Freiburg, Germany
2017 *Lichtsicht VI*, Bad Rothenfelde, Germany
2017 *Open Codes: The World as a Field of Data*, ZKM | Center for Art and Media Karlsruhe, Germany
2015 *Data Steel*, presented by Galerie Zdeněk Sklenář – at Bolt Tower, Dolní Vítkovice during the Colours of Ostrava Festival 2015, Ostrava, Czech Republic
2015 *Globale: Global Control and Censorship*, ZKM | Center for Art and Media Karlsruhe, Germany
2015 *Globale: Without Firm Ground – Vilém Flusser and the Arts* ZKM | Center for Art and Media Karlsruhe, Germany
2015 *Morphing*, the Nordic House, Reykjavík, Iceland
2014 *700IS Reindeerland Screening*, Slaughterhouse, Egilsstadir, Iceland
2014 Über das Morgen hinaus (Beyond Tomorrow), Quadrennial, IMAI, Düsseldorf, Germany
2013 Lichtsicht 4, 4th Projection Biennial, Bad Rothenfelde, Germany
2013 *Wagner Extase*, Telegrafenamt, Vienna, Austria
2013 *Why Don't We*, Czech Centre, Berlin, Germany
2012 *Cartographies of Hope: Change Narratives*, DOX – Centre for Contemporary Art, Prague, Czech Republic
2012 La Bienal de La Habana – 11th Havana Biennial, Havana, Cuba
2012 *Plakartive*, Bielefeld, Germany
2012 *Zeit(lose) Zeichen* (Time[less] Signs), Künstlerhaus, Vienna, Austria
2011 4th Moscow Biennale of Contemporary Art, Moscow, Russia
2011 *Declining Democracy*, Palazzo Strozzi, Florence, Italy
2011 *Global Contemporary: Art Worlds after 1989*, ZKM | Center for Art and Media Karlsruhe, Germany
2011 *Tracing Home*, SIGGRAPH, Vancouver, Canada
2011 *Windows upon Oceans*, State Museum of Contemporary Art, Thessaloniki, Greece
2010 *IV. Semana de Teatro Alemán en La Habana*, Havana, Cuba
2010 *DIDF CINMAI – International Interactive Design Forum and International Contemporary New Media Art*, Wuhan, China
2010 *Esse, Nosse, Posse: Common Wealth for Common People*, National Museum of Contemporary Art, Athens, Greece
2010 *Gangnam Media Pole*, Seoul, South Korea
2010 *Record > Again! – 40yearsvideoart.de – Part 2*, Edith-Ruß-Haus für Medienkunst, Oldenburg, Germany
2009 *20 Jahre ZKM,* ZKM | Center for Art and Media Karlsruhe, Germany
2009 *Collider: Interactivity and New Media*, Myers School of Art at the University of Akron, Ohio, USA
2009 *Contemporary Art from Germany and China (Zeitgenössische Kunst aus Deutschland und China – Gemeinsam in Bewegung*), Wuhan Museum of Art, China
2009 *Incheon International Digital Art Festival*, Incheon, Korea
2009 *KAMUNA*, Karlsruhe, Germany
2009 *Light Up the Night at the Complex*, Santa Fe, New Mexico, USA
2009 *Notation: Calculation and Form in the Arts*, ZKM | Center for Art and Media Karlsruhe, Germany
2009 *Uncharted: User Frames in Media Arts*, Santralistanbul Museum, Istanbul, Turkey
2009 *Windows upon Oceans*, Strasbourg, France
2009 *YOU_ser 2.0: Celebration of the Consumer*, ZKM | Center for Art and Media Karlsruhe, Germany
2008 VII. Festival tschechischer Kunst und Kultur (7th Festival of Czech Art and Culture), Berlin, Germany
2008 Bienal Internacional de Arte Contemporáneo de Sevilla, Spain
2008 *Mostra SESC de Arte*, São Paulo, Brazil
2008 *Urban Screens*, Melbourne, Australia
2008 *Welcome to Capitalism!*, DOX – Centre for Contemporary Art, Prague, Czech Republic
2007 VI. Festival tschechischer Kunst und Kultur (6th Festival of Czech Art and Culture), Berlin and Karlsruhe, Germany
2007 *Interferencia*, Barcelona, Spain
2007 *Sibiu: European Cultural Capital 2007*, Sibiu, Romania
2007 *YOU_ser: Century of the Consumer*, ZKM | Center for Art and Media Karlsruhe, Germany
2006 V. Festival tschechischer Kunst und Kultur (5th Festival of Czech Art and Culture), Berlin, Germany
2006 *Falling Life*, the National Museum of Contemporary Art, Bucharest, Romania
2006 *Landscapes of Desire*, Projections in the Quarry, Fertörakosz, Hungary
2006 *New Media Arts Festival*, Bangkok, Thailand
2007 *Columbus 2.0*, public facade, Wuhan, China
2005 IV. Festival tschechischer Kunst und Kultur (4th Festival of Czech Art and Culture), Berlin, Germany
2005 *Die Lange Nacht* (The Long Night), Autostadt, Wolfsburg, Germany
2005 *Light Art from Artificial Light*, ZKM | Center for Art and Media Karlsruhe, Germany
2005 *Projections in the Streets of Linz*, unofficial contribution to the Ars Electronica Festival, Linz, Austria
2005 *This Year in Jerusalem*, Robert Guttmann Gallery at the Jewish Museum in Prague, Czech Republic
2003 3rd Zlín Youth Salon, Zlín, Czech Republic
2003 *Svět jako struktura, struktura jako obraz* (World as Structure, Structure as Image), Galerie Klatovy, Klenová, Czech Rebublic
2000 2nd Zlín Youth Salon, Zlín, Czech Republic

Photo credit

ARCHIVE MICHAEL BIELICKY
pp.1, 75, 78, 81 [right], 85, 86, 88, 138-139, 140-141, 154, 155 [bottom], 157, 160 [top], 182, 184, 185, 186, 187, 188, 222-225, 279, 296, 369, 408 [bottom], 417, 454-455, 481, 504, 505, 530, 543, 544

PHOTO © LUC BERNHARD
pp. 449, 450, 452-453, 458-459

PHOTO © MICHAEL BIELICKY
pp. 10, 13, 21, 23, 28 [01], [02]; 29 [03], [04], 30-31 [05], 32 [06], 38-39 [12], 50-51 [22[, [23], [24], 60-61 [35], 64-65 [37], 66-67 [38], 81 [left], 82, 83, 96 [top, bottom], 107, 112 113, 119, 122-123, 128, 130, 134-135, 136, 144-145, 148-149, 152-153, 165, 168, 171, 172, 181, 183, 194 [middle, bottom], 196-221, 229, 234-235, 240-241, 244-245-, 247, 249, 251, 253, 255, 256-257, 261, 263, 264-265, 266-267, 268-269, 273, 275, 276, 282 [top], 295, 297, 298, 316, 318, 319, 320, 321, 322, 323, 326, 328, 341, 362, 364 , 366, 367, 405, 408 [top], 418 [top], 422, 425, 426, 427, 430, 431, 433, 438-439, 440-441, 442, 443, 444-445, 446-447, 451, 463, 464, 466, 475, 486-487, 487-488, 491, 494-495, 502, 503, 506-507, 508, 509, 516, 518, 519, 520, 521, 522-523, 528-529, 531, 532, 533, 534, 535

PHOTO © BENJAMIN BREITKOPF
pp. 510-511, 512-513, 514-515

PHOTO © FREDERICK CANTOR
pp. 4, 95, 410 [right]

PHOTO © PETER FISCHLI / DAVID WEISS
p. 476

PHOTO © SARKA HEJNOVA
pp. 161, 334 [middle, bottom], 336, 338

COLLAGE © PAUL KENIG
pp. 102-103, 106, 108-109, 114-115, 116-117, 118, 120-121, 124-125, 126-127, 129, 131, 132-133, 137, 142-143, 150-151, 238-239, 242-243, 246, 248, 250, 252, 254, 258-259, 260, 262, 270-271, 272, 274, 376-377, 378-379, 380-381, 382-383, 384-385, 388-389, 392-393, 394-395, 396-397, 398-399, 400-401, 402-403, 482-483, 490, 500-501

PHOTO © MARTIN POLÁK
pp. 524-525, 526-527

PHOTO © KAMILA B. RICHTER
p. 179

PHOTO © JOSEV SVOBODA
p. 160 [bottom right]

PHOTO © ZKM | KARLSRUHE, PHOTO: STEFFEN HARMS
p. 365

PHOTO © ZKM | KARLSRUHE, PHOTO: DORCAS MÜLLER
p. 16 [top]

PHOTO © ZKM | KARLSRUHE, PHOTO: TOBIAS WOOTTON
pp. 19, 20, 22, 26-27, 33 [07], 34, 35 [08], [09], 36, 37 [10], [11], 40 [13], 41 [14], 42 [15], 43 [16], 44-45[17], 46-47 [18], 48-49 [19], [20], [21], 52-53 [25], [26], 54-55 [27], 56-57 [28], [29], [30], [31], [32], 58-59 [33], [34], 62-63 [36], 68-69 [39], [40], [41], 70-71 [42], [43], [44-46], 72-73 [47], 325

The Exhibition
Michael Bielicky: Perpetuum Mobile

ZKM | Center for Art and Media Karlsruhe
October 13, 2019 – March 8, 2020

Curated by
Bettina Korintenberg

Curatorial assistance
Paul Kenig

Head of curatorial department
Philipp Ziegler

The Book:
Michael Bielicky: Perpetuum Mobile

Editors
Peter Weibel and Zdeněk Sklenář

Basic concept
Paul Kenig, Michael Bielicky

Editorial staff and project lead
Jens Lutz, Paul Kenig, Miriam Stürner, Patrick Trappendreher

Production management
Michal Petkov (Galerie Zdeněk Sklenář) and DCV

Design
studio +fronczek

Copy editing
Melanie Mallon, Jessica Peart, Gloria Custance

Translations
Paul Kenig, Sarah Clift, Lonnie Legg, Michal Petkov, Pepe Rojo

Image editing
dpi-factory, Krefeld

Printing and binding
optimal media, Röbel/Müritz

This publication is listed in the German National Bibliography by the German National Library. Detailed bibliographic data are available at http://dnb.d-nb.de.

Distribution and marketing
DCV sales@dcv-books.com

ISBN 978-3-96912-028-6
Printed in Germany

Published by www.dcv-books.com DCV

This publication is a cooperation between

zkm karlsruhe and

Galerie Zdeněk Sklenář

Founders of ZKM

Baden-Württemberg
Ministerium für Wissenschaft, Forschung und Kunst

Karlsruhe

Partner of ZKM

EnBW